PAGE 28

ON THE ROAD

...DE and insider tips

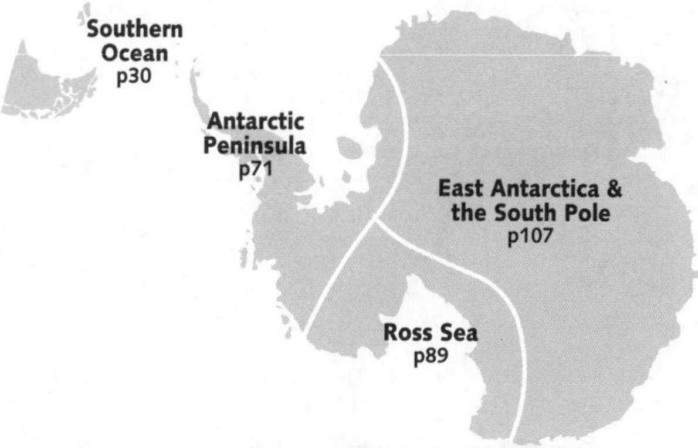
Southern Ocean p30
Antarctic Peninsula p71
East Antarctica & the South Pole p107
Ross Sea p89

PAGE 203

SURVIVAL GUIDE

VITAL PRACTICAL INFORMATION TO HELP YOU HAVE A SMOOTH TRIP

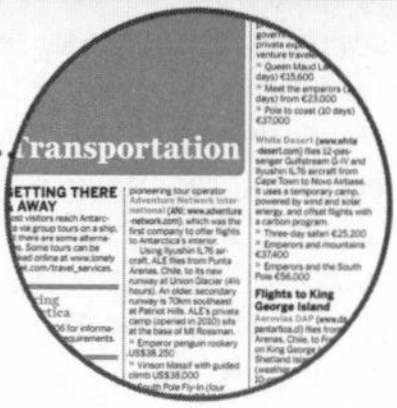
Transportation

THIS EDITION WRITTEN AND RESEARCHED BY

Alexis Averbuck

Adventure

Antarctica's surreal remoteness, extreme cold, enormous ice shelves and mountain ranges, and myriad exotic life forms invariably challenge you to embrace life fully. Everyone – scientist, support worker, government official and tourist alike – who comes to this isolated continent, must 'earn' it, whether by sea-voyage or flight. Ice and weather, not clocks and calendars, determine the itinerary and the timetable of all travel here. Expect experiences unlike any other, whether whale-watching across the open sea, spying a penguin rookery, or framing that perfect photograph of an awe-inspiring ice-form. Today, it's even possible for visitors to climb Antarctic peaks, or kayak icy waters. But there is nothing quite like the craggy crevasses of a magnificent glacier or the sheer expanse of the polar ice cap.

Wildlife

This continent, preserved by the Antarctic Treaty, is home to some of the world's most extraordinary species, adapted to life in their unique home. Some migrate far and wide, like the enormous whales, others remain close to the continent, like the Weddell seal and the emperor penguin. Millions of seabirds skim the Southern Ocean, the world's most abundant ocean...species like far-flung albatrosses and petrels circle these waters. Antarctic wildlife is generally

No place on Earth compares to this vast white wilderness of elemental forces: snow, ice, water, rock. Antarctica is simply stunning.

(left) Arches, Graham Land, Northern Peninsula.
(below) Penguin chicks.

unafraid of people. Visitors usually elicit no more than an uninterested yawn from seals and penguins focused on rearing their young and evading predators. The human reaction is, ironically, exactly opposite.

History

The names of explorers and their sovereigns and benefactors are written on Antarctica's shores. Renowned explorers from Cook to Amundsen and Scott all tried to penetrate this vast, mysterious land: each with varying degrees of success. Visitors can follow in their footsteps and imagine what it was like to forge through the pack ice on a creaking wooden boat or man-hauling sledges across the polar plateau. Some of their huts actually remain, preserved in frozen rime, to tell the story of adventures long past.

Inspiration

Antarctica possesses an unnamable quality. Call it inspiration, call it grandeur...it is simply the indescribable feeling of being a small speck in a vast, harshly beautiful land. A land where striated ice towers float among geometric pancake ice, literally untouched mountains rear from marine mist, and wildlife lives, year in and year out, to its own rhythms, quite apart from human concerns. To let our minds soar in a place nearly free of humankind's imprint: this is magic.

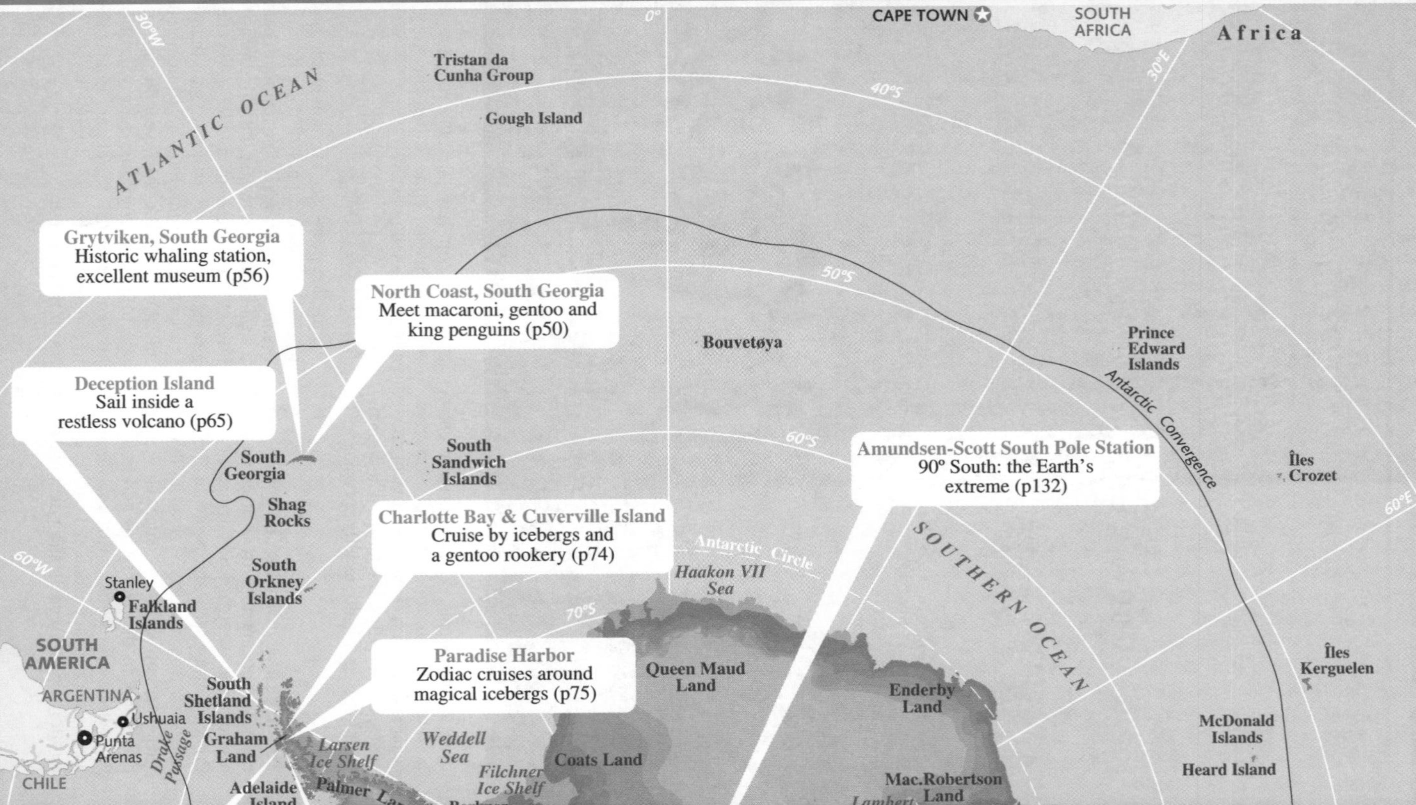

CAPE TOWN
SOUTH AFRICA
Africa
0°
30°W
30°E
40°S
50°S
60°S
70°S
60°W
60°E
ATLANTIC OCEAN
Tristan da Cunha Group
Gough Island
Grytviken, South Georgia
Historic whaling station, excellent museum (p56)
North Coast, South Georgia
Meet macaroni, gentoo and king penguins (p50)
Bouvetøya
Prince Edward Islands
Antarctic Convergence
Deception Island
Sail inside a restless volcano (p65)
South Georgia
South Sandwich Islands
Amundsen-Scott South Pole Station
90° South: the Earth's extreme (p132)
Îles Crozet
Shag Rocks
Charlotte Bay & Cuverville Island
Cruise by icebergs and a gentoo rookery (p74)
SOUTHERN OCEAN
Antarctic Circle
Haakon VII Sea
Stanley
Falkland Islands
South Orkney Islands
SOUTH AMERICA
ARGENTINA
Ushuaia
Punta Arenas
CHILE
Drake Passage
Paradise Harbor
Zodiac cruises around magical icebergs (p75)
South Shetland Islands
Graham Land
Adelaide Island
Larsen Ice Shelf
Weddell Sea
Filchner Ice Shelf
Queen Maud Land
Coats Land
Enderby Land
Mac.Robertson Land
Îles Kerguelen
McDonald Islands
Heard Island

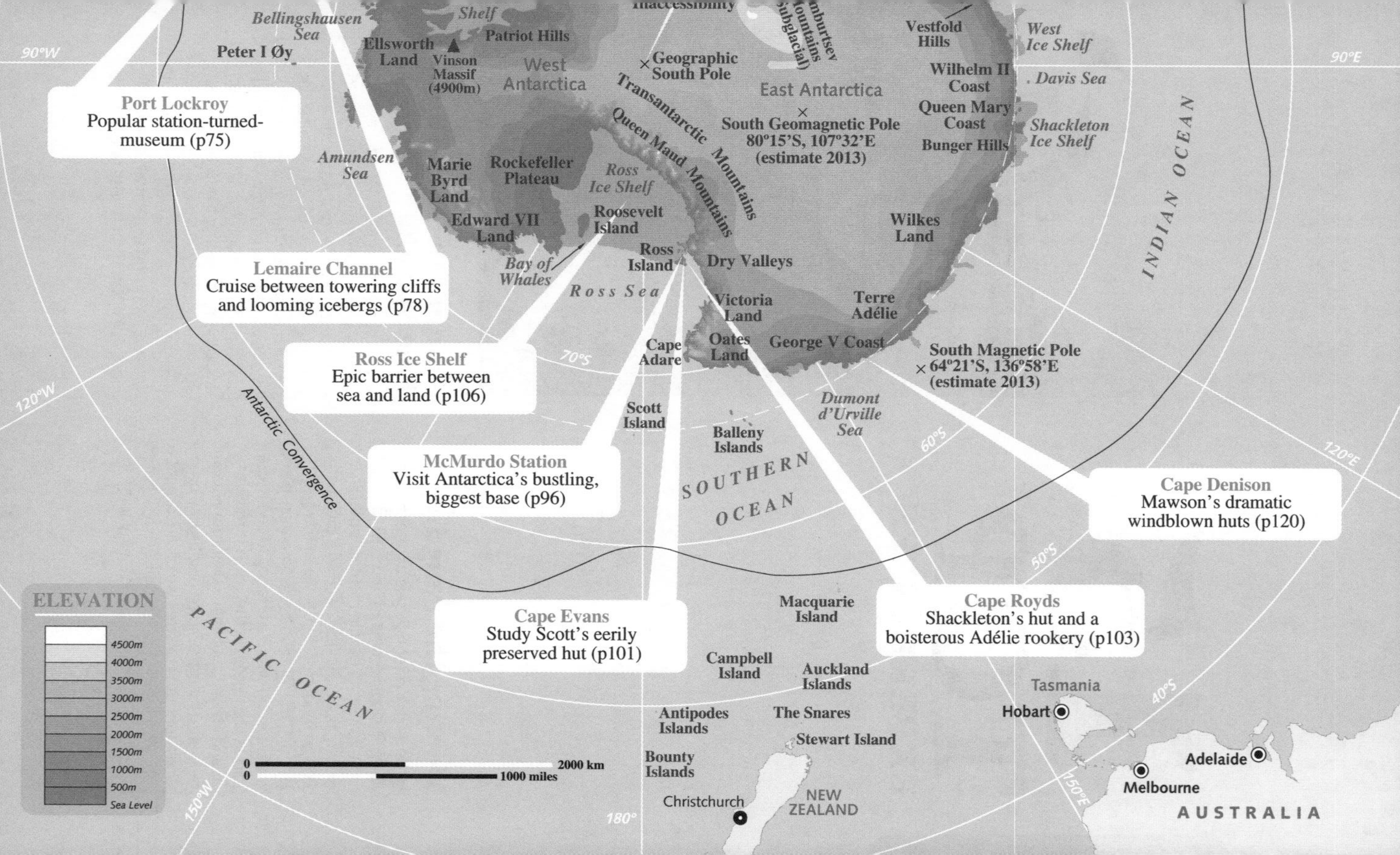

Port Lockroy
Popular station-turned-museum (p75)
Lemaire Channel
Cruise between towering cliffs and looming icebergs (p78)
Ross Ice Shelf
Epic barrier between sea and land (p106)
McMurdo Station
Visit Antarctica's bustling, biggest base (p96)
Cape Evans
Study Scott's eerily preserved hut (p101)
Cape Royds
Shackleton's hut and a boisterous Adélie rookery (p103)
Cape Denison
Mawson's dramatic windblown huts (p120)
Bellingshausen Sea
Peter I Øy
Ellsworth Land
Vinson Massif (4900m)
Patriot Hills
West Antarctica
Geographic South Pole
East Antarctica
South Geomagnetic Pole 80º15'S, 107º32'E (estimate 2013)
Transantarctic Mountains
Queen Maud Mountains
Vestfold Hills
Wilhelm II Coast
Queen Mary Coast
Bunger Hills
West Ice Shelf
Davis Sea
Shackleton Ice Shelf
Amundsen Sea
Marie Byrd Land
Rockefeller Plateau
Ross Ice Shelf
Roosevelt Island
Edward VII Land
Bay of Whales
Ross Island
Ross Sea
Dry Valleys
Victoria Land
Oates Land
Cape Adare
George V Coast
Terre Adélie
Wilkes Land
South Magnetic Pole 64º21'S, 136º58'E (estimate 2013)
Dumont d'Urville Sea
Scott Island
Balleny Islands
SOUTHERN OCEAN
INDIAN OCEAN
PACIFIC OCEAN
Antarctic Convergence
Macquarie Island
Campbell Island
Auckland Islands
Antipodes Islands
The Snares
Stewart Island
Bounty Islands
Christchurch
NEW ZEALAND
Tasmania
Hobart
Melbourne
Adelaide
AUSTRALIA
ELEVATION
4500m
4000m
3500m
3000m
2500m
2000m
1500m
1000m
500m
Sea Level
0 2000 km
0 1000 miles
90°W
120°W
150°W
180°
150°E
120°E
90°E
70°S
60°S
50°S
40°S

15 TOP EXPERIENCES

Meeting the Penguins

1 When you first lay eyes on these ever-anthropomorphized birds (p173),you'll *know* you've arrived in the Antarctic. From the tiny tuxedo-clad Adélie and the bushy-browed macaroni, to the world's largest penguin, the fabulously debonair emperor, the Antarctic offers a chance to see these unique creatures on their own turf: sea, ice and shore. Spot them shooting out of the water, tobogganing along the ice or in cacophonous rookeries which are a sight to behold: squawking, gamboling birds, hatching, molting and caring for their young. King penguins

Amundsen-Scott South Pole Station

2 First reached just 100 years ago by the valiant explorer Roald Amundsen during the Heroic Age of Antarctic exploration, the South Pole (p125) still embodies myth, hardship and glory. Today it is topped by a new high-tech station surrounded by cutting-edge astrophysical observation equipment (including a neutrino detector array buried approximately 1.9 km below the ice). To the visitor, a photo op with the flapping flags and globe-topped pole, is, indeed, a once-in-a-lifetime opportunity,

1

PETER SCOONES / GETTY©

2

SCOT JACKSON / NATIONAL SCIENCE FOUNDATION©

Cruising the Lemaire Channel

3 The sheer-sided Lemaire Channel (p78) is a perennial favorite for photography buffs and naturalists alike. Under pale-pink skies, glaciers tumble slow-motion to the sea from the mountains overhead. Your Zodiac glides past a floe topped by basking Weddell seals, another crowded by a noisy group of gentoo penguins. Nearby, an enormous female leopard seal sleeps off a recent meal. Small cruise ship passing through the Lemaire Channel

Cape Evans

4 Reaching Ross Island's Cape Evans (p101) isn't easy – but then again, it never was. Dog skeletons bleach on the sand in the Antarctic sun, chiding *memento mori* of Captain Robert Scott's death march from the Pole. Inside Scott's hut from that ill-fated *Terra Nova* expedition a collection of sledging pennants, rustling pony harnesses and a sighing wind evoke the doomed men who left here with high hopes of reaching the pole. Explore the captain's bunkroom, and peer at the perfectly preserved provisions and photographic supplies. Wooden cross near Scott's Hut

SCOTT DARSENY / LONELY PLANET IMAGES©

THOMAS PICKARD / AURORA PHOTOS / CORBIS©

Shackleton's Hut

5 Step inside Ernest Shackleton's *Nimrod* expedition hut at Cape Royds (p96) on Ross Island and enter an eerily preserved world from a century ago. Amazingly intact despite 100 years of blasting Antarctic storms, the wooden house is surprisingly homey. Colored glass medicine bottles line shelves, a fur sleeping bag rests on one of the bunks and tins of food with unappetizing names (boiled mutton, lunch tongue, pea powder) are stacked on the floor, awaiting diners who will never return. Adélie penguins fill the cape now, breeding in summer.

Paradise Harbor

6 The pragmatic whalers who worked in the waters of the Antarctic Peninsula at the beginning of the 20th century were hardly sentimental. Yet they named this harbor Paradise, obviously quite taken with the stunning icebergs and reflections of the surrounding mountains. Gentoos and shags call the area home, and a climb up the hill here offers magnificent glacier views. If you're lucky, perhaps you'll see one calving.

7

8

Grytviken, South Georgia

7 A tall granite headstone marking the last resting place of British explorer Ernest Shackleton, known to his loyal men simply as 'the Boss,' stands at the rear of the whalers' cemetery at Grytviken (p56). This old whaling station is still strewn with evidence of its past industry, and its South Georgia Museum gives insight into whaling life, as well as into South Georgia's history and wildlife. Meanwhile, seals wriggle outside the station's quaint, white-clapboard whalers' church.

Deception Island

8 Deceptive in more ways than one, with its secret harbor, slopes of ash-covered snow and hidden chinstrap penguin rookery at Baily Head, Deception Island (p65) offers the rare opportunity to sail inside a volcano. Now classified as having 'a significant volcanic risk,' Deception remains a favorite for the industrial archaeology of its abandoned whaling station, half-destroyed by an eruption-induced mud-flow and flood. Some will stop for a quick dip in the island's heated geothermal currents.

ROBERT HARDING WORLD IMAGERY / CORBIS©

WAYNE LYNCH / ALL CANADA PHOTOS / CORBIS©

Antarctic Museum at Port Lockroy

9 Each year, tens of thousands of visitors flock to Britain's beautifully restored Bransfield House, the main building of Base A, built at Port Lockroy (p75) during WWII. Not only does it offer the chance to spend up big at the well-stocked souvenir shop and to mail postcards at the busy post office, the museum's old wooden skis, clandestine 1944 radio transmitter and wind-up HMV gramophone are evocative artifacts of the explorers who once lived for years at this wilderness outpost.

Charlotte Bay & Cuverville Island

10 Ah, how do you choose a favorite among the Antarctic Peninsula's many gorgeous bays and inlets? Charlotte Bay (p74) is certainly a contender…like Paradise Harbor, it can become studded with recently calved icebergs, reflected on the smooth sea surface. Many cruises pop in for a look, and test everyone's supply of film or the size of their cameras' memory cards. Nearby Cuverville Island is home to one of the largest gentoo rookeries on the Ice; several thousand pairs share their exquisite views with you.

Whale Encounters

11 One of the major pay-offs of the long passage across the Southern Ocean is the chance to spot migrating whales (p168) circulating through krill-rich waters. Once nearer to land, if you're in a Zodiac, calling it whale-watching doesn't do it justice: you could be close enough to get a 'whale bath'. The whale exhales with a startlingly loud 'ffffffffffffff!' right next to your boat, leaving you bathed in fish-scented mist. Near the ice edge, look for orcas hunting in pods.

Cape Denison

12 Douglas Mawson's Australasian Antarctic Expedition didn't realize when it set up its base at East Antarctica's Commonwealth Bay, near Cape Denison (p120), in 1911 that fierce gravity-driven winds called katabatics make the place one of the windiest on Earth. Mawson later gave it the memorable moniker 'the home of the blizzard.' Even today, roaring winds that can top 160km/h may make getting ashore here impossible. But if you make it, you'll find the windblown huts of these explorers, clinging tenaciously to the land.

Orca emerging through the ice

RALPH HOPKINS / LONELY PLANET IMAGES©

DAN LEETH / ALAMY©

HOLDINGS LTD / ALAMY©

Kayaking

13 The Antarctic Peninsula's icy waters certainly number among the world's most extraordinary paddles. Imagine your blades cutting the clear surface of the subzero waters as you navigate between towering icebergs and brilliantly hued ice formations. Seals may zip through the water beneath you, and penguins congregate on the shore after a quick dip in the sea. Seabirds circle overhead from their clifftop nests, and you are surrounded by it all. There are numerous cruises that make kayaking possible.

McMurdo Station

14 Affectionately called Mac Town (p96), Antarctica's largest base, operated by the US, is the central hub for many transiting to the interior. As such, its rough-and-tumble array of buildings can seem like an international adult summer camp. Enormous C-5 cargo planes occasionally land on the sea-ice runway, but usually the base is simply a hive of small aircraft and snowmobiles, as scientists come and go from base camps and the central science buildings. Visitors can't help but pick up the infectious excitement of science in action.

Ross Ice Shelf

15 This towering sheet of ice, rising up from the Ross Sea, was the daunting barrier to many an Antarctic explorer. In fact, the Ross Ice Shelf (p106) was formerly known simply as the Barrier, even though its thinnest part – a mere 100m thick – faced the sea. Inland, where the glaciers meet it, the slab can be as much as 1000m thick. The whole floating ice shelf is an astounding 520,000 sq km and was on the routes taken by both Amundsen and Scott to the South Pole.

need to know

Area
» 14.2 million sq km – almost double the size of Australia

Visitors
» Tourists (2011): 26,519

» Staff (2011): 2101

» Ship crew (2011): 17,725

» Scientists & logistics support (summer): 4500

When to Go

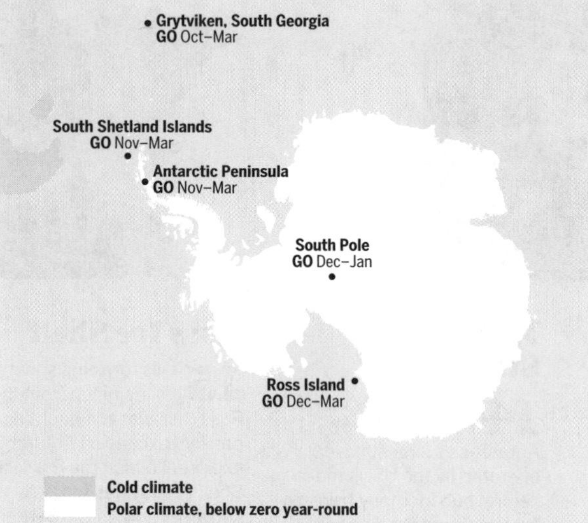

High Season
(Dec & Jan)

» Expect up to 20 hours of sunlight each day, and the main influx of Antarctic visitors

» Days are the warmest the continent will see

» Penguins hatch eggs and feed chicks; seabirds soar

Shoulder
(Nov & Feb-Mar)

» November: the ice breaks up and penguins court

» February and March: prime time for whale-watching, and penguin chicks are fledging

Low Season
(Apr-Oct)

» Continuous sunrise and sunset bring fantastic skies, bracketing midwinter, when 24-hour darkness reigns

» Winterovers find aurora australis, isolation and extreme temperatures

Your Budget

Budget less than US$10,000
» Cruises start at US$4500 for 10-day voyages (three days for the sub-Antarctic islands and the Antarctic Peninsula) with quad accommodations and shared bathrooms

» Fly-overs start at AU$999

Midrange US$10,000 to US$30,000
» 20-day voyages (Falklands, South Georgia, sub-Antarctic islands, Antarctic Peninsula) start at US$12,750

» Higher-end cabins: from US$16,000

» Fly-cruises start at US$10,000

Top End more than US$30,000
» High-end tours include 20-day cruises with balcony suite (US$32,995), inland flights to South Pole (US$42,950), and guided climbs of Vinson Massif (US$38,000)

Governance

» **Antarctic Treaty** (www.ats.aq) 50 signatory countries as of 2012.

Visas

» No visas required; permits required for tour operators, yachts, researchers, independent expeditioners from Antarctic Treaty signatory countries (see p206).

Communications

» Standard mobile phones don't work in Antarctica. Ships offer satellite communications for steep fees; service varies based on location and weather conditions.

Time

» There are no time zones. Most ships' clocks are based on ports of departure.

» **Chile**: GMT -4 hours

» **Argentina**: GMT -3 hours

Websites

» **International Association of Antarctica Tour Operators** (www.iaato.org) Responsible travel; loads of info

» **Antarctic Heritage Trust** (www.nzaht.org) Historic-hut conservation

» **Australian Antarctic Division** (www.antarctica.gov.au) General resource

» **Lonely Planet** (www.lonelyplanet.com/Antarctica) Info; traveler forum

» **Royal Geographical Society** (http://images.rgs.org) Photographic inspiration

Useful Terms & Acronyms

Traveling around the Ice you'll hear all sorts of acronyms and expressions thrown around. Here are a few of the main ones; see the Glossary (p210) for more.

» **ANARE** Australian National Antarctic Research Expeditions

» **Antarctic Circle** One of five major parallels of latitude, everything south is the Antarctic

» **Antarctic Convergence** (Polar Front) Region where colder Antarctic seas meet warmer waters of the north

» **ASPA** Antarctic Specially Protected Area

» **BAS** British Antarctic Survey

» **IAATO** International Association of Antarctica Tour Operators

» **IGY** International Geophysical Year 1957–58

» **IPY** International Polar Year 2007–09

» **NSF** National Science Foundation; section of US government in charge of the US Antarctic Program

» **USAP** US Antarctic Program

Money

» **Ships**: choose their currency, and usually have a system where you sign for your expenditures and pay at the end by cash or credit card

» **Station shops**: usually their national currency or US dollars

» **Chile**: Chilean peso

» **Argentina**: Argentine peso

» **Falkland Islands**: British pound and local pound (FK£; traded one-to-one)

» **ATMs/Banks**: Tourists won't be able to access ATMs or banks in Antarctica; take cash and credit cards

Traveling Responsibly

One of the biggest challenges of travel to Antarctica is how best to maintain the pristine environment.Tens of thousands of people visit the Antarctic Peninsula every year, and almost half of them visit the very same places. Antarctica is protected by the Antarctic Treaty (www.ats.aq) and its visitors guidelines are straightforward and easy to follow (see p163 for more details). Also, it is critical to book with an ecologically responsible tour operator in order to minimize pollution on sea and land (see p208 and www.iaato.org). Penalties for failing to follow the guidelines include fines of up to US$10,000 (for US citizens) or even imprisonment (for British citizens).

if you like...

Wildlife

From the sub-Antarctic islands to the ice-choked continent, Antarctica's fabled creatures thrive in their unique environment. Whale- and penguin-watching from ship or shore are thrilling. Spy beachmaster elephant seals noisily defending their turf. Or sit back and enjoy the sea birds whirling and calling alongside craggy cliffs.

Penguin rookeries Gregarious penguins of all sorts offer some of the most entertaining viewings (p173)

Whale-watching See minkes spout, orcas travelling in pods and, if you're superlucky, a mammoth blue whale, flukes aflare (p168)

Seal-spotting Find dense colonies of Antarctic fur seals and lone leopard or Ross seals (p171)

Seabird colonies Spot albatrosses, petrels, cormorants and more among the millions-strong contingent of seabirds circling the Southern Ocean (p175)

South Georgia Crammed with fauna, especially on the northern coast: elephant and fur seals, penguin colonies and seabirds galore (p51)

History

Follow in the footsteps of some of the world's greatest explorers, there's plenty to see from their pioneering expeditions.

Grytviken South Georgia's whaling station, museum, cemetery (with Shackleton's grave) and chapel (p56)

Port Lockroy The Antarctic Peninsula's most visited museum in a restored historic building (p75)

Shackleton's Hut Perfectly preserved and packed with cool relics from the Heroic Age of Antarctic exploration (p103)

Scott's Terra Nova Hut A chilling backdrop, eerily intact, of the doomed expedition (p101)

Mawson's Hut Australia's brave Mawson made the most of it on this windswept coast (p120)

Borchgrevink's Huts Oldest buildings in Antarctica and home to first winterovers (p91)

Museums Stanley (p43) and Ushuaia (p33) set the stage for life in the far south.

Nordenskjöld's Hut Oldest building on the Peninsula, and Nordenskjöld's home for an unplanned two years (p86)

Detaille Island Time capsule of 1950s Antarctic life (p79)

Adventure

Antarctica is a land made for adventure. Even just being there constitutes the adventure of a lifetime. But for those looking to skate closer to the edge, there's more – from inland mountain ranges to daring scuba diving.

Kayaking Hit the water for a thrilling paddle, under ice, cliffs and sky.

Mountaineering Antarctica's highest point, Vinson Massif (p81), is a clear draw, as are myriad remote ranges around the continent or the sub-Antarctic islands

Helicopter to the Dry Valleys A lucky few drop in on this otherworldly terrain (p94)

The South Pole Of course, the granddaddy of them all is the South Pole. Fly, or cross-country ski it (p125)

Deception Island thermal vents Want to swim in Antarctica? Stop by these volcanic thermal currents to ensure you stay alive (p68)

Scuba diving Expert divers head into the mysterious depths

TOBIAS BERNHARD / GETTY©

» Diver and jellyfish near Cape Evans, Ross Islands

Icebergs & Glaciers

Prepare to be WOW-ed by the dazzling array of light-struck ice formations around the Antarctic. Whether a wee floating berg, an enormous tabular iceberg, newly calved, or the crenulated tongue of a glacier, Antarctica has it all.

Paradise Harbor & Neko Harbor Freshly calved bergs reflect on the sea surface of two of Antarctica's most stunning bays. Climb high for a view of azure glaciers. (p75 and p74)

Lemaire Channel It's hard to choose...photograph the dramatic cliffs or the sparkling bergs? (p78)

Lambert Glacier & Amery Ice Shelf One of the world's largest glaciers and the mother of myriad tabular icebergs (p115)

Ross Ice Shelf Thundering icebergs calve from 'The Barrier,' as explorers used to call it (p106)

Hope Bay One of the Antarctic Peninsula's best spots for tabular icebergs (p82)

Ross Sea glaciers Track Shackleton, Amundsen and Scott's paths to the Pole ascending the Beardmore and Axel Heiberg glaciers (p127)

Science

Antarctica is a vast, unique landscape reserved for science. Researchers from all over the globe come to study the mysteries of the continent and of the universe. Once in a while you might spot these investigators at work.

Crary Laboratory Tour the aquariums at McMurdo's high-tech lab (p99)

The South Pole Supersophisticated measurements are taken here: from outer space (tele scopes, neutrino detectors) and underground (seismographic equipment) (p135)

King George Island Thirteen stations packed on one small island (p62)

Rothera & Palmer Stations Two busy Peninsula bases (p80 and p76)

Princess Elisabeth Antarctic Station Antarctica's first zero-emissions base (p112)

Mt Erebus One of only three volcanoes in the world with a permanent convecting magma lake (p105)

Mawson Station Oldest station south of the Antarctic Circle (p114)

The Remote

Even on Antarctica there are places that only the most fortunate or intrepid get to experience. It is a rare day when a non-scientist comes to most East Antarctic bases, and some sub-Antarctic islands are visited just a couple of times a year.

Vostok Station Site of thrilling science and the coldest temperatures on the Ice (p123)

Dome A Highest point on the Plateau; for years the Chinese kept only an unmanned robotic station here (p124)

Dry Valleys Empty but for microscopic life forms, bizarre lakes and wind-sculpted ventifacts (p94)

Cape Denison Mawson's wind-ravaged coast makes for difficult landings (p120)

Cape Adare Fascinating penguins and historic huts...but hard to reach (p91)

Weddell Sea Ships can't get very far, so few see its Ronne and Filchner Ice Shelves (p86)

East Antarctica & the Ross Sea The most remote parts of the continent, as are the surrounding islands

Pole of Maximum Inaccessibility As its name suggests: furthest point from anywhere (p134)

itineraries

Whether you've got six days or 60, these itineraries provide a starting point for the trip of a lifetime. Want more inspiration? Head online to lonelyplanet.com/thorntree to chat with other travelers.

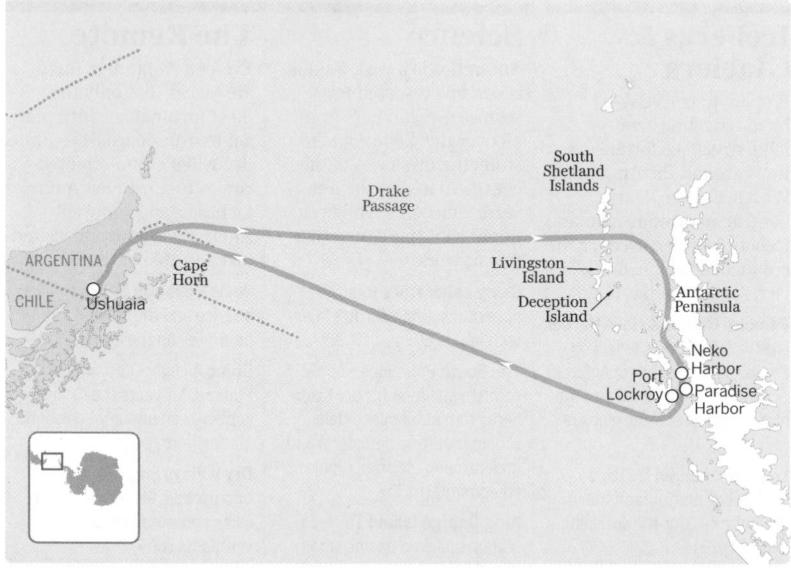

Seven to 14 days

The Antarctic Peninsula

The Antarctic Peninsula is an excellent introduction to Antarctica and its wildlife, and is the most popular trip to the Ice.

Cruises vary, but generally, starting from **Ushuaia**, Argentina, your ship crosses the **Drake Passage**. The duration of the crossing depends on vessel size and the weather – from as little as 1½ days, to as long as three or four days.

You might make your first landing at one of the **South Shetland Islands**. Popular stops include **Deception Island**, an active volcano with a hidden 'amphitheatre', which is home to the largest chinstrap rookery in the Peninsula region, and **Livingston Island**, with its penguins and wallowing elephant seals.

Next, you'll steam down to the Peninsula. You may take a Zodiac cruise in aptly named **Paradise Harbor** or along the rumbling glaciers above **Neko Harbor**, and head to the museum at **Port Lockroy**.

Homeward bound, keep an eye out for a glimpse of the fabled headland at **Cape Horn** off port side.

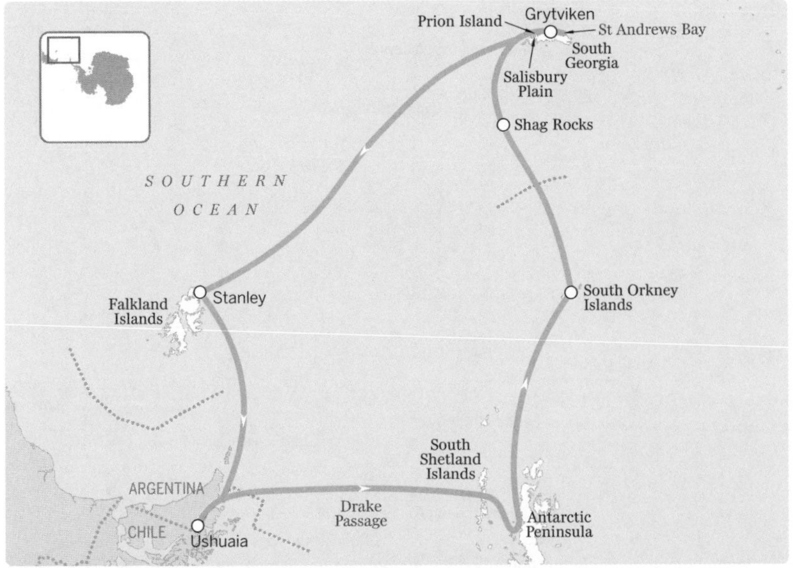

14 to 20 Days

The Peninsula, South Georgia & the Falkland Islands

This trip includes the popular Peninsula region, home to loads of amazing wildlife and scenery, as well as stunning, historical South Georgia, with its Shackleton connections and huge concentrations of king penguins and fur seals. You may also visit the lonely South Orkneys, pass by Shag Rocks, and spend a few days in the fascinating Falkland Islands, with its captivating wildlife and friendly folk. The route is increasingly popular despite the greater amount of time it requires at sea.

Departing from **Ushuaia**, Argentina, you may either head straight to the Peninsula and on to South Georgia (which has the advantage of following the prevailing westerly winds), or the route may be done in reverse (which means going against the westerlies, with often heavy head seas). Here, we'll go with the flow: head south across the **Drake Passage**, stop in the **South Shetland Islands**, and then head on to visit the **Antarctic Peninsula**; see the Antarctic Peninsula itinerary.

After leaving the Peninsula, head east (with following seas, resulting in a faster and more comfortable trip) to the **South Orkney Islands**, home of early sealers, whalers and bases – provided there's time and the weather cooperates. Next, cruise past the lonely, wave-thrashed **Shag Rocks** while looking for their eponymous bird life and occasional groups of whales feeding on the krill-rich waters.

Your first **South Georgia** landing is likely to be at **Grytviken**, home to an abandoned whaling station, museum and Ernest Shackleton's grave.

You won't be able to miss South Georgia's spectacular wildlife – it's everywhere! – but some of the highlights include **St Andrews Bay** and **Salisbury Plain** where you can watch the antics of king penguins by the thousand. Offshore **Prion Island** in the Bay of Isles is an excellent place to spy on the endangered and magnificent wandering albatrosses roosting on their nests.

On the way back to Ushuaia, call in at the **Falkland Islands**. You'll probably land at one or two of the outer islands, with their abundant penguins, seals and albatrosses, and spend half a day in the engaging capital, **Stanley**.

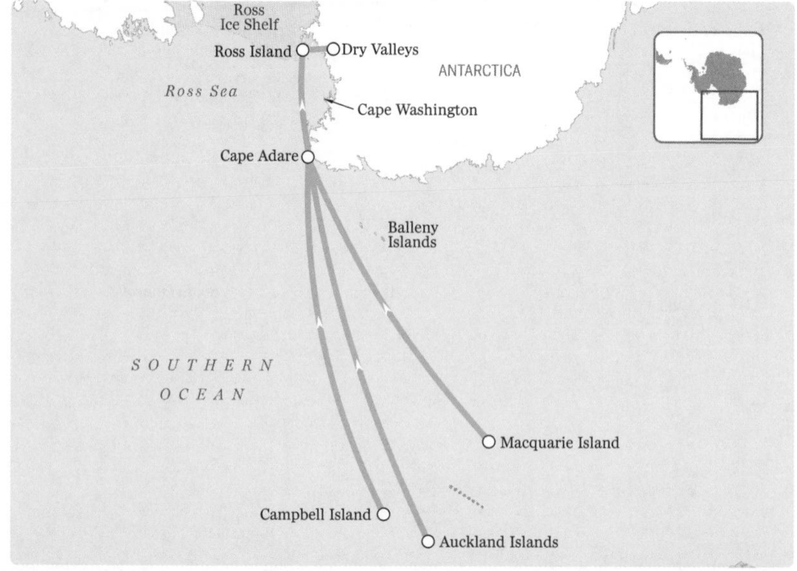

18 to 28 Days

The Ross Sea

This is Antarctica to another degree: cold and wind are magnitudes greater, tabular icebergs more abundant, wildlife scarcer. The Ross Sea area enjoys some of Antarctica's most spectacular terrain, and as the explorers' gateway to the South Pole, the region has the continent's richest historic heritage: the huts of the British Antarctic Expeditions led by explorers Robert F Scott, Ernest Shackleton and Carsten Borchgrevink. This itinerary also calls in at the busy US and New Zealand scientific research stations and several of the wildlife-rich peri-Antarctic island groups.

Starting from an Australian or New Zealand port, spend a couple of days rolling across the **Southern Ocean**, getting your sea legs and watching the abundant bird life. Depending on your route (and the unpredictable weather), you may stop at either **Macquarie Island**, **Campbell Island**, or the **Auckland Islands**, all famous for their breeding seabirds and windswept aspects. After a cruise past the shudder-inducing icebound coasts of the Balleny Islands, try for a quick visit to Antarctica's first buildings and an enormous Adélie penguin rookery at **Cape Adare** (if the wind allows). Turn to starboard and head south into the **Ross Sea** for a stunning view toward the floating, France-sized **Ross Ice Shelf**. You'll pass **Cape Washington**, with one of the largest emperor-penguin colonies in the world.

Next, visit **Ross Island**, site of **Mt Erebus** volcano, with its bubbling, steaming magma lake. If you're fortunate – and the pack ice permits – you'll hit the historic-hut trifecta, landing at Scott's *Discovery* hut at **Hut Point**, Shackleton's *Nimrod* hut at **Cape Royds** and Scott's *Terra Nova* hut at **Cape Evans**, to which Scott and his men would have returned had they not perished on the way back from the South Pole.

Most cruises visit one of Ross Island's human communities, the sprawling US **McMurdo Station** and/or New Zealand's ecofriendly **Scott Base** for a look at Antarctic scientific research and a bit of shopping. A very few with helicopter support offer a quick trip to the **Dry Valleys**, with ancient wind-formed ventifacts and bizarre lakes and ponds. Then it's time to turn north, and return to warmer climes.

Planning Your Antarctic Adventure

Top Activities

Wildlife-watching: whales, seals, seabirds and penguins
Shore visits: via Zodiac boats
Photography: flora and fauna, plus magnificent icebergs and terrain
Shipboard study: lectures by Antarctic experts, and wildlife or adventure videos
History appreciation: exploring historic huts and unique Antarctic museums

Way Off the Beaten Track

Cruise adventure activities: offered on select trips (usually for an extra US$600 or more): sea kayaking for experienced paddlers, scuba diving for advanced divers, or brief camping and mountain-climbing trips
Fly to the interior: climbing, skiing, camping and trekking for the ultrafit, experienced adventurer with plenty of time and money
Sail by private yacht: reach the Ice as few do

A trip to the world's most pristine and remote continent is a trip of a lifetime. You will have the chance to experience things that most only see on TV. Unless you're planning your own expedition, you'll visit Antarctica as part of a group tour, almost certainly on a ship. This has the advantage of combining your transportation, meals and accommodations all in the one vessel. It also means that no infrastructure has to be built ashore in Antarctica's delicate environment.

Nevertheless, the options can be daunting: this chapter is designed to help you plan your ultimate Antarctic adventure.

Booking Your Trip

When to Go

The Antarctic tour season is about five months, from November to March, with each offering its own highlights (see p14). Cruises later in the season may be less crowded; however, the longer you wait to go, the more wildlife will already have headed out to sea.

When to Book

It's wise to book your Antarctic journey early: January through May before the season you are planning to go. Tours fill quickly, and the sooner you book, the better selection you will have of accommodations and early-booking discounts.

ANTARCTICA ON A BUDGET

Getting to Antarctica is plain expensive. But short of getting a job there (all expenses paid!), there are still a few ways to keep costs down.

Some cruise companies offer steep discounts for early booking: for example, 25% on reservations made before April or May for the forthcoming season.

It's sometimes possible to find last-minute bargain bookings in Ushuaia when a ship has empty berths. However, most Antarctic ships are fully booked months in advance. Your best bet is very early (November and early December) and late in the season (mid-February onwards). Expect to pay at least US$4500; the 'last-minute' price is the same for all cabins, even, rarely, a suite! 'Last-minute' including South Georgia costs between US$6500 to US$8500. Check with **Ushuaia Turismo** (☎02901-436003; www.ushuaiaturismoevt.com.ar; Gobernador Paz 865, Ushuaia) and online at www.tierradelfuego.org.ar/antartida.

Types of Ships

Smaller ships (fewer than 100 passengers) offer far more time ashore, and guests are generally free to wander more. Larger ships offer greater comfort and less movement in heavy seas, and cross the Drake Passage much faster, though they cause greater environmental impact and pose rescue challenges in the case of an accident. Ships with fewer than 200 passengers have the right to land at most places. Those with over 500 passengers are not allowed to land at all. See p208 for a list of tour operators/ships.

The motion that causes seasickness is greater on upper decks, so a cabin on a lower deck (usually cheaper) may be more comfortable.

Costs

Antarctica isn't cheap. It's remote, and operating tours there is expensive. But price is only one factor in choosing a trip: sometimes a small increase in what you pay will get you a much more in-depth experience, important in what may be a once-in-a-lifetime trip.

Expect to pay at least US$5000, which buys you a bed in a four-person cabin with public bathroom facilities down the corridor, on a small-ship tour with only three or four days of landings in Antarctica. Not all ships offer these 'quad' accommodations. Prices rise quickly from there; high-end berths can cost eight times that much. Large ships (more than 400 passengers) may offer two-person cabins at similar prices to small-ship quads, but the experiences are very different.

Solo travelers pay extra for a single cabin (1.5 times the regular fare, or more). If you're willing to be matched with another solo traveler of the same gender, you each pay regular fare.

For more on price ranges, see Your Budget p14.

Refund Policies

Each operator varies, so check before booking. Some airfares are completely nonrefundable. Travel insurance (p205) is highly recommended and available from most operators. Broad cancellation ranges:

» >120 days prior: US$500 to US$750 fee

» 60-120 days prior: 20% to 50% of fare

» <90 days prior: no refund

What to Ask Your Tour Operator

☐ **How many days will you actually spend in Antarctica?** This may be *the* most important question. Many tours include nights in South America or the Falkland Islands. Crossing the Southern Ocean takes a couple of days each way. Ask how many days of landings are planned. For a bit more money, you may buy yourself several extra days.

☐ **What is included in the quoted price of the trip, and what is excluded?** Airfare? Most don't include it. Port taxes? They can add hundreds. How about fees (like Chile and Argentina's 'reciprocity fee' of US$140)?

☐ **What kind of ship is it?** An 'icebreaker' can push through much thicker ice than an 'ice-strengthened' vessel, but an icebreaker's shallower draft means it rolls more in heavy seas.

☐ **How many other passengers will be on board?** The smallest ships accommodate fewer than 60 passengers, while the largest carry more than 1000.

☐ **What kind of atmosphere prevails on board?** Smaller ships offer a more intimate experience, while on larger ships you can remain more anonymous.

☐ **What about rescue in case of an accident?**

☐ **Is the tour operator an International Association of Antarctic Tour Operators (IAATO) member?** IAATO is an industry group that promotes responsible travel to Antarctica.

☐ **Who are the other passengers?** Special-interest groups such as bird-watchers or alumni groups sometimes buy a large proportion of a ship's cabins. What language will most people speak?

☐ **Who are the lecturers?** The quality and enthusiasm of lecturers varies greatly from cruise to cruise. Delivering a top-quality talk is a special skill, blending knowledge, entertainment and good humor. Sometimes eminent scientists are poor lecturers. Is there a dedicated lecture hall aboard?

☐ **Does the ship carry helicopters?** Helicopters can go places inaccessible by Zodiac.

☐ **What communication options are on board?** Do they offer satellite phones, internet etc? What are the fees?

☐ **Can they accommodate any special requests?** Dietary restrictions, connecting cabins etc.

☐ **What are the baggage restrictions?**

Alternate Travel Options

Yacht Cruises

A small but growing number of visitors reach Antarctica aboard private vessels: sailboats equipped with auxiliary engines. A number of these yachts (see p209) sail to the Antarctic regularly, mostly from Ushuaia, Argentina, or Stanley, Falkland Islands. They primarily charter to private expeditions and commercial groups such as film crews but most also take fare-paying participants who help with sailing.

Sailing to Antarctica is not something one undertakes lightly. A reliable engine, a cabin heater, a hull strong enough to withstand collision with ice and rocks, and a generously dimensioned anchor and chain – together with an experienced crew – will increase the odds of a trouble-free cruise. It's also important to be certain you are physically and mentally capable of coping with several weeks of isolation under often-strenuous conditions. Also, make sure you carry ample supplies of food, fuel, clothing and spare parts and that you are completely self-sufficient for the duration of your cruise.

Permits are required for yachts visiting the Antarctic, so contact your charter company and national agency to find out what you need.

Other Options

» **Flights to the Interior** Several companies offer flights to the mainland, followed by guided adventures. These can include a flight or ski to the Pole, or climbing Vinson Massif. See p207.

» **Flyovers** Overflights are the quickest and least-expensive way to see Antarctica (13 to 14 hours, 10,000-km round trip). Although no landings are made, observing the continent from altitude provides a unique perspective – unavailable to those who remain at sea level. Individual buildings can be seen when stations are overflown, but it is impossible to observe individual animals, even with binoculars. Experienced guides are on board to answer questions. See p208.

» **Fly-Cruise** If you'd rather skip sailing the Drake Passage, you can hop a flight and then get on your cruise; see p208.

» **Resupply Vessels** The French sub-Antarctic islands are accessible by resupply vessel; see p209.

The Crossing

Crossing the Southern Ocean is the price you pay to reach Antarctica by ship. The weather can be stormy: no landmasses impede low-pressure systems circling Antarctica, so the westerly winds can reach great speeds and seas can get very rough.

More than 90% of Antarctic cruises visiting the Antarctic Peninsula sail from Ushuaia, Argentina, and cross the Drake Passage – 1000km of ocean between South America and Antarctica. The crossing generally takes two days. Smooth seas are known as the 'Drake Lake;' their opposite is called the 'Drake Shake,' also referred to as 'paying the Drake Tax.' Once your ship reaches the South Shetlands or the Peninsula, nearly all uncomfortable motion ceases.

Life Aboard a Polar Ship

Voyages to polar seas are different from other sorts of travel, and even seasoned 'cruisers' may need to adjust. It's completely normal to feel lethargic and sluggish during the several days of sailing required to reach Antarctica.

Typically, a printed bulletin is distributed each night listing the next day's planned activities. Attending educational lectures and video screenings prepares you for what's ahead. Other ship-board activities include seabird-watching, iceberg spotting, reading and getting to know your fellow passengers.

Many Antarctic ships maintain an 'open bridge,' welcoming passengers to the navigation and steering area. The bridge closes during tricky navigation and if a pilot is aboard or the ship is in port. Etiquette demands no food or drink be brought to the bridge, and going barefoot is not appreciated. Keep your voice down; excessive noise interferes with communication between the navigator and helmsman. Of course, don't touch anything unless invited to do so.

One further warning: sailors are a superstitious lot, and whistling anywhere on a ship is considered bad luck – seriously. Tradition says that a person whistling is calling up the wind, and that a storm will result.

Shipboard Safety

International law requires every ship to hold a lifeboat drill within 24 hours of sailing. These are serious and mandatory for all passengers. Each cabin should contain a sign or card explaining which lifeboat station the occupants should use. There will also be a life vest for each person in the cabin; these are usually equipped with a whistle and a battery-powered beacon light, which starts flashing automatically upon contact with water. The universal signal to proceed to lifeboat stations is seven short blasts on the ship's bell or horn, followed by a long blast. This signal may be repeated several times for the lifeboat drill. Since there's only one such drill held during each voyage, if you ever hear the signal a second time during your voyage, it's the real thing. Go immediately to your cabin to pick up your life vest and some warm clothing and then head straight to your lifeboat station to await instructions.

A fall overboard is often fatal. Always keep one hand free ('one hand for the ship') to grab a railing or other support should the ship roll suddenly. Take care not just when climbing ladders and stairs, but anywhere that a sudden slam into furniture could result in a fractured limb or skull – yes, it happens.

Doors can swing dangerously; don't curl fingers around door jambs. Decks can be

CLASSIC LITERATURE & PHOTOGRAPHY

For more top reads and movies see p138.

Classic Antarctic Literature

The Rime of the Ancient Mariner, Samuel Taylor Coleridge (1798)

The Monikins, James Fenimore Cooper (1835)

The Narrative of Arthur Gordon Pym, Edgar Allan Poe (1837)

20,000 Leagues Under the Sea, Jules Verne (1870)

Photography

The Heart of the Great Alone: Scott, Shackleton, and Antarctic Photography, David Hempleman-Adams, Emma Stuart, Sophie Gordon

The Great White South, Herbert Ponting

Antarctic Photographs, 1910–1916: Scott, Mawson and Shackleton Expeditions, Herbert Ponting and Frank Hurley

Poles Apart: Parallel Visions of the Arctic and Antarctic, Galen Rowell

The Lost Photographs of Captain Scott: Unseen Photographs from the Legendary Antarctic Expedition, David M Wilson

Antarctica, Eliot Porter

Cold – Sailing to Antarctica, Thijs Heslenfeld

WHAT TO BRING

As the saying goes: there's no bad weather, only inappropriate clothing. As a general rule, pack clothes you can layer; temperatures will probably vary during your trip (from -10°C in Antarctica to 30°C in Buenos Aires).

☐ **Windproof & waterproof jacket and trousers** Some high-end operators provide the parka

☐ **Knee-high waterproof boots (ie Wellingtons) with high-traction soles** Essential for landings, when you step into surf and walk through guano

☐ **Felt insoles for boots** Great insulation; take two sets and dry on alternate days

☐ **Wool socks with equal number of thin socks** (silk or polypropylene sock liners

☐ **Warm (wool, flannel or polar fleece) shirts and sweaters**

☐ **Warm, casual trousers** to fit under your waterproof pants

☐ **Full set of thermal or silk long underwear** For warmth without bulk

☐ **Casual clothes** Whatever can squeeze into your baggage allowance for on-board life

☐ **100% UV-filtering sunglasses** Sun reflection off ice and water creates lots of glare

☐ **Extra contact lenses or eyeglasses**

☐ **Warm gloves and glove liners** Liners are handy when removing thick gloves for photography

☐ **Hat** Polypropylene or wool, long enough to protect ears

☐ **Balaclava or scarf** Balaclava is more effective

☐ **Ski goggles** Preferred over sunglasses by some, but fogging can be a problem

☐ **Waterproof day-pack** or bag to go in your pack

☐ **Camera, telephoto lens, UV filters, spare batteries and chargers, and double the digital-photo storage capacity (or film) you think you'll need** Polarizing filters cut through glare in the water and darken skies; also bring waterproof/zip-close plastic bags for this gear

☐ **Binoculars**

☐ **Seasickness remedies** Pills, patches, acupressure bracelets

☐ **Sun block**

☐ **Flashlight** Useful inside dark historic huts

☐ **Earplugs** For sleeping on ships

☐ **Bathing suit and watershoes** (old tennis shoes will do) Only if you are going to the thermal waters at Deception Island

☐ **Patience** Weather, ice and unpredictable seas set the schedule, not calendars or clocks

slippery with rain, snow or oil; move carefully. Beware of raised doorsills, stanchions and other shipboard hardware.

Health

Medical resources here are limited. There are no public hospitals, pharmacies or doctor's offices. Ships and research bases have infirmaries, but usually with just a single doctor or nurse, and limited equipment. A life-threatening medical problem will require evacuation to a country with advanced medical care.

Ship's doctors treat problems arising *en voyage*, but are not available for routine consultations, nor are they equipped for elaborate medical intervention. These voyages to extreme climates can test the healthiest among us: make all necessary preparations before leaving; and if your health is shaky, consider postponing; see p205 for typical ailments.

Preparations

No special vaccines are required for travel to Antarctica, but everyone should be up-to-date on routine immunizations. Bring any medications in their original containers, clearly labeled, and, if required, syringes. Also bring a signed, dated letter from your physician describing all medical conditions and medications, including generic names.

Insurance

Find out in advance if your insurance plan makes payments directly to providers or reimburses you later for overseas health expenditures; and inquire of your tour operator what health facilities are available. If your insurance does not cover medical expenses abroad, or costly emergency evacuations (tens of thousands of dollars), consider organizing supplementary insurance; some tour operators require it.

regions at a glance

Antarctica's various regions are surprisingly diverse. The encircling Southern Ocean, with its rough-and-tumble sealing and whaling history, offers superb wildlife viewing, and the adventure of a magnificent sail. The Antarctic Peninsula, with its warm climate (for Antarctica!), combines super ice formations with the continent's most abundant seals, penguins, seabirds and whales.

Those rare few who make it to the Ross Sea side encounter well-preserved history, and experience dramatic land- and ice-scapes, like the towering Ross Ice Shelf, the bizarre Dry Valleys and steaming volcano, Mt Erebus. East Antarctica belongs to the vast, icy Polar Plateau. Its shores are rimmed with stations and seabirds, but the interior, including the Pole, is ice as far as your eye can see.

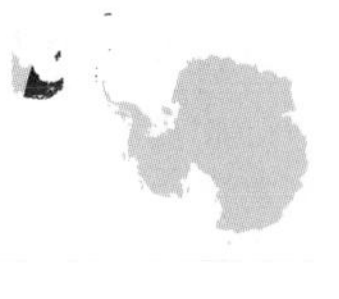

Southern Ocean

Wildlife ✓✓✓
History ✓✓✓
Adventure ✓✓✓

South Georgia & Falkland Islands

Vast seasonal colonies of seals, penguins and seabirds cram the shores of these isolated, windswept islands. Some beaches are so packed you won't even be able to land…content yourself with Zodiac-cruising alongside, as beachmaster seals defend their turf.

Southernmost Outposts

Imagine the early days of southern exploration as you visit museums in Ushuaia and Stanley, before heading to South Georgia's only whaling station open to visitors: Grytviken, where Shackleton and Wild are buried. The Orkneys and South Shetlands harbor some of the region's first bases.

Crossing of a Lifetime

Hold tight as you cross the roughest ocean in the world. When you reach relatively calmer waters you will cruise between islands first explored by hardy sailors aboard rough-hewn sealing ships.

p30

Antarctic Peninsula

Wildlife ✓✓✓
History ✓✓
Adventure ✓✓✓

Whales, Seals & Birds...Oh My!

Penguins chatter and breed, seals slip in and out of the sea, and seabirds gyre overhead. The Antarctic Peninsula region offers the very best of continental wildlife, and in abundance.

Preserved Bases

From Port Lockroy's popular museum to the deserted shores of Snow Hill Island with Nordenskjöld's hut, old science stations dot the Peninsula's shores. Detaille and Stonington islands' bases are mid-20th century time capsules.

Sailing Channels & Bays

This is your chance to really explore Antarctica. Glittering waterways weave between mountains, icebergs and glaciers. Some will go by Zodiac, others might opt for a kayak, but it's the dramatic landscape and abundant wildlife that bring you to the heart of Antarctica.

p71

Ross Sea

Wildlife ✓✓
History ✓✓✓
Landscapes ✓✓✓

Penguin Rookeries

From Cape Washington's emperor penguin colony to Cape Royds' and Cape Adare's Adélies, you can't go wrong if it's continental penguins you're after. Largely undisturbed, it is a privilege to witness these birds in the wild.

Historic Huts

Those tragic and dramatic tales that exemplify human courage, skill, fortitude, triumph and failure are written on the Ross Sea's shores. Shackleton, Amundsen and Scott all took their shots at the Pole from here, and before them Borchgrevink spent the first long, dark winter on the continent.

Geographical Phenomena

Extraordinary features begin at the towering, floating Ross Ice Shelf, continue on to volcanic Mt Erebus and hit land at the glaciers making their inexorable runs to the sea. They culminate in the exceptional Dry Valleys.

p89

East Antarctica & The South Pole

Adventure ✓✓✓
Science ✓✓✓
Isolation ✓✓✓

Reaching Pole

Truly, the accomplishment of a lifetime...a very lucky few get to experience standing at the absolute bottom of the world. Contemplate those who have come before you, and enjoy the marvel of knowing there is nowhere left to go...you are furthest south.

Scientific Terrain

East Antarctica is almost exclusively the province of scientists. Base camps dot the polar plateau at its highest points (Dome A, Dome C), Vostok and Pole, and ring its coastline. Cutting-edge experiments drill deep beneath the ice cap and reach out into deepest space.

Polar Plateau

This vast ice cap, thousands of meters thick, covers entire mountain ranges and subglacial lakes, now being explored for the first time. On its edges, oases of uncovered land offer shelter in an otherwise barren expanse.

p107

❯ **Every listing is recommended by our authors, and their favourite places are listed first**

❯ **Look out for these icons:**

Our author's top recommendation

A green or sustainable option

No payment required

See the Index for a full list of destinations covered in this book.

On the Road

Southern Ocean

Includes »

Best Places to Spot Wildlife

» North coast of South Georgia (p50)

» Livingston Island (p65)

» West Falkland (p48)

» Deception Island (p65)

Best Historical Sights

» Grytviken (p56)

» Falkland Islands Museum (p43)

» Museo Marítimo & Museo del Presidio (p33)

» Orcadas Station (p60)

Why Go?

The southern parts of the Atlantic, Indian and Pacific Oceans form the fifth ocean of the world, the Southern Ocean. Its wild waters surround Antarctica and isolate it geographically, biologically and climatically from the rest of the world. Scattered around these waters are the islands that early explorers and sealers encountered before they actually found Terra Australis Incognita.

Visit the rocky but fecund shores of the Falkland Islands and South Georgia, with abundant wildlife and history. Most cruises from South America call in at the South Shetland Islands or the South Orkney Islands, where people set up their first Antarctic outposts. Travelers from Australia, New Zealand and South Africa approach the continent from the Ross Sea side, with seabird-rich Heard and Macquarie islands.

Sailing these waters and sighting these windswept isles recreates the journeys of early adventurers.

Top Resources

» **South Georgia & South Sandwich official site** (www.sgisland.gs) Loads of info, including permit requirements.

» **South Georgia Heritage Trust** (www.sght.org) History/wildlife conservation group.

» **Falkland Islands** (www.falklandislands.com) Central source on the island group.

» **A Visitor's Guide to the Falkland Islands** By Debbie Summers with photos, excellent maps and interesting facts by a native Falklander. Published in 2005 by **Falklands Conservation** (www.falklandsconservation.com).

» **Antarctic Equipment** (www.antarcticequipment.com.ar) Last-minute equipment in Ushuaia.

» **Ushuaia Tourist Office** www.turismoushuaia.com

» **Antarctic Tourist Information** (www.tierradelfuego.org.ar/antartida) Argentina's Tierra del Fuego website includes Antarctic information.

USHUAIA

02901 / POP 57,000

Nearly 90% of all Antarctic tourists depart from Ushuaia in Argentina, thanks to the city's fortunate location almost directly across the 100km-wide Drake Passage from the Antarctic Peninsula.

A busy port and adventure hub, Ushuaia is a sliver of steep streets and jumbled buildings below the snowcapped Martial Range.

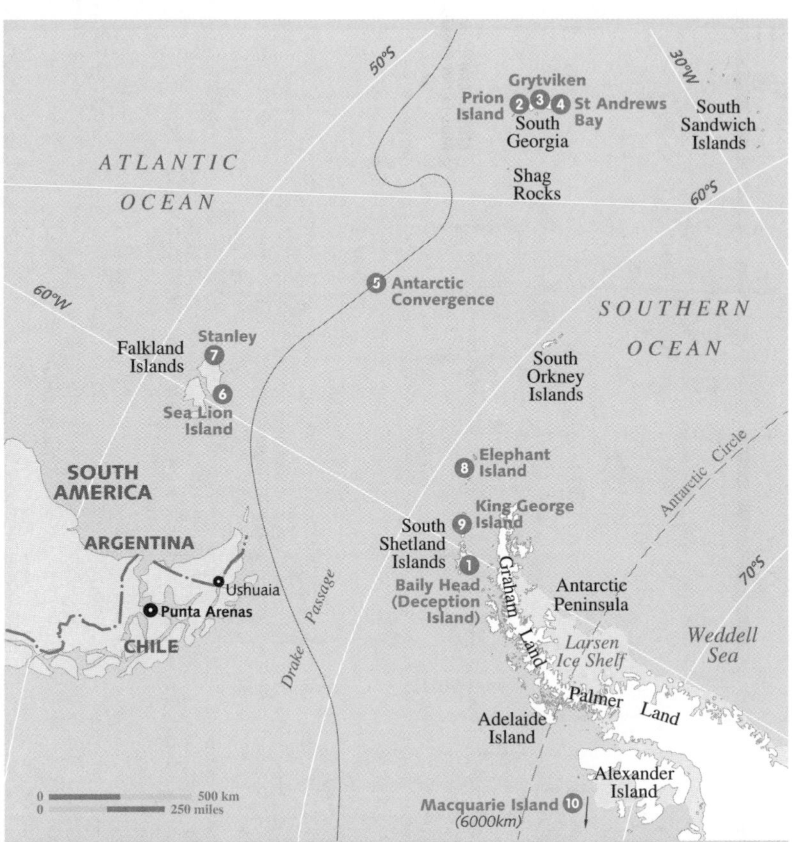

Southern Ocean Highlights

1. Brave surging swells to reach Deception Island's giant chinstrap rookery at **Baily Head** (p65)
2. View nesting albatrosses on **Prion Island** (p54)
3. Ring the bells in Grytviken's evocative old **Whaler's Church** (p56)
4. See hundreds of thousands of king penguins at **St Andrews Bay** (p59)
5. Cross the **Antarctic Convergence** (p49), the oceanographic boundary separating Antarctica from the rest of the world
6. See all five of the Falklands' penguin species at **Sea Lion Island** (p48)
7. Share a drink with locals or visit the **Falkland Islands Museum** (p43) in Stanley
8. Zodiac cruise off **Elephant Island** (p62), where members of Shackleton's *Endurance* expedition survived more than four months
9. Chat with winterovers at one of eight countries' Antarctic stations on **King George Island** (p62)
10. Visit four million penguins, including about 850,000 breeding pairs of royals, at **Macquarie Island** (p69).

Ushuaia

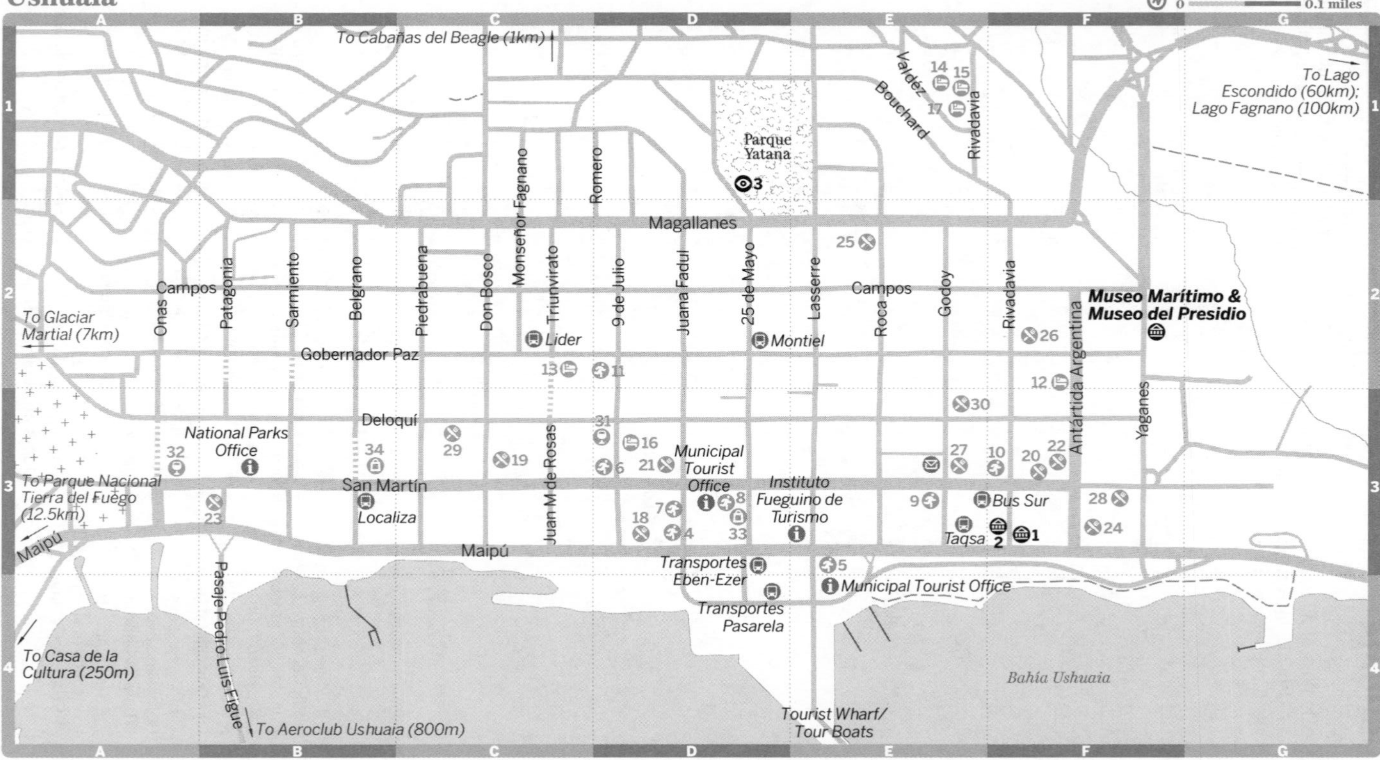
0 200 m
0 0.1 miles
To Cabañas del Beagle (1km)
To Lago Escondido (60km); Lago Fagnano (100km)
To Glaciar Martial (7km)
To Parque Nacional Tierra del Fuego (12.5km)
To Casa de la Cultura (250m)
To Aeroclub Ushuaia (800m)
Valdéz
Bouchard
Rivadavia
Parque Yatana
Magallanes
Campos
Onas
Patagonia
Sarmiento
Belgrano
Piedrabuena
Don Bosco
Monseñor Fagnano
Triunvirato
Romero
9 de Julio
Juana Fadul
25 de Mayo
Lasserre
Roca
Godoy
Antártida Argentina
Yaganes
Gobernador Paz
Deloquí
San Martín
Juan M de Rosas
Maipú
Pasaje Pedro Luis Figue
Museo Marítimo & Museo del Presidio
Lider
Montiel
National Parks Office
Municipal Tourist Office
Instituto Fueguino de Turismo
Bus Sur
Taqsa
Localiza
Transportes Eben-Ezer
Transportes Pasarela
Municipal Tourist Office
Tourist Wharf/ Tour Boats
Bahía Ushuaia

During the past 30 years, Ushuaia (pronounced 'oosh-wya') has expanded rapidly from a small village into a city of almost 60,000. Growth is only partly due to the influx of Antarctic tourists: this region of Tierra del Fuego attracts visitors in its own right, and high wages draw Argentines from all over to resettle in the world's southernmost city.

Sights

Paralleling the Beagle Channel, Maipú becomes Malvinas Argentinas west of the cemetery, then turns into RN 3, continuing 12km to **Parque Nacional Tierra del Fuego**. Most visitor services are on or near San Martín, a block from the waterfront.

The tourist office distributes a free city-tour map with information on the historic houses around town. **Casa Beban** (cnr Maipú & Plúschow; ⏲11am-6pm) was built in 1911 using parts ordered from Sweden, and sometimes hosts local art exhibits.

Museo Marítimo & Museo del Presidio MUSEUM
(☎437481; www.museomaritimo.com; cnr Yaganes & Gobernador Paz; admission AR$70; ⏲10am-8pm) Convicts were transferred from Isla de los Estados (Staten Island) to Ushuaia in 1906 to build this national prison, finished in 1920. The spokelike halls of single cells, designed to house 380, actually held up to 800 before it closed in 1947.

Antarctic exhibits include stuffed penguins, a fur-seal pelt, photos, and artifacts from the Nordenskjöld expedition's huts on Snow Hill Island (p86) and at Hope Bay. Antarctic fossils from Snow Hill and Seymour (p86) islands are also on view.

Perhaps the best collection of Antarctic ship models anywhere in the world is displayed throughout the museum. Also, remains of the world's narrowest-gauge freight train, which transported prisoners between town and work stations, sit in the courtyard. Guided tours are at 11:30am and 6:30pm.

Museo Yámana MUSEUM
(☎422874; Rivadavia 56; admission AR$25; ⏲10am-8pm) Small but carefully tended, with an excellent overview of the Yámana (Yahgan) way of life. Displays cover how they survived harsh weather without clothing, why only women knew how to swim and how campfires were kept in moving canoes. Expertly detailed dioramas (in English

Ushuaia

Top Sights
- Museo Marítimo & Museo del Presidio F2

Sights
- 1 Museo del Fin del Mundo F3
- 2 Museo Yámana F3
- 3 Parque Yatana D1

Activities, Courses & Tours
- 4 All Patagonia D3
- 5 Boat Tours E3
- 6 Canal Fun D3
- 7 Club Andino Ushuaia D3
- 8 Compañía de Guías de Patagonia D3
- 9 Rumbo Sur E3
- 10 Turismo Comapa F3
- 11 Ushuaia Turismo D2

Sleeping
- 12 Antarctica Hostel F2
- 13 Freestyle C2
- 14 Galeazzi-Basily B&B E1
- 15 La Casa de Tere B&B E1
- 16 Martín Fierro B&B D3
- 17 Posada Fin del Mundo E1

Eating
- 18 Almacen Ramos Generales D3
- 19 Bodegón Fueguino C3
- 20 Café Bar Tante Sara F3
- 21 Café-Bar Tante Sara D3
- 22 Chiko F3
- 23 El Turco B3
- 24 Kalma Resto F3
- 25 Kaupé E2
- 26 La Anónima F2
- 27 La Estancia E3
- 28 Lomitos Martinica F3
- 29 María Lola Restó C3
- 30 Placeres Patagónicos E3

Drinking
- 31 Dublin Irish Pub D3
- 32 Macario 1910 .... A3

Shopping
- 33 Boutique del Libro D3
- 34 Boutique del Libro B3

USHUAIA PRICE ICONS

Inflation in Argentina is rampant, running (unofficially) at around 25%. To avoid a shock, check current prices.

SLEEPING	DOUBLE ROOM
$	<AR$250
$$	AR$250-500
$$$	>AR$500

EATING	MAIN DISH
$	<AR$45
$$	AR$45-65
$$$	>AR$65

and Spanish) are based on bays and inlets of the national park.

Museo del Fin del Mundo MUSEUM
(☎421863; www.tierradelfuego.org.ar/museo; cnr Maipú & Rivadavia; admission AR$30; ⏲9am-8pm) Built in 1903, this former bank contains exhibits on Fuegian natural history, stuffed birdlife and the lives of natives and those in early penal colonies.

FREE **Parque Yatana** PARK
(Fundación Cultiva; ☎425212; cnr Magallanes & 25 de Mayo; ⏲3-6pm Wed-Fri) Part art project, part urban refuge, this city block of lenga forest has been preserved from encroaching development by one determined family.

Activities

Club Andino Ushuaia HIKING
(☎422335; www.clubandinoushuaia.com.ar, in Spanish; Juana Fadul 50; ⏲9am-1pm & 3-8pm Mon-Fri) Sells a map and bilingual trekking, mountaineering and mountain-biking guidebook. The club occasionally organizes hikes and can recommend guides. Unguided trekkers are strongly encouraged to register here or with the tourist office before hiking and after a safe return.

Cerro Martial & Glaciar Martial HIKING
(optional chairlift AR$55; ⏲10am-4pm) A hearty all-day hike from the city center leads up to Glaciar Martial, with fantastic panoramas of Ushuaia and the Beagle Channel. Alternatively, catch a taxi or jump aboard a minivan (AR$35, half-hourly, from 8:30am to 6:30pm) at the corner of Maipú and Juana Fadul.

Views are more impressive than the actual glacier. Follow San Martín west and keep ascending as it zigzags. When you arrive at the ski run 7km northwest of town, either take the *aerosilla* (chairlift) or walk another two hours. For the best views, hike an hour above the chairlift terminus. A refuge offers coffee, desserts and beer at the *aerosilla* base. Weather is changeable so take warm, dry clothing and sturdy footwear. Evening **canopy tours** (escuela@tierradelfuego.org.ar; Refugio de Montaña; AR$130; ⏲10am-5:15pm Oct-Jun) are by reservation only.

Beagle Channel BOATING
Navigating the Beagle Channel's gunmetal-gray waters, with glaciers and rocky isles in the distance, offers a fresh perspective and decent wildlife-watching. Find operators on the tourist wharf on Maipú between Lasserre and Roca. Harbor cruises are usually four-hour morning or afternoon excursions (AR$180 to AR$230) to sea lion and cormorant colonies. The number of passengers, extent of snacks and hiking options may vary between operators. A highlight is an island stop to hike and look at *conchales,* middens or shell mounds, left by the native Yahgan.

Aeroclub Ushuaia SCENIC FLIGHT
(☎421717, 421892; www.aeroclubushuaia.org.ar; 30min flight AR$443) Scenic flights over the channel.

Tours

Ushuaia is loaded with tour companies offering packages throughout the region, and to Antarctica.

All Patagonia GUIDED TOUR
(☎433622; www.allpatagonia.com; Juana Fadul 60) Amex rep offering moreconventional and luxurious trips.

Canal Fun ADVENTURE TOUR
(☎437395; www.canalfun.com; 9 de Julio 118) Run by hip young guys, these popular all-day outings include hiking and kayaking in Parque Nacional Tierra del Fuego (AR$425), and a multisport outing that includes a visit to a penguin colony (AR$785).

Compañía de Guías de Patagonia WALKING TOUR
(☎437753; www.companiadeguias.com.ar; San Martín 654) Excursions in the national park, full-day treks and ice-hiking on Glaciar Vinciguerra (AR$329), three-day treks to Valle Andorra and Paso la Oveja (AR$2026).

Nunatak Adventure ADVENTURE TOUR
(☎430329; www.nunatakadventure.com) Competitively priced adventure tours; has its own mountain base.

Rumbo Sur GUIDED TOUR
(☎422275; www.rumbosur.com.ar; San Martín 350) Ushuaia's longest-running agency specializes in conventional activities and bookings to Antarctica.

Turismo de Campo GUIDED TOUR
(☎437351; www.turismodecampo.com, in Spanish; Fuegia Basquet 414) Light trekking, Beagle Channel sailing trips and visits to Estancia Rolito near Río Grande. Variety of nine- to 12-night Antarctica passages.

Sleeping

Reserve ahead from January to early March. Check when booking for free arrival transfers. Most places offer laundry service. The municipal tourist office has lists of B&Bs and *cabañas* (cabins), and posts a list of available lodgings outside after closing time.

Hostels abound, all with kitchens and most with internet access. Rates typically drop by 25% in low season (April to October). Prices here include tax (21%) and are general high-season rates. Payment in cash sometimes gets a 10% discount.

Antarctica Hostel HOSTEL $
(☎435774; www.antarcticahostel.com; Antártida Argentina 270; dm/d AR$70/125; @) This friendly backpacker hub delivers with a warm atmosphere and helpful staff. It turns out that an open floor plan and beer on tap are conducive to making friends. Cement rooms are ample, with radiant floor heating.

Galeazzi-Basily B&B B&B $$
(☎423213; www.avesdelsur.com.ar; Valdéz 323; s/d with shared bath AR$190/280, d/tr/q cabin AR$390/450/520; @) The best feature of this elegant wooded residence is the hospitable family who makes you feel at home. Rooms are small but offer personal touches. Because beds are twin-sized, couples may prefer a modern cabin out back.

Cabañas del Beagle CABIN $$$
(☎432785; www.cabanasdelbeagle.com; Las Aljabas 375; 2-person cabin AR$1055, 2-night minimum) Couples in search of a romantic hideaway delight in these rustic chic cabins with heated stone floors, crackling fireplaces and full kitchens stocked daily with fresh bread, coffee and other treats. The personable owner, Alejandro, wins high praise for his attentive service. It's 13 blocks uphill from the center and accessed via Av Leandro Alem.

Freestyle HOSTEL $
(☎432874; www.ushuaiafreestyle.com; Gobernador Paz 866/868; dm without/with bath AR$80/90; @) With an MTV vibe you'll love (or not), this tricked-out hostel boasts modern dorms, a marble-countertop cooking area, and a sprawling living room with pool table and panoramic views. Brothers Emilio and Gabriel offer tips and tour connections.

La Posta HOSTEL $
(☎444650; www.laposta-ush.com.ar; Perón Sur 864; dm/d AR$85/135; @) Despite its location on the outskirts of town, this cozy guesthouse is hugely popular with young travelers thanks to warm service, homey decor and spotless open kitchens.

La Casa de Tere B&B B&B $$
(☎422312; www.lacasadetere.com.ar; Rivadavia 620; s/d AR$211/253, d with bath AR$337) Tere showers guests with attention and gives them the run of this beautiful, modern home with great views. Its three tidy rooms fill up fast. Guests can cook, and there's cable TV and a living room fireplace. It's a short, steep walk uphill from the center.

Posada Fin del Mundo B&B $$$
(☎437345; www.posadafindelmundo.com.ar; cnr Rivadavia & Valdéz; d without/with bath AR$422/527) This rambling family home exudes character, starting with a snug living room with folk art and expansive water views. Eight fresh, tiled rooms tend toward the small, but beds are long. Pricey for its category, but breakfast is abundant and there is afternoon tea and cakes.

Cabañas Aldea Nevada CABIN $$$
(☎422851; www.aldeanevada.com.ar; Martial 1430; d AR$520, 2-night minimum; @) This beautiful patch of lenga forest is discreetly dotted with 13 log cabins with outdoor grills and rough-hewn benches contemplatively placed by ponds. Interiors are rustic but modern, with functional kitchens, wood stoves and hardwood details.

Cumbres del Martial INN $$$
(☎424779; www.cumbresdelmartial.com.ar; Martial 3560; d/cabin AR$1160/1667; @) This stylish place at the base of Glaciar Martial has standard rooms with a touch of English cottage. Two-story wooden cabins are simply stunning, with stone fireplaces, Jacuzzis

and dazzling vaulted windows. Lush robes, massages and your country's newspaper delivered to your mailbox are some of the decadent extras.

Familia Piatti B&B B&B $$
(☎437104; www.interpatagonia.com/familiapiatti, in Spanish; Bahía Paraíso 812, Bosque del Faldeo; s/d/tr AR$240/335/395; @📶) If idling in the forest sounds good, head for this friendly B&B with down duvets and native lenga-wood furniture. Hiking trails nearby lead up into the mountains. The friendly owners are multilingual (English, Italian, Spanish and Portuguese) and can arrange transport and guided excursions.

Martín Fierro B&B B&B $$
(☎430525; www.martinfierrobyb.com.ar; 9 de Julio 175; s/d with shared bath AR$250/350, s/d AR$350/500; ⏱Oct-Apr; 📶) Spending a night at this charming inn feels like staying at the cool mountain cabin of a worldly friend who makes strong coffee and has a great book collection. The owner, Javier, personally built the interiors with local wood and stone; these days he cultivates a friendly, laid-back atmosphere.

Eating

Kalma Resto GOURMET $$$
(☎425786; www.kalmaresto.com.ar; Av Antártida 57; mains AR$55-105; ⏱8pm-midnight) Creating quite a stir, this tiny chef-owned gem presents Fuegian staples, like crab and octopus, in a refreshing new context. Roast lamb stews with earthy pine mushrooms meet summer greens and edible flowers fresh from the garden. Service is stellar, with young chef Jorge making the rounds of the few black-linen tables. For dessert, indulge in deconstructed chocolate cake.

Kaupé INTERNATIONAL $$$
(☎422704; www.kaupe.com.ar; Roca 470; mains AR$80-120) For an out-of-body seafood experience, head to this candlelit house overlooking the bay. Chef Ernesto Vivian employs the freshest of everything, and service is nothing less than impeccable. The tasting menu (AR$360 with wine and champagne) features two starters, a main dish and dessert, with standouts such as king crab and spinach chowder.

Bodegón Fueguino PATAGONIAN $$
(☎431972; www.tierradehumos.com/bodegon; San Martín 859; mains AR$32-82; ⏱Tue-Sun) The spot to sample hearty home-style Patagonian fare or gather for wine and appetizers. This century-old Fuegian home is cozied up with sheepskin-clad benches, cedar barrels and ferns. A *picada* (shared appetizer plate) for two includes eggplant, lamb brochettes, crab and bacon-wrapped plums.

María Lola Restó ARGENTINE $$
(☎421185; Deloquí 1048; mains AR$45-70; ⏱noon-midnight Mon-Sat) Locals pack this creative cafe-style restaurant overlooking the channel for homemade pasta with seafood or strip steak in rich mushroom sauce. Portions tend toward humongous: desserts can easily be split.

Chez Manu INTERNATIONAL $$$
(☎432253; www.chezmanu.com; Martial 2135; mains AR$55-90) If you are headed to Glaciar Martial, don't miss this gem, 2km on the way out of town. Chef Emmanuel puts a French touch on fresh local ingredients, such as Fuegian lamb or cold *fruits de mer* (seafood). The three-course set lunch is the best deal, and views are a welcome bonus.

Chiko SEAFOOD $$
(☎432036; Av Antártida Argentina 182; mains AR$38-65; ⏱noon-3pm & 7:30-11:30pm Mon-Sat) This popular 2nd-floor restaurant decorated with Chilean memorabilia is a clear boon for seafood lovers. King crab, *paila marina* (shellfish stew) and fish are done so well that you might not mind the uneven service.

Almacen Ramos Generales CAFE $$
(☎427317; www.ramosgeneralesushuaia.com; Maipú 749; mains AR$30-70; ⏱9am-midnight) The real draws of this ambience-rich general store are the croissants and crusty baguettes baked by the French pastry chef. There's also local beer on tap, wine and light, if pricey, sandwiches, soups and quiche.

La Estancia STEAKHOUSE $$
(☎431241; Godoy & San Martín; mains AR$40-90) For authentic Argentine *asado* (barbecue), it is hard to beat this reliable, well-priced grill. At night it's packed with locals and travelers alike, feasting on whole roast lamb, juicy steaks, sizzling ribs and heaping salads.

El Turco CAFE $
(☎424711; San Martín 1410; mains AR$22-55; ⏱noon-3pm & 8pm-midnight) Nothing fancy, this classic Argentine cafe nonetheless charms with reasonable prices and swift bow-tied waiters game to try out their French on tourists. Standards include

milanesa (breaded meat), pizzas and roast chicken.

Placeres Patagónicos CAFE $$
(☎433798; www.patagonicosweb.com.ar; 289 Deloquí; mains AR$29-60) This stylish cafe-deli serves up wooden cutting boards piled high with homemade bread and mouth-watering local specialties: smoked trout and wild boar. Coffee arrives in a bowl-sized mug.

Café-Bar Tante Sara CAFE $$
(☎433710; www.cafebartantesara.com.ar; cnr San Martín & Juana Fadul; mains AR$40-80) Popular for its bubbly atmosphere, this corner bistro has a sister branch near the intersection of San Martín and Rivadavia and is often packed with locals having coffee and pastries.

Lomitos Martinica FAST FOOD $
(San Martín 68; mains AR$22-32; ⏲11:30am-3pm & 8:30pm-midnight) Cheap and cheerful, this greasy spoon with grillside seating serves enormous *milanesa* sandwiches and a cheap lunch special.

La Anónima SUPERMARKET $
(cnr Gobernador Paz & Rivadavia) Offers cheap take-out.

Drinking & Entertainment

Dublin Irish Pub BAR
(☎430744; www.dublinushuaia.com; cnr 9 de Julio & Deloquí) Dublin doesn't feel so far away with the lively banter and free-flowing local Beagle beers at this dimly lit foreigners' favorite. Occasional live music.

Macario 1910 PUB
(☎422757; www.macario1910.com; San Martín 1485; sandwiches AR$22; ⏲6pm-late) A welcoming pub with polished wood and leather booths, local Beagle beer and above-average pub fare.

Küar Resto Bar PUB
(☎437396; www.kuar.com.ar; Av Perito Moreno 2232; ⏲6pm-late) This chic new log cabin-style bar welcomes the 'after-ski' crowd for fresh cocktails, local beer and tapas. The real highlight, especially at sunset, is the jaw-dropping views over the water. Cab it a few kilometers outside of town.

Casa de la Cultura PERFORMING ARTS
(☎422417; cnr Malvinas Argentinas & 12 de Octubre) Hidden behind a gym; hosts occasional live-music shows.

Shopping

Boutique del Libro BOOKS
(☎432117, 424750; 25 de Mayo 62; ⏲10am-9pm) Outstanding selection of Patagonia and Antarctica-themed material; there's a branch at San Martín 1120.

Information

EMERGENCY **Hospital Regional** (☎107, 423200; cnr Fitz Roy & 12 de Octubre)

IMMIGRATION OFFICE (☎422334; Beauvoir 1536; ⏲9am-noon Mon-Fri)

MONEY **Cambio Thaler** (San Martín 209; ⏲10am-1pm & 5-8pm Mon-Sat, 5-8pm Sun) Convenience equals slightly poorer exchange rates. Several banks on Maipú and San Martín have ATMs.

TOURIST INFORMATION **Administración de Parques Nacionales** (National Parks office; ☎421315; San Martín 1395; ⏲9am-4pm Mon-Fri)

Instituto Fueguino de Turismo (Infuetur; ☎421423; www.tierradelfuego.org.ar; Maipú 505) Ground floor of Hotel Albatros.

Municipal tourist office (☎432000, at airport 423970, outside of Tierra del Fuego 0800-333-1476; www.turismoushuaia.com, in Spanish; San Martín 674) Very helpful, with English- and French-speaking staff, message board and multilingual brochure. Lodging, activities and transport info. Also at airport and pier.

Getting Around

TO/FROM AIRPORT To/from the modern airport (USH), 4km southwest of downtown, cost AR$25. Charter taxis for around AR$140 per hour.

BUS & SHUTTLE Local bus service along Maipú. Hourly ski shuttles (AR$70 round-trip) from the corner of Juana Fadul and Maipú to resorts along RN 3 (9am to 2pm daily). Resorts provide transportation from downtown Ushuaia.

CAR Rental rates for compact cars, including insurance, start at around AR$464 per day. Some may not charge for drop-off in other parts of Argentine Tierra del Fuego.

Localiza (☎430739; Sarmiento 81)

CAPE HORN

Most Antarctic tour ships sail to and from Ushuaia, which means that passengers may catch sight of the fabled Cape Horn (Cabo de Hornos) – and, rarely, land there. Cape Horn is a synonym for adventure and the romance of the old days of sailing – although for most of the poor sailors attempting to double the

Horn, there was no romance on a cold winter ocean with a gale blowing.

From a European point of view, Cape Horn was discovered in January 1616 by Dutchmen Jakob Le Maire and Willem Schouten, sailing in the ship *Unity*. They named the cape after their ship *Hoorn,* which had accidentally burned at Puerto Deseado on the Patagonian coast.

Horn Island, where the famous cape forms its southernmost headland, is just 8km long. The cape itself rises to 424m, with striking black cliffs on its upper ramparts.

Landings at Cape Horn are very infrequent. They are expensive to attempt (ships must have a Chilean pilot for navigation in the shoal-filled offshore waters) and the weather seldom cooperates. Chilean authorities routinely refuse requests to make landings – or even to approach closely. When permission is granted, landings are usually made in the westward of the two bays located east of the cape. A steep wooden staircase of about 110 steps leads to high ground above the beach.

Cabo de Hornos Light is a white fiberglass-reinforced plastic tower 6m high with a red band around it. It's automated, but a nearby Chilean naval observation station, consisting of two huts with a conspicuous radio antenna about 1600m northeast of the light, is home to a few lone officers. The small wooden chapel is called **Stella Maris**, or 'Star of the Sea.'

A **stone monument** on a plinth surrounded by heavy iron chains honors the ancient mariners who rounded Cape Horn.

Another monument, in the form of a large **abstract sculpture**, depicts – in the negative space formed by four steel plates – a soaring albatross. It commemorates those lost in the treacherous seas off this headland.

The great Andean condors can be seen here, as well as Magellanic penguins, which nest in burrows in the moss and tussock grass.

ISLAS DIEGO RAMIREZ

These Chilean islands, located 100km southwest of Cape Horn, became the most southerly known land in the world when they were discovered on February 12, 1619 by two brothers, Bartolomé and Gonzálo de Nodal, sailing in *Nuestra Señora de Achoa* and *Nuestra Señora de Buen Succeso,* on a Portuguese expedition. The brothers named the archipelago for their expedition's cosmographer, and the islands held their 'southernmost' distinction for more than 150 years, until Cook discovered the South Sandwich Islands in 1775.

Islas Diego Ramirez comprise two small groups of islands: northerly Isla Norte and four smaller islands; and the southerly pair, 93-hectare Isla Bartolomé (maximum elevation 190m) and Isla Gonzálo (38 hectares and 139m), separated by a 400m channel, along with a dozen other smaller islands and rocks.

At **Caleta Condell**, a small cove on the northeast side of Isla Gonzálo, the Chilean Navy established a small meteorological station and lighthouse in 1951.

Macaroni, rockhopper and Magellanic penguins breed here, and kings and chinstraps occasionally visit.

Islas Diego Ramirez are critically important for albatrosses. As the southernmost albatross breeding ground in the world, the islands account for some 20% of the world's black-browed albatrosses (55,000 pairs) and 23% of the world's grey-headed albatrosses (17,000 pairs), according to a 2002 nest survey.

FALKLAND ISLANDS

The Falkland Islands are a popular addition to many Antarctic voyages, but they're well worth seeing on their own for their spectacular populations of penguins, seals and albatrosses. Surrounded by the South

LAST-MINUTE ANTARCTICA

Haven't booked your trip yet? Last-minute bookings can be made through **Ushuaia Turismo** (☎02901-436003; www.ushuaiaturismoevt.com.ar; ushuaiaturismo@speedy.com.ar; Gobernador Paz 865). Rent gear in the same building at **Antarctic Equipment** (www.antarcticequipment.com.ar). For Antarctica information, consult the very helpful **Oficina Antártida** (Antarctica tourist office; ☎02901-430015; www.tierradelfuego.org.ar/antartida) at the pier.

For cruise companies, see p208. Many local tour companies offer packages.

Falkland Islands

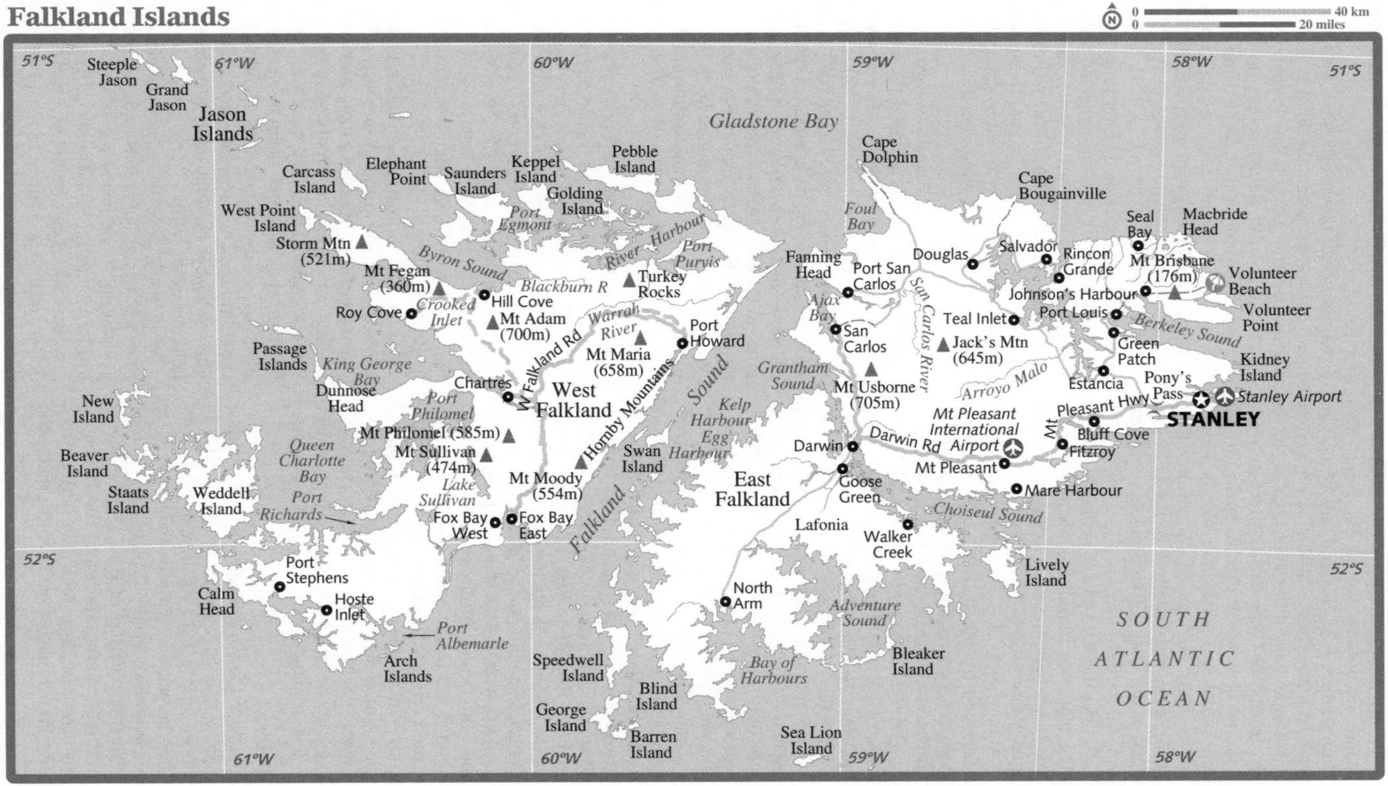

0 – 40 km
0 – 20 miles

51°S
61°W
60°W
59°W
58°W
52°S

Steeple Jason
Grand Jason
Jason Islands
Gladstone Bay
Pebble Island
Keppel Island
Golding Island
Saunders Island
Elephant Point
Carcass Island
West Point Island
Port Egmont
River Harbour
Port Purvis
Storm Mtn (521m)
Byron Sound
Mt Fegan (360m)
Hill Cove
Blackburn R
Turkey Rocks
Roy Cove
Crooked Inlet
Mt Adam (700m)
Warrah River
Port Howard
Mt Maria (658m)
Passage Islands
King George Bay
Falkland Rd
Chartres
West Falkland
Hornby Mountains
Dunnose Head
Port Philomel
New Island
Mt Philomel (585m)
Mt Sullivan (474m)
Lake Sullivan
Queen Charlotte Bay
Beaver Island
Staats Island
Weddell Island
Port Richards
Mt Moody (554m)
Fox Bay West
Fox Bay East
Falkland Sound
Swan Island
Kelp Harbour
Egg Harbour
Port Stephens
Calm Head
Hoste Inlet
Port Albemarle
Arch Islands
Speedwell Island
George Island
Blind Island
Barren Island
Cape Dolphin
Foul Bay
Fanning Head
Port San Carlos
Ajax Bay
San Carlos
San Carlos River
Grantham Sound
Mt Usborne (705m)
Douglas
Cape Bougainville
Salvador
Rincon Grande
Seal Bay
Macbride Head
Mt Brisbane (176m)
Volunteer Beach
Volunteer Point
Johnson's Harbour
Port Louis
Berkeley Sound
Teal Inlet
Jack's Mtn (645m)
Green Patch
Kidney Island
Arroyo Malo
Estancia
Pony's Pass
Stanley Airport
STANLEY
Pleasant Hwy
Mt Pleasant International Airport
Darwin Rd
Mt
Bluff Cove
Fitzroy
Darwin
Goose Green
Mt Pleasant
Mare Harbour
East Falkland
Choiseul Sound
Lafonia
Walker Creek
Lively Island
North Arm
Adventure Sound
Bay of Harbours
Bleaker Island
Sea Lion Island
SOUTH ATLANTIC OCEAN

Atlantic and by centuries of controversy, the islands lie 490km east of Patagonia. Two main islands, East Falkland and West Falkland, and more than 700 smaller ones cover 12,173 sq km, about the same area as Northern Ireland or Connecticut. Alternately settled and claimed by France, Spain, Britain and Argentina, the Falkland Islands (known as the Islas Malvinas in Argentina) have been an overseas territory of the UK since 1833, a status the Argentines have fought and still contest.

Besides the five types of penguin (gentoo, king, macaroni, Magellanic and rockhopper) that breed here, there are many other birds equally interesting and uncommon.

About 60% of Falklanders are native born, some tracing their ancestry back six or more generations. Today more than 80% of the 3140 Falklanders (sometimes called 'Kelpers') live in Stanley, and about 1200 British military live at Mt Pleasant base. The rest of the islanders live in 'Camp,' the name given to all of the Falklands outside Stanley.

Since the advent of large sheep stations in the late 19th century, rural settlement in the Falklands has consisted of tiny hamlets built near sheltered harbors where coastal shipping could collect the wool clip.

The Falklands retain their rural character: the islands are laced with 400km of roads, but there's not one traffic light. Interesting 'stone runs' of quartzite boulders descend from many of the ridges and peaks on both East and West Falkland. Among the 13 endemic plants are several unusual species, including snake plant *(Nassauvia serpens)*, with its long stalks and tiny leaves, and Felton's flower *(Calandrinia feltonii)*, a caramel-scented, magenta-blossomed annual until recently thought to be extinct in the wild. Vanilla daisy *(Leuceria suaveolens)*, while not endemic, is still interesting – its flowers smell remarkably like chocolate. There are no remaining native land animals.

The Falklands operate on GMT -3 hours.

History

Although there's evidence that Patagonian Indians may have reached the Falklands in canoes, and a 1522 Portuguese chart indicates knowledge of the islands, they were officially discovered on August 14, 1592, by John Davis, master of HMS *Desire*, during an English naval expedition. The Falklands' Spanish name, Islas Malvinas, derives from early French navigators from St Malo, who called the islands 'Les Malouines' after their home port.

No European power established a settlement until 1764, when the French built a garrison at Port Louis on East Falkland, disregarding Spanish claims under the papal Treaty of Tordesillas that divided the New World between Spain and Portugal. Unbeknownst to either France or Spain, Britain set up a West Falkland outpost at Port Egmont, on Saunders Island, in 1765. Spain, meanwhile, discovered and then supplanted the French colony after an amicable settlement. Spanish forces next detected and expelled the British in 1767. Under threat of war, Spain restored Port Egmont to the British, who only a few years later abandoned the area without, however, renouncing their territorial claims.

For the rest of the 18th century Spain maintained the islands as one of the world's most secure penal colonies. After it abandoned the colonies in the early 1800s, only whalers and sealers visited, until the United Provinces of the Rio de la Plata (as Argentina was formerly known) sent a military governor in the early 1820s to assert its claim as successor to Spain. Later, a naturalized Buenos Aires entrepreneur named Louis Vernet initiated a project to monitor uncontrolled sealers and sustainably exploit local fur seal populations.

Vernet's seizure of three American sealing vessels in Berkeley Sound triggered reprisals from US naval officer Captain Silas Duncan, commanding the corvette *USS Lexington*, who vandalized the Port Louis settlement beyond restoration in 1831. After Vernet's departure, Buenos Aires kept a token force there until early 1833, when it was expelled by Britain.

Under the British, the Falklands languished until the mid-19th century, when sheep began to replace cattle, and wool became an important export. Founded by Samuel Lafone, an Englishman from Montevideo, the Falkland Islands Company (FIC) became the islands' largest landholder. Other immigrant entrepreneurs occupied all other available pastoral lands in extensive holdings by the 1870s.

Woolraising was very successful and spawned similar operations in South America. Nothing stood in the way of sheep (the foxlike warrah, the island's only native mammal, was wiped out; bounties were placed on birds felt to be a threat to sheep) and the native tussock grass was soon overgrazed. By the late 1800s, the island's ecology was tottering and the amount of exhausted land needed to sustain each sheep was growing. The deliberate introduction of cats and the accidental introduction of rats devastated small bird populations.

Land overuse brought problems, and so did land ownership. From the 1870s to the 1970s the islands were a near-feudal society with landowners in London and islanders as poorly paid laborers. Since all the land had been parceled out in the early days of British rule, islanders could not acquire any. Even publicly owned land was minimal; apart from a few outlying islands, the Falklands today are almost devoid of parks and reserves. Things began to change in the late 1970s when the sale and subdivision of large landholdings was encouraged in order to slow high rates of emigration.

In WWI the Battle of the Falkland Islands was fought southeast of Stanley. The biggest impact on island life, however, came with the invasion of the Falklands by Argentina in 1982.

THE FALKLANDS WAR

Although Argentina had persistently affirmed its claim to the Falklands since 1833, successive British governments never publicly acknowledged that claim until the late 1960s. By then, the British Foreign & Commonwealth Office (FCO) and Argentina's military government of General Juan Carlos Onganía had reached an agreement, to begin in 1971, that gave Argentina a significant voice in matters affecting Falklands transportation, fuel supplies, shipping and even immigration.

Islanders and their supporters in Britain saw the Argentine presence as ominous. Only a few years earlier, right-wing guerrillas had hijacked an Aerolíneas Argentinas jetliner, which crash-landed on the Stanley racecourse (the islands had no airport then). Afterward, the guerrillas briefly occupied parts of town. Concerned about Argentina's chronic political instability, Falklanders suspected the FCO of secretly arranging transfer of the islands to Argentina.

This process dragged on for more than a decade, during which Argentina's Dirty War gave Falklanders good reason to fear increasing Argentine presence.

On April 2, 1982, the military government of General Leopoldo Galtieri invaded the nearly undefended Falklands. The seizure briefly united Argentina and made Galtieri a hero, but he never anticipated British Prime Minister Margaret Thatcher's decisive response.

Experienced British troops landed at San Carlos Bay, routing ill-trained and poorly supplied Argentine conscripts. The most serious battle took place at Goose Green on East Falkland, but the Argentine army's surrender at Stanley averted the capital's destruction. A total of 635 Argentines and 255 Britons died in the 11-week war, along with three Falkland Island women killed by a stray British mortar round.

Some of the war's longest-lasting legacies are the 25,000 Argentine landmines that render certain beaches and pastures strictly off-limits. The minefields have not prevented the return of penguins, which are too light to set off the charges.

THE FALKLANDS TODAY

Argentina and Britain restored diplomatic relations in 1990, and following the war, Britain showed greatly renewed interest in the islands. Falklanders received full British citizenship, and Britain also allowed the Falklands government to declare a 150 nautical mile (278km) Conservation and Management Zone around the islands, giving the Falklands lucrative control over fishing and oil-exploration rights in that area.

The Falklands are administered by a governor appointed by the Foreign & Commonwealth Office in London. In local affairs, the eight-member elected Legislative Council (Legco) exercises power over most internal matters. Four of the eight members come from Stanley, with the remainder representing Camp. Britain controls defense and international relations.

Tensions between Argentina and the UK once again escalated in 2012, the 30th anniversary of the war, with Argentina complaining to the UN over the deployment of British military ships to the islands, and the British irate over a controversial Argentine Olympic ad insinuating the islands belong to Argentina.

Climate

The islands' climate is temperate, with frequent high winds. Maximum temperatures rarely reach 24°C, while even on the coldest winter days the temperature usually rises above freezing. Average annual rainfall at Stanley, one of the islands' most humid areas, is only 600mm.

Getting There & Away

AIR **LanChile** (www.lan.com) operates one weekly flight (Saturday, 1¾ hours) from Punta Arenas, Chile to **Mt Pleasant International Airport** (MPN), occasionally stopping in Rio Gallegos, Argentina, en route. From other countries, connect to the LanChile flight in Santiago, where it originates.

Britain's Royal Air Force makes six flights per month from RAF Brize Norton in Oxfordshire, England (20 hours). Only 28 seats on each flight are reserved for nonmilitary personnel; book well ahead, particularly during summer. You can choose to stay over at the refueling stop on tiny Ascension Island in the South Atlantic. Book with **Falkland Islands Government Office** (☎44-20-7222-2542; travel@falklands.gov.fk; Falkland House, 14 Broadway, Westminster, London, SW1H 0BH, UK).

BOAT The vast majority of visitors arrive by ship, often on voyages that also visit South Georgia and the Antarctic Peninsula (p208).

Getting Around

Expedition or cruise ships generally make several short visits to settlements on outlying islands of East or West Falkland, and sometimes Stanley.

AIR Most travel around the islands is done by air because the road network is limited. **Falkland Islands Government Air Service** (FIGAS; ☎500-27219; figas.fig@horizon.co.fk) operates on-demand service from the Stanley airport, a surfaced runway 5km east of town. Reservations specify a date but not usually a flight time. FIGAS may delay a flight until other passengers join the group. To find out when you're actually flying, phone FIGAS, get the daily fax that goes out to each FIGAS destination, or listen to the radio announcement each evening, which includes not only the flight schedule, but also each passenger's name and itinerary! On rare occasions, usually around holidays, flights are heavily booked. Its eight-seater Britten-Norman Islander aircraft offer great views; flights rarely climb above 600m.

CAR Hiring a car is impractical for ship visitors, since the minimum hire period is three days. Off-road driving is strictly prohibited, so nearly all sights around Stanley are out of reach.

TOURS Stanley-area sites can be visited by hiring local guides (with vehicles). It can still be a long walk to some sites from the nearest road.

Stanley

POP 2200

The Falklands' capital, Stanley, is little more than a village. Despite rapid growth since 1982, the old part of town retains its colorful charm. Bricks were expensive to ship and difficult to make locally, while the local stone proved tricky to quarry, so Stanley's builders used timber from shipwrecks, metal cladding and corrugated iron for walls as well as roofs, and then painted all of it in bright hues. Flower-bedecked gardens and patriotic flags add to the vivid colors, which contrast with the surrounding moorlands. The old pubs are reminders that some Falkland traditions remain unchanged.

Stanley's picturesque and compact layout makes it an excellent place to explore on foot. The old shipwrecks along the waterfront provide interest on a harborside stroll. With more time, you can climb to the high points around the harbor, which were the scene of fierce fighting in the closing days of the Falklands War.

History

Stanley was founded after Lord Stanley (1799–1869), a British colonial secretary, in 1842 instructed the Falkland's first governor, Richard Moody, to investigate the potential of the site as a new capital to replace Port Louis. Stanley grew slowly as a supply and repair port for ships rounding Cape Horn en route to the California Gold Rush. It expanded more rapidly when sheep replaced cattle in the late 19th century. Despite its occupation by thousands of Argentine troops from April 2 to June 14, 1982, during the Falklands War, Stanley escaped almost unscathed.

Sights

Christ Church Cathedral CHURCH

The great peat slip of 1886, a landslide which killed two people and damaged numerous buildings, wiped out Stanley's Holy Trinity Church. The foundation stone for its replacement was laid in 1890 and the new, massive brick-and-stone Christ Church Cathedral opened in 1892. With its brightly painted, corrugated-metal roof and attractive stained-glass windows, the cathedral is the town's most distinguished landmark. Plaques on its walls honor the memory of local men who served in the British Forces in WWI and WWII, as well as the great and good of the Falklands.

The **stained-glass windows** are the church's most vivid feature. As you enter from the main door you face the Post Liberation Memorial Window with the Falklands crest and the islands' motto, 'Desire the Right.' Below are the crests of the various British forces involved in the 1982 conflict and, below that, illustrations of three features of the Falklands and South Georgia: the Cathedral and Whalebone Arch represent Stanley; a typical farm settlement represents Camp; and Grytviken's church and surrounding mountains represent South Georgia. At the other end of the same wall is the charming Mary Watson window, dedicated to a much-loved district nurse standing with her bicycle at the ready.

For the cathedral's centenary in 1992, members of the congregation stitched pictorial hassocks. The collection, picturing many aspects of life in the Falklands, has grown to more than 50 of the cushioned 'kneelers.'

On the small grassy square next to the cathedral, the **Whalebone Arch** was built in 1933 to commemorate the centenary of British rule in the Falklands. Made from the jawbones of two blue whales, it was presented by the South Georgia whaling stations.

Falkland Islands Museum MUSEUM
(☎27428; www.falklands-museum.com; Holdfast Rd; admission £3) Open whenever tour ships are in port, the museum building was constructed for the Argentine representative of LADE (Lineas Aereas del Estado; an airline operated by the Argentine air force), which operated air services here until 1982. The museum contains artifacts from everyday life, natural history specimens and a fine collection relating to the islands' shipwrecks. Outside displays include the **Reclus Hut**, originally fabricated in Stanley then shipped to Antarctica and set up on the Reclus Peninsula in late 1956. Forty years later it was dismantled and brought back here.

Government House HISTORIC BUILDING
Perhaps Stanley's most photographed landmark, rambling Government House has been home to London-appointed governors since 1845 and was briefly occupied by the Argentine commander Menendez during the 1982 occupation. Government House is set back about 50m from Ross Rd West by a lush flower garden fronting the glassed-in conservatory. The house has an interesting architectural history with numerous revisions.

1914 Battle of the Falklands Memorial LANDMARK
This obelisk, just past Government House, commemorates a WWI naval engagement. On December 8, 1914, nine British ships, refueling in Stanley, quickly responded to the sighting of five German cruisers that had surprised them earlier in southern Chile. The British sank four of the cruisers in the battle, in which 1871 Germans lost their lives. Just 10 British seamen were killed.

1982 Falklands War Memorial LANDMARK
In front of the Secretariat on Ross Rd, this wall carries the names of the 252 British military personnel and three Falklands civilians who died in the Falklands War. Designed by a Falkland Islander living overseas, it was paid for by public subscription and built with volunteer labor. Ceremonies are held here every June 14.

Stanley Cemetery & Memorial Wood CEMETERY
At the east end of Ross Rd, Stanley Cemetery holds among its graves the tombstones of three young Whitingtons, children of an unsuccessful 19th-century pioneer. Other surnames, such as Felton and Biggs, are as common in the islands as Smith and Jones are in the UK. The cemetery is fronted by the **Cross of Sacrifice**, a memorial to islanders who lost their lives in WWI and WWII.

Immediately beyond the cemetery is Memorial Wood, where a tree has been planted for each member of the British forces who died in the 1982 Falklands War.

Maritime History Trail HISTORIC WALK
Information panels point out some of Stanley Harbour's most interesting ship remains. For example, *William Shand, Snow Squall* and *Egeria* are all incorporated into the Falkland Island Company's East Jetty, visible from the Public Jetty.

In all, more than 100 shipwrecks dot Falklands waters, but not all the hulks around Stanley Harbour are the result of wrecks. Some ships were simply abandoned, and others suffered that most depressing of shipping fates: they were 'condemned.' Stanley was less than five years old when the California Gold Rush prompted an explosion of shipping around Cape Horn. Inevitably, many vessels ran into trouble rounding that notoriously storm-wracked headland and put into Stanley for repairs. Not all damaged ships could be repaired. A despairing owner reported that Stanley was 'dreaded by shipmasters being notorious for its heavy charges and leisurely way of work.' Many leftover ships were turned into floating warehouses. Others can still be seen, for they were sunk and built into town piers or roofed over to make ramshackle buildings.

Stanley

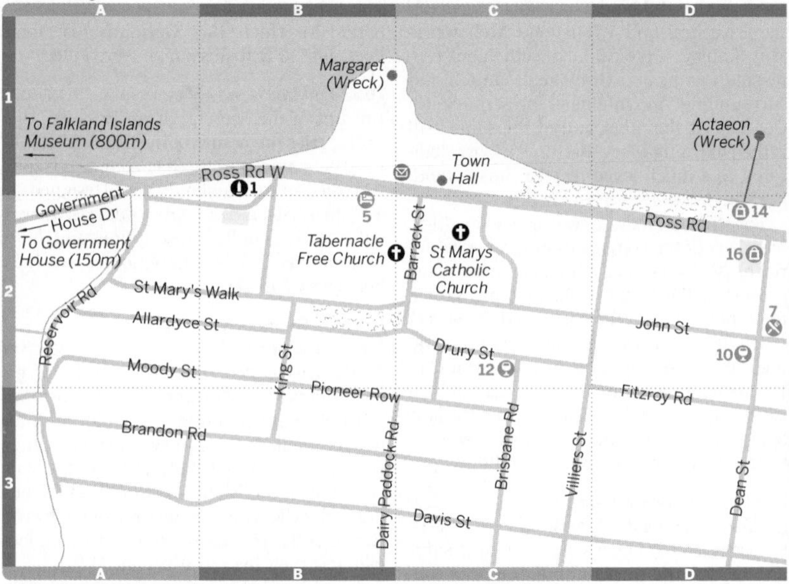

The advent of reliable steamships around the 1890s began to kill Stanley's ship repair operations; the opening of the Panama Canal in 1914 was the final blow.

Sleeping & Eating

In addition to the hotels listed here, there are five B&Bs and two guesthouses (see www.falklandislands.com). Most restaurants open when ships are in town, and serve fish and chips, burgers and the like.

Malvina House Hotel HOTEL, RESTAURANT ££
(21355; www.malvinahousehotel.com; 3 Ross Rd; s/d incl breakfast £109/144;) The original Malvina House was built on this site in the 1880s by sheep farmer John James Felton, who named it for his youngest daughter. All rooms are smoke-free and have direct-dial phones and satellite TV. Three larger harbor-view suites cost an additional 20%. Its fine **restaurant** (dinner mains £17-20; noon-1:30pm & 7-9pm), in the glassed-in conservatory at the front of the hotel, is the best eatery in town. Starters include dishes like upland goose parfait. Main courses range from duck breast to Falklands-inspired dishes like slow-braised local lamb. Lunch (mains £7 to £8) runs from build-your-own burger to fried chicken. The **Beagle Bar** adjoins.

Shorty's Motel & Diner MOTEL £
(22861; www.shortys-diner.com; West Hillside, Snake Hill; s/d incl breakfast £42/55;) East of the town center, this motel has two basic doubles and four twins with TVs. The **restaurant** (mains £7; 9am-8pm) serves diner-style breakfast and burgers (including the traditional Chilean sandwich known as a *chacarero*), full meals, baguettes and paninis.

Michelle's Café CAFE £
(Philomel Hill; mains £4-6; 8:30am-1:30pm Mon-Thu, 8:30am-1:30pm & 5:30pm-12:30am Fri & Sat) Serves tea, coffee, cakes, burgers and daily specials.

Bread Shop BAKERY, SNACKS £
(Dean St; 7:30am-1:30pm) Pick up bread, snacks and light meals; there's another branch opposite Globe Tavern.

Woodbine Café CAFE £
(29 Fitzroy Rd; mains £4-7; 10am-2pm Tue-Sat, 6-8pm Mon, Wed & Fri) Serves Cornish pasties, sausage rolls, pies, fish and chips, chicken, burgers, sandwiches and hot dogs.

Drinking

Stanley's pubs offer the opportunity to down a pint with locals and they remain open when cruise ships are docked.

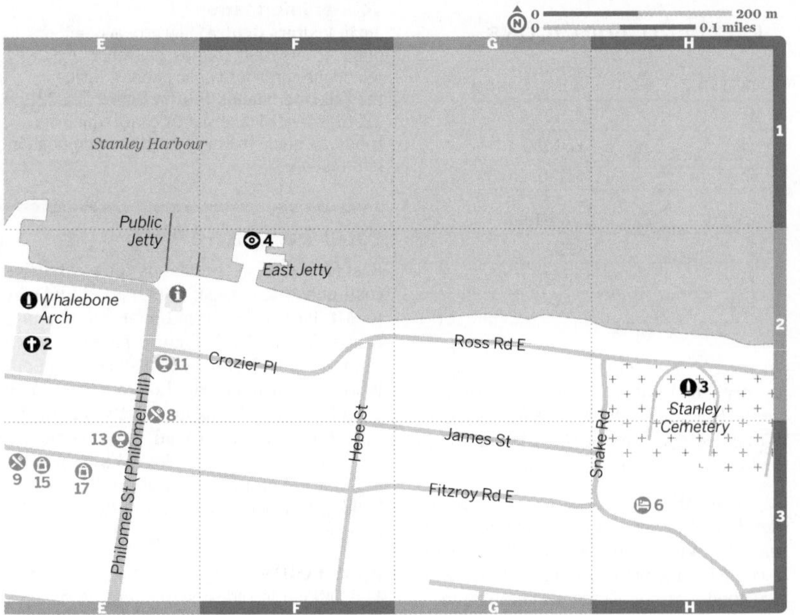

Stanley

Sights
1 1982 Falklands War Memorial ... B1
2 Christ Church Cathedral ... E2
3 Cross of Sacrifice ... H2
4 William Shand, Snow Squall, Egeria ... F2

Sleeping
5 Malvina House Hotel ... B2
6 Shorty's Motel & Diner ... H3

Eating
7 Bread Shop ... D2
Malvina House Restaurant ... (see 5)
8 Michelle's Cafe ... E2
Shorty's Motel & Diner ... (see 6)
9 Woodbine Café ... E3

Drinking
Beagle Bar ... (see 5)
10 Deano's Bar ... D2
11 Globe Tavern ... E2
12 Rose Hotel ... C2
13 Victory Bar ... E3

Shopping
14 Capstan Gift Shop ... D2
15 Falkland Collectibles ... E3
16 FIC West Store ... D2
17 Pink Shop ... E3

Globe Tavern PUB
(cnr Crozier Pl & Philomel St) The best-known pub, it also serves bar meals including fish and chips. The beer garden out back is great when the sun is shining.

Victory Bar PUB
(cnr Philomel St & Fitzroy Rd) Probably the most popular local pub, it's said to be the place where most Stanley gossip gets reviewed over a beer.

Rose Hotel PUB
(Brisbane Rd) Opened as the Rose Public House in the 1860s.

Deano's Bar PUB
(John St) Selection of beers and hamburgers, fish and chips and other snacks.

Shopping

Stanley shops almost always open when a cruise ship docks. Falklands' knitwear,

FALKLAND PRICE ICONS

SLEEPING	DOUBLE ROOM
£	<£60
££	£60-150
£££	>£150

EATING	MAIN DISH
£	<£10
££	£10-20
£££	>£20

jewelry incorporating polished semiprecious Falklands' pebbles and astringent diddle-dee jam, one of the islands' unique flavors, all make good souvenirs.

Capstan Gift Shop SOUVENIRS
(Ross Rd) Jam-packed emporium with a great selection of postcards, books and locally produced gear like woolen wear and craftwork; also goods with no Falklands connection.

Falkland Collectibles SOUVENIRS
(Fitzroy Rd) From stamps to banknotes and phonecards.

FIC West Store SUPERMARKET
(Ross Rd) Video rentals, stationery, books, newspapers and magazines.

Pink Shop SOUVENIRS, BOOKS
(33 Fitzroy Rd; closed Tue & Sun) Gifts, woolens, Falklands' and general-interest books, wildlife prints by the owner-artist, and work by other Falklands' artists.

Information

Internet Access

Available at rear of Jetty Visitors Centre, wi-fi hotspots and Cable & Wireless PLC.

Money

There's no ATM. Most Stanley businesses accept Visa, MasterCard and cash or traveler's checks in British pounds, US dollars or euros. Falklands currency is valueless outside the islands.

Standard Chartered Bank (21352; Ross Rd; 8:30am-3pm Mon-Fri) Changes currency and traveler's checks.

Telephone & Fax

Cable & Wireless PLC (20804; Ross Rd; 8am-4:30pm Mon-Fri) Identified by its satellite dish, it operates phone, telegram, internet and fax services, and sells phonecards.

Tourist Information

Jetty Visitors Centre Main arrival point; has public toilets; sells stamps, souvenirs and telephone cards for public phones. Inside is the **Falkland Islands Tourist Board** (22215, 22281; www.falklandislands.com), which distributes a guide to Stanley and accommodation information.

East Falkland

East Falkland has the islands' most extensive road network, consisting of a good highway to Mt Pleasant International Airport and Goose Green. Only slightly larger in area than West Falkland, East Falkland's population is much larger, though once you're out of Stanley things are pretty quiet. The northern part of the island is rolling and often mountainous and is joined by a narrow isthmus to Lafonia, the southern half of East Falkland, which is flat and dotted with innumerable lakes and ponds.

PORT LOUIS

The Falklands' oldest settlement, Port Louis dates from the French foundation of the colony by Louis de Bougainville in 1764. One of its oldest buildings is the ivy-covered 19th-century **farmhouse**, still occupied by farm employees. Scattered nearby are ruins of the French governor's house and fortress and Louis Vernet's settlement. Visit the **grave of Matthew Brisbane**, Vernet's lieutenant, murdered by gauchos after British naval officer JJ Onslow left him in charge of Port Louis in August 1833. Brisbane, who twice survived being shipwrecked, was also the master of *Beaufoy,* which accompanied James Weddell's *Jane* on his furthest south of S 74°15´ in February 1823, when Weddell discovered his namesake sea. In 1842 James Clark Ross dug up Brisbane's body from the rough grave in which the Indians had buried it and reinterred it, giving it a wooden marker. That grave marker, now in the Falkland Islands Museum, was replaced in 1933 by a marble stone.

VOLUNTEER BEACH

This popular excursion from Stanley boasts the largest **king penguin colony** in the Falklands, where the photogenic kings are at the northern limit of their range. King penguins were reported here in the early 18th century, but by the late 1800s they had been virtually wiped out in the exploitation of the Falklands' wildlife. The first return of king penguins to the beach was recorded in 1933, but by 1967 there were just 15 breeding pairs. Since then the numbers have steadily grown, and the most recent count found more than 500 breeding pairs. There's also a small but growing colony on Saunders Island.

Large colonies of gentoo (850 pairs) and Magellanic (several hundred pairs) penguins also inhabit Volunteer Beach, and during the summer Falklands Conservation posts a warden here. In February, the pale pink and very sweet teaberries that grow near the beach ripen and can be eaten fresh.

From Volunteer Beach it's a couple of hours' walk to **Volunteer Point** at the end of the promontory. Both the beach and the point are named for *Volunteer,* the ship in which American sealer Edmund Fanning visited Port Louis in 1815. An offshore breeding colony of southern fur seals can be seen through binoculars, and elephant seals are sometimes found on the beaches.

SAN CARLOS

British forces in the 1982 war first came ashore at San Carlos settlement at the south end of San Carlos Water. Before it was subdivided and sold to half a dozen local families in 1983, San Carlos was a traditional large sheep station.

The excellent small **museum** in San Carlos chronicles rural life, looks at the islands' natural history, and covers the Falklands War, in particular the landings from San Carlos Water. Many of the battles took place just a stone's throw from the museum.

Continue through San Carlos to the immaculate **British War Cemetery** close to the water's edge. A total of 252 British servicemen died during the conflict; the cemetery has just 14 graves from the war. Some casualties remained in their sunken ships, but most were returned to Britain where Falklands' combatants are commemorated at the Falkland Islands Memorial Chapel in Pangbourne, Berkshire.

Across San Carlos Water are the ruins of the **Ajax Bay Refrigeration Plant**, a madcap 1950s Colonial Development Corporation project that failed because Falklands sheep are bred for wool, not mutton.

MT PLEASANT

After the Falklands War, British military personnel were housed in and around Stanley until **RAF Mt Pleasant** was completed in 1986. At its post-1982 peak, the base staff numbered more than 2000 and even today there are about 1200, making it the second-biggest population center in the islands. Some visitors arrive and depart via the Mt Pleasant International Airport. The base includes the world's longest hallway (800m Millennium Corridor) and a public bar, restaurant, cinema and shops, which are open to visitors.

DARWIN

Situated at the narrow isthmus separating Lafonia from the northern half of East Falkland, Darwin is named after the young Charles Darwin, who visited the Falklands from 1833 to 1834 on HMS *Beagle* and spent a night ashore close to where the settlement is today. Darwin later became the center of the FIC's Camp operations, but by 1920 the farm site had become too small for the thriving settlement and there were water shortages. Over a two-year period most of the population was shifted to nearby Goose Green. Today Darwin is little more than a big lodge building and a smaller, older building housing two flats. Close to the lodge is a fine restored **stone corral** built in 1874.

FALKLANDS WAR SITES

Approaching Goose Green from Stanley, the well-kept **Argentine cemetery** from the 1982 war is just off the road to the left (south). The heaviest ground fighting of the Falklands War took place around here. Simple white crosses mark the 234 graves; nearly half are unmarked because many conscripts did not wear identification tags, or their comrades took them to return to relatives. A little further down the road there's a small **memorial** to three British soldiers close to the road, and a little further back another one marks where 'H' Jones, the British hero of the assault on Goose Green, was killed. Close to the Darwin lodge a larger **memorial** honors the British troops of 2 Para Battalion who died in the attack. There's a fine view down to Goose Green from the memorial.

GOOSE GREEN

Goose Green, with some 80 residents, is the largest settlement in Camp. It once had a population of up to 250, but today many houses are empty, though the shop and school still operate. In the middle of the settlement lies the **community hall** where more than 110 residents, ranging in age from three months to over 80, were held for nearly a month by the Argentines until they were released by British troops. Goose Green is one of the farms owned by the government-operated Falkland Landholdings Corporation; it runs 75,000 sheep.

SEA LION ISLAND

The Falklands' southernmost inhabited island is little more than 1km across at its widest, but has more wildlife in a smaller area than almost anywhere in the islands. It features all five species of Falklands' penguins, enormous colonies of cormorants, giant petrels and the 'Johnny Rook' (more properly, the striated caracara *Phalcoboenus australis*), one of the world's rarest birds of prey. Sea Lion Island is the most important breeding ground in the Falklands for southern elephant seals; every spring more than 500 females haul ashore to give birth. The sea lions that give the island its name are far less numerous, however: even at peak times there are fewer than 100 of them.

Sea Lion's isolation, and the fact that it has no introduced rodents or cats, has undoubtedly contributed to the continuing abundance of wildlife. **Sea Lion Lodge** (32004; www.sealionisland.com; high season incl full board s/tw £175/160; closed Apr-Aug; @) markets itself as 'the most southerly British hotel in the world.' This wild outpost offers creature comforts in the way of snug rooms, central heating, shared guest lounges and even a small putting green.

BLEAKER ISLAND

The northern part of Bleaker Island is a wildlife sanctuary; the rest is a sheep farm. Rockhopper, gentoo and Magellanic penguins are resident, along with king cormorants, elephant seals and sea lions.

West Falkland

Port Howard is West Falkland's oldest farm, dating back to 1866, and also the largest privately owned farm in the Falkland Islands. About 25 people live on the 81,000-hectare station, which has 40,000 sheep and 800 cattle. **Port Stephens'** rugged headlands, the most scenic part of the Falklands, are open to the blustery South Atlantic. Thousands of rockhopper penguins, cormorants and other seabirds breed on the exposed coast. West Falkland's only proper road runs from Port Howard on Falkland Sound to Chartres on King George Bay, but there's also a system of rough tracks.

PEBBLE ISLAND

Elongated Pebble, off West Falkland's northern coast, has varied topography, a good sampling of wildlife and extensive wetlands. There are also more than 10,000 purebred Corriedale sheep. Pebble is thought to be named for the beautiful agate stones found on the beaches at the island's west end.

During the Falklands War about 350 Argentine troops had come to the island to establish an air base. On the night of May 14, 1982, a contingent of 45 SAS troops landed by helicopter, stealthily made their way to the airstrip and destroyed or damaged all of the 11 aircraft. As a result, the 25 islanders were locked in the settlement's main house for 31 days, released only to keep the farm in shape each morning.

KEPPEL ISLAND

The Patagonian Mission Society (now called the South American Missionary Society) established an outpost on Keppel Island in 1853 to catechize the Yámana people from Tierra del Fuego and teach them to become potato farmers instead of hunter-gatherers.

The mission was controversial because the government suspected that the Yámana had been brought against their will, but it lasted until 1898, despite the their susceptibility to disease. One Falklands' governor attributed numerous Yámana deaths from tuberculosis to their 'delicacy of constitution,' but it's likely that hard physical labor, change of diet, European-introduced diseases and harsh living conditions in their damp stone houses played a greater role in the Yámanas' demise. The mission was undoubtedly prosperous, however, and by 1877 it was bringing in an annual income of nearly £1000 from its cattle, sheep and gardens.

Keppel is now exclusively a sheep farm. The former chapel is a wool shed, while the stone walls of the Yámana dwellings remain in fairly good condition. Keppel is also a good place to see penguins.

SAUNDERS ISLAND

The first British garrison on the Falklands was built in 1765 at **Port Egmont**. In 1767, after France ceded its colony to Spain, Spanish forces dislodged the British from Saunders and nearly precipitated a war between the two countries. After the British left voluntarily in 1774, the Spaniards razed the settlement, including its impressive blockhouse. Remaining are jetties, extensive foundations and some of the buildings' walls, plus garden terraces built by British marines. The numerous rockhoppers breeding on the island have actually clawed grooves into rocks as they clamber out of the surf; gentoo, king and Magellanic penguins also breed here.

CARCASS ISLAND

Despite its off-putting name, Carcass is a scenic little island with a good variety of wildlife, including a small gentoo rookery and large colonies of Magellanic penguins, which even nest beneath the home of Rob and Lorraine McGill, the owners. Because the island has never had cats, rats or mice, small birds are abundant. The island takes its name from HMS *Carcass,* which, along with HMS *Jason,* established Port Egmont on Saunders Island in 1766–67.

WEST POINT ISLAND

West Point, owned by Lilly and Roddy Napier, is unusual for having large plantations of tussock grass, replanted by a forward-thinking farmer of the early 20th century. A 2.5km walk past the main house of the settlement brings you to a dramatically cliffed promontory called **Devil's Nose**, on the west coast, where 500 breeding pairs of rockhopper penguins and 2100 pairs of black-browed albatrosses nest in a natural amphitheater with the sea as its stage.

JASON ISLANDS

Stretching 65km off the west coast of West Falkland, this chain is among the westernmost in the Falklands. The Jasons take their name from HMS *Jason,* dispatched to survey the Falklands in 1766. The archipelago's largest islands are **Grand Jason**, 11km long and about 3km across, and, to the west, **Steeple Jason**, 10km long and 1.5km wide at its broadest. Both are uninhabited nature reserves owned by the Wildlife Conservation Society in New York City. Steeple Jason is home to the largest colony of black-browed albatrosses in the world: 113,000 pairs nest in a vast colony that continues for 5km along the island's windward western coast. There are also 65,000 pairs of rockhoppers.

NEW ISLAND

The Falklands' most westerly inhabited island is also a unique wildlife area, with large colonies of penguins, albatrosses, petrels and seals.

The island comprises two properties. **New Island South** is cared for by the New Island South Conservation Trust, which promotes the study of ecology and conservation. **New Island North**, owned by Tony and Kim Chater, is also operated as a nature reserve.

In the late 18th century New Island's excellent harbors and rich wildlife resources turned it into an important base for North American whalers and sealers. The island's name originated from the voyagers' New England home ports: New York, New Bedford, New London and others.

A Norwegian whaling company sent *Admiralen,* the first modern floating factory ship to reach the southern regions, and began whaling at New Island on Christmas Eve, 1905. The whaling firm Salvesen's of Leith (in Scotland) operated a shore-based whaling station from 1908 to 1916. There weren't enough whales nearby, so the company subsequently operated on South Georgia. A few **ruins** of the station remain about 3km south of the settlement on the eastern coast.

Beached in **Settlement Harbour** lies *Protector,* built in Nova Scotia in the late 1930s/early 1940s as a minesweeper for the Canadian navy. She was brought down to the Falklands for a local sealing venture, and was eventually run onto the beach here.

Just up the beach, **Barnard Memorial Museum** incorporates the remains of a rough stone hut built by Captain Barnard, marooned here after a disastrous encounter with the crew of a shipwrecked British vessel in 1813. All but two of the shipwreck survivors took over Barnard's ship, leaving him and four other men stranded here for almost two years. But just as the pirates were sailing away, the British gun-brig *Nancy* arrived and took her as a prize of war. Barnard and his fellows, meanwhile, were left behind until December 1814.

On the island's precipitous western coast are large colonies of rockhoppers, king cormorants and black-browed albatrosses, as well as a large rookery of southern fur seals. Gentoo and Magellanic penguins also breed on New Island.

ANTARCTIC CONVERGENCE

At some point on your way to Antarctica you will pass over the Antarctic Convergence, also known as the Antarctic Polar Front. The ocean south of the convergence differs greatly from northern waters in salinity, density and temperature. A great mixing occurs where northern and southern waters meet, with nutrients from the seafloor being brought to the surface, making the convergence a highly productive area for algae, krill and the other small creatures at the base of the Antarctic food web.

The exact location of the Antarctic Convergence varies slightly throughout the year, and also from year to year. Despite what you may hear, there's very little sign that you are actually crossing the Convergence. The sea does not get rougher, and there is usually no change in its appearance. The primary indicator is a dip in the water temperature, a change that the ship's instruments will detect, although you almost certainly will not.

North of this seasonally and longitudinally varying line, the summer surface seawater temperature is about 7.8°C, while south it is 3.9°C. During winter it drops to approximately 2.8°C north of the Convergence and to just 1.1°C south of it. For more on the Southern Ocean see p159.

SOUTH GEORGIA

The island of South Georgia, one of the first gateways to Antarctica, was the center for the huge Southern Ocean whaling industry from 1904 to 1966. Several important expeditions to Antarctica called at the whaling stations en route to or from the continent, notably those of Shackleton. Each station has a cemetery or burial site (www.wildisland.gs).

With its sharp, heavily glaciated peaks, crescent-shaped South Georgia (170km long and 40km wide at its broadest) presents a rugged appearance. The Allardyce Range forms the island's spine. The highest point is Mt Paget (2934m), first ascended in 1964. Glaciers cover 57% of the 3755 sq km island.

Visiting ships focus on South Georgia's northeastern coast, with its many fjords and fantastic wildlife breeding beaches. Thanks to the high mountains, this coast is protected from the prevailing westerlies, which is why all of the whaling stations were built on this side of the island.

History

London-born merchant Antoine de la Roche was probably the first to sight the island in April 1675 while sailing from Peru to England. Captain James Cook made the first landing on January 17, 1775, when he named it the Isle of Georgia after King George III and claimed it for his majesty.

Because it is north of S 60°, South Georgia is not part of the area covered by the Antarctic Treaty. In 1908 the British government consolidated earlier claims into a territory called Falkland Islands Dependencies (South Georgia, the South Orkneys, the South Shetlands, the South Sandwich Islands and Graham Land on the Antarctic Peninsula); now they are a British Overseas Territory.

SEALING AT SOUTH GEORGIA

When Cook's account of South Georgia was published in 1777, his descriptions of fur seals there set off a stampede of British sealers, who began arriving in 1786. Americans followed shortly after, and within five years there were more than 100 ships in the Southern Ocean taking fur-seal skins and elephant-seal oil. A large elephant seal yielded one 170L barrel of oil (although a big bull could produce double that).

SOUTH GEORGIA IN BOOKS & FILM

» *A Visitor's Guide to South Georgia* (2005), Sally Poncet & Kim Crosbie. Good overview of the island's history, wildlife, government and research, plus descriptions of 25 sites commonly visited by tourists.

» *Antarctic Oasis: Under the Spell of South Georgia* (1998), Tim and Pauline Carr. Well-written photographic book by a couple who lived on their yacht at Grytviken for many years.

» *The Island of South Georgia* (1984), Robert Headland. Definitive study of the island, its history and geography.

» *Antarctic Encounter: Destination South Georgia* (1995), Sally Poncet. Wildlife and history through the eyes of three boys who explore it with their parents by yacht.

» *The Living Edens: Paradise of Ice, South Georgia Island*, BBC Natural History Unit. Amazing look at South Georgia's wildlife.

The British sealer *Ann,* for example, took 3000 barrels of elephant-seal oil and 50,000 fur-seal skins from South Georgia in 1792–93. In 1877–78 alone, the American sealer *Trinity* took 15,000 barrels of seal oil. In 1909, when the American ship *Daisy* stayed for five months in what was probably the last fur-sealing visit to South Georgia, only 170 fur seals could be found.

So complete was the fur seal hunt that by the 1930s the population of *Arctocephalus gazella* was probably at its lowest extreme, with only about 100 left. Over the next 80 years the species made an astounding recovery. Today there are more than three million fur seals at South Georgia.

ANTARCTICA'S WHALING CAPITAL

South Georgia whaling began in 1904, when the Compañía Argentina de Pesca, a Norwegian company based in Buenos Aires, established the first Antarctic whaling station at Grytviken. Using only one whale-catching ship, the Compañía took 183 whales in its first year. This modest start quickly became an enormous industry that generated millions of kroner and marked the beginning of South Georgia's permanent inhabitation.

Eventually six shore stations were built – at Grytviken, Ocean Harbour, Leith Harbour, Husvik, Stromness Harbour and Prince Olav Harbour – plus an anchorage for floating factory ships at Godthul. Grytviken was the first and longest-running station, operating until 1965. It was able to remain open longer than the others in part because it also processed elephant seals, which provided nearly 20% of the station's total oil production.

During 1925–26, one of South Georgia's peak seasons, there were five shore stations, one factory ship and 23 whale-catching ships. They caught 1855 blue whales, 5709 fin whales, 236 humpbacks, 13 sei whales and 12 sperm whales, which produced 404,457 barrels of oil. The largest animal ever recorded (at just over 33.5m), a female blue whale, was caught at Grytviken in the 1911–12 season.

The Great Depression, combined with a barely nascent whale conservation awareness, slowed the booming whale-hunting business. By the 1931–32 season, Prince Olav and Stromness stations closed for good, while Husvik Harbour and Leith closed temporarily.

By 1961–62 the Norwegian companies that once dominated the trade – a 1909 census at Grytviken found that 93% of the 720 whalers were Scandinavian – could no longer make a satisfactory profit. Hoping to make money on frozen whale meat, Japanese investors took over the South Georgia whaling operations the next season, but soon also found it unprofitable and closed the last shore station, Grytviken, in 1965.

South Georgia's total whale catch from 1904 to 1966 included 41,515 blue whales, 87,555 fin whales, 26,754 humpbacks, 15,128 sei whales and 3716 sperm whales: a total of 175,250 animals. Land stations, however, accounted for *just 10%* of the total Antarctic whale catch. For more on Antarctic whaling, see p181.

SOUTH GEORGIA AT WAR

War intruded on South Georgia in 1982. On March 25 Argentine naval vessel *Bahía Paraíso,* later to become infamous for spilling fuel (p78) at Anvers Island along the Antarctic Peninsula, arrived at Leith Harbour and set up a garrison in a clear challenge to Britain's sovereignty over South Georgia. On April 3 *Bahía Paraíso, Guerrico* and their accompanying helicopters landed 200 Argentine soldiers at King Edward Point, which was defended by just 22 Royal Marines. After a two-hour battle in which several Argentines were killed and two Argentine helicopters were shot down, the Argentines captured the station and took the marines and the station's scientists to Argentina as prisoners.

In response, London dispatched six ships, including the nuclear submarine HMS *Conqueror.* This force retook King Edward Point on April 25, and the Argentine garrison at Leith Harbour the next day. An Argentine submarine, *Santa Fé,* was sunk; 185 Argentines were taken prisoner and later released in Uruguay. During the Falklands War the Royal Navy used South Georgia as a base.

For an account of the war at South Georgia, read Roger Perkins' fascinating *Operation Paraquat* (1986).

Sights & Activities

South Georgia's wildlife is varied and abundant. The fur seal population (over three million) is found mainly on the northwestern coast, and during breeding season it crowds the beaches to the extent that landings are difficult without disturbing the seals or being bitten.

More than five million pairs of macaroni penguins nest on the island. The largest king penguin rookery (300,000 birds) lies on the

South Georgia Island

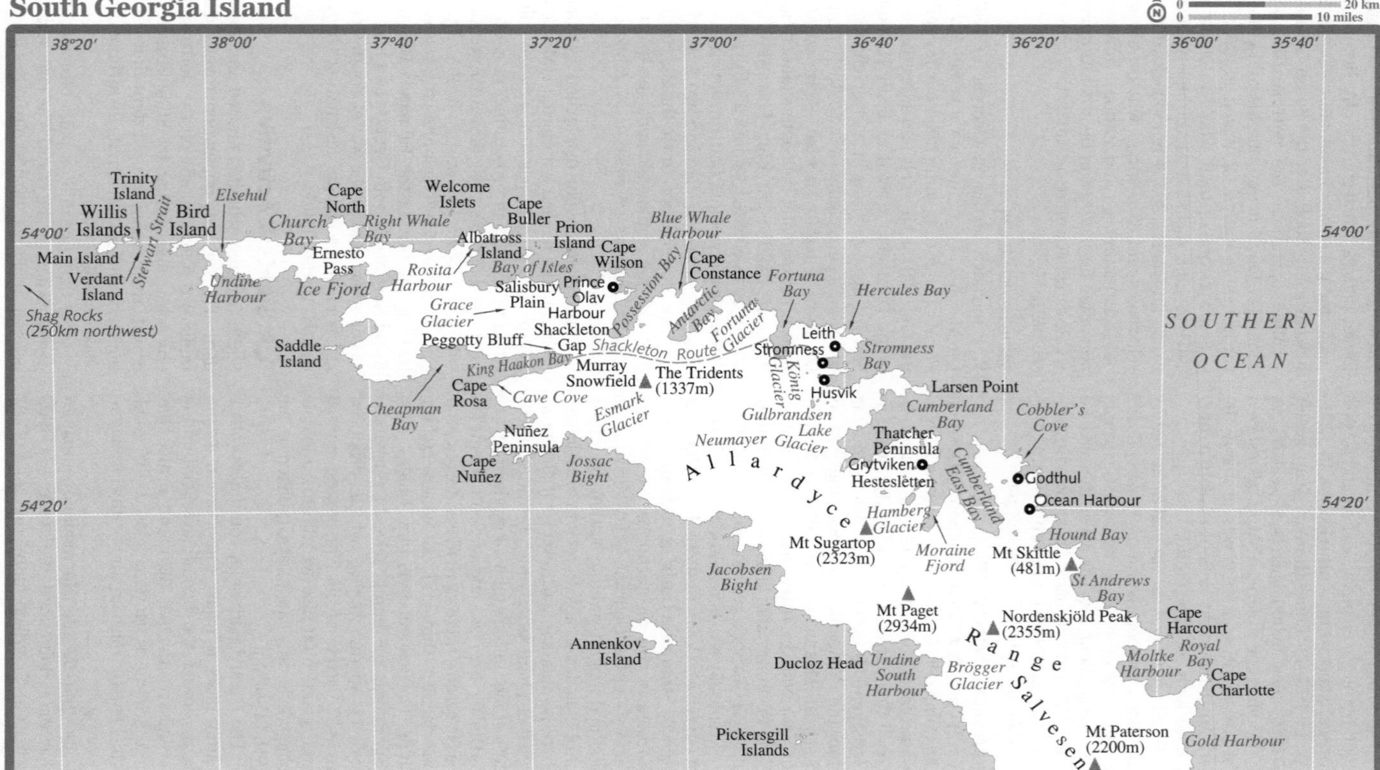

beach at St Andrews Bay. Kings also nest in vast numbers at Salisbury Plain.

Prion Island is home to magnificent wandering albatrosses and thousands of burrowing seabirds which thrive, since there are none of the destructive rats introduced to South Georgia by early visitors. Four other rat-free islands also harbor enormous seabird populations, but they are off-limits to tourist landings: **Cooper Island** off the southeastern coast, **Annenkov Island** off the southern coast, **Albatross Island** in the Bay of Isles, and Bird Island off South Georgia's northwestern end.

South Georgia has two additional fascinating bird species: the South Georgia pipit, the only songbird in Antarctica, and the South Georgia pintail, the world's only known carnivorous duck. South Georgia's 3000 reindeer were introduced by whalers in 1911 and are confined by glaciers to two regions of the island.

WILLIS ISLANDS

Named after Cook's midshipman Thomas Willis, described as a 'wild and drinking midshipman,' who made the first sighting on January 14, 1775, these islands rise out of the sea to an altitude of 551m (the highest point on Main Island). Also in the group are Trinity Island, Verdant Island and several smaller islands. Remarkably these islands have no permanent snow or ice.

Though there are not many fur seals on the Willis Islands now, it is thought that they provided sanctuary for the tiny population which survived 19th-century sealers and were the progenitors of the seal explosion on South Georgia in recent decades. The Willis group is free of rats and as a result is home to burrowing and ground-nesting birds, such as small petrels and prions, as well as South Georgia's unique pipit.

Black-browed albatrosses (34,000 pairs or a third of South Georgia's total population) and grey-headed albatrosses (25,000 pairs of South Georgia's 80,000) nest here. Perhaps half of South Georgia's 2.5 million pairs of macaroni penguins also live here.

BIRD ISLAND

Because it is free of rats, Bird Island boasts an incredible diversity of wildlife, including 27 of South Georgia's 31 breeding bird species. Captain Cook named Bird Island 'on account of the vast numbers that were upon it.' Unfortunately, it is off-limits to tourism.

THE SHACKLETON TREK *TONY WHEELER*

Ernest Shackleton's crossing of South Georgia was first repeated in 1964 by a British military group – they hauled sleds and hit terrible weather including a 36-hour blizzard in which a gust of wind snapped in two a ski stuck upright in the snow outside their tents. The crossing has since been done by a number of private expeditions and tourist groups. Typically, the crossing involves two nights camping en route, although an extra night should be allowed for – and if conditions are especially severe the crossing can take much longer.

It's only 35km from Peggotty Camp to Stromness, but the walking distance is about 50km. In good conditions it would not be particularly difficult: the maximum altitude reached is about 650m and, apart from the sharp drop down from the Tridents, the ascents and descents are fairly gentle.

Conditions on South Georgia, however, are unlikely to be good. Shackleton's achievement in making this walk in 36 hours nonstop, with miserable equipment and while still exhausted after his voyage to South Georgia, was amazing – but he was also fortunate to have good weather; indeed, virtually the only good weather for months.

In many ways the conditions for the walk were even better in 1916 than they are now. Global warming and glacial retreats have made the terrain at some points along the walk much more difficult. In his account of making the IMAX film about *Endurance*, William Blake commented that elite mountaineers Conrad Anker and Reinhold Messner, with modern equipment and clothing, still required more than 10 hours to cross the Crean Glacier, while Shackleton's team needed just five. The smooth snowfield of Shackleton's era has become a heavily crevassed glacier.

The walk varies with the time of year. In November or December, walkers may face wilder weather, but more snow cover can make for easier walking. Later in the season, reduced snow cover can lead to more crevasses to negotiate and may involve more floundering through deep, soft snow. However, some areas may be snow-free, making walking easier.

Aurora Expeditions (www.auroraexpeditions.com.au/alpine-crossing) is a cruise operator who offers this trek.

Tony Wheeler is the co-founder of Lonely Planet Publications.

Bird Island's **BAS field station** is a dream posting for biologists (12 in summer and four in winter) who come to study the island's 50,000 breeding pairs of penguins, 14,000 pairs of albatrosses (including fewer than 1000 pairs of wandering albatrosses), 700,000 nocturnal petrels and 65,000 breeding fur seals, which cover the beaches during the height of the breeding season.

ELSEHUL

Elsehul – 'Else's Cove' in Norwegian – is separated from Undine Harbour on the south coast by an isthmus less than 400m wide. Like Undine Harbour, Elsehul is one of South Georgia's main breeding grounds for fur seals. During the November to March breeding season the beach is so crowded with aggressive bulls and cows that landings are impossible. Zodiac cruises, however, offer great views of the hectic activity on the beach as well as three sealer's try-pots. Macaroni and gentoo penguins, along with thousands of petrels and smaller albatrosses, nest here.

RIGHT WHALE BAY

Right Whale Bay has another jam-packed fur seal beach. The beach is long enough and the area behind the beach extensive enough that a landing may be possible. A large king penguin colony extends back from the beach at the eastern end of the bay.

BAY OF ISLES

One of the most popular regions of South Georgia, this wide bay contains several interesting islands including Albatross Island (closed to visitors) and **Prion Island**, two important bird breeding grounds because they are rat-free. Both are nesting sites for wandering albatrosses and giant petrels and have large populations of South Georgia pipits. Due to previous visitor pressure on the wandering albatross, visitors to Prion Island must remain on a boardwalk. The island closes to visitors during peak fur seal breeding season (November 20 to January 7).

SALISBURY PLAIN

Salisbury Plain is a huge, flat expanse of green spreading out in front of Grace Glacier. As many as 250,000 king penguins converge here during the molting season, making it South Georgia's second-largest king rookery. Climb the tussock-covered hillside to enjoy wonderful views, not only of the rookery, but also of the beautiful island-studded bay. Elephant and fur seals also haul out on these beaches to breed, give birth and molt.

PRINCE OLAV HARBOUR

Just outside the mouth of Possession Bay, Prince Olav Harbour was named by whalers for the crown prince of Norway. It was originally called 'Ratten Hafen' (rat harbor) by the sealers and whalers, for the terribly destructive brown rat which first came to South Georgia here in 1800. There are no penguin rookeries, so it is not heavily visited.

The whaling factory ship *Restitution* operated here from 1911 to 1916, as did a shore station from 1917 to 1931. This could have been the endpoint of Ernest Shackleton's famous 1916 trek across South Georgia, rather than the much longer hike he and his companions made to Stromness. Shackleton, however, thought this whaling station would already be closed for the winter.

The three-masted *Brutus* was deliberately towed here from Cape Town and beached to serve as a coaling hulk. Although the whaling station is off-limits, the **cemetery** on the hillside above *Brutus* beach, with six handsome iron crosses, may be visited.

POSSESSION BAY

Captain Cook landed here on January 17, 1775, and took possession of the island for His Majesty King George III. Because Possession Bay is not well charted, visiting ships treat it with some trepidation. A fine glacier tumbles into the bay on the southeast corner, occasionally calving icebergs into the bay.

FORTUNA BAY

Shackleton's party descended from the **Fortuna Glacier** on to the west side of this bay, followed the edge of the bay round to the east, then climbed over the saddle to drop down to Stromness.

Fortuna Bay was named for *Fortuna,* the Compañía Argentina de Pesca's first whalecatcher, brought to South Georgia by Carl Anton Larsen when he established the whaling station at Grytviken in 1904. There's a large king penguin colony at the head of Fortuna Bay, along with many elephant and fur seals. Beneath an outcrop on the western end of the beach is a **sealer's cave**. Light-mantled sooty albatrosses nest on the cliffs above the beach.

HERCULES BAY

Named for a Norwegian whaling boat that took shelter from a storm here, this bay is an excellent place to see macaroni penguins.

LEITH HARBOUR

South Georgia's largest whaling station, Leith Harbour is named for Leith in Scotland, home of the Salveson whaling company that ran this station. During the whaling era, Leith had a cinema and whalers would follow the track round from Stromness to catch an evening movie. Today its rusting ruins are closed to visitors, but a Zodiac cruise offers good views of the flensing plan and other structures. Landings can be made south of the station to visit the **cemetery** where 57 men were buried between 1917 and 1961.

STROMNESS

Most famous as the finish of Shackleton's epic crossing of South Georgia, Stromness began as an anchorage for the floating factory ship *Fridtjof Nansen II* in 1907. A shore station began operating in 1913, but in 1931 it was converted to a ship repair yard until it closed in 1961.

HUSVIK

The floating factory *Bucentaur* was moored at Husvik (house cove) in 1907 and operated until 1913. The shore station (off-limits to visitors) opened in 1910 and closed in 1960 when much of the equipment was dismantled and moved to Grytviken.

Sitting securely on the slipway, the 32m, 179-ton *Karrakatta* was hauled out of the water so her coal-fired boiler could provide steam to power an adjacent engineering workshop. A hole was cut in her hull and a steam pipe connected to the workshop.

South of the station, and outside the prohibited zone, lies the **Manager's Villa** and the **cemetery**.

Dammed by the Neumayer Glacier, **Gulbrandsen Lake**, in the mountains 3km southwest of Husvik, is one of South Georgia's largest and most spectacular lakes. Icebergs sometimes float across its surface, but the lake periodically and suddenly drains completely. Terraces above the shore mark earlier water levels.

GRYTVIKEN

South Georgia's only whaling station that can be visited (hazardous material and dangerous structures were removed by the government at a cost of £7.5 million), Grytviken is the island's first and longest-running station. It operated from 1904 to 1965.

Although a whole whale could be butchered in as little as 20 minutes, it was sometimes hard to keep pace with the catcher boats! As many as four dozen whales might be brought in at once, with the whole of Grytviken Bay covered by carcasses, which were inflated with compressed air to keep them afloat. Working overtime to keep up meant double pay.

Alcohol was banned, but illicit stills produced homemade aquavit. Crime was not a big problem at Grytviken; the jail was used mainly to house visiting expeditions.

South Georgia Museum MUSEUM

(http://sgmuseum.gs) When entering the wonderful South Georgia Museum, be sure to look up to see the wandering albatross mounted overhead. Unless you're a scientist, this is the closest you'll come to one of these magnificent birds, and their size is startling.

The museum is housed in the former station manager's house, built in 1916 by the Norwegians. It's filled with fascinating exhibits on South Georgia's history and wildlife. The shop sells an amazing array of clothing, souvenirs and books.

The Kino (cinema) was built in 1930 slightly in front of the Whaler's Church. A storm destroyed it in 1994 and the remains were removed in 2002, but the signboard and projector are in the museum.

The **football pitch** (soccer field) remains, but not the tennis court.

Whalers' Church CHURCH

The restored Whalers' Church, consecrated on Christmas Day, 1913, is a typical Norwegian church. Indeed, it was originally erected in Strømmen before being dismantled and shipped here. Inside are memorials to Grytviken's founder, Carl Anton Larsen, and to Shackleton, whose funeral was held here. Visitors are invited to go upstairs to ring the two bells. Grytviken's first pastor, Kristen Löken, lamented that 'religious life among the whalers left much to be desired.' The church has been used for a few baptisms (13 births have been registered on the island) and marriages, but it has been used most often for funerals.

Whalers' Cemetery CEMETERY

Shackleton's grave is the highlight of the whalers' cemetery at Grytviken. 'The Boss' is buried at the left rear of the graveyard. On the back of the granite headstone (engraved with the nine-pointed star that Shackleton used as a personal emblem) is one of his favorite quotations, from the poet Robert Browning: 'I hold that a man should strive to the uttermost for his life's set prize.'

In November 2011, Frank Wild's ashes were buried alongside Shackleton's after a ceremony in the church attended by Shackleton's and Wild's descendants. Wild was Shackleton's 'right-hand man'

There are 63 other graves here, several of which may belong to 19th-century sealers. Most belong to Norwegian whalers, including nine who died in a 1912 typhus epidemic. One grave holds the remains of an Argentine soldier killed during the Falklands War. The cemetery's abundant dandelions come from seeds in the soil, some of which was imported from Norway to allow the dead whalers to be buried in a bit of home. The cemetery is surrounded by a fence to keep molting elephant seals from scratching against the gravestones.

The cross on the hillside above commemorates Walter Slossarczyk, third officer on Filchner's *Deutschland* expedition, who committed suicide at Grytviken in 1911; he rowed off in a ship's dinghy one night and never returned: the boat was found three days later. The cross higher up the hill commemorates 17 men who died when their fishing vessel *Sudurhavid* sank off the island in 1998. The hillside is a good place to take panoramic photos of the station, but it's quite steep.

GODTHUL

Named 'Good Cove' by the Norwegian sealers who began working here in about 1905, Godthul never had a shore whaling station. Instead, a floating factory with two attendant catchers anchored here in the summers from 1908 to 1917 and from 1922 to 1929. Today an amazing number of whale and elephant seal bones litter the rocky beach, and several wooden boats used in flensing whales alongside the factory ship are now falling to pieces among the tussock.

GRYTVIKEN WHALING STATION OPERATIONS *ROBERT BURTON*

Grytviken means 'Pot Cove' and is named for the sealers' try-pots that were discovered there. As a 'bay within a bay,' it is the best harbor in South Georgia and was chosen by the Norwegian captain Carl Anton Larsen as the site of the first whaling station in Antarctic waters. On November 16, 1904, Larsen arrived with a small fleet of ships to build a factory, and whaling started five weeks later. Although the company was Argentine-owned, the whalers were mostly Norwegians. Huge profits were made at first, but Grytviken was eventually forced to close because whales had become so rare. The station underwent a massive cleanup in 2004–06. Several buildings, larger machinery and three beached sealing vessels remain.

During Grytviken's first years only the blubber from the whale was utilized. Later, meat, bones and viscera were cooked to extract the oil, leaving bone and meat-meal as important by-products.

Life for the station workers was arduous. The season ran from October to March, and the workers put in 12-hour days. As many as 300 worked here during the industry's heyday. A few stayed over winter to maintain the boats and factory.

The timber flensing plan was in the large open space between the two main jetties. Whale carcasses were brought to the iron-plated whale slip at the base of the plan and hauled onto the plan by the whale winch. (The 40,815kg electric winch has been removed from the top of the plan.) The blubber was slit by flensers armed with hockey stick–shaped flensing knives. Strips of blubber were then ripped off the carcass, like the skin from a banana, by cables attached to steam winches, which you can still see.

The blubber was minced and fed into the blubber cookers, the 12 large vertical cylinders on the right of the plan. Each cooker held about 24 tonnes of blubber, which was cooked for approximately five hours to drive out the oil. The oil was piped to the separators for purification by centrifuging, and finally into tanks behind the station. About 25 fin whales (each 18m) could be processed in 24 hours. They would yield 1000 barrels (160 tonnes) of oil.

When the whale had been flensed, the meat, tongue and guts were cut off by the lemmers (who took their name from the Norwegian word for 'dismember'), drawn up the steep ramp on the left of the plan to the meat cookery and dropped into rotating cookers. The head and backbone were dragged up another ramp (now gone) at the back of the plan to the bone cookery, where they were cut up with large steam saws and also cooked.

After oil extraction, the remains of the meat and bone were dried and turned into guano for animal feed and fertilizer. In later years meat extract was made by treatment with sulfuric acid in a plant next to the blubber cookery. Meat extract was used in dried soups and other prepared foods.

Along the shore, past the boilers and guano store (now gone), lies *Petrel*. Built in 1928, she was used for whaling until 1956 and then converted for sealing. The catwalk connecting the bridge to the gun platform has been removed and the present gun is a recent addition. In this area of the station were the engineering shops, foundry and smithy, all of which enabled the whalers to repair their boats. Further along was the piggery, the meat freezer and, on the hillside, the hydroelectric power plant. On the shore are the burnt-out remains of the wooden barque *Louise*, a sailing ship built in 1869 at Freeport, Maine. She came to Grytviken in 1904 as a supply ship and remained as a coaling hulk, until she was burned in a training exercise by the UK's garrison at King Edward Point in 1987.

Robert Burton was the director of South Georgia's museum from 1995 to 1998.

OCEAN HARBOUR

This whaling station, opened in 1909, was until 1955 known as New Fortuna Bay, probably after the Norwegian-Argentine whaling ship *Fortuna* that helped establish Grytviken in 1905. In 1920 the station's leaseholder amalgamated with Sandefjords Hvalfangerselskab and nearly everything here was taken to Stromness. Old sealing try-pots can still be seen at the site, however, along with the station's toppled narrow-gauge locomotive.

Ocean Harbour's most notable relic is *Bayard,* a 67m iron-hulled three-master built in 1864. *Bayard* was moored at the station's coaling pier in 1911 when high winds tore the 1300-ton ship loose and swept her across the harbor, where she grounded. A large colony of blue-eyed shags nests in the tussock grass which thrives on the rotting decks.

SHACKLETON AT SOUTH GEORGIA

Ernest Shackleton's name is inextricably linked with South Georgia, and visits to the island often include landings at places associated with his expeditions.

Grytviken is the most important and most visited. Shackleton first stopped here in November 1914 on his way south with *Endurance*. From the whalers he learned that it was a bad ice year in the Weddell Sea. Although he delayed his departure by several weeks, the ice got his ship nevertheless.

At tiny **Cave Cove**, at dusk on May 10, 1916, Shackleton and his five companions made landfall after their amazing 16-day, 1300km crossing from Elephant Island in the lifeboat *James Caird*. It had been 522 days since they left South Georgia. The men immediately fell to their knees at a freshwater stream, 'drinking the pure, ice-cold water in long draughts that put new life into us,' Shackleton wrote in *South*. The cave, at the left side of the head of the cove, is just an overhang of the cliff. When Shackleton and his men stayed here, 5m-long icicles hung down in front of the cave mouth. The men supplemented this cover with *James Caird*'s sail, and spread tussock grass on the ground to cushion their sleeping bags. They also feasted on albatross chicks (albatrosses still nest on the slopes opposite the cave). Frank Worsley later recalled: 'By jove, they were good, damn good!' At Cave Cove, too, occurred one of the several miracles of the *Endurance* saga: *James Caird*'s rudder, which had been lost just as they arrived at South Georgia, came floating back into the cove on the returning tide. Today, a discreet plaque commemorating Shackleton and his men, left by the Irish 'South Aris' expedition of 1997, is bolted to the cliff wall to the left of the cave.

After five days at Cave Cove, Shackleton and his crew sailed *James Caird* deeper into **King Haakon Bay**, making camp on the northern shore by overturning the boat on the sand at a place they named **Peggotty Bluff**, after the family in Dickens' *David Copperfield* whose home was made from a boat. Hundreds of elephant seals lay on the beach, and Shackleton wrote, 'our anxieties with regard to food disappeared.' Shackleton reflected soberly on 'the many tragedies written in the wave-worn fragments of lost vessels.' Even now, the beach is littered with wood, ropes, buoys and other debris swept into the bay by the westerlies.

Before dawn on May 19, Shackleton, Worsley and Tom Crean began their crossing of the island's 1800m range and ice crevasses – the first time this was done, as people had only penetrated 1km from the coast.

After 36 hours they neared Stromness, but impassable ice cliffs forced them to lower themselves down an icy, 9m waterfall. Arriving at the station on May 20, 1916, their long beards, matted hair and ragged clothes caused the first three people they met to flee in disgust.

The whaling station manager, Thoralf Sørlle, gave them food, shocking news of the progress of WWI, and a bath. 'I don't think I have ever appreciated anything so much as that hot bath,' Worsley wrote in his book *Endurance*. 'It was really wonderful and worth all that we had been through to get it.' The manager's villa still stands at the station's southern end.

Shackleton returned to Grytviken in 1922. This time southbound on *Quest,* he died of a heart attack aboard his ship, moored alongside the whaling station, early on the morning of January 5. A few hours before, he wrote his final diary entry, ending on a poetic note: 'In the darkening twilight I saw a lone star hover, Gem like above the bay.' Even as his body was en route home to Britain, his widow Emily decided he should be buried at South Georgia. Today, his grave in the Grytviken whalers' cemetery is one of South Georgia's highlights for many visitors, along with the Memorial Cross erected by his *Quest* shipmates in 1922 at Hope Point, across King Edward Bay from the cemetery.

Among eight graves at the small **cemetery** (though it is unknown which grave is his) is the final resting place of Frank Cabrail, steward of the New London, Connecticut sealer *Francis Allen,* who drowned on October 14, 1820. His is the oldest recorded grave on South Georgia, though earlier burials almost certainly took place.

ST ANDREWS BAY

Here at South Georgia's largest **king penguin rookery** as many as 300,000 raucous, smelly kings congregate on 3km of gravel and black-sand beach. High surf, however, can prevent landings. This is also South Georgia's largest **elephant seal breeding beach**, with as many as 6000 cows hauled out at the height of the season. The three glaciers behind the beach are all in significant retreat.

MOLTKE HARBOUR

At this harbor in Royal Bay, German scientists participating in the International Polar Year of 1882–83 spent more than a year studying local geology, magnetism, zoology and the Transit of Venus. Their expedition ship *Moltke* was the first powered vessel to reach South Georgia. Foundations of their eight buildings can still be discerned. King and gentoo penguins and blue-eyed cormorants all breed at **Royal Bay**.

GOLD HARBOUR

Joining exceptional wildlife with fabulous scenery, Gold Harbour has 25,000 breeding pairs of king penguins, interspersed with several hundred pairs of gentoos. Antarctic terns, southern giant petrels and beautiful light-mantled sooty albatrosses are also found here. Fur seals are not quite as numerous as at many other South Georgia beaches.

Gold Harbour is thought to take its name from the pyrite, or 'fool's gold,' found by Filchner's German Antarctic Expedition, which stopped here in 1911.

COOPER BAY

Named for Robert Pallisser Cooper, Captain Cook's first lieutenant on HMS *Resolution* during his 1775 visit, this bay has some 20,000 chinstrap penguins, the island's largest colony. Many thousands of macaroni and gentoo penguins, along with several hundred pairs of kings, also breed here.

DRYGALSKI FJORD

Named for the leader of the 1901–03 German Antarctic Expedition, this rat-free inlet at South Georgia's extreme southeast shelters birds like the South Georgia pipit and smaller burrowing petrel and prion, and snow petrel. The fjord extends 14km into the island's interior, ending at **Risting Glacier** where ship captains must maneuver a tight turn-around. Steep-sided **Larsen Harbour**, named for Norwegian explorer and whaler Carl Anton Larsen, is the first indentation on the south side of Drygalski Fjord. It is 4km long and the most northerly breeding site of the Weddell seal.

Information

Visitors over 16-years of age to South Georgia are charged a fee of £110. Visits must be approved in advance. Tour companies handle paperwork for passengers, but yachts must apply to the **Executive Officer of the Government of South Georgia and the South Sandwich Islands** (☎500-28200; fax 500-28201; info@gov.gs; Government House, Stanley, Falkland Islands FIQQ 1ZZ, UK) and pay separate harbor fees (download guidelines at www.sgisland.gs).

Websites

Official South Georgia & South Sandwich (www.sgisland.gs)

South Georgia Heritage Trust (www.sght.org)

SOUTH ORKNEY ISLANDS

Usually visited en route to or from the Antarctic Peninsula from South Georgia, the South Orkneys consist of four major islands (Coronation, the largest, and Signy, Powell and Laurie), along with several minor islands and rocks, and the Inaccessible Islands (29km west).

Covering 622 sq km, the group is 85% glaciated. The highest point, 1265m Mt Nivea, was first scaled in 1955–56; it takes its name from the snow petrel *(Pagodroma nivea),* which breeds in the area.

South Orkney weather is cold, windy (westerlies) and overcast. On average the sun shines fewer than two hours a day.

The islands were discovered jointly by American sealer Nathaniel Palmer sailing in *James Monroe* and British sealer George Powell in *Dove,* on December 6, 1821. Powell named the islands Powell's Group and took possession for the British crown the next

SHAG ROCKS: WHALE HEAVEN

Whales occasionally congregate in great numbers near Shag Rocks, south of South Georgia, as they feed on megaswarms of krill. In just 90 minutes on a 2006 voyage, visitors saw six humpbacks, seven seis, eight southern rights, 25 orcas and 150 fin whales. In April 2008, a fisheries vessel saw more than 500 whales feeding on a krill mega-swarm several kilometers long.

day on Coronation Island. Weddell, who visited in *Jane* in February 1822, gave the islands their present name in recognition of their position at the same latitude in the south that Britain's Orkney Islands occupy in the north.

Sealing wiped out the local population of seals, and as late as 1936 a visitor found just one solitary fur seal.

Britain declared the South Orkneys part of its Falkland Islands Dependencies in 1908, a territorial claim challenged by Argentina in 1925.

In 1933 the South Orkneys became one of the first Antarctic regions to receive tourists, when an Argentine naval voyage to relieve the Laurie Island meteorological station brought visitors.

Besides Laurie and Signy Islands, **Shingle Cove** on Coronation Island is often visited, offering excellent wildlife-viewing.

LAURIE ISLAND

In 1903 Scottish explorer William Spiers Bruce wintered on mountainous Laurie Island, where he helped set up a meteorological station. The ruins of his stone hut, **Omond House**, are still visible at the end of the beach. When Bruce departed in February 1904 the station was turned over to Argentina's Oficina Meteorologica, which has operated it ever since, making it the oldest continuously run research facility in Antarctica.

Renamed **Orcadas Station** in 1951, it accommodates 45 people in the summer, 14 in winter. A three-room **museum** in the Casa Moneta (built in 1905) features a replica of an early hut interior, as well as an array of artifacts, some from Bruce's expedition. Chinstraps, Adélies and gentoos nest nearby.

On Jessie Beach, north of the station, a small **cemetery** contains 10 graves marking the final resting places of men from Argentina, Germany, Norway, Scotland and Sweden. Three are memorials to Argentines who disappeared from the station together in 1998.

SIGNY ISLAND

Whaling in the South Orkneys began in January 1912, when the Norwegian company Aktieselskabet Rethval deployed the factory ship *Falkland* at Powell Island. The captain who took the first whale, Petter Sørlle, surveyed the South Orkneys in 1912–13 and named Signy Island after his wife.

Floating factory ships visited the archipelago until 1914–15, and then again from 1920–30. *Tioga,* the first ship to undertake open-ocean whaling in Antarctica, was wrecked at Signy in 1913. A Norwegian shore station opened on Signy in 1920–21.

The shore station at Signy took the *skrotts* (stripped carcasses) cast off by the floating factories and extracted the remaining oil (60% of a whale's oil is in its meat and bones), and made meat and bone meal.

In 1946–47 Britain established a meteorological station, Base H, at Factory Cove, site of the old whaling station. Over the years, its successor, **Signy station**, expanded its program to include biological studies. The station is located on a site with particularly rich plant life, including steep moss-covered terraces rising behind it. A **marine biology aquarium** is in the station's wooden Tønsberg House. Formerly a year-round base, it is now open from November to April with a maximum population of 10. Automated equipment continues data collection in the off-season. **Cemetery Flats** is the site of five graves from the whaling days.

Signy's fur seals have rebounded dramatically. In 1965 there were practically none; in 1995 researchers estimated that 22,000 lived on the island, which is just 6.5km by 5km. Some studies suggest this is due to having less competition from whales for krill.

SOUTH SHETLAND ISLANDS

Thanks to their spectacular scenery, abundant wildlife and proximity to Tierra del Fuego, the South Shetlands are one of

Antarctica's most visited areas. This major group of islands is just half a day's cruise across the Bransfield Strait from the Antarctic Peninsula, and all cruises stop here.

The South Shetlands stretch 540km from northeast to southwest and include four major groupings as well as 150-odd islets, skerries and rocks. The islands are about 80% glaciated and cover 3688 sq km. The archipelago's highest point is Smith Island's Mt Foster (2105m), first climbed in 1996.

Most distinctive of the South Shetlands is Deception Island, a beautiful 'restless' volcano which was the site of a whaling station and the first Antarctic flight.

History

William Smith, sailing in the British ship *Williams,* was blown off course while rounding Cape Horn for Valparaiso, Chile, and discovered the islands on February 19, 1819, but made no landing. He returned later in the year and landed on King George Island on October 17, claiming the islands for King George III.

On Christmas Day that same year, the first British sealing ship arrived (with Joseph Herring, who had been the mate of *Williams* when the islands were discovered). A veritable navy descended upon the seal-rich islands the next year.

During the summer of 1819–20, the senior British naval officer for the western coast of South America, William Henry Shirreff, chartered *Williams* and placed Edward Bransfield aboard as senior naval officer. Smith and Bransfield surveyed the island group and today the strait between the South Shetlands and the northwestern coast of the Antarctic Peninsula bears Bransfield's name. Bransfield landed on both King George Island (January 22, 1820) and Clarence Island (February 4) to claim them for the new sovereign, King George IV.

Smith returned to the South Shetlands for a fifth time during the summer season of 1820–21, this time on a sealing voyage. His two vessels took an extraordinary 60,000 fur-seal skins.

An incredible 91 sealing ships operated in the South Shetlands during that season, most of them British or American, and the fur seals were almost completely gone by the end of 1821. It was half a century before sealers visited the islands again in great numbers. From 1871–74 a handful of American sealing ships took another 33,000 fur seals from the slowly recovering populations. By 1888–89 the American sealer *Sarah W Hunt* reported taking just 39 skins in a season.

Death visited the sealers as well as the seals: with so many vessels operating in

South Shetland Islands

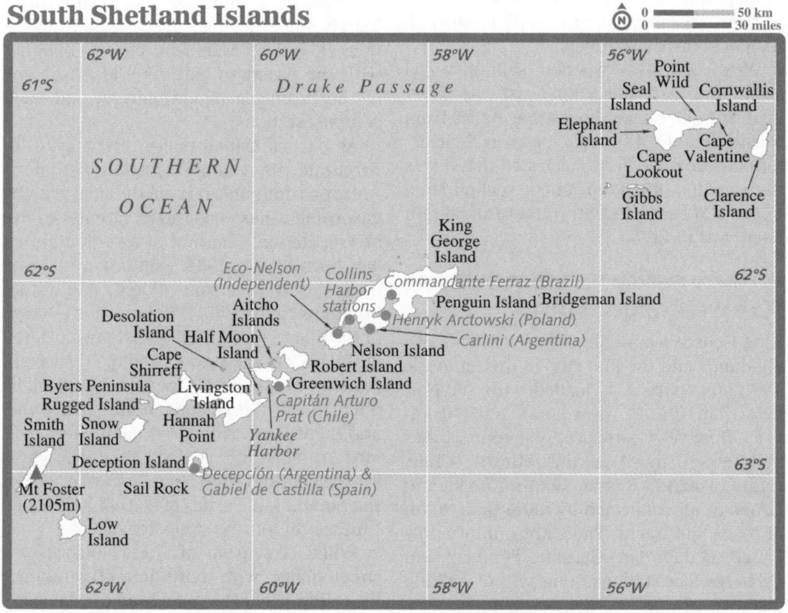

such treacherous waters, there were many wrecks – six ships foundered between 1819 and 1821 alone.

Elephant Island

Elephant Island is located at the South Shetlands' northeastern end. It was originally named 'Sea Elephant Island' by the British sealers who first charted it in the early 1820s, because of its abundance of elephant seals. The island itself bears a superficial resemblance to an elephant's head and trunk.

It was here that 22 members of Shackleton's *Endurance* expedition, stranded in 1915 after their ship was crushed in the Weddell Sea pack ice, spent 135 days. At **Point Wild**, on the northern coast 10km west of Cape Valentine (the island's easternmost point), where the men lived beneath two upturned boats, a monolith with a bust of Piloto Pardo, commander of the Chilean navy cutter *Yelcho,* commemorates the rescue on August 30, 1916. Landings are difficult; heavy surf often prevents even Zodiac tours, and if it is calm, the beach may be too crowded with fur seals and chinstraps to go ashore.

At **Cape Lookout**, a 240m-high bluff on the southern coast, there are chinstrap, gentoo and macaroni penguins.

Elephant Island is also home to moss colonies, dated at more than 2000 years old, with peat nearly 3m deep.

Wreckage of a wooden sailing vessel found on the southwestern coast was examined in 1999, raising hopes that it was from Nordenskjöld's *Antarctic,* or even Shackleton's *Endurance*. Tests suggested that it was the remains of a Connecticut sealing ship, *Charles Shearer,* lost en route to the South Shetlands in 1877.

King George Island

King George Island, the largest of the South Shetlands and the first stop in the Antarctic for many tourists, is loaded with stations. Less than 10% of the island's 1295 sq km is ice-free, yet it supports year-round bases maintained by Argentina, Brazil, Chile, China, Poland, Russia, South Korea, and Uruguay, all connected by more than 20km of roads and tracks. There are summer-only Dutch, Ecuadorian, German, Peruvian and US bases. The stations, some within walking distance of one another, are here because King George Island is so accessible to South America. Thus it's a smart spot for countries to build stations and perform scientific research, thereby earning the status of a consultative party, or full member, of the Antarctic Treaty.

Before the island's station-building boom began, whalers (p181) set up operations at Admiralty Bay on the southern coast in 1906. See the p57 for more on whaling.

In 1972 *Lindblad Explorer,* the first passenger ship built specifically for polar cruising, ran aground in Admiralty Bay. The 90 passengers were rescued by a Chilean naval vessel, and a German tugboat towed the ship off the rocks 18 days later.

Among the most popular landing sites on King George Island today is **Turret Point**, at the eastern end of King George Bay on the island's southern coast. The point takes its name from a group of prominent rock stacks above the beach, a nesting area for Antarctic terns. You'll also find chinstraps, Adélies, blue-eyed shags and southern giant petrels.

PRESIDENTE EDUARDO FREI MONTALVA STATION

Chile constructed this station, known as 'Frei,' in 1969 on the nearly ice-free Fildes Peninsula at the island's southwestern tip, and 10 years later added **Teniente Rodolfo Marsh Martin station** less than 1km across the peninsula. Frei has since incorporated Marsh, thus the station's name appears either as Frei or Marsh on charts. Together with the Escudero base, Frei/Marsh is one of the Peninsula region's largest and most complex stations.

As part of Chile's policy of trying to incorporate its claimed Territorio Chileno Antártico into the rest of the country, the government has encouraged families to live at Frei station. The first of several children was born here in 1984. Families are housed in a group of cream-colored single-story buildings called **Villa Las Estrellas** (Village of the Stars), built in 1984, that are clustered at the back of the station. Today, Frei accommodates as many as 170 people, but normally only 110 live here (mostly military personnel and their dependents). Among the few civilians are air-traffic controllers and teachers for the children, who make up nearly 25% of the population. Parties of station kids sometimes greet tourists upon arrival.

When seen from afar, Frei looks like a small village, with more than 40 buildings, including 15 chalets painted in bright colors on the hillside. In the center, red-orange buildings include a hospital, school, bank, post office and tourist shop. The original base complex, also in the center, houses a supermarket, canteen, kitchen and recreation area. Frei also has a chapel and large gymnasium (the scene of a weekly soccer tournament played among the local stations).

The station's Marsh section includes a 1300m compacted-gravel runway, a hangar, a garage, a hostel, a control tower and parking for three wheeled Hercules C-130 aircraft, which have landed here since 1980.

The first UN Secretary-General to visit Antarctica, Ban Ki-moon, was greeted at Frei on November 9, 2007 with a glass of scotch served with 40,000-year-old ice.

Not until 1995 was a scientific annex added to Frei's sprawl. The five blue-roofed buildings of the summer-only **Professor Julio Escudero base** lie along the bottom of a steep hill southeast of Frei.

BELLINGSHAUSEN STATION

Russia set up this base in 1968 and it is now separated from Frei by a small stream. After a fuel-tank farm was established, Bellingshausen became a major fuel depot for the Soviet Antarctic fishing fleet.

Bellingshausen has a maximum capacity of 50 and a winter population of 13. The station consists of 15 one-story buildings built on stilts and painted silver and red. The *banya* (sauna), showers and washing machines are located in the power station, where warm water is produced using the waste heat from the generators.

The station underwent a remarkable cleanup in 2002, with more than 1350 tonnes of scrap metal and other waste cleared from the beach in front of the station and removed to Uruguay and the UK. Every season since then, small additional amounts of waste have been removed.

On the hills north of Bellingshausen is **Holy Trinity**, the first Orthodox church in Antarctica, preassembled of cedar and larch in Siberia and sanctified in February 2004. The 15m-tall church, complete with three small onion domes, a church bell and a handsome interior with hand-painted icons, holds 30 worshippers. They are led in weekly services by the church's priest and his assistant, both Bellingshausen residents. Many visitors enjoy the unusual Antarctic experience of smelling natural wood and frankincense. Holy Trinity's first wedding took place in February 2007 between a Chilean member of Frei station and the daughter of a Russian mechanic at Bellingshausen.

SURF'S UP

A group of surfers surfed at Elephant Island in February 2000 while visiting on a passenger yacht. They wore fleece-lined neoprene undersuits, oversuits and drysuits with specially fitted hoods.

ARTIGAS STATION

Uruguay's base, established in 1984, accommodates 14 in winter and 60 in summer. Named for Uruguay's national hero, José Gervasio Artigas, an early leader who redistributed land and abolished slavery, the station sits about 200m north of a wreck of a wooden sailing ship.

CHANG CHENG STATION

China's 'Great Wall of China' station was established in 1985 and accommodates 45 people, but recent winter crews have numbered about 12. During the 1987-88 season hundreds of domestic pigeons were freed in a 'Dove of Peace' ritual. Nearly all froze to death the same day.

KING SEJONG STATION

South Korea named its base at Marian Cove close to Maxwell Bay after a 15th-century Korean king who was also a scientist and inventor. Built in 1987–88, the collection of orange buildings accommodates 90 people in summer, 17 in winter.

CARLINI STATION

Argentina built this station, formerly named Jubany, but renamed in 2012 after biologist Alejandro Carlini, at Potter Cove in 1953. Backed by **Three Brothers Hill** (210m), it has been a year-round facility since 1984 and accommodates 80 people (20 in winter). The summer-only **Dallman Laboratory** was opened in 1994 by Argentina, the Netherlands and Germany: the first multinational research facility in Antarctica.

HENRYK ARCTOWSKI STATION

Poland's station, opened in 1977, was named for a geologist on Adrien de Gerlache's *Belgica* expedition and houses up to 50 people. Female visitors were once presented with small bouquets of flowers grown in the station greenhouse, but this has been discontinued because growing nonfood plants now requires special permission under the Antarctic Treaty. Station members still grow vegetables using Antarctic soil, with penguin guano fertilizer.

The **iron cross** on the hill behind the station marks the grave of filmmaker Wladzimierz Puchalski, who died here in 1979.

A well-illustrated English-language brochure sold at the station provides a brief history. Several walking routes emanate from the station. The large gentoo and Adélie rookeries are off-limits because they are encircled by protected moss beds. A **tourist information center** built from recycled wood is on the unnamed point beneath the small yellow-and-red striped **lighthouse**.

The US has operated the small summer-only **Pieter J Lenie field station**, near Arctowski station, since 1985. It's also called 'Copacabana.'

COMMANDANTE FERRAZ STATION

Brazil's station on Admiralty Bay, opened in 1983–84, is located between an old whaling station and the site of the abandoned British Base G (removed in 1996). Ferraz's distinctive orange-roofed, pine-green buildings accommodated 60 people, but a fire in 2012 gutted the station and killed two. At the time of research, the Brazilian government planned to rebuild.

Mt Cross lies behind the station, and a small **cemetery** contains several graves and memorials. Circumnavigate the sensitive bed of lichens nearby, whose boundaries are marked in stone. Also nearby is a composite whale 'skeleton' on a moss bed, which contains the bones of no fewer than nine whale species.

Penguin Island

Just offshore from Turret Point, Penguin Island was named by Bransfield in 1820. Its highest point, 170m **Deacon Peak**, with its red cone, is easily identifiable. It's easy to climb to the extensive crater at the summit, and so many people do that a path is worn into the ground early each season. There's also a meltwater lake in a former volcanic crater where you may see chinstrap penguins.

Nelson Island

Nelson Island is home to **Eco-Nelson** (www.econelson.org), or 'Vaclav Vojtech Base,' a private base run by a Czech man, Jaroslav Pavlíček. The three plywood buildings opened in 1989 and are staffed almost continuously with between one and nine residents. It is run on 'green' principles: detergents, soap, toothpaste and shampoo are banned, and wind turbines generate power, though diesel and wood are also burned. Residents live on local fish, seaweed and mussels and (imported) rice. They study remote survival skills, carry out whale watches and collect rubbish on the beach.

Greenwich Island

As early as 1820, circular **Yankee Harbor**, on the island's southwestern side, was an important anchorage for sealers, who knew it as Hospital Cove. A stone-and-gravel spit extends nearly 1km in a wide curve, protecting Yankee Harbor and making it a favorite yacht anchorage. The spit is an ideal place for walking; look for an old sealer's try-pot on this strand. Further up the beach, by the Argentine *refugio* (refuge) built in the 1950s, several thousand pairs of gentoos nest. A small plaque commemorates Robert McFarlane, a British sealer who operated in the region in 1820 in his brigantine *Dragon*.

Chile's **Capitán Arturo Prat station**, a collection of orange buildings on Discovery Bay on Greenwich's northern coast, was opened in 1947 as Soberania station, and later renamed to honor the Chilean naval hero.

The station accommodates up to 15 personnel and has a small **museum** displaying photos, early expedition equipment and whaling artifacts. A bust of Prat stands outside, and nearby is a cross and shelter commemorating the 1960 station leader, who died while in charge. A cross and shrine to the Virgin of Carmen, erected in 1947, is also in the vicinity.

Ecuador's bright red **Pedro Vicente Maldonado station**, completed in 1998, operates in summer only, and accommodates 18 people.

Half Moon Island

Crescent-shaped Half Moon, just 2km long, lies in the entrance of Moon Bay on the eastern side of Livingston Island. Here the Argentine navy operates the summer-only **Cámara station**, built in 1953. Landings are usually made on the wide sweeping beach east of the station. A handsome wooden boat lies derelict on the shore below the chinstrap colony. In 1961 21 tourists were stranded here for three days when the landing craft from their chartered vessel *Lapataia* was damaged.

Livingston Island

Livingston Island was the first land sighted in the Antarctic when William Smith saw it in February 1819. The island's prominent 1700m central peak, **Mt Friesland**, is often obscured by cloud; it was first climbed in 1992 by a pair of Spaniards.

The island was a major early 19th-century sealing center, and the remains of shelters and artifacts have been found on many beaches. The entire **Byers Peninsula** on the island's western end is protected, because it contains the greatest concentration of 19th-century historical sites in Antarctica.

British Captain Robert Fildes, who survived the wrecks of two ships while sealing in the South Shetlands in the early 1820s, wrote about the superabundance of fur seals and reported that English sealers had taken more than 95,000 fur-seal skins from Livingston's northern coast alone. In January 1821 as many as 75 sealers lived ashore at **Cape Shirreff**.

After the seals' near extinction, fur seals were not observed again until 1958, when a small colony was discovered at the cape. It has since grown to be perhaps the largest in the South Shetlands.

Antarctica's worst loss of life occurred in September 1819 near Cape Shirreff when the 74-gun *San Telmo,* a Spanish man-of-war sailing from Cadiz to Lima, encountered severe weather while crossing the Drake Passage and lost her rudder and topmasts. Although taken in tow by an accompanying ship, the hawsers parted and the ship was lost along with 650 officers, soldiers and seamen. An anchor stock and spars were found by sealers in 1820, and in the same year Weddell found evidence that survivors of a shipwreck had lived for a period on the island. A cairn on Livingston's northern coast at Half Moon Beach, named by sealers in 1820, commemorates those lost.

Hannah Point, on Livingston's south coast, is an extremely popular stop, with its large chinstrap and gentoo rookeries and the occasional macaroni pair nesting among them. The point is named after the British sealer *Hannah* of Liverpool, wrecked in the South Shetlands on Christmas Day, 1820. Be careful of southern giant petrels nesting in the area; they are skittish and will abandon eggs or chicks if nervous.

On a hill above the Hannah Point landing beach, a prominent red vein of jasper runs through the rock. From this lookout you can survey a sheltered beach on the opposite side of the point where elephant seals bask and young male fur seals spar. If elephant seals are at the lookout, do not approach them. They may retreat over the cliff, to their deaths onto the rocks below. Tourists have done this in the past, which accounts for the place's nickname, Suicide Wallow.

Walker Bay is occasionally used as a landing site instead of the overvisited Hannah Point to its east. On Walker's broad beach is a fascinating collection of fossils left by researchers on a tablelike rock among a group of boulders. There are also seal jaws and teeth, and penguin skulls and skeletons. This open-air museum is right below the squarish outcrop on top of the ridge above.

Just east of Hannah Point lies Spain's **Juan Carlos Primero station**, a summer-only base established in 1987–88, which accommodates up to 19 people. It has one of the few alternative-energy systems at an Antarctic station, using both solar power and wind generators, which can provide as much as 20% of the station's needs.

Bulgaria's **St Kliment Ohridski station** is less than 2km northeast of Juan Carlos Primero. A summer-only station, accommodating 20, it was built in 1988, operated for only a year, then reopened in 1993. It's named for St Kliment of Ohrid (840–916), a scholar and bishop who helped introduce the Cyrillic alphabet to Bulgaria.

Deception Island

Easily recognized on any map by its broken-ring shape, Deception Island's collapsed volcanic cone provides one of the safest natural harbors in the world, despite periodic eruptions.

To reach this secret haven, however, vessels must navigate a tricky 230m-wide break in the volcano's walls, known since the early 19th-century sealing days as **Neptunes Bellows** for the strong winds that blow through this strait. A British visitor to Deception in the 1920s called the Bellows 'a veritable death-trap to the uninitiated,' thanks to hull-piercing Ravn Rock (named by Charcot in

1908 for the whale-catcher *Ravn*), which lies just 2.5m beneath the surface in the center of the narrow channel. The 'deceptive' entrance to the island has been known since the early 19th century, when it was called Hell's Gates or Dragon's Mouth.

The southern headland, called **Entrance Point**, harbors evidence of how dangerous the constricted channel can be: the wreck of the British whale-catcher *Southern Hunter*, which ran aground on New Year's Eve, 1957, while avoiding an Argentine naval vessel steaming in through the Bellows. The British whalers yelled for help after hitting the rocks, but the Argentines assumed that the shouting and waving was part of the New Year's celebrations and continued past. Nearby is the site where the cruise ship *Nordkapp* ran aground in February 2007, ripping a 25m gash along the hull of the vessel and ending the cruise for her 280 passengers.

As you enter the harbor, notice the striking colors of the rock faces on either side. Watch too for the pintado petrels that nest on the cliffs on the starboard side of the entrance; the birds often wheel above the sea.

Upon reaching this interior sea, visitors may land at **Whalers Bay** on a black-sand beach cloaked in mysterious white clouds of sulfur-scented steam. Dig your boots into the sand to find heat escaping from subterranean volcanic vents. The island's sloping, snow-covered walls, which reach 580m, rise above the beach.

Few marine animals venture into Port Foster, because volcanic vents heat the water. Chinstraps are Deception's most common penguins, with several rookeries exceeding 50,000 pairs each. Rookeries are on the southwestern coast at **Vapour Col** and on the eastern coast at **Macaroni Point** and **Baily Head** (also called Rancho Point), a natural amphitheater with a melt stream running through it. Visiting Baily Head, home of perhaps the largest chinstrap rookery on the Peninsula, can be difficult due to heavy surf even in calm seas. Just south of Baily Head, the seastacks named **Sewing Machine Needles** once included a natural rock arch; it collapsed in 1924 after an earthquake.

History

Early sealers used Deception's 12km-wide harbor as a base. Nathaniel Palmer, who first explored the island and discovered its inner harbor, is thought to have seen the Antarctic Peninsula in 1820 from the break in the caldera wall at **Neptunes Window**, known to sealers as 'the Gap.'

Chanticleer, commanded by Captain Henry Foster, entered the 190m-deep harbor now known as **Port Foster** in 1829. The ship anchored at Pendulum Cove and magnetic experiments were performed there for two months. Besides Webster, the first scientist to visit the Antarctic, *Chanticleer* also carried Lieutenant Edward Kendall, who made the first survey of the island and some of the first paintings of Antarctica.

THE WHALING STATION

In 1906 a joint Norwegian-Chilean whaling company established by Captain Adolfus Amandus Andresen, a Norwegian-born immigrant to Chile, began using an area on the northern side of the caldera at Whalers Bay as a base for *Gobernador Bories,* his floating factory ship. Andresen was accompanied by his wife, family and pets: a parrot and an Angora cat. His company, the Sociedad Ballenera de Magallanes, was based in Punta Arenas and used Whalers Bay for 10 years. In 1907 the company's ship was joined by two more Norwegian and one Newfoundland factory ship.

Britain, which had formally claimed the island in 1908 as part of the Falkland Islands

DEADLY DEBRIS

Dumping any trash overboard south of S 60° is prohibited by the agreements of the Antarctic Treaty, but some vessels ignore these regulations. One researcher estimates that debris in the Southern Ocean increased 100-fold between 1992 and 2002. Every year, thousands of Antarctic seabirds and marine mammals are killed or injured by debris.

Detritus from fishing boats is the main cause of Southern Ocean debris. Fur seals become entangled in plastic, particularly in net fragments, packaging bands and six-pack rings. They slowly strangle fur seals as they grow.

Seabirds can be killed or injured when they eat plastic and other debris that cause intestinal blockages or starvation.

Dependencies, gave a 21-year lease to Hvalfangerselskabet Hektor A/S, a Norwegian whaling company, in 1911. One of the reasons for granting the license was to utilize the estimated 3000 whale carcasses that littered the shores of Port Foster. They had been abandoned by ships that had stripped them of their blubber but were unable to process the meat and bones, which contain 60% of a whale's oil. Hektor established a shore station at Whalers Bay in 1912, although it was not fully operational until 1919.

In the 1912–13 season, 12 floating factories, 27 catcher boats and the shore station operated at Whalers Bay, processing more than 5000 whales. The whalers called the station **New Sandefjord** after the Norwegian whaling town.

The shore station closed in 1931, partly because of a slump in whale oil prices and partly because technology had advanced. Floating factories could efficiently process a whale at sea, especially once the stern slipway was invented, allowing the whole carcass to be hauled aboard.

Today, where the beach is more than 300m wide in places, several wooden huts stand disintegrating. Flensing boats and water barges lie buried to their gunwales in black volcanic sand. Huge boilers and tanks that once processed and held the whale oil now stand rusting under the southern sky.

A **whalers' cemetery** once held the graves of 45 men but is now buried under several meters of sand from a *lahar* (mudslide) released in 1969 when a volcanic eruption melted the glacier above. Sharp-eyed visitors wandering in the area behind the station may find one of the cemetery's simple wooden coffins (empty), which was tossed about by the massive wave of mud and water. Nearby is a wooden cross.

The mostly intact **FIDASE building** housed the Falkland Islands and Dependencies Aerial Survey Expedition (FIDASE), which spent two seasons (1955–56 and 1956–57) taking aerial photographs of the South Shetlands and northern Peninsula for mapping purposes. Using Canso flying boat aircraft, FIDASE photographed nearly 90,000 sq km of territory.

Far down the beach toward the corrugated steel **aircraft hangar** built in 1961–62, a **cross** commemorates Tømmerman (carpenter) Hans A Gulliksen, who died in 1928. There was once a north–south runway alongside the hangar.

Just west of the old hangar, toward the point and **Kroner Lake**, is a no-entry area protected by the Antarctic Treaty. No boundaries are marked, but to be safe, don't wander past the hangar toward the point. Go up the hill behind the hangar instead, to get a view into a small volcanic cone.

FIRST FLIGHT BY WILKINS

Australian Hubert Wilkins and his pilot Carl Ben Eielson made the first powered flight in Antarctica on November 16, 1928, taking off from a hand-cleared runway in Wilkins' Lockheed Vega monoplane *Los Angeles* and flying for 20 minutes. A month later, on December 20, they took off in his other Vega, *San Francisco,* and flew 11 hours and 2100km to about S 71°20' along the Peninsula.

TERRITORIAL DISPUTES

Deception's strategic location and superb harbor have made it a contested piece of real estate. A British naval operation, mounted in 1941 to thwart German raiders, destroyed coal and oil-fuel depots at the whaling station. In 1942 Argentina sent its naval vessel *Primero de Mayo* to the island to take formal possession of all territory south of S 60° between W 25° and W 68°34'. The ship repeated the possession ceremony at two other island groups and left behind copper cylinders containing official documents claiming the islands for Argentina.

In January 1943, Britain dispatched HMS *Carnarvon Castle* to Deception, where it removed evidence of the Argentine visit, hoisted the Union Jack and returned the copper cylinder and its contents to Argentina through the British ambassador in Buenos Aires. Two months later, *Primero de Mayo* was back, removing the British emblems and repainting the Argentine flag. At the end of 1943 the British once again removed Argentina's marks. In February 1944 Britain established a permanent meteorological station, **Base B**, in former whaling-station barracks.

Today, the ruins of the base's surviving main timber building, **Biscoe House**, can be seen to the west of the whaling station at Whalers Bay. Biscoe was badly damaged by the 1969 mudslide, which carried away several sections of its walls. But the building once housed a tightly knit group of expeditioners posted to the island for two-year stints. Their bar, the scene of many convivial evenings, was decorated with plaques, flags, spirit-bottle labels and the snipped-off ends of visitors' neckties, a cherished base tradition.

The wrangling between Argentina and Britain continued after the establishment of Base B, and the Argentines built their own base Decepción in 1948. In 1952 the Argentines and Chileans both built refuge huts on Britain's airstrip (formerly Wilkins'). The British navy removed the huts the next year and deported two Argentines to South Georgia. In 1953–54 a detachment of Britain's Royal Marines arrived to 'keep the peace' and spent four months on Deception. In 1955 Chile formalized its presence on Deception, building its station at Pendulum Cove. In 1961 Argentina sent President Arturo Frondizi to show the country's official interest in the island. Today, all three countries claim the island.

Currently, Deception's only regularly open stations are summer-only. Spain's **Gabriel de Castilla station**, on the southern side of Fumarole Bay, accommodates 12. About 1000m west is Argentina's **Decepción station**.

Volcano

The volcano that formed Deception is today classified as 'a restless caldera with a significant volcanic risk.' A violent explosion 10,000 years ago blew about 30 cu km of molten rock from the island, and the volcano's summit collapsed to form the caldera, now flooded. In 1923 water in Port Foster boiled and removed the paint from ships' hulls, and in 1930 the floor of the harbor dropped 3m during an earthquake. Two 1967 eruptions forced the evacuation of the Argentine, British and Chilean research stations, and the Chilean station was destroyed. More eruptions occurred in 1969, forcing another round of evacuations and damaging the British station. Five station members, the island's only occupants at the time, escaped a hail of volcanic bombs and falling cinders by carrying pieces of corrugated iron over their heads. They were rescued the same day by a helicopter from a Chilean ship. There were further eruptions in 1970. In summer 1991–92, with increased seismic activity and increased water temperatures at the island, some ships thought it prudent not to enter Port Foster. Spanish scientists presently monitor seismographs on the island about three months each summer.

At **Pendulum Cove**, named for the experiments performed there by Captain Foster, you can doff your clothes and go 'bathing.' A small stream trickling into the harbor here is geothermally heated and a small area where the scalding water mixes with the frigid water provides space for a few people to lie down together in relative comfort. The ruins of Chile's **Presidente Pedro Aguirre Cerda station**, destroyed here by the 1967 eruption, are located behind the beach, but they're off-limits. Although no boundaries are marked, entry is forbidden to protect the abundant mosses.

Telefon Bay is a spectacular place to view the results of volcanic activity. It is named for the whaling supply vessel *Telefon,* which ran aground in 1908 at the entrance to Admiralty Bay on King George Island and was repaired here in 1909.

Sail Rock

Striking-looking Sail Rock, 11km southwest of Deception, is often seen on the horizon while crossing the Bransfield Strait. With its eerie resemblance to a black-sailed pirate ship, the 28m-high rock attracts much attention.

OTHER PERI-ANTARCTIC ISLANDS

No expedition will take in all the peri-Antarctic islands. Voyages from Australia, New Zealand or South Africa often stop at Macquarie Island or Heard Island and New Zealand's sub-Antarctic islands. Resupply vessels visiting **Îles Kerguelen**, **Îles Crozet**, **Île Amsterdam** and **Île St Paul** take tourists.

Tristan da Cunha and **Gough Island** are usually visited on 'repositioning' cruises, en route to/from the northern hemisphere. Landings on any of the 11 rarely visited volcanic **South Sandwich Islands** are extremely difficult, except by helicopter. **Bouvetøya**, **Peter I Øy** and **Scott Island** are visited only rarely.

Heard & McDonald Islands

World Heritage–listed Heard and McDonald Islands, an external territory of Australia, consist of the main volcanic island of Heard, the tiny Shag Islands (11km north) and the McDonald Islands (43km west). No known human-introduced species are present on Heard and McDonald Islands, so extensive quarantine restrictions require anyone going

ANTARCTICA'S FIRST TOURISTS

» The first Antarctic tourist flight, by LAN Chile in 1956, flew over the South Shetlands and the Antarctic Peninsula.

» Two of the earliest cruises to Antarctica, by the Argentine ship *Les Eclaireurs*, reached the South Shetlands in January and February 1958.

» In 1959 the Argentine ship *Yapeyú* and the Chilean vessel *Navarino* both took passengers to the South Shetlands.

» In the earliest mass visit to the Antarctic, Spanish cruise ship *Cabo San Roque* carried 900 passengers to the South Shetlands and the Peninsula in 1973.

ashore to wear clean footwear and clothing. All landings require a permit from the **Australian Antarctic Division** (www.aad.gov.au).

Heard is roughly circular, with the 10km-long **Laurens Peninsula** extending northwest and the 7km **Elephant Spit** extending east. Australia's only active volcano, **Big Ben**, erupted in 1910, 1950, 1985 and 1992. Its summit, the island's highest point, is Mawson Peak (2745m). The island covers 390 sq km and is 80% glaciated, although many glaciers are retreating dramatically. The mean annual temperature is 1.4°C.

Sealer's Corner, at the northwestern end of **Corinthian Bay**, was first used by elephant-sealers in about 1850. The **ruins** of a stone hut, originally built half-buried in the sand for protection from the wind, are clearly visible. Not as easily discerned are several **graves** with thin wooden boards for markers and piles of rocks in the shape of bodies.

As Heard's prime hunting ground during the sealing era, Elephant Spit's low sand-and-shingle beach is named for its abundance of elephant seals, with around 40,000 coming ashore each year for breeding – more than 15,000 pups are born annually. You may see fur seals, and gentoo and king penguins.

In 1908 Heard and McDonald Islands were annexed by Britain. On December 26, 1947, this sovereignty was transferred to Australia. Also on this date, the first of the Australian National Antarctic Research Expeditions (ANARE) established a base at **Atlas Cove** on Heard's northwestern coast, using a WWII naval landing craft driven onto the beach and unloaded through bow doors. The first wintering party's experiences are chronicled in Arthur Scholes' *Fourteen Men: The Story of the Antarctic Expedition to Heard Island* (1952).

Today little remains besides the **cross** commemorating Alistair 'Jock' Forbes and Richard Hoseason, who died in 1952 while returning from an ill-fated journey down island. While walking along the beach beneath the ice cliff fronting the **Baudissin Glacier**, a wave swept them into the sea. Hoseason drowned, and Forbes died of exposure while trying to return to the station over the glacier. The cross is off-limits as it's located in the midst of protected plant life.

Remnants of the **Admiralty Hut**, built by the British in 1929 as a refuge for shipwrecked mariners, still stands at Atlas Cove.

More than a million pairs of macaroni penguins breed on Heard. Long Beach on Heard's south coast may have the world's largest colony. There are also approximately 1000 Heard Island sheathbills (a subspecies) in the islands, and less than 1000 pairs of the endemic Heard shag *(Phalacrocorax nivalis)*.

Macquarie Island

Nicknamed 'Macca' and located halfway between Tasmania and Antarctica, Macquarie's leading attractions are its residents: 100,000 seals, mainly elephant seals; and four million penguins, including about 850,000 breeding pairs of royals, which breed nowhere else.

The first recorded sighting of Macquarie was on July 11, 1810, by sealing brig *Perseverance*. They named the island after Lachlan Macquarie, governor of the Australian colony of New South Wales (of which Tasmania was then a part) and collected 80,000 fur-seal skins. After the sealing era, ships began calling at Macquarie again in the mid- to late-1870s, when king and royal penguins were killed and boiled for their oil. Each bird yielded about half a liter. Royals were preferred because their oil was not as highly saturated with blood, which tended to ferment and ruin the oil. Today, Macquarie is a Tasmanian State Reserve. Permits to land must be obtained in advance from the **Tasmanian Parks and Wildlife Service** (www.parks.tas.gov.au). A fee of not less than A$150 per person is charged for landing, and is included in cruise prices. Parks rangers oversee visits, and strict regulations govern how many people come ashore at once.

Rising in steep cliffs to a plateau 240m to 345m high, Macquarie is 34km long and between 2.5km and 5km wide, covering 128 sq km. The highest point, 433m **Mt Hamilton**, is named for Harold Hamilton, biologist on Douglas Mawson's 1911–13 expedition. Small lakes dot the plateau. Judge and Clerk Rocks lie 16km north; Bishop and Clerk Rocks, 28km south.

Macquarie's climate is one of the most equable (least-changing) on Earth. Mean annual temperatures range from 3.3°C to 7.2°C. Strong westerlies blow nearly every day. There is no permanent snow or ice cover. The yearly precipitation (91cm) is spread out over more than 300 days in a variety of forms: snow, rain, hail, sleet, mist and fog – sometimes all in the same day.

Vegetation at low altitude is dominated by tussock grass, with short grasslands and feldmark communities higher up. There are no trees or shrubs, but there are two species of 'megaherb' on the island, one of which can grow up to 1m high. The yellow-flowering Macquarie Island cabbage was once eaten by sealers to prevent scurvy.

Among Macquarie's unusual features are the 'featherbeds,' waterlogged areas on the coastal terraces, where subsurface drainage is poor, and which only just support a person's weight. Also known as 'quaking mires,' they are actually floating patches of vegetation covering lenses of water, which can be more than 6m deep.

The island is the only place on Earth where rocks from the Earth's mantle, 6km below the ocean floor, are actively exposed above sea level by the gradual but continuing upthrust of the plate. With all of this seismic activity, large earthquakes occur often. Macquarie was granted World Heritage status in 1997, primarily because of its geological values.

Whalers and sealers brought horses, donkeys, dogs, goats, pigs, cattle, ducks, chickens and sheep to Macquarie, although none survive today. Rats, mice, cats, rabbits and wekas (a flightless bird from New Zealand) did thrive – and in recent years have heavily impacted the island's ecology. Although wekas were eradicated in 1988, the rats, mice and rabbits are still numerous and problematic.

When Mawson landed a scientific party here during his Australasian Antarctic Expedition of 1911–14, he was met by the crew of *Clyde*, shipwrecked a month earlier and prepared to defend their sealing rights against what they initially thought were rival sealers. Once the mix-up was straightened out, the party Mawson left on the island used a wireless relay station set up on Wireless Hill in the first two-way communication with the Antarctic continent. The transmissions were: news of the death of Mawson's sledging companions (sent from Commonwealth Bay to Macquarie), and word of Robert Falcon Scott's death (sent from Macquarie to Antarctica).

Other expedition leaders who stopped at Macquarie include Bellingshausen (who traded one of the sealers three bottles of rum for two live albatrosses, 20 dead ones and a live parrot), Wilkes, Scott and Shackleton.

In 1948 a scientific station was established by ANARE at the isthmus on the site occupied by Mawson's men in 1911. About 15 to 20 people winter at the **ANARE station**; up to 40 spend the summer there.

New Zealand's Sub-Antarctic Islands

New Zealand maintains five sub-Antarctic island groups as National Nature Reserves: the **Antipodes**, **Auckland**, **Bounty**, **Campbell** and **Snares** groups. These islands teem with wildlife, particularly seabirds, which nest by the millions. Ten species of penguin have been recorded, and four species breed there regularly.

All are managed by the **New Zealand Department of Conservation** (DOC; www.doc.govt.nz). Entry is by permit only; all groups must be accompanied by a DOC representative. The number of visitors each year is limited to several hundred.

Antarctic Peninsula

Includes »

Best Historical Sights

» Port Lockroy (p75)
» Detaille Island (p79)
» Stonington Island (p81)
» Snow Hill Island (p86)

Best Scenery

» Lemaire Channel (p78)
» Paradise Harbor (p75)
» Charlotte Bay (p74)
» Cuverville Island (p74)
» Danco Island (p74)

Why Go?

The most accessible part of the continent, the beautiful Antarctic Peninsula extends a welcoming arm north toward South America's Tierra del Fuego as if beckoning visitors. And intrepid travelers do come, for the Antarctic Peninsula, the warmest part of the continent (facetiously called the 'Banana Belt') is Antarctica's major breeding ground for seabirds, seals and penguins.

With its dramatic landscapes of steep snow-covered peaks often plunging straight into the sea, and with narrow iceberg-studded channels weaving between countless islands and the mountainous mainland, the Peninsula also offers some of Antarctica's most stunning scenery.

In recent decades, tourist landings have concentrated on sites along the western coast of the central Peninsula; relatively few ships of any sort visit the Weddell Sea, on the Peninsula's eastern side. It has, indeed, earned its reputation as an ice-choked ship-eater. Shackleton's *Endurance* is only the most famous example of the half-dozen vessels crushed there.

Top Resources

» *Two Men in the Antarctic* (1939), Thomas W Bagshawe. Gripping tale by one of two young men who wintered (alone on the continent) at Waterboat Point.

» *Swimming to Antarctica* (2004), Lynne Cox. Fascinating autobiography by the Neko Harbor swimmer.

» *The Ferocious Summer* (2008), Meredith Hooper. Global warming, penguins and the Peninsula.

» *The Crystal Desert* (1992), David G Campbell. Ecologist's three summers studying the life of the Antarctic Peninsula.

» **UK Antarctic Heritage Trust** (UKAHT; www.ukaht.org) Maintains sights on the Peninsula, including Port Lockroy.

» **Polar Times** (www.americanpolar.org)

Antarctic Peninsula Highlights

1 Photograph eye-popping scenery around the **Lemaire Channel** (p78), **Paradise Harbor** (p75) and **Charlotte Bay** (p74)

2 Listen to 200,000 braying Adélie penguins on **Paulet Island** (p83)

3 Knock back a throat-burning pepper vodka at the convivial bar of Ukrainian station **Academician Vernadskiy** (p79)

4 Send a postcard at UK base-turned-museum, **Port Lockroy** (p75)

5 Step inside a time capsule of 1950s British Antarctic life at Base W on **Detaille Island** (p79)

6 Search for fossils on **Seymour Island** (p86) to show your fellow visitors (remember, you can't remove anything!)

7 Explore Nordenskjöld's hut, the Peninsula's oldest remaining building, at **Snow Hill Island** (p86)

8 Spot Adélie penguins and human children at **Esperanza Station** (p82)

9 Inspect old science stations at **Stonington Island** (p81)

10 See science in action at **Palmer Station** (p76), **Rothera Station** (p80) or space-aged **Halley VI** (p87)

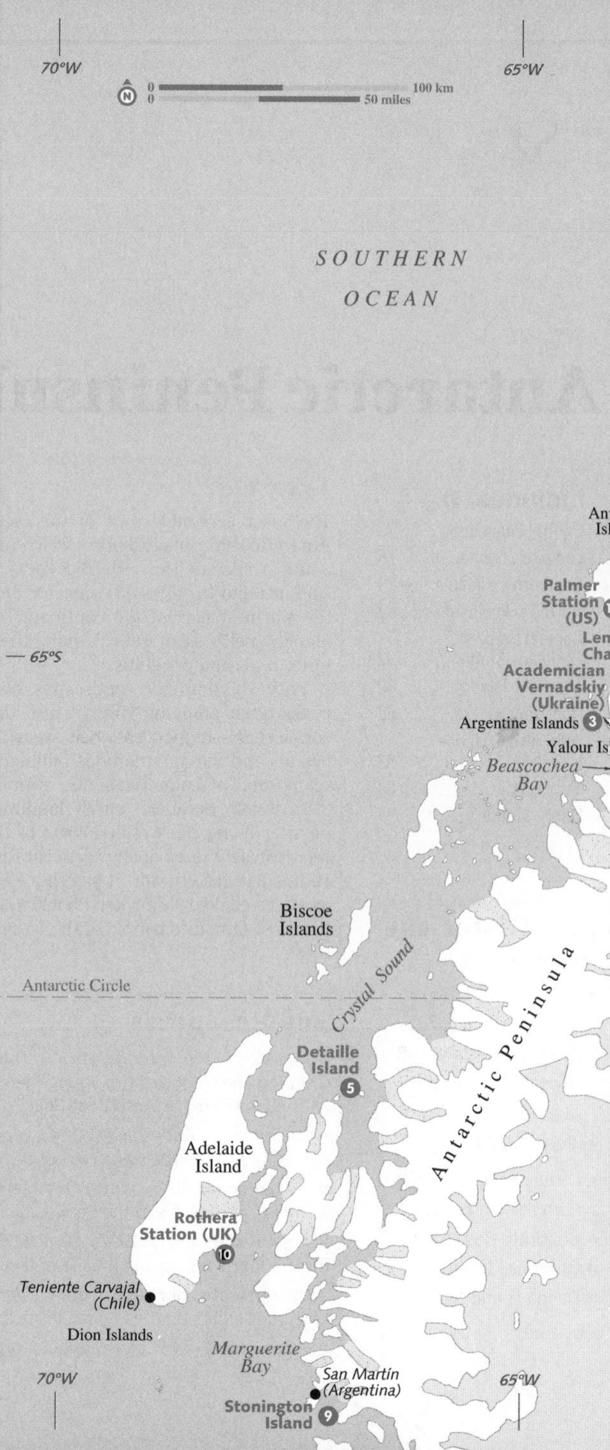

Drake Passage
60°W
55°W
South Shetland Islands
King George Island
Nelson Island
Robert Island
Greenwich Island
Livingston Island
Bransfield Strait
Smith Island
Snow Island
Deception Island
D'Urville Island
Bransfield Island
Joinville Island
Low Island
Astrolabe Island
Esperanza Station (Argentina)
8 Antarctic Sound
General Bernardo O'Higgins (Chile)
Cape Legoupil
Hope Bay
Dundee Island
2 Paulet Island
Trinity Peninsula
Hoseason Island
Trinity Island
Orleans Strait
Brown Bluff
Anderson Island
Devil Island
Botany Bay
Erebus & Terror Gulf
Davis Coast
Vega Island
Brabant Island
James Ross Island
6 Seymour Island
7 Snow Hill Island
Gerlache Strait
1 Charlotte Bay
Cape Sobral
1 Paradise Harbor
65°S
Cape Fairweather
Robertson Island
Weddell Sea
Cape Disappointment
Larsen Ice Shelf
60°W
Halley VI Station (1200km) 10
55°W

CENTRAL PENINSULA

The majority of Antarctic cruises frequent several beautiful spots surrounding the Anvers Island area. These closely arrayed sights offer a multitude of opportunities to snap great photos, record video of icebergs calving, and visit some of humankind's southernmost settlements. All while spying on penguins in their natural habitat.

Charlotte Bay

Some feel that Charlotte Bay, often filled with recently calved icebergs and one of the most beautiful spots along the Peninsula, rivals Paradise Harbor in beauty. It's named for the fiancée of the second-in-command of de Gerlache's 1897–99 expedition. At its entrance, **Portal Point** is the former site of a British Antarctic Survey hut, built in 1956, now relocated to the Falkland Islands Museum in Stanley.

Cuverville Island

Discovered by de Gerlache in 1897–99, and named after JMA Cavalier de Cuverville, a vice admiral in the French navy, this black, half-dome-shaped, 250m-tall island is a popular stop. Its several large gentoo rookeries (totaling several thousand pairs) comprise one of the largest gatherings of gentoos in Antarctica.

University of Cambridge researchers studied the impact of their presence and the presence of tourists on the penguins from 1992 to 1995. After monitoring the gentoos' heart rates and observing skuas and other species, they concluded that well-conducted groups, with tourists observing guidelines (p163), had no detectable effects on the penguin's breeding behavior or success.

The slopes above the landing beach shelter extensive and deep beds of moss, which shouldn't be stepped on, and snow algae stain the hillsides (see the boxed text, p88).

Danco Island

Danco Island, 1.5km long, has a wide, sloping cobblestone beach. It was charted by de Gerlache in 1897–99 and later named for the expedition's geophysicist, Émile Danco, who died in the Antarctic. **Base O**, built by the British in 1955–56 and occupied as a surveying base until 1959, was demolished and removed in 2004 after four decades as a refuge hut. Six concrete foundation blocks, one with a plaque, remain. Gentoos nest right up to the summit of Danco's 180m peak. Zodiac cruising in the ice-choked channels around the island can be spectacular.

Rongé Island

De Gerlache named this island for Madame de Rongé, a wealthy contributor to his expedition. It is home to several large colonies of gentoos and chinstraps. The cave on the hillside may have sheltered early sealers. The small archipelago called **Orne Islands** just north of Rongé Island was probably named by early-20th-century whalers working in the area. It is home to a colony of chinstraps.

Neko Harbor

A continental landing deep in Andvord Bay, Neko was discovered by de Gerlache, but takes its name from Norwegian whaling ship *Neko,* which operated in the area between 1911 and 1924.

A nearby glacier often calves with a thunderous roar, offering dramatic video footage.

The small orange hut with the Argentine flag on the side is a *refugio* (refuge hut), built in 1949 and named 'Captain Fleiss.' Hundreds of gentoos nest on the hillside.

As you gaze over Neko's iceberg-filled waters, recall American long-distance swimmer Lynne Cox, who in December 2002 swam nearly 2km (in 25 minutes) in the 0.5°C waters here – a fatal stunt for almost anyone else. Cox spent many years training in superchilled waters, but doctors say that she is also physiologically unique.

Useful Island

Probably named for its 'useful' location 3km west of Rongé Island in the Gerlache Strait, this small but interesting island has gentoos and chinstraps nesting right up to the top. In fact, since the high ground loses its snow cover first, it's preferred by the birds for their nests. Penguins willing to trek more than 100m in elevation over snow and rocks get a head start raising chicks. The summit is marked by an Argentine beacon (a metallic orange cylinder that's 2m tall).

Waterboat Point

Although it appears to be an island, Waterboat Point is separated from the Peninsula only at high tide. At low water, it's possible to walk across a stretch of rocks to the mainland.

From January 1921 to January 1922 British researchers Thomas W Bagshawe (only 19 years old) and Maxime C Lester (22) spent a year at Waterboat Point recording meteorological, tidal and zoological data. At the time they were the only people living on Antarctica.

They were part of the smallest Antarctic expedition ever mounted, a four-man effort led by John Cope; the other member was Hubert Wilkins. The expedition was supposed to be much larger, but funds were tight. The other two abandoned the project, but the young men decided to proceed. They supplemented insufficient stores with penguin and seal meat, living in a rough shelter they constructed in part from an upturned water boat left by Norwegian factory ship *Neko* about eight years before. There's almost nothing left of the **ruin** of Bagshawe's and Lester's hut, but it's a protected historic site.

Chile's air force built **Presidente Gabriel González Videla Station** in 1951 amid a large gentoo rookery that covers almost the entire area, including the site of Bagshawe and Lester's huts. Occupied now only intermittently in the summer, the station is named for the Chilean president who, in 1948, became the first head of state to visit Antarctica – with an entourage of 140 that included his wife and daughters! Station members used to keep pigs, sheep and chickens, all of which roamed freely, 'an incongruous scene in the Antarctic,' as a 1964 visitor recalled.

Paradise Harbor

With its majestic icebergs and reflections of the surrounding mountains in the water, Paradise Harbor is undeniably beautiful. Even the early-20th-century whalers operating here recognized its extreme splendor, as its name indicates.

This is a favorite place for Zodiac cruising around the ice calved from the (receding) glacier at the head of the bay. You may pass beneath blue-eyed shags nesting on cliffs, which can be colored blue-green by copper deposits, emerald green by moss and orange or yellow by lichens.

The original portions of Argentina's **Brown Station** (formerly called Almirante Brown) were destroyed on April 12, 1984 by a fire set by the station's physician-leader, who didn't want to stay another winter. Station personnel were rescued by US ship *Hero*. Gentoos nest among the ruins.

Climb the hill for a great view of glaciers. The broken memorial stone commemorates Jostein Helgestad, who died in 1993 on Monica Kristensen's private expedition when his snowmobile plunged down a crevasse en route to the South Pole.

Port Lockroy

De Gerlache named **Wiencke Island** in 1897–99 for Carl August Wiencke, a young seaman who fell overboard and drowned while trying to clear *Belgica*'s scuppers.

An 800m-long harbor on the west coast of Wiencke, Port Lockroy is one of the most popular tourist stops in Antarctica, thanks to **Base A**, the former British station-turned-museum on tiny **Goudier Island**, operated by the UK Antarctic Heritage Trust (UKAHT; www.ukaht.org).

Visits are usually made in conjunction with landings at the gentoo rookery at nearby **Jougla Point**, where other highlights include blue-eyed shags and a composite whale skeleton reconstructed on the shore.

History

Port Lockroy was discovered by Belgian explorer Adrien de Gerlache in 1899, but remained unnamed and uncharted until Jean-Baptiste Charcot arrived in February 1904. It's named after Edouard Lockroy, vice president of France's Chamber of Deputies, who helped Charcot secure expedition funds.

Until about 1931 Port Lockroy was a major harbor for whalers. Around the landing site, chains and eyebolts and the date '1921' inscribed in the rock can be seen; these were moorings for *Solstreif*, one of 11 factory ships that anchored and processed whales here.

After Argentine navy ship *Primero de Mayo* left a cylinder at Port Lockroy in 1943 claiming the harbor and all territory between W 25°W and W 68°34′ south of S 60°, Britain moved to uphold its rival claim. In 1943–44 a secret British naval operation, unofficially called 'Operation Tabarin' (for a bawdy Parisian nightclub), removed the Argentine emblems and established Base A. Some of the timber used in its construction was salvaged from platforms and rafts left by the whalers, and also from Deception Island's abandoned whaling station.

Base A was staffed almost continuously until 1962 (normal occupancy was four to nine people, with the usual tour of duty lasting about 2½ years!) but then fell into disrepair.

Sights

Bransfield House HISTORIC BUILDING

Britain beautifully restored the original station building, Bransfield House, the main building of Base A, in 1996. Displays on the station's history hang inside. Artifacts include clothing from Operation Tabarin, a clandestine 1944 radio transmitter, a wind-up HMV gramophone with Noel Coward 78 rpm records, and wooden skis purchased from the Grytviken Whaling Station Stores on South Georgia in 1957. A scientific highlight: a restored 'Beastie' (an early apparatus for upper-atmospheric research). Don't miss the full-length portrait of Marilyn Monroe painted on the back of the generator-shed (gift shop) door, a memory aid for lonely winterers during Antarctica's all-male era.

Three UKAHT staff members live at Port Lockroy in the summer to maintain the historic site. They also run a busy **post office** (about 70,000 items are hand-stamped each year) and a well-stocked souvenir shop, with the proceeds funding museum operations. Surplus profits help pay for the conservation of other British historic sites on the Peninsula. The shop accepts US dollars, British pounds, euros and credit cards (no American Express).

To manage the number of visitors, UKAHT allows up to 350 people to visit per day, but no more than 60 are allowed ashore at once. The hut is the staff members' temporary home; respect their personal areas.

Goudier Island ROOKERY

Goudier Island is home to 800 pairs of gentoos. Monitoring of their breeding success since 1995 has found no discernible impact from tourists, who tramp past their nests by the thousands each year. Breeding success seems more closely linked to local environmental conditions, such as snow cover or the availability of krill. Indeed, the gentoos seem to care little about Bransfield House; in the beginning of the summer, the snow can be as high as the building's eaves, and the penguins attempt to nest on the roof.

Anvers Island

Mountainous Anvers Island, 70km long, was discovered by de Gerlache in 1898 and named for the Belgian province of the same name.

Sights

Palmer Station BASE

Palmer was built in 1968 on the island's southwest coast to honor American sealer Nathaniel B Palmer, who in 1820 was one of the first to see Antarctica. The new station replaced the prefabricated wooden huts of 'Old Palmer,' established in 1964 about a kilometer across Arthur Harbor from the present station. Old Palmer itself superseded Britain's **Base N**, occupied from 1955 to 1958 (no longer in existence).

Palmer accommodates 44 people in summer but only about 25 people winterover. The station is accessible by sea year-round and is resupplied by ship every six weeks.

Palmer comprises two main buildings, as well as a boathouse, a dive locker, workshops, a clean-air laboratory, a sauna and storage buildings all placed close together. The three-story **BioLab** includes a laboratory, a dining area, offices and communications and sleeping facilities. The two-story **GWR building** (the acronym stands for garage, warehouse and recreation) also houses generators, sleeping facilities, a small medical facility and the station store.

Research focuses on long-term monitoring of the marine ecosystem (mainly seabirds and krill), atmospheric studies and the effects of increased ultraviolet radiation (caused by the ozone hole) and climate change on marine and terrestrial communities.

Only 12 ship visits are permitted annually to avoid disruption to research. Tourists get a walking tour, including an interesting peek into two **aquariums** filled with anemones, mollusks, sea urchins, krill and fish. You may also shop at the station **store** (which accepts credit cards and US dollars) and taste the locally famous 'Palmer brownies' in the dining room.

You can't overlook the **leaping orca mural** on the station's giant fuel tank. Palmerites

Anvers Island Area

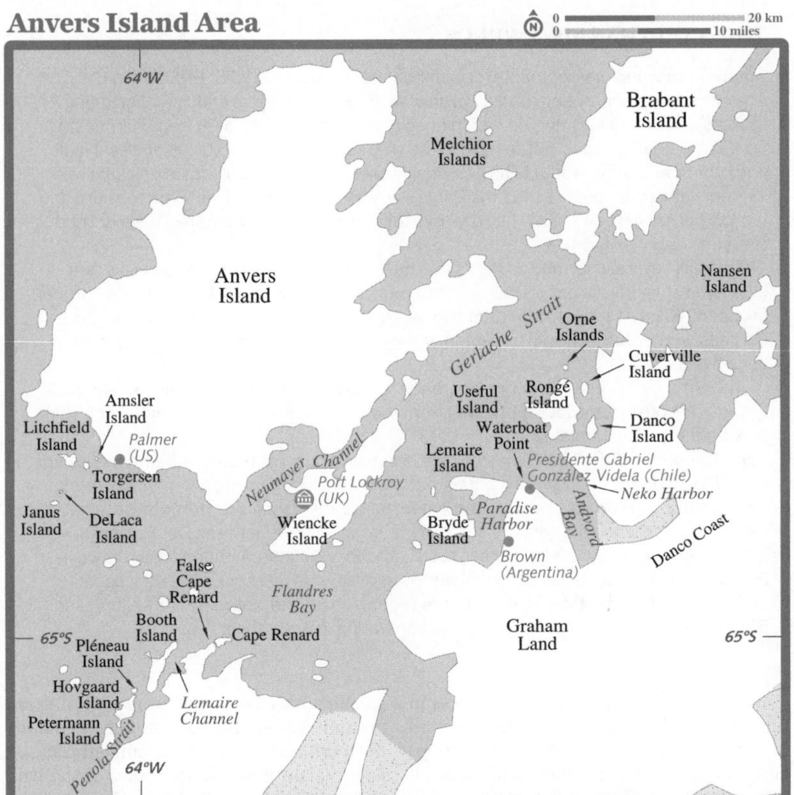

sometimes watch outdoor movies projected onto the side of the tank, when weather permits. Also, look for the metal krill **weathervane** atop the sauna.

Torgersen Island ROOKERY

The Adélie rookery just offshore is often visited in conjunction with Palmer. Since 1974, however, the Adélie population here has dropped by 60% to fewer than 3300 pairs, due to climate-induced changes in sea ice and snowfall.

At **Litchfield Island**, just west of Torgersen, the Adélies are already gone. The rookery had been monitored since 1974, when there were about a thousand breeding pairs. Paleoecological evidence indicates that the penguins had been breeding there for at least 600 years, with up to 15,000 pairs nesting on the island each year. By November 2007 there were no more.

Melchior Islands

Sixteen of the small Melchior Islands, located between the much-larger Anvers and Brabant islands well down the west side of the Antarctic Peninsula, are named for letters of the Greek alphabet: Alpha to Omega. On Lambda Island the first **lighthouse** built by Argentina in the Antarctic, called Prim–ero de Mayo, was erected in 1942, and is now a historic site.

Booth Island

Y-shaped Booth Island – discovered by a German expedition in 1873–74 and named for either Oskar Booth or Stanley Booth, or both, who were members of the Hamburg Geographical Society – forms the western side of the Lemaire Channel. Its highest point is 980m Wandel Peak.

THE BAHÍA PARAÍSO WRECK

Antarctica's worst environmental disaster occurred on January 28, 1989, when the 131m Argentine naval supply ship *Bahía Paraíso*, with 234 passengers and crew (including 81 tourists), ran into a submerged rock pinnacle off DeLaca Island, 3km from Palmer station. The pinnacle ripped a 10m gash in the ship's hull, spilling 645,000L of diesel fuel and other petroleum products and creating a slick that covered 30 sq km. No one was injured. Palmer residents towed the *Bahía Paraíso*'s unmotorized lifeboats to shore and fed the passengers and crew. Two nearby cruise ships and an Argentine vessel carried everyone out of Antarctica.

The spill severely harmed seabirds and the marine environment. Skua chicks and blue-eyed shag chicks each experienced a mortality rate of nearly 100%. Adélie numbers dropped 16% that season. Mollusks and macroalgae were also immediately damaged. Perhaps worst of all, the spill disrupted or destroyed research that in some cases went back two decades.

In 1992 a joint Argentine-Dutch operation recovered most of the remaining 148,500L of fuel and some hazardous lubricants from the submerged tanks (although some still leak from the wreck today).

In the course of the 1990s most local marine communities recovered, with the exception of the blue-eyed shags, which have not been able to regain their former numbers.

Today, *Bahía Paraíso*'s nearly submerged hulk is still visible. From Palmer station, as well as from approaching vessels, the rusty hull can be seen between DeLaca and Janus Islands, in front of and slightly closer to DeLaca. Vessels enter Arthur Harbor between Bonaparte Point and Janus Island. Sharp-eyed observers can spot a 3m-long section of *Bahía*'s hull at high tide. At low tide, the section above the waterline is 10m long and 50cm high – a reminder of the dangers of operating in Antarctica.

Booth Island is one of very few places in the Antarctic Peninsula where three species of penguin (Adélie, gentoo and chinstrap) nest alongside one another, and most of those places are off-limits to tourism.

Charcot's French Antarctic Expedition aboard *Français* spent the winter of 1904 at **Port Charcot** (the explorer named it for his father) on Booth's northwest end. A cairn, pillar and plaque from the expedition are protected as a **historic site**.

Lemaire Channel

So photogenic that its nickname is 'Kodak Gap,' this steep-sided channel runs 11km between the mountains of Booth Island and the Peninsula. The passageway is quite deep – more than 140m for most of its length – and at just 1600m wide it's only visible once you're almost inside.

The channel was discovered by a German expedition in 1873–74, but wasn't navigated until December 1898, when de Gerlache's *Belgica* sailed through. In a decidedly odd choice, de Gerlache named it for Belgian adventurer Charles Lemaire, who explored the Congo. Ice sometimes blocks the way, so ships may be forced to retreat and sail around Booth Island. At the Lemaire's northern end are two tall, rounded peaks at **False Cape Renard**. The taller of the pair, at 747m, was summited by a German team in 1999.

Pléneau Island

Almost 1km long, this island is home to thousands of gentoos. It was named by Charcot during his 1903–05 expedition for photographer Paul Pléneau. When Charcot changed his plans at the last minute (he had originally intended going to Greenland), Pléneau replied by telegram, as described in William J Mill's book *Exploring Polar Frontiers* (2003), in a way that would gratify any leader: 'Where you like. When you like. For as long as you like!'.

Petermann Island

Home to the **world's southernmost gentoo colony**, 135m-high Petermann Island, at S 65°10´, is one of the most southerly landings most cruises make. Just under 2km, the island was discovered by an 1873–74 German whaling and sealing expedition in the steamship *Grönland*, led by Eduard Dallman, who named the island for German geographer August Petermann. Adélies, gentoos and blue-eyed shags nest here, and snow algae (see boxed text p88) are abundant.

Charcot's expedition of 1908–10 wintered aboard *Pourquoi Pas?* at **Port Circumcision**, a cove on the island's southeast coast. It was discovered by Charcot on New Year's Day 1909 and named for the holy day Feast of the Circumcision (January 1), when tradition says Christ was circumcised. A **cairn** built on **Megalestris Hill** (named after an obsolete species name for the South Polar skua) can still be seen, as can an Argentine **refuge hut** built in 1955. Near the hut is a **cross** commemorating three BAS (British Antarctic Survey) men who died in 1982 attempting to cross the sea ice back to Faraday Station from Petermann.

Yalour Islands

This group of islands, 2.5km in extent, was named by Charcot for Lieutenant Jorge Yalour, an officer of the Argentine navy ship *Uruguay,* which rescued the Swedish Antarctic expedition in 1903. About 8000 pairs of Adélies nest here. There are often beautiful examples of orange lichens and green mosses, as well as small clumps of Antarctic hairgrass.

Argentine Islands

Discovered by Charcot on his *Français* expedition and named after the Argentine Republic in thanks for its help, the islands offer several sheltered yacht anchorages.

Sights

Academician Vernadskiy Station BASE

This Ukrainian base, which accommodates 24 people, is located on Galindez Island. Transferred from the UK in 1996 for £1 (look for the actual coin embedded in wood between the taps at the station bar), it was previously called Faraday (after Michael Faraday, the English discoverer of electromagnetism). The station now commemorates Vladimir Vernadskiy, first president of the Ukrainian Academy of Sciences.

A popular remnant from the station's British era is the **pub**, with a dartboard, billiards table and a magnificent carved wooden bar – built by station carpenters who were supposed to be working on something else. The pub is richly decorated with flags, banners and photographs from visiting ships and neighboring stations. One oddity is the pub's large collection of bras, periodically added to by visitors. Sample the *gorilka,* a tongue-burning pepper vodka made locally – say *Budmo!* (Ukrainian for cheers) and then drink it down in one.

Among the unusual souvenirs for sale in the Vernadskiy **shop** is a bottle of 'low-ozone air,' collected locally and officially labeled.

One important upgrade to the station was made soon after the transfer: the Ukrainians added a **sauna**.

Long-running weather records kept at the station show that mean annual temperatures along the Peninsula's west coast have risen by about 2.5°C since 1947. Local ice cover has declined, and the number of plants (such as Antarctic hairgrass and Antarctic pearlwort) in the vicinity has increased, possibly as a result of the warming.

Wordie House HISTORIC BUILDING

Built in 1947 as the first part of what would later become Faraday, this protected historic site, restored in the late 1990s by BAS, sits about 1km from the station. The original base here was established in 1934 by the British Graham Land Expedition. It was washed away by a tsunami in about 1946. The rooms have been returned to their early-1950s appearance and contain period artifacts such as Tilley lamps, bunks, sacks of anthracite and a stove, but also some more recent foodstuffs, perhaps left by visiting yachties. Signs describing the building's history line the walls.

SOUTHERN PENINSULA

South of the Antarctic Circle, few cruise ships make it this far. But those yachties who do will find vast, deserted stretches of sea coast, several interesting historic stations, and two active bases, including the UK's Rothera Station.

Detaille Island

Because of its location just south of the Antarctic Circle, tiny Detaille Island is commonly the goal of expedition leaders on 'Circle crossing' cruises, but landings often cannot be made due to high winds and seas. Detaille is the site of Britain's **Base W**, built

TENNIS, ANYONE?

Tennis has played a curious role in Detaille's history: it is the first place south of the Antarctic Circle where the game was played. After opening the 1956 Olympics in Melbourne, the Duke of Edinburgh visited several British Antarctic bases. A keen tennis player in his retinue had racquets and balls but because the balls did not bounce on Detaille's snow, the game was modified to 'continuous volleying.' Prince Philip and others in the party (including 69-year-old Sir Raymond Priestley, who had earlier worked in Antarctica with both Ernest Shackleton and Robert Scott) joined in. The group formed the first Antarctic Tennis Club, complete with their own club ties.

in 1956 and hurriedly evacuated in summer 1958–59. Thanks to the men's hasty departure and the necessity that they take little with them, Base W is an eerily preserved time capsule of 1950s Antarctic life.

The base had been intended to host dog-sledging survey parties which would cross the sea ice to the nearby Antarctic Peninsula, but the ice was dangerously unstable. When Base W was vacated, heavy sea ice prevented resupply ship *Biscoe* from approaching closer than 50km, despite the assistance of two US icebreakers. So the men were forced to close up the base, load sledges with only their most valuable gear and use dog teams to reach the ship (a touch of irony).

As the dogs were being brought aboard *Biscoe,* one named 'Steve' escaped and ran back towards Detaille. Since time was short, the men reluctantly abandoned the dog to its fate. Three months later, the men at Britain's Horseshoe Island base 100km to the south were surprised to see Steve come running up, healthy and happy.

Today Base W's cozy wooden main building can be visited by small groups. Heavy wooden skis in racks line the main corridor, mattresses remain on the bunks, and a pair of woolen long-johns hangs on a line over a small kerosene heater, awaiting an owner who will never return. A poignant stack of typed radio messages lying on a top bunk reveals the isolation the expeditioners experienced during their two-year stint here. 'My new roses are looking very bonny,' a mother wrote to her son John, while another offered, 'We all hope you and your companions are keeping well and enjoying your new base.'

Adelaide Island

This large (140km long, 30km wide), heavily glaciated island, with mountains up to 2565m high, was discovered by *Biscoe* in 1832 and named for Queen Adelaide of England, also namesake of South Australia's capital. Most ships venturing this far south sail to the west of Adelaide as the island-choked channel between it and the mainland may be impassable.

Sights

Rothera Station BASE

The UK's Rothera, built in 1975, occupies a small peninsula on Adelaide's southeast coast. A 900m gravel airstrip and hangar were added in 1990–91, making Rothera a regional logistics center for British Antarctic operations using Twin Otter aircraft. The station is also resupplied by ships using the 60m Biscoe Wharf built in 1990–91. Rothera accommodates up to 130 people in the summer and an average of 21 in winter. The station takes its name from Rothera Point, itself named for John Rothera, a surveyor with the British program in the 1950s.

Rothera's main building, **Bransfield House**, includes the station dining room, bar, library, offices, labs and an elevated 'operations control tower.'

The last sledge dog teams at Rothera are commemorated in the two dormitories. **Admirals House**, opened in 2001, has en suite rooms for two people, while **Giants House**, opened in 1997, has rooms for four people with communal bathrooms.

Bonner Laboratory, named for eminent polar biologist Nigel Bonner and completed in 1997, was destroyed by a fire caused by an electrical fault on September 28, 2001. The lab, rebuilt at a cost of £3 million, reopened in January 2004. It includes an emergency compression chamber in case of diving accidents, and a cold-water aquarium in which researchers have noted the dramatic effects that even slight warming can have on key species in the Antarctic marine environment (see p194). Just a 2°C rise in the water temperature rendered three species unable to defend themselves from predators.

Teniente Carvajal BASE

Britain established **Base T** at the southwest tip of Adelaide Island in 1961 but closed it in 1977 when the skiway deteriorated, and moved operations to Rothera. Base T was transferred in 1984 to Chile, which renamed it Teniente Luis Carvajal Villaroel Antarctic base, usually known simply as Teniente Carvajal.

Marguerite Bay

This extensive bay was discovered by Charcot on his 1909 expedition and named for his wife.

The **Dion Islands** at the northern end of Marguerite Bay are home to the only emperor penguin rookery in the Antarctic Peninsula region, but they are a protected area and closed to tourists.

Argentina's **San Martín Station**, the most southerly Peninsula station, was established in 1951 on Barry Island in the Debenham Islands, between Adelaide and Alexander islands. Closed between 1960 and 1975, it now accommodates 20 people.

Stonington Island

Named for the home port of Connecticut sealer Nathaniel Palmer, Stonington Island is an Antarctic ghost town. Two abandoned stations, about 200m apart, are rarely seen by tourists, being so far south. They get occasional visitors from Rothera and San Martín stations.

Sights

Base E HISTORIC BASE

The UK's Base E, established in 1945–46 and used until 1975, consists of two wooden huts and some steel-mesh dog pens. The larger, two-story hut served as sleeping quarters, while the smaller was a generator shed. A **cross** on the point commemorates two Britons who died while waiting out a storm in a snow-hole during a field trip in 1966.

East Base HISTORIC BASE

East Base was built during aviator Richard Byrd's third Antarctic expedition, the US Antarctic Service Expedition of 1939–41. It was also used in 1947–48 by the private Ronne Antarctic Research Expedition, which included the first women to winter in Antarctica, Edith Ronne and Jennie Darlington. Unfortunately their husbands, who were also on the expedition, quarreled, so out of loyalty they did not speak to one another either! After the Ronne expedition departed, the UK used East Base until 1975.

The US government funded a historic preservation program at East Base in 1990–91. A small display of artifacts has been set up in one of the three base buildings, marked as a **museum**.

NORTHERN PENINSULA

The seldom-visited northern peninsula includes parts of Graham Land, which British

VINSON MASSIF: ON TOP OF THE BOTTOM OF THE WORLD

Antarctica's highest peak is 4900m Vinson Massif. The mountain (20km long by 13km wide) is in the **Sentinel Range** in the **Ellsworth Mountains**, near the base of the Antarctic Peninsula. It was discovered in 1958 by US Navy aircraft and is named for Congressman Carl Vinson of Georgia, who influenced the US government to support Antarctic exploration from 1935 to 1961. Thanks to the mountaineering pilgrimage of the 'Seven Summits' (scaling the highest peak on each continent), Vinson is also Antarctica's most-climbed mountain.

On December 18, 1966, four members of a private US expedition led by Nicholas B Clinch made the first ascent. Over the next few days, the expedition also reached the summits of Antarctica's second-, third- and fourth-highest peaks: neighboring Tyree (4845m), Gardner (4686m) and Shinn (4661m), respectively.

Since 1985, Adventure Network International has guided over 600 climbers to Vinson's summit. The time required ranges from two to 14 days, depending on weather, and the climber's experience and fitness level. Vinson's neighbor, Mt Tyree, only 52m lower, is regarded as the continent's most challenging peak, but dozens of other Antarctic mountains remain virgin.

explorer John Biscoe discovered and named for James RG Graham, First Lord of the Admiralty, and terminates with the Trinity Peninsula on its northernmost point, named by Edward Bransfield in 1820. Claimed by Britain, Chile and Argentina as part of their Antarctic territories, its three bases include General Bernardo O'Higgins base (Chile), one of the oldest on the Peninsula, and Esperanza Station (Argentina), where the first person was born in Antarctica.

General Bernardo O'Higgins Station

One of the oldest stations on the Peninsula, Chile's General Bernardo O'Higgins Station stands 80m offshore from the ice-cliffed **Cape Legoupil** on a small island. It was established in 1948 and inaugurated by Chilean president Gabriel González Videla. A jetty provides easy access, and a wooden plank and wire suspension pedestrian **bridge** links the island to the mainland.

The station, which accommodates 50, is operated by the Chilean army; meteorological and sea-temperature data are collected. A modern three-story structure built in 1999–2000 houses all living and office spaces, plus water and wastewater facilities. There is a small **museum** in the stores building.

Gentoos breed successfully among the buildings of the station, which was originally constructed amid the rookery. These may be some of the most-acclimated-to-people penguins in Antarctica – you must step over them to reach the bridge. They nest on the station doorstep, and are unperturbed by helicopter operations. Monitoring by station personnel shows that many of the nests are in the same location as when the station was built in 1948.

The separate **German Receiving Station** on the island was built by Germany in 1988–89. It acquires data from European Remote Sensing satellites via a white 9m parabolic dish next to the bay. It is occupied four to five months per year, with a staff of 12. At other times, O'Higgins personnel provide caretaking.

An **ice runway** on the nearby glacier serves DHC-6 Twin Otters flying from Chile's Frei Station.

Astrolabe Island

Discovered by Jules-Sébastien-César Dumont d'Urville's 1837–40 expedition and named for his chief ship, this infrequently visited, 5km-long island is home to several thousand pairs of chinstraps.

The **Dragon's Teeth**, a small group of huge rocks, lie off the northeast coast; cruising between them is known, naturally, as 'flossing.'

Hope Bay

On the northernmost tip of the Peninsula, Hope Bay is home to one of Antarctica's largest **Adélie rookeries** – housing 125,000 pairs, along with a few gentoos. The entrance to Hope Bay, reached via Antarctic Sound, is often filled with tabular icebergs.

Sights

Esperanza Station BASE

Argentina built this base in 1951, though a naval post was established here in 1930. Esperanza was significantly expanded in 1978

CLIMATE CHANGE & THE PENINSULA

The western peninsula is one of the most rapidly warming places on the planet (see p162). The average wintertime temperature in the Palmer area has risen more than 6°C over the past 50 years. This has resulted in a decrease in winter sea-ice extent and caused glaciers to recede, changing the local landscape dramatically. The site of 'Old Palmer' was revealed in 2004 to be a separate island, not part of Anvers Island. The former gap separating the islands had been covered by the Marr Ice Piedmont, but when it receded a distinct island emerged. The new 2km-long island was named Amsler Island in 2007 to honor two American marine biologists, husband and wife Chuck and Maggie Amsler.

Among the many changes as local weather warms, chinstrap and gentoo penguins are increasing in numbers, while the more cold-loving Adélies are decreasing (by 85% since 1974).

Palmer Station Long Term Ecological Research (http://pal.lternet.edu) studies the region's changes.

and women and children began to reside year-round as part of Argentina's efforts to establish 'sovereignty' over Antarctic territory. Silvia Morello de Palma, the wife of Esperanza's station leader Army Captain Jorge de Palma, was flown in from Argentina when she was seven months pregnant. She gave birth to Emilio Marcos de Palma, the first native-born Antarctican, on January 7, 1978. Over the next five years, four more boys and three girls were born here.

Today some 20 children live with their families year-round at the station, which can accommodate up to 100 people. Most personnel are military, and about 35% of Esperanza's population is made up of spouses and children. With a chapel, bank, post office, infirmary, gravel soccer field, graveyard, 1.5km of gravel roads, and 13 chalets housing families, it is more village than scientific station – there are only two modest laboratories.

Close to the jetty and behind ropes are the ruins of a **stone hut** where three members of Nils Otto Gustav Nordenskjöld's Swedish Antarctic expedition spent a desperate winter in 1903, surviving on seal meat. Nordenskjöld named the bay in honor of these three men. Esperanza staff rebuilt the hut in 1966–67; a small **museum** of relics is in one of the station's buildings. Other historic equipment is kept outside near the stone hut.

An **ice runway** on the nearby Buenos Aires Glacier serves DHC-6 Twin Otters flying from Marambio Station about 20 times a year.

Ruperto Elichiribehety Station BASE

On the hill about 500m from Esperanza is **Trinity House**, a hut remaining from Base D, built by the UK in 1944–45 and closed in 1963. It was transferred to Uruguay in 1997 and is now named Ruperto Elichiribehety Station after the captain of Uruguayan steam trawler *Instituto de Pesca No 1,* which Shackleton used in his second of three unsuccessful attempts to reach the Elephant Island castaways. The summer-only facility accommodates 12.

Crosses in the nearby **cemetery** commemorate two men lost in a 1948 fire.

Joinville & D'Urville Islands

Joinville is the largest of the three islands at the Peninsula's tip. It was discovered in 1838 by Dumont d'Urville, who named it for a French nobleman, François Ferdinand Phillipe Louis Marie d'Orléans, Prince de Joinville. At the foot of the reddish-colored 300m-high Madder Cliffs (named for the red vegetable dye called madder) at Joinville's western end are 45,000 nesting pairs of Adélies. Joinville's northerly neighbor, D'Urville Island, was charted by Nordenskjöld in 1902 and named for Dumont d'Urville.

Dundee Island

Dundee Island, 5km northwest of Paulet, was discovered in 1893 by British whaler Captain Thomas Robertson, who named it for his home port in Scotland.

At Dundee, millionaire American aviator Lincoln Ellsworth (p154) and copilot Herbert Hollick-Kenyon took off on the first trans-Antarctic flight on November 22, 1935, heading for the Bay of Whales on the Ross Ice Shelf, and sighting and naming the Eternity and Sentinel Ranges on the way. The 3700km flight was intended to last 14 hours. Poor weather stretched the trip to two weeks, during which they established four separate camps.

Their Northrop Gamma monoplane, *Polar Star,* ran out of fuel 25km from the Bay of Whales, and they trekked for eight days to reach it. Australia, meanwhile, urged on by Douglas Mawson and John King Davis, dispatched a ship which met the explorers at Byrd's former base, Little America II, where the two had been living comfortably for nearly a month.

Paulet Island

About 100,000 pairs of Adélies nest on this circular volcanic island, and there are also blue-eyed shags and southern giant petrels. Paulet is just 2km in diameter but its distinctive cone is 353m high.

It was discovered by James Clark Ross' expedition of 1839–43 and named for the Right Honorable Lord George Paulet, a captain in the Royal Navy.

On February 12, 1903, Nordenskjöld's ship *Antarctic,* which had been crushed by the Weddell Sea pack ice for weeks, finally sank 40km from Paulet. The 20 men sledged for 16 days to reach the island, then built a 10m by 7m hut on the northeast coast, where all but one survived the winter.

BASE LIFE

Those lucky few who get to spend an extended length of time on the Ice are usually scientists and their support staff. Depending on where you are based, you can have a wide range of experiences. Stations have varying facilities: from primitive huts to well-insulated modern bases with high-tech labs and cushy amenities like saunas and bars. Food at regularly restocked stations can even include fresh produce.

Small bases are often staffed only by scientists, while large ones, like McMurdo, have a bustling crew of support staff, from hairdressers to heavy-equipment operators. Staff usually stay for up to a year, while some scientists may come for just the few weeks of their observations. No matter the scenario, though, you'll usually discover a lively sense of camaraderie, and depending on the size of the station, an active social life. McMurdo in summer operates several bars (base members volunteer to bartend) and holds well-attended dances, crafts classes, and sporting events. But winter is a completely different story.

Wintering in Antarctica

Wintering on an Antarctic base can be a life-changing experience. Cut off from the rest of the world for up to eight months (especially on bases outside of the Peninsula) with no flights, boats, or people coming or going can produce interesting effects. Combine that with the lack of sunlight and the amazing physical conditions, and things are extraordinary indeed.

After a station closes the sun begins its continuous sunset circle around the horizon – a glorious sight: wherever you turn, soft colors fill the sky and reflect off the ice. And there is a giddy sense of potential and excitement. The 'noise' of the 'outside world' can no longer touch you, and the people around you will be your companions for the long haul. The first day you walk outside at lunch and see a night sky, filled with more stars than you've ever seen in your life (like a field of white dotted with black, as opposed to the other way round) is absolutely thrilling.

At first, people tuck in and develop friendships and hobbies, acquire new skills, and explore nearby terrain. But as the season advances, the entire group usually begins to experience the effects of long-term sensory deprivation. (At some bases even an emergency medical evacuation is impossible...) There is hardly any precipitation, no plant life, the same people day in and day out (often taking communal meals) and nary a fresh vegetable in

Today, the **ruins** (a pile of stones and some roofing timbers) are populated by Adélies. Above them is a 100m-long ovoid melt lake. Marked by a cross, the **grave** of Ole Christian Wennersgaard, a seaman from the expedition who died of heart disease in 1903, lies along the shore 300m east of the hut, but it can't be reached without disturbing the nesting penguins.

Brown Bluff

Brown Bluff is an ice-capped, flat-topped 745m extinct volcano on the Peninsula's northeastern tip. The original diameter of the volcano has been calculated at 12km to 15km; it's approximately one million years old. The bluff takes its name from a striking cliff of reddish-brown rock on its north face. Several hundred gentoos and 20,000 Adélies nest here; rock slides onto the 3km-long beach sometimes wipe out groups of them.

WEDDELL SEA

As you round the northern extent of the Antarctic Peninsula, the Weddell Sea side of the peninsula is surprisingly different from its western side (where mountains often soar straight from the sea). On the Weddell side, the mountains rise further back and are fronted by vast, snow-free gravel planes reminiscent of Australia's deserts or the American Southwest (although without vegetation!). James Weddell discovered the sea in February 1823 and named it 'King George IV Sea' for the British sovereign. German Antarctic historian Karl Fricker proposed the name Weddell Sea in 1900. All but the most powerful icebreakers are usually pre-

sight. Oddly, despite the complete isolation, finding privacy becomes a real concern...you are surrounded by people almost all the time. And the same ones. Escaping your fellow station members can be all but impossible in a place where safety requirements mean that you often cannot stray far from home without at least one companion and a radio.

This profound experience allows life to impact you deeply. The sight of astronomical phenomena, like the aurora australis, are magnificent, and any chance at a 'boondoggle' – a trip off-station for fun – is greedily snatched up. With the slow pace of work-life over these long months, there is time for hanging out, and friendships form in the unlikeliest places. People's behavior can alternate between fraternal and hermitlike.

While some stations maintain traditions each year (like a viewing of *The Thing* or *The Shining*, or creating a 'Midwinter Book' as did Robert Scott and Ernest Shackleton with poems, paintings and photographs by station members), many people find their attention spans shrink. All those good intentions of reading Shakespeare's complete works or learning a foreign language ablate like the Antarctic moisture.

In recent years, the advent of email and other internet-based communications have, of course, done a lot to ameliorate the isolation. And old-timers come prepared, knowing what to bring to help them through the lean times of midwinter. But still, the first sight of a warming glow on the horizon can make a grown man dance. There is something primal about seeing the sun after months without, and the heaviest hearts lift immediately. From that point on, even as folks can't wait to get off the Ice or see a new face when the station opens, there is a wistfulness, a value placed on the last few weeks or months alone, together. The sun rises continuously on the horizon...sometimes creating incredible tableaux: a full moon behind you, a golden sun in front, and the ice colored all shades from indigo to butter-yellow. It's also at this time, with its cold, cold air that light plays super tricks, refracting through clouds and creating glowing prisms of emanating color.

Then, quickly on the sun's heels comes the rambunctious return of outsiders for the start of summer, followed by winterovers' exit to a fecund land (like New Zealand in springtime). Many of the friendships formed on the Ice endure for life and the experiences remain searingly vibrant.

(See also Station Life, p130; Wintering at the South Pole, p133; and Vostok's Winterovers: Vostochniki, p124).

vented from traveling in the Weddell Sea. Others have tried – and paid the price.

Vega Island

Nordenskjöld named this island for the ship *Vega*, used by his uncle Baron AE Nordenskiöld, who made the first crossing of the Northeast Passage in the Arctic in 1878–79.

On October 12, 1903, Nordenskjöld encountered the three missing members of his party, who had wintered at Hope Bay, at a place they renamed Cape Well-Met on Vega's north coast.

The first discoveries of Antarctic dinosaurs were made here and on nearby James Ross Island (see p95).

In the summer, snowmelt waterfalls stream down the steep cliff face of Vega's north coast to the scree slopes below – a breathtaking sight.

Devil Island

This narrow island, just under 2km long, was named by Nordenskjöld for its low peaks at each end. It lies just off the north coast of Vega Island, over which it gives good views, and is home to 8000 Adélies.

James Ross Island

Until 1995 an ice shelf permanently connected this 65km-long island to the Antarctic mainland but then the ice shelf collapsed. Greenpeace vessel *Arctic Sunrise* made the first circumnavigation of the island through the never-before passable **Prince Gustav Channel** in February 1997.

Nordenskjöld named this island for its discoverer, Ross, who sighted it in 1843 but thought it was part of the Antarctic Peninsula because of the connecting ice shelf. The 'James' in the island's name distinguishes it from Ross Island in the Ross Sea, but all are named for the wide-ranging explorer.

Marine fossils and fossilized wood can be found on the island's west coast. Fern fossils and other plant-stem impressions can be found at nearby **Botany Bay**, named for the fossil flora collected there by British researchers in 1946 on the Trinity Peninsula.

Seymour Island

Remarkable for its lack of snow and ice cover, Seymour Island is 20km long and between 3km and 9km wide. It remains ice-free because it lies in the lee of high mountains on neighboring James Ross and Snow Hill Islands. Ross discovered Seymour in 1843 and named it after British Rear Admiral George Seymour. Carl Anton Larsen determined in 1892–93 that it was an island.

Seymour is the only place in Antarctica where rocks ranging in age from about 120 million to 40 million years are known. As such, the island contains one of the most important records of the circumstances surrounding the worldwide 'extinction event' 65 million years ago that wiped out 70% of the world's species, including the dinosaurs.

In December 1902 Nordenskjöld, wintering at nearby Snow Hill Island, made some striking fossil discoveries on Seymour Island. He found the bones of a giant penguin, bolstering earlier fossil finds made by Larsen in 1893. This find was confirmed in 1975 by Dr William J Zinsmeister. These penguins stood almost 2m tall and may have weighed as much as 135kg. Among the 800 fossils Zinsmeister found are starfish, crabs, crinoids, corals and nearly 200 new mollusks, among them a 4m-long ammonite. Another interesting find: a sea turtle that lived 40 to 45 million years ago and was the size and shape of a Volkswagen Beetle.

More than 20,000 Adélies breed at **Penguin Point** on the south coast.

Marambio Station, built in 1969–70, accommodates 22 people in winter and 150 in summer. Operated by Argentina's air force, it has a 1200m airstrip where C-130 Hercules can land most of the year. In summer Twin Otters and helicopters transport supplies and personnel to outlying stations and camps. North of Marambio are barren-looking landscapes rich in invertebrate fossils.

Snow Hill Island

This descriptively named 395m-high island was discovered by Ross in 1843; he called it simply 'Snow Hill' because he was uncertain of its connection with the mainland. Nils Otto Gustav Nordenskjöld (p146) set up a winter base in February 1902 and determined its insular nature.

Sights

Nordenskjöld Hut HISTORIC HUT

The Swedish South Polar Expedition's prefabricated black-walled hut, the Antarctic Peninsula's oldest remaining building, is a protected historic site. This dwelling, in which five Swedish and one Argentine scientist spent an unplanned two years (see the boxed text), sits on a fragile beach terrace easily eroded by footsteps.

The 6m x 8m hut contains three double bunks, a kitchen and a central living room. Two large metal signs in Spanish describe the site's history, as do leaflets in English inside the hut. Two angled wooden planks, original to the design, support the northeast wall. The Argentine government, whose Marambio Station on Seymour Island is 21km northeast, maintains the hut. No more than five people are allowed in the hut at a time, with no visits between 7pm and 8am.

Behind the hut is a snowless ravine, where fossils of clams and ammonites can be plucked from the gravel to show to one another (but not taken!).

Emperor Penguins ROOKERY

On the fast ice about 400m from the low ice cliffs on Snow Hill's south coast is Antarctica's northernmost (and most accessible) emperor penguin rookery. First sighted from a small aircraft in 1997, it was finally visited in 2004 by a Russian icebreaker carrying tourists. The colony is estimated to hold more than 4000 breeding pairs.

Ronne Ice Shelf

Together with its eastern neighbor, the Filchner Ice Shelf, the Ronne Ice Shelf forms the Weddell Sea's southern coast. It was discovered by American naval commander Finn Ronne, leader of the private Ronne Antarctic Research Expedition in 1947–48,

NORDENSKJÖLD: A TALE OF LUCK & SURVIVAL

Poor weather often confined Nordenskjöld's Snow Hill party to its small hut, but in December 1902 they were able to sledge to Seymour Island, where they found striking fossils. By then the men were getting distinctly anxious about their ship, *Antarctic*, which should have arrived.

Antarctic, trying unsuccessfully to reach the men at Snow Hill, stopped at Hope Bay to drop off three men, who would hike the 320km to Snow Hill. The ship then sailed around Joinville Island and south, becoming caught in the pack ice, whose relentless grip inexorably crushed it. *Antarctic* sank on February 12, 1903, 45km from tiny Paulet Island; the crew spent 16 days sledging provisions and small boats to land.

The three men left at Hope Bay, meanwhile, found their route to Snow Hill Island blocked by open water, so they settled down to wait for *Antarctic*'s return, according to a prearranged plan. The Swedish Antarctic Expedition was now split into three groups, two in very rough conditions, with none aware of the others' fates.

The Hope Bay trio eked out the winter in a primitive hut, living primarily on seal meat, then set out again for Snow Hill on September 29, 1903. By sheer luck, Nordenskjöld and Ole Jonassen were dog-sledging north from Snow Hill on a research journey at the time. The two groups met on October 12. Nordenskjöld was so struck by the Hope Bay men's remarkable appearance (they were completely soot-blackened, and wearing odd masks they had fashioned to prevent snow blindness) that he wondered if they were from a previously unknown race. They renamed the point of their rendezvous 'Cape Well Met.'

Antarctic's crew, meanwhile, wintered on Paulet Island. They built a stone hut and killed 1100 Adélies for food before the birds left for winter. On October 31, the ship's captain, and a veteran explorer, Carl Anton Larsen led a group of five others in an open boat to search for the trio at Hope Bay. Finding a note the three had left at their hut, Larsen decided he would have to follow by sea the route that the Hope Bay men were taking to Snow Hill Island.

Since the expedition had disappeared, three search parties had been dispatched. Argentina sent *Uruguay* in 1903, and on November 8 they found two Snow Hill Island men camped at Seymour Island. They all did the short trek to Snow Hill, arriving, by incredible coincidence, only a few hours ahead of Larsen and his group. After a joyful reunion, all that was left to do (on November 11) was pick up the remaining *Antarctic* crew back on Paulet Island. They had just finished collecting 6000 penguin eggs, their first surplus food supply.

and named for his wife, Edith, who accompanied the expedition at the last minute and spent a difficult year at Stonington Island.

Germany's summer-only **Filchner Station**, established on the Ronne Ice Shelf in 1982, accommodated 12 people. But the calving of an enormous iceberg that took the station with it was observed via satellite on October 13, 1998. Fortunately the station was unstaffed at the time.

Filchner Ice Shelf

When Wilhelm Filchner discovered this ice shelf in January 1912, he named it after his emperor, Kaiser Wilhelm, who decided that the honor should return to Filchner. **Berkner Island**, separating Filchner from the Ronne Ice Shelf, is often the start of trans-Antarctic ski trips.

Argentina's **Belgrano II Station**, built in 1979 on a 50m nunatak 120km from the coast, accommodates 18 people year-round. Its predecessor, General Belgrano Station, was built on the Filchner Ice Shelf as a meteorological center by the Argentine army in 1954–55 and became a scientific station in 1969–70. The original Belgrano Station was abandoned in January 1980, having been nearly destroyed by snow buildup; it subsequently floated out to sea when the ice shelf calved.

Halley Station

British scientists first measured the ozone depletion (see p162) of the Antarctic

PINK SNOW

Though popular imagination represents snow as white, it can often have a pink, red, orange, green, yellow or gray cast. The phenomena is caused by snow algae, single-celled organisms that live atop snowfields around the world, including many places in the Antarctic Peninsula.

Snow algae have been remarked upon for at least 2000 years, since Aristotle wrote about snow that was 'reddish in color' in his *History of Animals*. In alpine areas of North America, snow algae's color and fruity scent create what hikers call 'watermelon snow.' In Scandinavia, it's known as 'blood snow.' Although people avoid eating it for fear of diarrhea, one study of seven volunteer subjects found no incidence of illness.

Somehow 350 species of snow algae manage to survive in this harsh, acidic, freezing, nutrient-starved, ultraviolet-seared environment. Snow algae tends to live in either high altitudes or high latitudes and reproduces by remarkably hardy spores, which can withstand very cold winters and very dry summers. Researchers are investigating snow algae's pharmacological potential.

Near penguin rookeries, of course, there's another reason for the snow's pinkish-orangish tinge: guano!

stratosphere at Halley Station in 1982, but the values they recorded were so low that they doubted their instruments and collected three more years of data before publishing their results in 1985.

Named after astronomer Edmond Halley, this is the most southerly British Antarctic station. Halley was established in 1956 on the floating 200m-thick **Brunt Ice Shelf** and requires renewal every decade or so as it approaches the ice edge. To date, three stations (built in 1966, 1972 and 1982) have calved off, and one (1989) is buried and closed.

Halley V was built in 1994 and is currently about 10km from the ice edge. With a population of about 70 in summer and 16 in winter, it's built on stilts above the ice surface, which moves about 2m a day! The stilts are jacked up annually in a week-long process so the station can be maintained 2m above the snow surface.

Construction of **Halley VI** began in 2007 at a site near Halley V and is nearing completion (as of summer 2011–12). The new station is designed to avoid the fate of its predecessors by being built atop 'jackable' legs that rest on skis instead of foundations, allowing it to be towed (in separate units) by bulldozer to a different location – up to many kilometers away – when necessary.

The US$74 million station will consist of seven prefabricated, blue single-story units and a red central double-story unit – all connected by short corridors, making it resemble a space-age train with legs. The central unit will include a dining room, kitchen, gym and library. When Halley VI is operational, Halley V will be removed.

Ross Sea

Includes »

Best Historical Sights

- » Scott's *Terra Nova* Hut (p101)
- » Shackleton's *Nimrod* Hut (p103)
- » Borchgrevink's *Southern Cross* Hut (p91)
- » Erebus Chalice at Chapel of the Snows (p99)

Best Photo Ops

- » Dry Valleys (p94)
- » Mt Erebus (p105)
- » Erebus Glacier Tongue ice caves (p98)
- » Cape Royds ice edge (p103)

Why Go?

The explorers of the Heroic Age who sailed the Ross Sea region's ice-choked waters gained a crucial foothold here for exploration of the interior. Around the Ross Sea, Antarctica's richest historic heritage is on full display. Most stirring of all are Robert Scott's and Ernest Shackleton's wooden huts left behind on Ross Island. Carston Borchgrevink's huts at Cape Adare, the first structures ever built on the continent, remain today for those lucky enough to get ashore.

Antarctica's largest modern-day outpost, McMurdo Station, sits alongside diminutive, eco-friendly Scott Base, but the region's scree-covered shores and enormous Ross Ice Shelf are mostly the domain of Weddell seals and Adélie and emperor penguins. The steaming volcano, Mt Erebus, and the mysterious and otherworldly Dry Valleys are two additional prizes won by travelers persistent and fortunate enough to reach this relatively remote part of Antarctica.

Top Resources

- » *Icy Heritage: Historic Sites of the Ross Sea Region*, David Harrowfield. Details on 34 sites. Available from AHT.
- » *The Worst Journey in the World* (1922), Apsley Cherry-Garrard. Classic chronicle of horrible mid-winter trip to Cape Crozier.
- » *The Longest Winter: Scott's Other Heroes* (2011), Meredith Hooper. Gripping account of Scott's Northern Party's trials in winter snow cave.
- » *Water, Ice and Stone* (1995), Bill Green. Geochemist's account of working in the Dry Valleys.
- » **New Zealand Antarctic Heritage Trust** (www.nzaht.org) Extensive hut/expedition information.
- » **Antarctic Sun** (http://antarcticsun.usap.gov) The newspaper of the US Antarctic Program (USAP).

Ross Sea Highlights

1. Feel the chill of the ghosts of the polar party who never returned to **Scott's Terra Nova Hut** (p101)
2. Puzzle over fantastic natural wind-sculptures in the **Dry Valleys** (p94)
3. Peer into marine aquariums at McMurdo station's **Crary Lab** (p99) to see local sealife up close
4. Shuttle between Shackleton's *Nimrod* hut and the Adélie penguin rookery at **Cape Royds** (p103)
5. Watch steam drift lazily from the lava lake at **Mt Erebus** (p105)
6. Visit one of the world's **largest emperor penguin rookeries** (p92) at Cape Washington
7. Land atop the magnificent **Ross Ice Shelf** (p106) via helicopter and look for orcas along the ice edge
8. After exploring **Borchgrevink's huts**, photograph **Antarctica's largest Adélie penguin colony** (250,000 pairs!) at Cape Adare (p91)
9. Visit the museum at **Scott Base** (p101)
10. Fly over giant, crevassed **Beardmore Glacier** (p95) on your way to the Pole

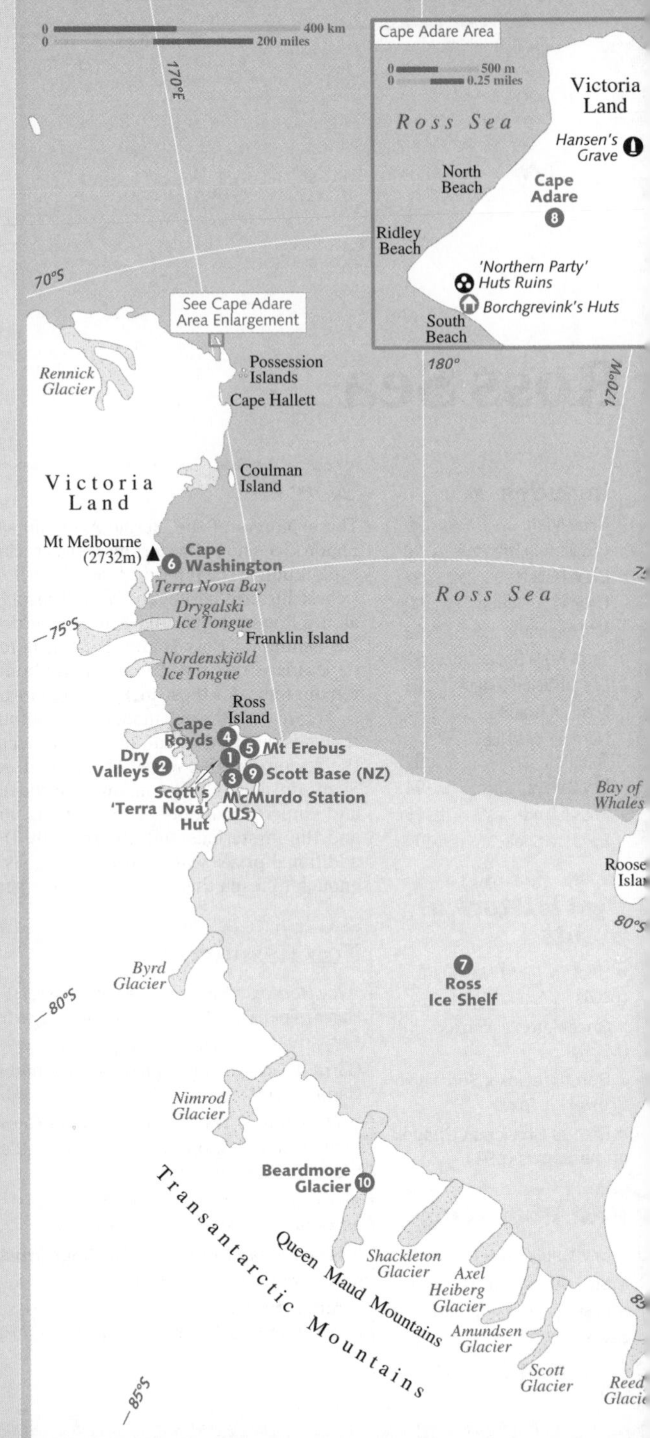

Cape Adare

This northernmost headland at the entrance to the Ross Sea was named for Britain's Viscount Adare, member of parliament for Glamorganshire, by his friend James Clark Ross, who discovered the cape in 1841. Sprawled across the shore is **Antarctica's largest Adélie rookery** – 250,000 nesting pairs – as well as two sets of historic huts. Unfortunately, Cape Adare is an extremely difficult landing, typically with heavy surf and strong offshore winds (200-500 people make it yearly). Because of the penguin rookery, helicopters cannot be used except very late in the season.

On January 24, 1895, a party including expedition leader Henrik Johan Bull went ashore at Cape Adare in what they claimed was the first landing ever made on the continent outside the Peninsula. Carsten Borchgrevink (assistant biologist on the expedition) said he was the first ashore but the captain of *Antarctic,* Leonard Kristensen, said the same. Alexander Tunzleman (a boy recruited in Stewart Island) may, however, have preceded both: he claimed to have got off first to steady the boat for the captain to disembark. However, it is unclear where sealers had landed earlier (see p142), and Dumont d'Urville landed off of Terre Adélie in 1840, so their claim may be spurious.

Borchgrevink's Huts HISTORIC HUT

In February 1899, four years after Kristensen's landing, Borchgrevink (see p146) was back at Cape Adare as the leader of the *Southern Cross* expedition. It took the men two weeks to erect two prefabricated structures, the remains of which can be seen today just back from **Ridley Beach**, which Borchgrevink named for his mother. These two huts are the oldest buildings in Antarctica.

Southern Cross departed to winter in New Zealand, and the 10 men left behind were the first to winter in Antarctica. Although they were the only humans on the continent, they had the company of 90 sledge dogs, the first ever used in Antarctica. The expedition also pioneered the use of kayaks for sea travel, and the Primus stove, a lightweight, portable pressure stove invented in Sweden six years before that was carried by nearly every expedition that followed. It is still in use today.

They experienced a death, an almost disastrous fire and a narrow escape from coal-fume asphyxiation. For the full tale, read Borchgrevink's *First on the Antarctic Continent.*

Borchgrevink's huts have outlasted the 'Northern Party' huts, though they are 12 years older, because they were built from sturdier materials: interlocking boards of Norwegian spruce.

The accommodations hut, which housed all 10 men, was 5.5m by 6.5m. Upon entering, an office/storeroom is to your left and a darkroom is to your right. Both were once lined with furs for insulation. Continuing inside, a stove stands to the left, a table and chairs are on the left past the stove, and five of the double-tiered coffinlike bunks line the remaining wall space. Borchgrevink's bunk was in the back left corner, on the top. The hut had papier-mâché insulation and a single double-paned window. Be sure to look out for the fine pencil drawing of a young woman on the ceiling above one of the bunks.

The stores hut, to the west, is now roofless. It contains boxes of ammunition that Borchgrevink brought in case the expedition encountered large predators such as polar bears. (He was the first to winter on the continent, remember. He didn't know what might be out there.) Coal briquettes and stores' barrels litter the ground outside this hut.

Today the huts are completely surrounded by an Adélie penguin colony, and care must be taken to avoid disturbing the animals. The Antarctic Heritage Trust (AHT) conserves the huts, and only four people (including the AHT representative, who will accompany your cruise or come over from Scott Base) are permitted inside the Cape Adare huts at one time. Only 40 people are allowed in the area of the huts at one time.

Hansen's Grave GRAVE

The *Southern Cross* expedition's zoologist, Norwegian Nicolai Hansen, died on October 14, 1899, probably of an intestinal disorder: the first human death on the continent. Tragically, Hansen married shortly before leaving for Antarctica and had a daughter, Johanne, whom he never saw.

His deathbed wish was to be buried on the ridge above Ridley Beach, so the expeditioners built a coffin and dynamited a grave for the first-known human burial on the continent. Dragging Hansen's heavy coffin up the steep incline was a major effort.

When *Southern Cross* returned, a graveside memorial was held and an iron cross and brass plaque were attached to a boulder on the site. Later, when Victor Campbell's men used the ridge as a lookout for *Terra Nova,* one of them spelled out Hansen's name with white quartz pebbles. Visitors to the site in 1982 restored the inscriptions.

Unfortunately, the safest route up the 350m ridge is blocked by an Adélie penguin colony, so the grave site is effectively off limits unless your ship has a helicopter.

'Northern Party' Huts HISTORIC HUT

Almost nothing remains of the hut built by Victor Campbell, a member of Scott's *Terra Nova* expedition of 1911–14 (see p151). What little does remain lies east of Borchgrevink's huts. The prefabricated building, originally standing 6.4m by 6.1m, once housed six men.

Possession Islands

Ross discovered this group's two main islands, Foyn and Possession, on January 10, 1841, after pushing *Erebus* and *Terror* through the Ross Sea pack ice to open water. He was quite surprised to sight land because he had hoped to sail west from the Ross Sea to the area where the South Magnetic Pole was calculated to lie. At that time, the pole was, in fact, well inland.

Despite his disappointment, Ross landed a boat two days later on Possession Island and claimed it for Queen Victoria. An engraving of the event shows penguins lined up even on the highest ridge of the island. Indeed, the thousands of Adélies that nest on both islands still climb to the top of Possession's small hill.

In 1895 Borchgrevink found a lichen here, the first plant discovered in Antarctica.

A century later, in February 1995, a small modern wreck of unknown origin was discovered on the western side of Possession Island: a mystery.

Cape Hallett

Cape Hallett was discovered by Ross in 1841 and named for Thomas Hallett, *Erebus*' purser. When a scientific station jointly run by the US and New Zealand was built in January 1957 as part of the International Geophysical Year, 8000 Adélie penguins were moved to another part of the cape to make way for the base. The station accommodated 11 Americans and three New Zealanders for the winter.

The base was operated year-round until 1964, when it became a summer-only facility after fire destroyed the main science building, and was then closed in 1973. Since the late 1970s the abandoned buildings have gradually been removed to allow the Adélies to return. A stained, white, domed refuge building is all that remains.

Cape Hallett can usually only be visited by Zodiac; helicopter landings are not permitted while penguins occupy their rookery.

Cape Washington

More than 20,000 breeding pairs of emperors live on the sea ice here in one of the two largest **emperor penguin rookeries** in Antarctica. The cape was discovered in 1841 by Ross, who named it for Captain Washington of the Royal Navy, secretary of the Royal Geographical Society from 1836–40.

Mt Melbourne

This 2732m cone is one of the very few volcanoes on the Antarctic continent itself. Almost all the others – including Mt Erebus, Mt Siple and Deception Island – are on off-lying islands. Like the Australian city of the same name, this active volcano commemorates Lord Melbourne, British prime minister in the 1830s and '40s. Like so many other features in the Ross Sea region, Ross discovered it in 1841.

Terra Nova Bay

This 65km-long bay was discovered by Scott's *Discovery* expedition and named after the relief ship *Terra Nova* (later used in Scott's ill-fated attempt at the Pole). Italy operates **Mario Zucchelli Station**, which accommodates 90 people during summer. The station, a collection of blue buildings with orange trim, was established in 1986–87 and was known as Baia Terra Nova until 2004, when it was renamed to honor the longtime director of the Italian Antarctic program.

The base's first building is known as the 'Pinguinattollo,' an imaginative conjunction of *pinguino* (penguin) and *scoiattolo* (squirrel). The interior walls are entirely covered with inscriptions, drawings and

THE SOUTHERN LIGHTS *FELICITY ASTON*

It starts with the faintest of smudges in the night sky – so indistinct that, at first, it could almost be a stray wisp of cloud. But as you watch, the smudge deepens, becomes more solid and blushes green. Suddenly a clear arc of color pierces the dark between the stars. Diffuse rays fall from space in ephemeral curtains that flicker and dance as if being blown by a gentle celestial breeze and the sky erupts into one huge abstract canvas of swirling green and rippling gold, of shimmering red and exploding violet. The light floats across the heavens, brightening to ferocity one minute, then fading away to blackness. Despite the furious riot of color and light above, the only noise you hear is the rush of your breath and the rustle of your clothing. The cold pinches your cheeks and claims your fingers, but still you stand, transfixed by a spectacle as mesmerizing as staring at the embers of an open fire. The display can last for hours, and although the cold will inevitably force a retreat, it is difficult to tear yourself away.

Named after the Roman goddess of the dawn, aurora can occur both in the north (aurora borealis) and in the south (aurora australis). Since ancient times, Arctic peoples have explained the mysterious northern lights in a variety of ways: from torches carried by souls on their way to the spirit world, to the reflection of swarms of herring in the polar seas. Certain tribes in North America believed that a handclap would frighten auroras away, while whistling would bring them closer.

Scientists travel to the Antarctic specifically to study auroras – and the cause of the phenomenon is in many ways as astonishing as the display itself. Millions of miles away, the sun produces electrically charged particles that are blown outwards across the solar system in a continuous 'solar wind' (see p200).

As the solar wind passes Earth, the charged particles are attracted by the Earth's magnetic field and are drawn toward its two geomagnetic poles. As the particles pass through the atmosphere, they interact with atoms, molecules and ions in the upper atmosphere, causing them to release energy as light. Green light is a result of the particles colliding with oxygen molecules, while red and purple light is caused by collisions with nitrogen.

The northern and southern lights occur simultaneously and are almost identical mirror images of each other, but the aurora australis holds a particular mystique because so few people have been lucky enough to observe it. The majority of people visit Antarctica in austral summer when daylight hides auroral activity. It is only dark enough to see the aurora australis from April to October. Even then, a full moon or cloudy skies will reduce visibility.

The best locations for watching the aurora australis are in some of the most inaccessible parts of Antarctica. Most aurora australis occur in a thick ring (known as the Auroral Zone) around the south geomagnetic pole (near Vostok station). The exact position of the Auroral Zone moves from day to day but usually covers the coast of Queen Maud Land, crosses Marie Byrd Land in West Antarctica, then spreads over the Southern Ocean as far as Macquarie Island. Only very rarely does it venture over the Peninsula, making this an unlikely place to spot the southern lights.

For more on auroras, visit University of Alaska Fairbanks Geophysical Institute (www.gedds.alaska.edu).

Felicity Aston (www.felicityaston.co.uk) spent three years at Rothera station as a British Antarctic Survey meteorologist; in 2012 she became the first woman to ski across the continent alone.

the signatures of dozens of visitors and staff over the years. The new Pinguinattollo is a large wooden chalet, with a granite fireplace fueled (somewhat surprisingly, given the extreme fire danger here) by wood scraps.

A sea-ice runway, opened in 1990, is used by about 10 Hercules flights per season.

Drygalski Ice Tongue

Discovered by Scott in 1902 and named for the German explorer (see p148) with whom Scott coordinated operations before his first expedition, this ice tongue is the seaward extension of the David Glacier. It ranges from 14km to 24km wide and is nearly 50km long.

Franklin Island

Ross landed on this 11km-long island on January 27, 1841, claiming the Victoria Land coast for Queen Victoria. He named the island itself for John Franklin, governor of Van Diemen's Land (Tasmania) and an explorer himself, who had shown the expedition considerable hospitality when it called in at Hobart in 1840 on the way south.

Affixed to only this tiny island in the Antarctic, Franklin's name is writ much larger in the history of the Arctic. In 1845 he took *Erebus* and *Terror,* the very same vessels Ross used to explore here, on a doomed expedition to chart more of the Northwest Passage. Rescuers searching for his missing ships also made major discoveries that they named after him.

Franklin Island is home to a large **Adélie rookery**.

Nordenskjöld Ice Tongue

Discovered by Scott's National Antarctic Expedition of 1901–04, this ice tongue is named for Swedish explorer Nils Otto Gustav Nordenskjöld (see p146). It is the seaward extension of the **Mawson Glacier**.

Dry Valleys

The Antarctic Dry Valleys are some of the most unusual places on Earth. Huge, desolate and magnificent spaces, they resemble terrain from other planets and hold some of the world's most extraordinary living forms in the rarest of conditions.

Part of the valleys' otherworldly appearance is due to their bizarre, wind-sculpted rocks. These ventifacts are highly polished on their windward surfaces, and some have been wind-carved into pocked boulders or thin, delicate wafers. Others fit into your hand so well that they resemble smoothly ground primitive tools.

The valleys cover 3000 sq km, and as with other Antarctic landscapes, it can be difficult to comprehend their scale. What appears to be a nearby mountainside or glacier could actually lie hours away.

The Dry Valleys (some Americans call them the 'McMurdo Dry Valleys') were formed when the land uplifted at a faster rate than glaciers could cut down through it. Eventually, high necks at the head of each valley stopped the glaciers altogether.

Valley air is so moistureless that there is no snow or ice. Such ice-free areas in Antarctica are called 'oases,' and there are about 20 others (including the Bunger, Larsemann and Vestfold Hills of East Antarctica). For an oasis to form there must be a retreating or thinning ice sheet, and a large area of exposed rock from which snow ablates due to solar radiation absorbed by the rock. Despite the oft-quoted statement that no rain has fallen there for at least two million years, it has indeed rained in the Dry Valleys (including in 1959, 1968, 1970 and 1974).

Scientists believe the Dry Valleys are the nearest equivalent on Earth to the terrain of Mars. NASA performed extensive research here from 1974 to 1976 before sending the Viking Lander spacecraft to Mars.

From north to south, the three main Ross Sea Dry Valleys are **Victoria**, **Wright** and **Taylor**. There are also several smaller valleys. Tourists generally fly by helicopter into Taylor Valley, the most accessible from the Ross Sea. Large sections of the others are protected under the Antarctic Treaty, and access is restricted or forbidden, even to scientists.

History

Robert Scott accidentally discovered the first of the Dry Valleys in December 1903 and named it for geologist Griffith Taylor. Scott and two others had sledged up the Ferrar Glacier to the East Antarctic Ice Sheet. On their return, they became lost in thick cloud and descended the wrong valley. Because they were equipped for sledging, not hiking, they were forced to turn back after a brief exploration. In *The Voyage of the Discovery,* Scott wrote:

> I cannot but think that this valley is a very wonderful place. We have seen today all the indications of colossal ice action and considerable water action, and yet neither of these agents is now at work...

Wildlife

Although the valleys appear lifeless, they harbor some of the most remarkable organisms on Earth. In 1976 American biologists discovered algae, bacteria and fungi growing *inside* Dry Valley rocks. This 'endolithic' vegetation grows in the air spaces in porous

ANTARCTICA DURING THE 'AGE OF REPTILES'

DR WILLIAM R HAMMER

The first Antarctic terrestrial vertebrate fossil was discovered in 1967. Since the finding of that single jaw fragment in Early Triassic age sediments (245 million years old) near the Beardmore Glacier, four different Mesozoic finds have been collected.

The Early Triassic assemblage is dominated by synapsids, an extinct group of animals that link primitive reptiles to mammals. Perhaps the best-known member is *Lystrosaurus*, a small herbivore also found on most of the other southern continents and in China and Russia.

In 1985 a vertebrate community of Middle Triassic age (235 to 240 million years old) was found near the first Early Triassic *Lystrosaurus* site in the central Transantarctic Mountains. This find is dominated by larger synapsids than those from the Early Triassic and includes the wolf-sized carnivore *Cynognathus* and a large kannemeyerid synapsid related to *Lystrosaurus*. Two large capitosaurids, *Paratosuchus* and *Kryostega collinsoni*, with skulls nearly a meter long, also lived during the Middle Triassic. *Kryostega collinsoni* is a new genus and species found only in Antarctica.

The first discoveries of Antarctic dinosaurs were made during the late 1980s in Late Cretaceous (65 to 70 million years old) deposits on James Ross and Vega islands. These remains included partial skeletons of a nodosaurid ankylosaur (armored dinosaur) and a hypsilophodontid (a small herbivorous ornithopod dinosaur). A few small limb pieces have also been referred to the Theropoda (carnivorous dinosaurs).

In 1998 a single tooth from a hadrosaur (duck-billed dinosaur) was discovered on James Ross Island, and in 2003 a fragmentary specimen of a small (1.8m long) dromeosaurid theropod was found on Vega Island.

In addition to the terrestrial animals, large extinct marine plesiosaurs have been found on islands near the Antarctic Peninsula. These long-necked animals with paddle-shaped fins (made famous as the Loch Ness Monster) are not dinosaurs but lived concurrently. One of the more spectacular plesiosaur specimens was discovered on Vega Island in 2005. It is a nearly complete, well-preserved juvenile plesiosaur that was apparently killed by a volcanic eruption.

Uniquely Antarctic Dinosaurs

A fourth terrestrial vertebrate community was found in 1990, again near the Beardmore Glacier. This Early Jurassic (190 to 200 million years old) find includes the nearly 7m-long bipedal carnivorous dinosaur, *Cryolophosaurus* ('frozen-crested reptile'). Represented by the most complete dinosaur skeleton found in Antarctica, *Cryolophosaurus* is the first dinosaur known to be unique to the continent (the Cretaceous dinosaurs are too incomplete to determine whether or not they represent new genera). The Latin 'cryo' was included in the name because although Antarctica wasn't frozen when the dinosaur lived, we nearly froze to death while collecting it.

Ribs of a prosauropod were in the mouth of the cryolophosaur when it died, leading to the assumption that the carnivore may have choked to death on its last meal. Prosauropods were smaller (7.5m long) predecessors to the well-known large sauropods *(Apatosaurus, Brachiosaurus)* of the later Jurassic. A new taxon was named (*Glacialisaurus hammeri),* the second dinosaur known to be unique to Antarctica.

After the *Cryolophosaurus* died along an Antarctic riverbank 200 million years ago, smaller carnivorous theropods scavenged the skeleton. Gnaw marks were found on some of the bones, and small broken theropod teeth were collected nearby. Other members of Jurassic fauna are represented by single elements, including a tooth from a rodentlike synapsid and the upper arm of a small pterosaur (flying reptile).

These finds suggest that Antarctic climates were relatively mild during the Mesozoic, and that connections existed between Antarctica and the other southern continents.

Dr William R Hammer, Chair of the Geology Department, Augustana College, for whom Glacialisaurus hammeri was named, and who discovered Cryolophosaurus with William Hickerson.

rocks. Light, carbon dioxide and moisture penetrate the rock, and the rock protects the organisms against excessive drying and harmful radiation. Some of these plants are believed to be 200,000 years old.

There is abundant microfauna in the soils, primarily bacteria, yeasts, protozoa and nematodes. Picture an ecosystem teeming with as much life as Africa's Serengeti Plain – with its vast migrating herds – all of it invisible to the naked eye.

For example, two or three nematode species occupy the top of a very simple food chain. (Nematodes are millimeter-long, cylindrical worms and the most numerous creatures on Earth: four out of five animals is a nematode.) Nematodes need water to move, feed and reproduce, but one type, *Scottnema,* survives the winter in dry saline soils by coiling up into a state of reversible dormancy called anhydrobiosis (literally 'life without water'). Individuals can remain dormant for years (60!), and then become active within minutes of getting wet.

Mummified seals and the occasional carcass of a wayward Adélie penguin have been found in the Valleys (as far as 50km from the sea). These remains freeze-dry in the extreme aridity, and then erode in the scouring wind, just like the ventifacts.

Lakes & Ponds

A collection of unusual ponds and lakes within the Dry Valleys also harbors life (at least, some of them do). In Taylor Valley, **Lake Hoare** is permanently covered by 5.5m-thick ice but dense mats of blue-green algae carpet its bottom. **Lake Bonney** is freshwater at its surface, and at its bottom is 12 times more saline than the sea. Saltwater **Lake Fryxell**, 5km long, is the third main lake in Taylor Valley. **Lake Chad**, a smaller Taylor Valley lake named for the African lake of same name, is so filled with magnesium that it acted as a laxative for the explorers who discovered and drank from it.

Wright Valley's **Lake Vanda**, named for a sled dog, is 60m deep and 25°C at its bottom. It has been intensively investigated for many years for its two ecosystems: the top 45cm (beneath 4m-thick ice) is nutrient-poor freshwater; below that is saline water four times as salty as seawater. The two layers support quite different microbial communities.

Antarctica's longest river, the 30km meltwater stream called the **Onyx River**, flows into Lake Vanda from the glacier at the end of the valley; it's one of very few rivers in the world to flow inland from the coast.

Don Juan Pond, also in Wright Valley, is only 10cm deep and just 100m wide by 300m long. It is a near-saturation solution of calcium chloride, and evaporates completely at times. It takes its name not, alas, from the legendary lover, but from two US Navy aviators named Don and John who helped the first field party studying the pond. White crusts of calcium salt crystals and of a rare mineral called antarcticite (calcium chloride hexahydrate) precipitate on Don Juan Pond's shores. Up to 19 times saltier than seawater, this is the most saline water body on Earth, remaining unfrozen even at -55°C.

Ross Island

Since both New Zealand and the US have their principal Antarctic stations on Ross Island, in summer it becomes a hub of activity, with science groups passing through on their way to field camps all over this side of the continent, and to the South Pole. It's also the location of three famous historic huts, Mt Erebus and several penguin rookeries.

MCMURDO STATION

McMurdo Station, Antarctica's largest encampment, has the unruly feel of a bustling frontier town, but with helicopters and icescapes. Backed by the looming active volcano, Mt Erebus, the sprawling US station is home to more than 1100 people during the summer and hosts a multinational assortment of many more researchers in transit to field camps and the Pole. More than 100 buildings blanket the nearly 4 sq km between Hut Point and Observation Hill. Water, sewer, telephone and power lines all run aboveground in a crisscrossing array. The industrial-looking station can be an overwhelming sight after Antarctica's clean white icebergs and lack of human presence. Approximately 250 people winterover at McMurdo to maintain the sprawling station and prepare it for the next busy summer season when the base refills to capacity.

Established in 1956, McMurdo takes its name from **McMurdo Sound**, which Ross named in 1841 after Lieutenant Archibald McMurdo of the ship *Terror*. The settlement was large right from the start: 93 men wintered the first year.

Called Mac Town (or just 'Town') by residents, the station *does* have the feel of

Ross Island

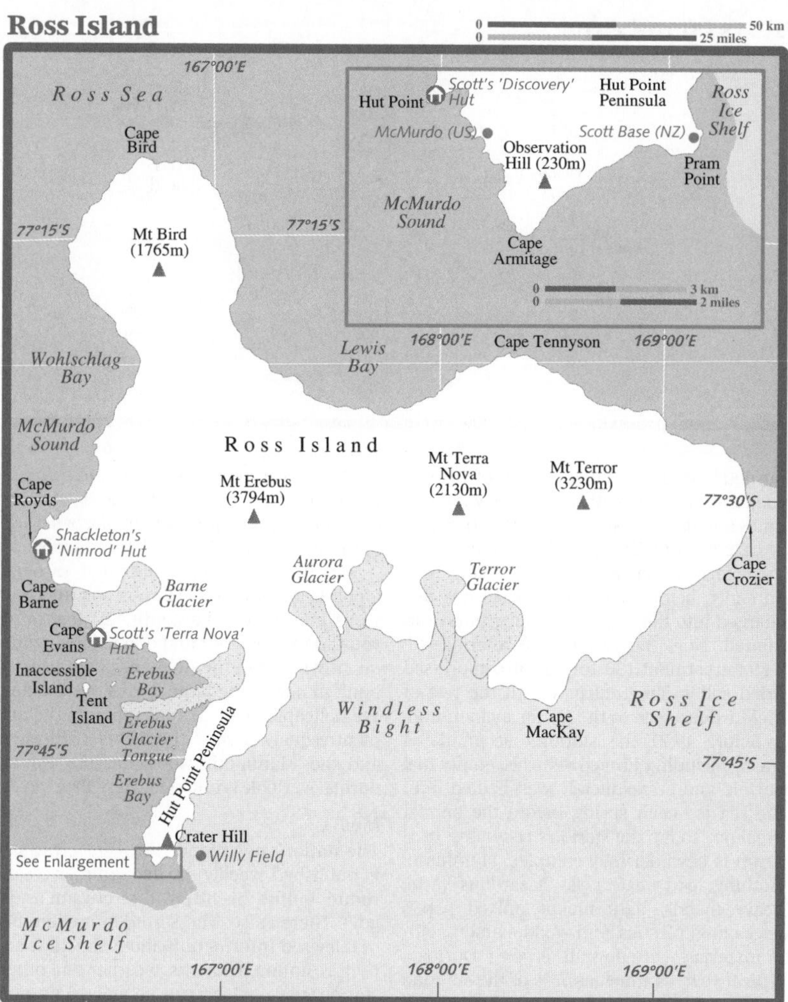

a bustling metropolis. Some 250 vehicles, including a fleet of 100 snowmobiles, help people get around, but not very quickly: the station speed limit is 30km/h. Although New Zealand time is used in the Scott Base/McMurdo Station area, driving is American-style, on the right.

Facilities

McMurdo has its own hospital, church, post office (not for tourist use), library, 42-member fire department with two stations, barbershop, video store and ATMs (not for tourist use). There's the **Coffeehouse** (formerly the Navy Officer's Club) and two clubs: the smokers' bar, **Southern Exposure**, and the nonsmoking **Gallagher's** (commemorating a McMurdo resident and former bartender who died in 1997). There is a diving recompression chamber, a 220m-long ice pier, and a fuel-tank farm with a total capacity of 30 million liters.

USAP has worked hard to minimize McMurdo's impact on the environment. A seawater reverse-osmosis **desalination plant** meets peak station demand of some 300,000 liters per day. Waste heat recovered from the desalination system saves about 1.6 million liters of fuel that would otherwise be

Ross Island Area

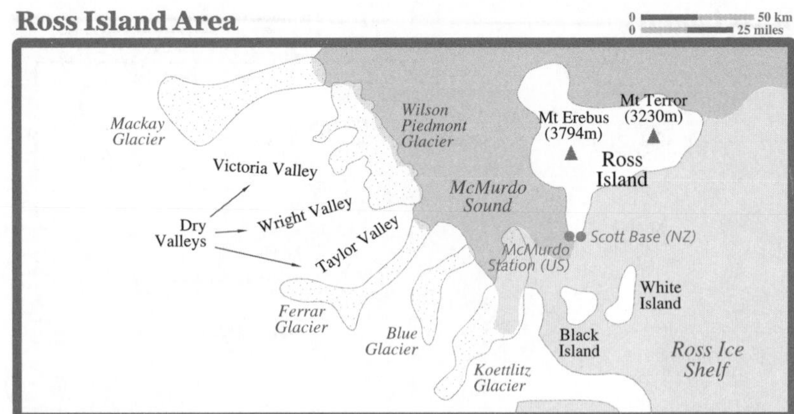

burned to heat buildings. Also, as of 2010, in cooperation with Scott Base, three wind turbines augment the station's electricity needs.

In 2003 the US opened a sewage-treatment facility that handles 35 million liters annually; before that, raw sewage was discharged into the sea after being ground and diluted. Now the residue left after wastewater treatment (30 tonnes of compressed dried solids) are returned with the rest of McMurdo's waste to the US for incineration.

Before 1990 the station's accumulated trash (including junked vehicles, empty fuel barrels and scrap metal) was hauled onto the sea ice each spring before the annual breakup. Today the station's **recycling program** is bewilderingly complex: aluminum, clothing, food waste, glass, hazardous waste, heavy metals, light metals, mixed paper, packaging, plastics, and wood – among other materials – are now all recycled. During a typical year, as much as 75% of the station's solid waste (over 2000 tonnes annually) is recycled, three times the rate achieved by the average US city.

A less successful endeavor was the continent's only large **nuclear-power plant**: a 1.8-megawatt experimental reactor, known colloquially as 'Nukey Poo.' It was deployed on Observation Hill in December 1961 and went online in March 1962. Unfortunately, the reactor experienced numerous problems and, in 1972, faced with a large repair bill, the US shut it down. Eventually, some 10,000 tonnes of radioactively contaminated soil and rock were removed from the site.

McMurdo's hydroponic **greenhouse** uses hand pollinating, since there are no insects (and none can be imported, due to environmental restrictions), and thousands of watts of artificial light to produce 1600kg of lettuce, herbs, tomatoes and cucumbers annually.

McMurdo housing is allocated through a points system, in which position and previous months on the continent determine your berth. Scientists and others moving frequently between the field and town usually bunk in one of the large dorms overlooking the helicopter pad. Two of these dorms are picturesquely named the 'Hotel California' and the 'Mammoth Mountain Inn.' Newer dorms overlook Winter Quarters Bay.

Media

The station's newspaper, the *Antarctic Sun,* is published weekly during summer (year-round online at http://antarcticsun.usap.gov). There's also 'The Scroll,' four channels of televised information about the day's activities, announcements, weather and other station news, which can be viewed on one of the station's several hundred TVs. Other media include Radio McMurdo (104.5 on your FM dial), National Public Radio (93.9), two TV broadcast channels, 11 and 13, plus two channels of movies (chosen on-station), 24 hours a day. Direct-dial, in-room phone service is available from many rooms in McMurdo.

Recreation

In summer, recreation opportunities for station personnel abound: aerobics, basketball, bingo, bowling, chili cook-offs, country dancing, cross-country skiing, darts, hiking, soccer, softball, table tennis, tae kwon do, volleyball, weight-lifting and yoga. Residents can even borrow bicycles to cruise around town. For golfers, there is the McMurdo Open tournament. For runners, events include an annual **marathon** (full- and half-marathon) for which many spend months training. Some ski instead of run.

Sunday science lectures, computer classes, cardiopulmonary resuscitation (CPR) training, Alcoholics Anonymous meetings, town choir rehearsals, the **Ross Island Drama Festival**, the **Ross Island Art Show**, the **Icestock Music Festival** with local talent, meetings of the **McMurdo Historical Society** and even occasional tours of Scott's *Discovery* hut are also offered.

Outings go to beautiful **ice caves** at the **Erebus Glacier Tongue**, made accessible by winter sea ice. These caves are formed during summer by wave action eroding the ice.

Residents may win a special lottery to go on an extraordinary day trip: the South Pole station. This unique reward (on a space-available flight) is known locally as a 'sleigh ride.'

Sights

Tourists will catch only glimpses of the station's busy life while visiting the places listed below, and through a **guided walking tour** of **Mac Weather** (the weather-observations center) and **Mac Ops** (the communications center), which are in the same building, and a hospitality stop at the Coffeehouse.

Chapel of the Snows — CHURCH

The white Chapel of the Snows, a 64-seat house of worship with a pretty, penguin-motif stained-glass window and an organ, is the third chapel raised at McMurdo (the first two were destroyed by fire). Christmas Eve is celebrated with an unusual midnight service with sunlight streaming in the window behind the altar. The **Erebus Chalice**, which first traveled to Antarctica with Ross in 1841, may be the oldest Antarctic relic on the continent. This beautiful silver and gilt chalice used during Communion spends the winter months at Christchurch Cathedral in New Zealand, and each summer is loaned to the McMurdo chapel.

Crary Science & Engineering Center — LABORATORY

Symbolically numbered 'Building 1,' the Crary Science & Engineering Center (CSEC), usually just called the 'Crary Lab,' is named for Albert P Crary, a geophysicist and glaciologist who was the first person to visit both the North and South Poles. The 4320 sq m building, completed in 1991, houses work space for biological studies, earth science and atmospheric science. The equipment is state of the art, with facilities as good as those found at major research universities. It's a bit disconcerting to go straight from a penguin rookery to a place where scientists have digital keycards to their offices, but then again, this is the Big City! The Crary Lab also has a darkroom, freezers for processing ice cores, an electronics workshop, a seismic observatory that monitors Mt Erebus, and a library. There are three types of **meteorites** on display in the Crary Lab, while three large **aquariums** offer the rare chance to see Antarctic marine life without having to scuba dive beneath the sea ice. Depending on what biologists have collected recently, you might get to look at Antarctic krill, starfish, isopods, sea spiders or even some of the big Antarctic cod, with their unique 'antifreeze' blood (see p179).

Building 155 — COMMUNITY CENTER

Building 155 is McMurdo's indoor Main St, and the long central corridor is known as Hwy 1. Along it are the dining facility (still known as the Galley from navy days), personnel offices, the recreation department, barbershop, housing offices, personnel berthing, and the main public computer lab. Bulletin boards advertise all kinds of activities.

Station Store

The Station Store, along Hwy 1, sells postcards, T-shirts and other souvenirs, and accepts credit cards and US dollars. Liquor

BOWL MCMURDO

The drab Quonset hut known as **Building 63** is McMurdo's oldest surviving building. It houses the weight room, bouldering cave, crafts rooms, ceramics studio – and, in the basement, McMurdo's famous bowling alley. Two lanes with rare antique Brunswick manual pinsetters, one of the few such alleys left, are staffed by volunteers. Perhaps because the lanes are distinctly warped, strikes are sometimes rewarded with the bashing of a large cymbal. During the alley's dedication ceremony on July 19, 1961, stuffed penguins were set up as pins.

and cigarette prices are reasonable, at least compared to those aboard your ship, but clerks won't sell them to you, because it would deplete station stock. USAP doesn't carry tourist mail, so you can't send postcards from McMurdo. Also, tourists are not allowed to use the station's two ATMs or payphones.

Derelict Junction SHUTTLE STOP

Just west of Building 155 is Derelict Junction (widely known as DJ), a wooden bus stop where summer-only 24-hour shuttles depart to the airfields and Scott Base.

Airfields RUNWAYS

Three different airfields, each operating at different times of the year, serve McMurdo. An **ice runway** on the McMurdo Sound sea ice close to the station is used by wheeled aircraft in October, November and early December. There's one local hazard: penguins and seals occasionally wander across the runway, requiring an official, trained 'escort' off the field.

Later in December, as summer temperatures weaken the sea ice, flight operations shift to **Williams Field**, a 3000m skiway on the Ross Ice Shelf. Also known as Willy Field or just 'Willy,' it was named for Richard T Williams, who died during Operation Deep Freeze I (1955–56) when his 30-tonne tractor broke through sea ice off Cape Royds. Willy Field resembles a small Antarctic station, with a collection of buildings all mounted on sleds for rapid deployment. 'Willy' is 16km from the station so there's an airport shuttle: a huge TerraBus vehicle (nicknamed 'Ivan').

A third airfield, the **Pegasus ice runway** (named for *Pegasus,* a US Navy C-121 Super Constellation that crashed nearby during the 1970–71 season; everyone aboard survived the crash, and the wrecked plane is still there today), is about 25km (45 minutes' drive) from McMurdo. Since 2002 a compacted-snow runway at the Pegasus site allows large wheeled aircraft to land at McMurdo. About 100 flights from Christchurch arrive each year: C-130 Hercules, C-5 Galaxies, C-141 Starlifters, C-17 Globemasters and LC-130 ski-equipped Hercules. While most arrive between early October and late February, some land in late August during the end of winter, in an operation called 'Winfly,' or Winter Fly-In, when the first wave of summer staff arrive to help reopen the station.

HUT POINT

Scott's Discovery Hut HISTORIC HUT

Scott's National Antarctic Expedition (see p147) built this hut in February 1902 on aptly named Hut Point. The prefabricated building, purchased in Australia, is of a type still found in rural Australia, with a wide overhanging veranda on three sides. It was originally painted a terracotta color, but wind has scoured it bare. Despite the building's expense and the effort required to erect it, Scott's men never used it for accommodations because it was difficult to heat efficiently. Instead, it was used for storage, repair work and as an entertainment center (called 'The Royal Terror Theatre').

In fact, the *Discovery* Hut was used more heavily by several later expeditions. Shackleton's *Nimrod* expedition, based at Cape Royds, found it a convenient en route shelter during sledge trips to and from the Ross Ice Shelf in 1908, as did Scott's *Terra Nova* expedition in 1911.

The Ross Sea party of Shackleton's ill-fated *Endurance* expedition benefited most: they holed up here from time to time in 1915 and 1916. The men, unaware of vast quantities of stores buried in the ice that had accumulated in the hut, nearly starved – despite the hidden bounty lying literally underfoot. They did find a bit of food, cigars, crème de menthe, sleeping bags and a pair of long underwear. The interior of the hut is soot-blackened and smells from the smoky blubber stove they used trying to stay warm.

Because it is the hut closest to McMurdo Station and has received the most visitors (and light fingers) over the years, the relatively barren *Discovery* hut is the least interesting of the three Ross Island historic sites. The AHT estimates that 1000 people visit the hut each year and there are few remaining artifacts. The hut sharply conveys the hardships endured by the early explorers. As you enter, stores line the right-hand wall. The central area is occupied by a stove, piles of provisions and a sleeping platform. A square hole in the floor was used for pendulum experiments. A mummified seal lies on the open southern veranda.

For conservation purposes, only eight people are permitted inside at a time, and only 40 are allowed in the area of the hut.

Vince's Cross MEMORIAL

About 75m west of the *Discovery* Hut, an oak cross stands as an enduring memorial to Able Seaman George T Vince, who fell to his death over an ice cliff into McMurdo Sound on March 11, 1902.

OBSERVATION HILL

This 230m volcanic cone on the edge of town is often called simply 'Ob Hill.' It is surmounted by a 3.5m **cross** that was raised on January 20, 1913, in memory of the five men who perished on Scott's return from the South Pole: Henry Bowers, Edgar Evans, Laurence Oates, Robert Scott and Edward Wilson. Its fading inscription is the closing line from Tennyson's poem *Ulysses:* 'To strive, to seek, to find, and not to yield.' The cross has been blown over at least twice. At the last re-erection, in January 1994, it was set in a concrete base.

PRAM POINT

Pram Point, on the southeast side of Hut Point Peninsula, was named by Scott's *Discovery* expedition because getting from there to the Ross Ice Shelf in summer requires a pram (small boat).

Scott Base BASE

Compared to McMurdo's 'urban sprawl,' just 3km away by gravel road, New Zealand's Scott Base looks positively pastoral. An orderly collection of lime-green buildings, Scott Base – named for Robert Scott – was established in 1957 by Edmund Hillary as part of Fuchs' Commonwealth Trans-Antarctic Expedition (TAE). Three original buildings from that era survive: two small magnetic huts, and another structure built in 1956 and known variously as the Mess Hut, Hut A or the TAE Hut. It housed not only the mess but also the base leader's room and the radio room. It is preserved as a historic monument and now houses a small **museum**.

Scott Base accommodates 11 winterers and up to 90 people in summer. In 2004 New Zealand built the Hillary Field Centre, a two-story, 1800 sq m heated storage building, the largest single construction project ever undertaken at Scott Base.

The base **flagpole** incorporates an interesting historic relic: part of the flagpole from Scott's *Discovery* Hut, found on the ground near the hut and presented by the Americans at McMurdo to Hillary in 1957.

As part of a major wind-power project, three **wind turbines** were installed on **Crater Hill** and became fully operational in early 2010. The turbines, which are also connected to McMurdo's grid, should reduce the diesel required for power generation by approximately 463,000 liters per year and should cut annual CO^2 emissions by 1242 tonnes. Currently they provide about 90% of Scott Base's power and 15% of McMurdo's. Toilets at Scott are flushed with seawater to reduce freshwater consumption.

Tourists can easily overwhelm a smaller Antarctic station like Scott Base, where staff must dedicate themselves to visitors when a ship is in. Still, the New Zealanders are very friendly and several hundred people visit annually. Once a week, Scott Base hosts 'American night,' when McMurdo residents are welcome; it's a way to contain visits from its more populous neighbor. Conversely, the relatively few Kiwis have an open invitation to events at McMurdo.

Although there are no mail facilities at Scott Base, there are two public telephones in the foyer of the Command Centre. Use phone cards purchased in the base shop, call collect (reverse charges) or use a credit card. The shop accepts New Zealand and US currencies, Visa, MasterCard and American Express.

CAPE EVANS

Terra Nova Hut HISTORIC HUT

Scott's hut from the *Terra Nova* expedition is steeped in an incredible feeling of history. Here, dog skeletons bleach on the sand in the Antarctic sun, evoking thoughts of Scott's death-march from the Pole. Stand at the head of the wardroom table and recall the famous photo of Scott's final birthday, with his men gathered around a huge meal and their banners hanging behind.

Erected in January 1911 at the place Scott named Cape Evans (after his second-in-command, Edward Evans), the prefabricated hut sits on what Scott called Home Beach. It stands close to the shore of McMurdo Sound and measures 14.6m long and 7.3m wide. The largest of the three historic huts on Ross Island, it accommodated 25 men in fairly crowded conditions. A long, narrow building stands in front of the hut; it held the latrines, with segregated facilities for officers.

After Scott's last expedition, 10 members of the Ross Sea party of Shackleton's *Endurance* expedition (see p153) were stranded here in May 1915, when their ship *Aurora* was blown from its moorings. Their arduous task was to lay depots for the party crossing the continent from the Weddell Sea side to use on the second half of their journey. Because *Endurance* was crushed, the

DON'T MISS

THE HISTORIC HUTS

Only by entering the historic huts of explorers can one truly sense what it must have been like on early expeditions. In black-and-white photos of the era, explorers crowd around a table or pack together in groups of bunks. When you step inside Scott's hut at Cape Evans, you suddenly realize that those men didn't crowd together just for the photographer – this was how they lived every day. Note also the rough construction of the huts' interiors – the buildings were only expected to be in use for two or three years, so they were built in a hurry.

Today, the huts are all locked. A representative of New Zealand's Antarctic Heritage Trust (AHT; www.nzaht.org), which maintains and conserves the huts and establishes visitor guidelines, accompanies you into the hut. They're also very familiar with the huts and can point out things visitors would otherwise miss. One tip: keep backpacks, life jackets and other gear away from huts so their modern look doesn't spoil photos.

depots were never used. The men here passed a very difficult 20 months before *Aurora*'s crew was able to bring the ship back.

To enter the hut you pass through an outer porch area. To the left are the stables on the hut's beachfront side. Still in the porch today are a box of penguin eggs, piles of seal blubber, shovels and implements hanging on the walls, and geologist Griffith Taylor's bicycle.

Inside the hut proper, which was insulated by seaweed sewn into jute bags, you'll be standing in what the expedition called the mess deck. In keeping with Royal Navy practice, Scott segregated expedition members into officers and men. The mess deck housed the men: Crean, Keohane, Ford, Omelchenko, Gerov, Clissold, Lashly, Edgar Evans and Hooper. To the right lies the galley with a large stove.

Continuing further into the hut, past what was once a dividing wall made out of packing cases, you'll come to the wardroom. Straight in back is the darkroom and Ponting's bunk. To the right is the laboratory, along with Wright's and Simpson's bunks. To the left of the wardroom table from front to back of their alcove were: Bowers (top bunk) and Cherry-Garrard (bottom bunk); Oates (top bunk, with only floor space beneath); and Mears (top bunk) and Atkinson (bottom bunk). To the right of the wardroom table were (front to back): Gran (top bunk) and Taylor (bottom bunk); a small geology lab; Debenham (top bunk, with nothing beneath); and Nelson (top bunk) and Day (bottom bunk). A note about Day's bunk: Dick Richards used it during Shackleton's Ross Sea party's occupation. Look for the depressing notation he made on his bunk wall after three of the party's members had died:

> RW Richards August 14th, 1916
>
> Losses to date -
>
> Hayward
>
> Mack
>
> Smith

The back left corner of the hut is the sanctum sanctorum. Scott's bunk, to the left, is separated from the bunks of Wilson and Edward Evans by a work table covered with an open book and a fading stuffed emperor penguin.

Throughout the hut are provisions and photographic supplies. There's a strong, not unpleasant musty smell, like that of dusty old books and pony straw. Boxes hold candles that could still be used today. The name brands on many of the supplies remain familiar, with label designs that are hardly changed even now. Be sure to look for the telephone, which connected this hut with the *Discovery* Hut using bare wire laid across the sea ice.

The site has undergone an extensive AHT restoration project over recent years and is slated for completion in 2014. Between 700 and 800 visitors land at Cape Evans yearly, making it the most frequently visited Ross Sea tourist site. Only 12 people are permitted inside the hut at one time, and only 40 people are allowed ashore at once.

OTHER SITES

During the site's occupation by Shackleton's Ross Sea party, three members perished while returning from a depot-laying trip. Reverend Arnold Spencer-Smith died of scurvy on March 9, 1916, and two others, Aeneas Mackintosh and Victor Hayward, vanished in a blizzard while walking on thin sea ice on May 8, 1916. The cross on **Wind Vane**

Hill commemorates them. Two of *Aurora*'s **anchors** remain embedded in the sand on Home Beach, one directly in front of the hut, the other 25m north of it.

Environmental organization Greenpeace had a year-round base at Cape Evans between 1987 and 1992. It was dismantled and removed in 1991–92. A rather difficult to locate **Greenpeace Base Plaque** is now all that marks the site. Walk north up the beach to find it.

CAPE ROYDS

Scott named the cape for *Discovery*'s meteorologist, Charles Royds. Besides being the home of Shackleton's hut, Cape Royds also harbors a **rookery** of 4000 Adélies that is the southernmost of the 160-odd Adélie rookeries around Antarctica. The small pond in front of Shackleton's hut is called **Pony Lake**, because the expedition kept its ponies tethered nearby.

Shackleton's Hut HISTORIC HUT

Shackleton erected this structure on his *Nimrod* expedition in February 1908. Fifteen men lived in the hut, which is much smaller than Scott's at Cape Evans, and the feeling inside is still very atmospheric. All of Shackleton's men left here alive (unlike Scott's hut), and apparently they left in a hurry: when members of the *Terra Nova* expedition visited in 1911, they found socks left hanging to dry and a meal still on the table. Members of the Ross Sea party of Shackleton's 1914–17 *Endurance* expedition also stopped by, commandeering tobacco and soap, among other treats.

Since these long-ago stopovers (snow filled it during one long interval between visits) the hut underwent an extensive AHT conservation project (2004–08). The weatherproofed result completely retains the hut's historical appeal.

As you step inside, if you're tall, duck so you don't hit your head on the acetylene generator over the entryway. It once powered the hut's lamps.

Unlike Scott, Shackleton imposed no division between officers and men at Cape Royds, although as 'The Boss' he did invoke executive privilege to give himself a private room near the hut's front door. Ask your AHT guide to point out Shackleton's signature (which may or may not be authentic) in his tiny bunk room. It's upside down on a packing crate marked 'Not for Voyage' which he had made into a headboard for his bunk.

A freeze-dried buckwheat pancake still lies in a cast-iron skillet on top of the large stove at the back of the hut, beside a tea kettle and a cooking pot. Colored glass medicine bottles line several shelves. One of the few surviving bunks, to the left toward the back, has its fur sleeping bag laid out on top. Many tins of food with unappetizing names such as Irish brawn (head cheese), boiled mutton, Army Rations, Aberdeen marrow fat, lunch tongue and pea powder lie on the floor (near the walls), along with still-bright-red tins of Price's Motor Lubricant. A bench piled with mitts and shoes stands on the right. The dining table, which was lifted from the floor every night to create extra space, is gone. It may have been burned by a later party that ran out of fuel.

In January 2010, in a sensational find, conservators unearthed three crates of Shackleton's Mackinlay's whiskey and two crates of brandy from under the hut. After they had been thawed in Christchurch, in 2011 the master blender at Whyte & Mackay (owners of the Mackinlay's brand) in

ICEBERG NAMES

Large icebergs – those at least 10 nautical miles (18.5km) long – are given code names that sound like those used for military aircraft: C-16, B-15A, and so on. The codes derive from the quadrant of Antarctica where the icebergs were originally sighted, often by satellite. 'A' designates the area from 0° to W 90° (Bellingshausen/Weddell Seas), 'B' the area from W 90° to 180° (Amundsen/eastern Ross Seas), 'C' the area from 180° to E 90° (western Ross Sea/Wilkes Land), and 'D' the area from E 90° to 0° (Amery Ice Shelf/ eastern Weddell Sea).

After an iceberg is sighted, the US National Ice Center assigns a quadrant letter and a number based on its point of origin. C-16, for example, is the 16th iceberg tracked in quadrant C since the center began tracking big bergs in 1976. Large icebergs are tracked even after they split, until the pieces are too small to be seen by satellite. Such pieces get a suffix letter after their original name, so B-15A is the first fragment to calve from iceberg B-15.

ANTARCTICA'S HOT SPOTS *DR PHILIP KYLE*

Beneath the icy exterior of Antarctica is a dynamic continental geologic plate. Tectonic forces are at work within the Antarctic plate, and in places the continent is slowly being torn apart by rifting, much like East Africa. As the Earth's crust is extended and thinned, deep hot mantle rises and partially melts to form basaltic magma, which rises and is often stored within the crust in magma chambers. Where the magma reaches the surface, it is erupted as lava or volcanic ash and volcanoes are formed.

Active volcanoes are found today in three areas of Antarctica: the western Ross Sea, West Antarctica and along the Antarctic Peninsula. There remains a high probability that significant volcanic eruptions could occur at any time in Antarctica.

In the western Ross Sea region, most volcanism occurs on or along the front of the Transantarctic Mountains. Many small volcanic vents have been detected beneath the Ross Sea as magnetic anomalies, but none of these vents are currently active. Among a group of volcanic cones and domes called the **Pleiades**, high in the Transantarctic Mountains of northern Victoria Land, is a very young-looking dome, which probably erupted less than 1000 years ago. **Mt Melbourne** near Terra Nova Bay has steaming ground at its summit and an ash layer showing it erupted less than 250 years ago.

In Marie Byrd Land of West Antarctica, only **Mt Berlin** is considered active. There is also a possibility that an eruption is currently ongoing beneath the ice of the West Antarctic ice sheet. Airborne studies have shown a circular depression consistent with the melting of the ice by a volcanic vent. The presence of a volcano beneath the depression is confirmed by studies that show magnetic rocks typical of volcanoes.

In the Antarctic Peninsula region, volcanic **Deception Island** lies at the south end of Bransfield Strait.

Mt Erebus

Antarctica's best-known volcano is **Mt Erebus**, a stratovolcano on Ross Island, discovered by Ross in 1841. Ross noted in his journal that Erebus was erupting, '...emitting flame and smoke in great profusion...some of the officers believed they could see streams of lava pouring down its sides until lost beneath the snow.' Erebus is one of the largest volcanoes in the world, ranking among the top 20 in size.

Erebus has many unusual features, the most notable being a permanent convecting lake of molten magma with a temperature of 1000°C (the only others are Erta Ale in Ethiopia and Nyiragongo in Congo). In late 2007 the lake was 35m in diameter. The magma, which is very rich in sodium and potassium, is called phonolite. This name comes from German and refers to rocks that ring like a bell when hit.

EREBUS CRYSTALS

Unique to Erebus is the occurrence of large crystals in the magma. They can exceed 10cm in length and take many different forms. Easily eroded out from the soft glassy matrix of volcanic bombs erupted from the volcano, the crystals litter the upper crater rim like a carpet. They are of a mineral type called feldspar and belong to the anorthoclase variety.

Scotland analyzed and replicated the expedition's whiskey precisely!

Outside the hut lie the remnants of the pony stables and the garage built for the Arrol-Johnson motorcar (Antarctica's first car). Shackleton had brought Siberian ponies, unfortunately unsuited to Antarctic labor: they managed to pull loads a considerable distance but did not have the stamina or versatility of dogs. Pony oats spill from feed bags onto the ground. One of the car's wheels leans up against a line of provision boxes, its wooden spokes scoured by the wind. Two wooden doghouses sit nearby.

On the hut's south side, the wood has weathered to a handsome bleached grey. Boxes of rusting food tins stand against the side and back. Although rust has completely destroyed the labels, one wooden carton is literally spilling its beans.

Cables running over the hut lash it to the ground, and the AHT put on a new roof in the summer of 2005–06. The front door is also a replica, made of the same Scots pine timber as the original.

The anorthoclase is spectacular, and among the most perfect and largest crystals found in volcanic rocks anywhere on Earth.

ICE TOWERS

Erebus' summit features beautiful fumarolic ice towers. From sea level these can be observed with binoculars on the upper summit plateau of the volcano. The ice towers represent places where heated gases, rich in water, vent to the surface along fractures. When the gas reaches the cold air, the water freezes and forms bizarre shapes of varying size. Beneath the ice towers it is common to find tunnels and caves melted into the underlying snow and ice. These ice caves are warm and steamy and in some cases feel like a sauna. Access to the cave system can be difficult and may require an abseil (a rappel) of more than 20m. During the summer, when the sun dips toward the horizon around midnight, the ice towers look spectacular, as steam slowly ascends through the hollow towers and vents out the top.

ERUPTIONS

Small eruptions are common from Erebus' magma lake, occurring six to 10 times daily during the mid-1980s and 1990s. Eruptive activity declined between 2000 and 2004 but was at a high level in 2005 and 2006 before going 'quiet' again in mid-2007. Activity was observed once again in 2010. The eruptions are referred to as Strombolian eruptions, after the volcano Stromboli near Sicily. Only rarely are volcanic bombs ejected from the lake onto the 600m-diameter crater rim. In March 2007 several bombs destroyed scientific equipment on the rim.

In September 1984 there was a four-month episode of more violent eruptions that showered bombs more than 3km from the vent inside the crater. Scientists had to abandon a small research facility near the crater rim while volcanic bombs – some as big as cars – rained down around the summit crater. The bombs whistled as they fell, but the most memorable part of the eruption was the sound of the sharp explosions that threw the bombs from the volcanic vent. (Upon landing, the bombs crackle as they cool. The interior of the bombs can be very hot, and if you break one open, you can pull the plastic hot lava out like taffy candy.)

SEISMIC MEASUREMENTS

Today a network of about a dozen seismic stations (which have continuous GPS, microphones and meteorological sensors) monitors Erebus, recording its small explosions and the earthquakes within its bowels. Between 2000 and 2004 the seismometers recorded tremor events generated by collisions between huge icebergs that broke from the Ross Ice Shelf. The seismometers should allow scientists to predict the next episode of eruptions. While there's no evidence in the geologic record of huge eruptions of the magnitude of the 1980 eruption at Mt St Helens in the US, the presence of volcanic ash from Erebus in blue ice near the Transantarctic Mountains several hundred kilometers from the volcano attests to its potential for larger eruptions.

Dr Philip Kyle, Professor of Geochemistry at the New Mexico Institute of Mining and Technology and Director of the Mount Erebus Volcano Observatory (erebus.nmt.edu), has spent 40 field seasons in Antarctica and returns annually to Mt Erebus to monitor its activity

Cape Royds is the least visited of the Ross Island historic huts (about 700 people yearly). For conservation reasons only eight people are permitted inside at one time, and only 40 are allowed ashore at once.

MTS EREBUS & TERROR

Impressive Mt Erebus, the world's most southerly active volcano, is 3794m high. Its lazily drifting plume of steam is a familiar sight throughout the Ross Sea region.

Mt Erebus was first climbed in 1908 by a party from Shackleton's *Nimrod* expedition. A geological curiosity, Erebus emits about 80g of metallic gold crystals each day. It is also one of only a handful of volcanoes in the world with a permanent convecting-lava lake. Researchers developed a DNA-testing technique to reduce crime-solving delays by using an enzyme from a microorganism found at a volcanic vent on Erebus.

In the area near Erebus' summit crater, the atmosphere's acrid mix of hydrochloric and hydrofluoric acids and sulfur dioxide caused volcanologists to give it the nickname 'Nausea Knob.'

Mt Erebus is infamous as the site of Antarctica's worst air tragedy. All 257 people aboard Air NZ flight 901 were killed when their DC-10 slammed into Mt Erebus on November 28, 1979. The Antarctic Treaty countries have declared the crash site a tomb. One edge of the site is marked by a stainless-steel cross.

Mt Terror (3230m) is an extinct volcano which is separated from Mt Erebus by Mt Terra Nova.

CAPE CROZIER

Site of the first **emperor penguin rookery** ever discovered (by Scott in 1902), Cape Crozier is named for Commander Francis Crozier, captain of *Terror,* one of the two ships on Ross' expedition, which first sighted the cape. Besides the emperors incubating their eggs on the sea ice, Cape Crozier is home to 300,000 Adélies.

Cape Crozier is inextricably linked with the infamous 36-day, 105km midwinter trek from Cape Evans made by three members of Scott's *Terra Nova* expedition in 1911. Apsley Cherry-Garrard eloquently chronicled the trip in his classic *The Worst Journey in the World* (1922). With Edward Wilson and 'Birdie' Bowers, he braved 24-hour darkness and temperatures as low as -59°C – so cold that his chattering teeth broke off in his mouth and he began 'to think of death as a friend.' This was undertaken so that they could be the first to collect emperor penguin embryos. The three eggs they gathered are in London's Natural History Museum (along with 40,000 other rarely displayed specimens from the *Terra Nova* expedition).

Ross Ice Shelf

Covering 520,000 sq km, an area roughly the size of France, the Ross Ice Shelf was discovered on January 28, 1841, by Ross, who called it the Victoria Barrier in honor of Queen Victoria. Since then it has been called many things, namely the Barrier, the Great Barrier, the Great Ice Barrier, the Great Southern Barrier, the Icy Barrier, the Ross Ice Barrier and, these days, the Ross Ice Shelf.

Its mean ice thickness is 335m to 700m, but where glaciers and ice streams meet it, the shelf is up to 1000m thick. At the ice front facing the Ross Sea, it's less than 100m thick. It is rather hard to believe, but the whole ice shelf is actually *floating.*

It moves as fast as 1100m per year, and calves an estimated 150 cu km of icebergs annually, out of its total of 23,000 cu km of ice. In 1987 a berg measuring 155km by 35km calved from the eastern side.

Another giant iceberg, named B-15, calved in March 2000. Measuring 298km by 37km and covering an area of about 11,000 sq km, it was the largest iceberg ever recorded. Although an iceberg sighted by USS *Glacier* in 1956 was reported to be 335km by 97km and covering nearly 32,500 sq km, researchers now believe these measurements were incorrect and that the berg was far smaller.

Scientists regard the calving of gigantic bergs as part of a normal process in which the ice sheet maintains a balance between constant growth outward from the continent and periodic loss by icebergs breaking off. The recent acceleration of the calving, though, is due to the effects of climate change (see p162).

The Ross Ice Shelf has inspired many awe-struck responses. The blacksmith aboard *Erebus* in 1841 was uncharacteristically moved to write a couplet:

> Awful and sublime, magnificent and rare
>
> No other Earthly object with the Barrier can compare.

Ross himself wrote in 1847, six years after discovering it:

> ...this extraordinary barrier of ice, of probably more than a thousand feet in thickness, crushes the undulations of the waves, and disregards their violence: it is a mighty and wonderful object, far beyond anything we could have thought or conceived.

Borchgrevink found the shelf to be much smaller than when Ross discovered it. In fact, at a place located at about W 164° (Scott later called it 'Discovery Inlet,' after his ship), the ice shelf was only 4.5m above the sea. In 1900 Borchgrevink landed stores, sledges and dogs here. With two members of his expedition, William Colbeck and Per Savio, he trekked to S 78°50', then the furthest south ever reached.

Roosevelt Island, 130km long and 65km wide, is completely covered by ice and is identifiable mainly by a central ridge of ice 550m above sea level. The island, of which the northernmost point is just 5km south of the Bay of Whales, was discovered by Byrd in 1934 and named for Franklin D Roosevelt.

East Antarctica & the South Pole

Includes »

Best Places for Science

» Amundsen-Scott South Pole Station (p132)

» Vostok Station (p123)

» Dome A and Kunlun Station (p124)

Best Wildlife

» Scullin & Murray Monoliths (p115)

» Dumont d'Urville Station (p120)

Why Go?

Severe and spectacular, East Antarctica is the land of the polar plateau and the continent's coldest temperatures. The icebound coast, with its massive ice shelves, is broken up by the occasional ice-free oasis, or teeming seabird or emperor penguin colonies.

Only a small number of research stations are scattered along these difficult-to-reach shores, and visitors appear so rarely that they are generally welcomed with open arms.

Inland East Antarctica, the heart of the ice cap, is only rarely visited by tourists. Several important research stations take advantage of the vast, thick ice sheet and its high, dry, freezing conditions: perfect for astronomy and physics.

Among them is the Amundsen-Scott South Pole Station. To reach here, you'll fly over magnificent glaciers, yawning crevasse fields, and the most barren snow on Earth as you cross the polar plateau to reach the mighty Geographic South Pole.

Top Resources

» *The South Pole* (1912), Roald Amundsen. Polar technician's triumph in reaching 90° South.

» *Scott's Last Expedition* (1913), Captain Robert F Scott. Firsthand account, published posthumously.

» *The Home of the Blizzard* (1915), Sir Douglas Mawson. The explorer's own account of survival and discovery.

» *South with Mawson* (1947), Charles F Laseron. Life on windswept Cape Denison.

» **US Antarctic Program** (www.usap.gov) Pole webcam.

» **Amundsen-Scott South Pole Station** (www.southpolestation.com) Unofficial South Pole info and trivia.

» *La marche de l'empereur* or *March of the Penguins* (2005) Directed by Luc Jacquet.

» *Antarctica* or *Nankyoku monogatari* (1983). Directed by Koreyoshi Kurahara. Music by Vangelis.

» *South* (restored 1998). Directed by Frank Hurley.

East Antarctica & The South Pole Highlights

1. Go around the world in seconds at the **Geographic South Pole** (p132)
2. Visit Mawson's 'Home of the Blizzard' at **Commonwealth Bay** (p120)
3. Tour futuristic-looking **Amundsen-Scott South Pole Station** (p129) and learn about cutting-edge experiments like IceCube (p132)
4. Honor the explorers whose coffins are bolted to bare rock at **Buromskiy Island cemetery** (p117)
5. Gape at **emperor penguins** (p117) brooding their chicks on the coast

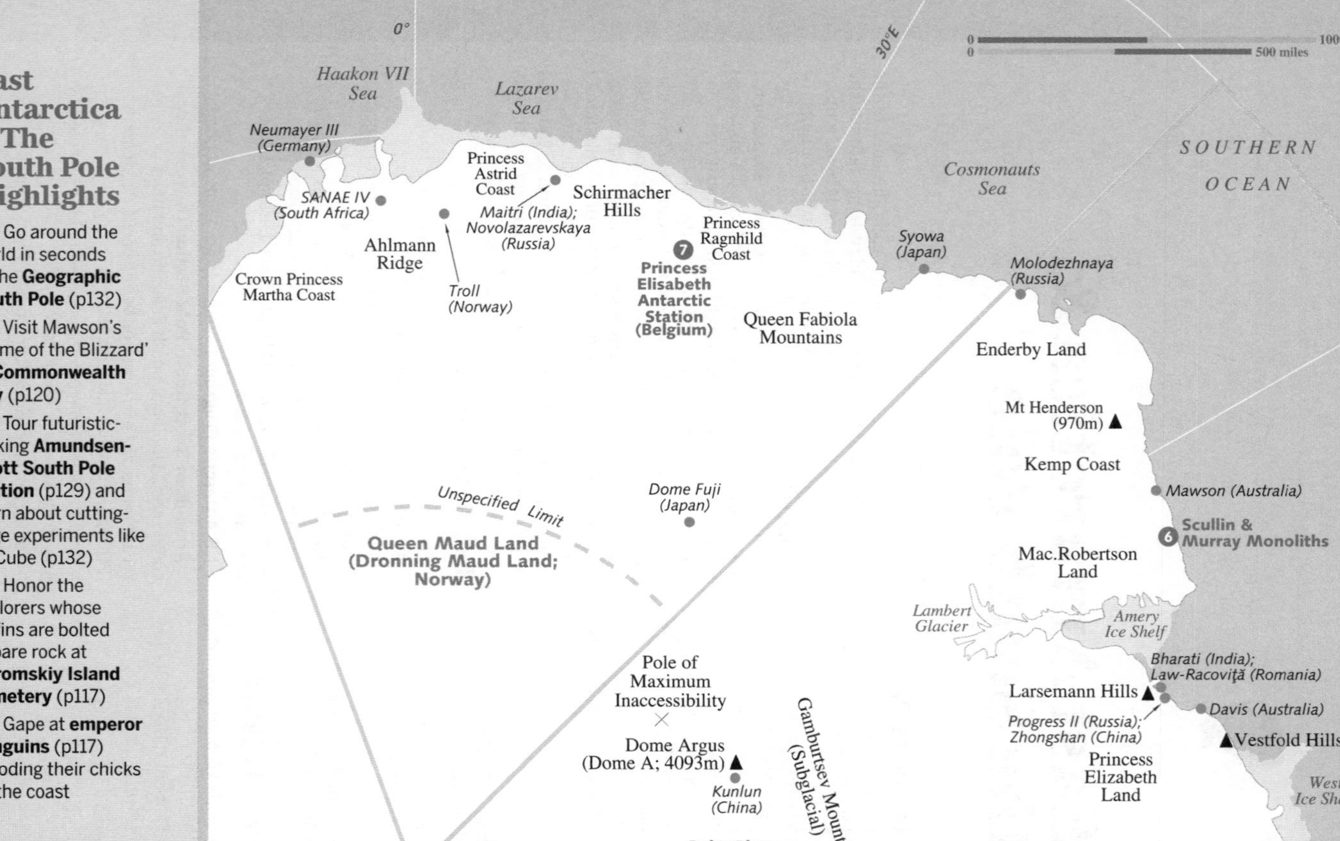

6 Cruise past the seabird colonies at **Scullin & Murray Monoliths** (p115)

7 See Antarctica's first zero-emission base at Belgium's **Princess Elisabeth Antarctica Station** (p112)

8 Scan the vast, white **polar plateau** (p129) and recall the pole-seekers' agonizing struggles

9 Visit **Vostok Station** (p123), where ancient ice cores are extracted and the first subglacial lake was tapped

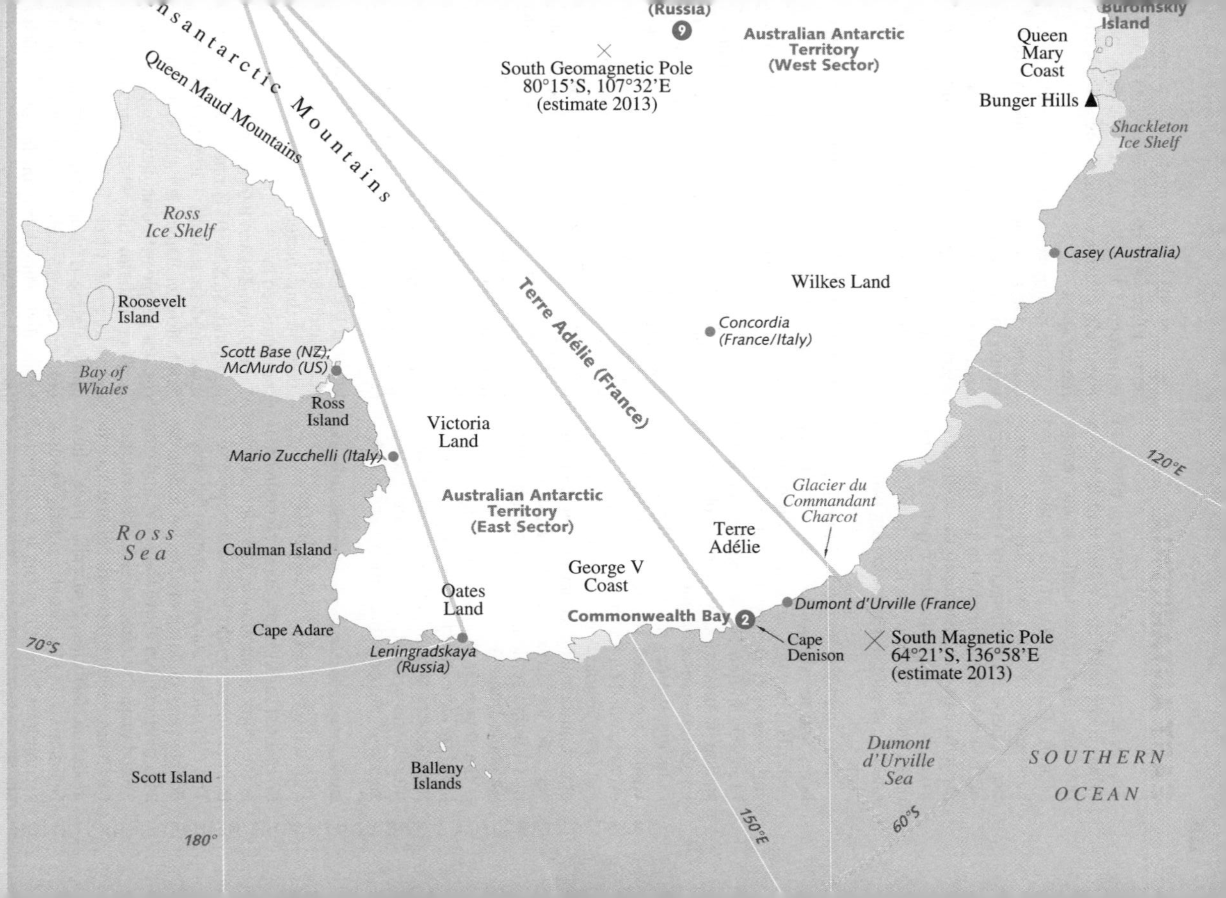

nsantarctic Mountains
Queen Maud Mountains
(Russia)
9
South Geomagnetic Pole
80°15'S, 107°32'E
(estimate 2013)
Australian Antarctic Territory (West Sector)
Queen Mary Coast
Buromskiy Island
Bunger Hills
Shackleton Ice Shelf
Ross Ice Shelf
Roosevelt Island
Casey (Australia)
Wilkes Land
Terre Adélie (France)
Concordia (France/Italy)
Scott Base (NZ); McMurdo (US)
Bay of Whales
Ross Island
Victoria Land
Mario Zucchelli (Italy)
120°E
Glacier du Commandant Charcot
Australian Antarctic Territory (East Sector)
Terre Adélie
Ross Sea
Coulman Island
George V Coast
Oates Land
Dumont d'Urville (France)
Commonwealth Bay
2
Cape Adare
Cape Denison
South Magnetic Pole
64°21'S, 136°58'E
(estimate 2013)
70°S
Leningradskaya (Russia)
Dumont d'Urville Sea
SOUTHERN OCEAN
Scott Island
Balleny Islands
180°
150°E
60°S

EAST ANTARCTICA

East Antarctica – as US Antarctic historian Edwin Swift Balch first called it in 1904 – is the name most often used for this remote section of the continent, all in the eastern hemisphere. It's also called Greater Antarctica because it's the larger of the two parts of the continent separated by the Transantarctic Mountains. Getting to this extremely isolated part of Antarctica requires a long, often difficult voyage, so it is visited by just one tourist ship (or occasionally two) each year.

The coastline harbors fantastical icebergs and ice shelves as well as sheltering seabirds, penguins, and the occasional scientist/research facility. Belgium's Princess Elisabeth Station is the first zero emission station in Antarctica; Norway's Troll is a major air-transportation hub.

Inland, stations dot the ice shelf. Russia's Vostok registered the lowest temperature ever recorded on Earth and sits atop subglacial Lake Vostok. France and Italy jointly operate Concordia, famed for its very deep and very old ice cores. And the latest, China's new Kunlun station, is at Antarctica's highest point, Dome A.

Starting near 0°, the following sites are listed by increasing longitude east, with stations located well inland listed last. Most of these bases are only visited by scientists or guests of the operating nation.

Neumayer III Station

Completed in February 2009, Neumayer III is the third generation of German stations built on the 200m-thick **Ekström Ice Shelf**. The €26 million station is one prefabricated double-story building erected on a 68m by 24m platform, 6m above the snow, and connected to a subsurface garage. The structure combines research, operational and accommodation facilities. Hydraulic piles allow Neumayer III to be raised regularly as snow accumulates beneath, giving it an expected life of 25 years.

Neumayer III augments its power generators with one 30kW wind turbine, and will eventually have a complete wind farm to cover most of its needs.

The first Georg von Neumayer station was built in 1981 and named after one of the promoters of the First International Polar Year in 1882–83. After it was buried by drifting snow, its replacement was completed about 10km away in 1992. Neumayer II was constructed 12m beneath the surface, but eventually became unsound due to the shifting ice sheet.

Nine people generally winterover. In December 1990 the first all-female group to winter in Antarctica staffed Neumayer. Two meteorologists, two geophysicists, two engineers, a radio operator, a cook and a doctor (also station leader) spent 14 months on the Ice, including nine months in complete isolation.

SANAE IV

SANAE IV (South African National Antarctic Expedition) sits like a long red-and-white millipede atop a nunatak called **Vesleskarvet** (Norwegian for 'little barren mountain') on the **Ahlmann Ridge**, 170km from the coast – hence the station's nickname 'Vesles.' The landscape around Vesles is relatively barren, with only a few lichens and mites on site, but skuas and snow petrels visit regularly in summer. The station perches just 50m from the edge of a 210m cliff, and on clear days offers dramatic views over the ice sheet and of surrounding nunataks and the Ahlmann Ridge peaks to the south.

The first SANAE base was occupied in 1959 and SANAE II and SANAE III followed. The latter, closed for wintering in 1994, was built on the **Fimbul Ice Shelf** and over the years had been buried by 14m of drifting snow. It thus became unsafe because the snow crushed it.

Built from 1993 to 1997 at a cost of 64 million rand, SANAE IV is one of Antarctica's most modern stations – it even includes a two-helicopter hangar, a bathroom with access for people with disabilities and a sauna large enough for the whole winter team. Consisting of three linked double-story units totaling 176m in length, the station is built on stilts 3.5m above the rock. Occupied by its first wintering team in 1997 (which included Dr Aithne Rowse, the first South African woman to overwinter in Antarctica), the station accommodates about 10 people in winter and more than 90 in summer.

Thanks to its small but excellent **hospital**, SANAE IV can serve as a surgical facility for the other research stations in Queen Maud Land, if necessary.

A wide range of research is conducted at SANAE IV, including invasion biology/ecology, geology, geomorphology and atmospheric sciences.

SANAE IV has recorded wind speeds as high as 208km/h, but the wind can blow even harder than that. After an anemometer was ripped from its anchor during a storm in 2006, meteorologists estimated that the wind speed reached 230km/h. A storm in 2003 blew a Ski-doo snowmobile over the Vesles cliff.

Controversy over the coloring of SANAE erupted in 2001. The station was blue on the bottom to absorb solar energy and help keep the area beneath it snow-free, and the roof was orange for visibility from the air. Because these colors, with the station's white sides, were the colors of the apartheid-era South African flag, politicians demanded change. The colors were impregnated into the fiberglass panels, so epoxy marine paint was used to paint the blue part of the station 'alert red'.

SANAE is resupplied by trains of tracked vehicles loaded from ships at the ice-shelf edge. In 2000 the station lost six empty 8.5-tonne fuel tanks after the calving of the section of the ice shelf on which they stood.

About 1km from the station is a 1200m smoothed-snow **airstrip**; most flights travel via Novolazarevskaya Station.

Troll Station

Norway's Troll Station was built as a summer-only facility in 1990 on a 'low' area between two peaks 250km from the Queen Maud Land coast, but still sits at an elevation of 1300m. In February 2005 Norway's queen (the first queen to visit Antarctica) inaugurated Troll as a year-round station. Troll takes its name from the surrounding jagged mountains, said to resemble the homes of mythical trolls.

Troll accommodates up to seven people during the winter, and 40 in summer in a tent camp. When Norwegian Prime Minister Jens Stoltenberg visited Troll in early 2008 with 40 officials, scientists and reporters, he impressed Antarcticans by declining a bed in the station, choosing instead to sleep outdoors in a tent.

Troll serves as a major hub of the **Dronning Maud Land Air Network Project** (DROMLAN), a cooperative transportation agreement between 11 countries with stations in East Antarctica. A 3km blue-ice **runway** located 7km northwest of Troll allows long-range aircraft to fly between Antarctica and Cape Town, South Africa. DROMLAN's other major hub is Russia's Novolazarevskaya, 350km northeast of Troll, but the runway there becomes inoperational in midsummer due to melting. Passengers fly six hours from Cape Town to either Troll or Novolazarevskaya, then transfer to smaller aircraft for their final destination.

Schirmacher Hills

Much of this narrow strip of land, 17km long and 3km wide, is ice-free year-round, making it an 'oasis.' Dotted with as many as 180 lakes and ponds, the terrain is hillocky with a maximum elevation of 228m. The hills, discovered by a secret Nazi Antarctic expedition dispatched to claim territory for Germany in 1938–39, are named for Richardheinrich Schirmacher, who flew an expedition seaplane, and are home to two research stations.

MAITRI STATION

Maitri (Hindi for friendship), a long U-shaped tan-colored building with a large Indian flag over the entrance, was built in 1989 on adjustable telescopic legs. It is located some 80km inland from the coast, and replaces India's first Antarctic base, Dakshin Gangotri, which was initially established as

SHOCKING!

Static electricity discharge is a problem at many inland stations in Antarctica. It's especially strong at SANAE IV, thanks to the very dry air and high winds. During storms, the base acts like a gigantic battery, storing up a charge. Putting one's hand as far as 10cm from a window causes a mini bolt of 'lightning' to arc across the gap. Fluorescent tubes brought close to windows light up on their own. Station members particularly feel the discharges when they are forced to go outdoors in a storm, getting continuous shocks every time they touch a grounded object. This static can also ruin electronic devices like MP3 players, memory sticks and digital cameras.

SELF-APPENDECTOMY

Antarctica's most celebrated surgery took place at Novolazarevskaya in 1961. Physician Leonid I Rogozov successfully removed his own appendix in an operation lasting one hour and 45 minutes. Rogozov had first noticed the symptoms of acute appendicitis the day before, but no nearby station had an aircraft, and poor weather would have prevented a flight anyway. The next day, his fever increased. 'An immediate operation was necessary to save the patient's life,' he wrote later in *Information Bulletin of the Soviet Antarctic Expedition*. 'The only solution was to operate on myself.' Half-reclining in bed with his weight on his left hip, the doctor anesthetized his abdomen with novocaine and made a 12cm incision. Using a mirror held by one of two assistants – and sometimes working entirely by feel – he excised the diseased appendix and placed antibiotics into his abdomen. 'General weakness became severe after 30 to 40 minutes, and vertigo developed, so that short pauses for rest were necessary,' he wrote. Nevertheless, he concluded the surgery at midnight. A week later, the wound was completely healed.

a refuge hut in January 1982. In 1984 another Gangotri was constructed further inland, in the Schirmacher Hills, and the first group wintered over there. Gangotri, which was becoming buried in ice, is now used as a supply base, transit camp and ice-core storage. Maitri's winter and summer complement is 25 and 65, respectively.

In 2008 an Israeli tourist, Ram Barkai, swam a distance of 1km in the 1°C waters of nearby Dlinnoye (Long) Lake, and claimed the record for the world's most southerly swim.

NOVOLAZAREVSKAYA STATION

Located at the southeastern tip of the Schirmacher oasis and on the shores of **Lake Stantsionnoye**, Russia's Novolazarevskaya Station is named for Mikhail Petrovich Lazarev, who was second-in-command of Fabian von Bellingshausen's expedition of 1803–06, and captain of the supply ship *Mirnyy*. The station is 80km from the Lazarev Sea coast, but only 4.5km east of India's Maitri Station.

Soviet/Russian activity in the area dates back to the establishment of Lazarev base in 1958. In its very first year of operation (1961), a storied self-surgery took place (see the boxed text).

In 1979 the current station replaced the old one, which included a sty for pigs fed on kitchen scraps. The station's seven single-story buildings are built on steel struts 1m to 2m above the ground and are connected by wooden boardwalks. A wooden Russian Orthodox **cross** marks the grave of the radio operator who died during winter in 1996.

About 25 people overwinter at 'Novo' and there are about 60 summer personnel. Despite its latitude (S 71°), weather at 'Novo' can be quite mild. In the summer, solar radiation from the surrounding rocks makes it warm enough to sunbathe in the nude – scientists in the mid-1960s even fell asleep during this unusual Antarctic activity!

A somewhat less surprising pastime for personnel features the station's beloved Russian **bathhouse**, or *banya*, in which as many as six people can steam at 100°C and beat each other with birch boughs – before running outside to roll in the snow.

A 2780m ice-sheet **runway** for ski and wheeled aircraft sits 15km south of 'Novo,' at an elevation of 550m. It is a major hub of the Dronning Maud Land Air Network Project in conjunction with Troll Station.

Princess Elisabeth Antarctica Station

On February 15, 2009 Belgium opened the Princess Elisabeth Antarctica Station (www.antarcticstation.org), the first zero-emission polar science station; it emits no carbon dioxide at all. The octagonal steel structure is built on stilts sunk into the permafrost on **Utsteinen Nunatak** north of the **Sør Rondane Mountains**.

The station is completely energy self-sufficient, being powered by solar energy (both photovoltaic and thermal solar panels) and wind energy (nine wind turbines). It's made of eco-friendly materials, and all on-site practices aim to minimize energy consumption and waste production. Bioreactors recycle all wastewater as many as five times for use in showers and toilets before it is ultracleaned and disposed of. The building itself is designed to maximize energy efficiency: marvelously, the station requires no heating other than the sun and the heat generated by people and the station's regular electrical appliances. The electrical system itself is run on a 'Smart Grid' (energy prioritizing system) to direct energy use to where it is most needed.

The Belgians designed the station for an expected life of 25 years and use it in summer to accommodate 25 to 40 people for studies in glaciology, climatology, geology and astronomy, among other endeavors.

Syowa Station & Dome Fuji

A collection of about 50 brightly colored structures, Japan's Syowa Station was established in 1956–57 and has been used continuously since then except for a four-year period from 1962–65. The 'mother station' of the Japanese Antarctic Research Expedition, it's built on the northern half of **East Ongul Island**, 4km offshore.

Syowa's main building, built in 1992, is a four-story structure topped by a domed skylight. With a winter complement of 31 people, Syowa has adopted the practice of using gray water from dishwashing and showers for station toilets, reducing water consumption.

Like most long-established Antarctic stations, Syowa has grown in size tremendously over the years, increasing from three buildings with a floorspace of 184 sq m in 1957 to 48 buildings (plus other outdoor facilities) totaling 5931 sq m in 2001.

The first live TV transmission from Antarctica was broadcast from Syowa to Tokyo from January 28 to February 3, 1979.

Part of the research done at Syowa in recent years is a study of microclimates in moss beds. In 1996 Japanese scientists were startled to find a 20cm-high flowering plant growing in a rock fissure about 25km south of Syowa, creating concern that global warming might be behind the plant's ability to thrive. That concern was greatly increased in 2004 when a graduate student at the station found a stalk of rice growing in a narrow gap between rocks.

Large numbers of snow petrels nest in nearby **Yukidori Valley** (protected by the Antarctic Treaty).

Some 1000km south of Syowa is 3810m-high **Dome Fuji**. Japan opened a small summer station here in 1995, and began drilling cores from the ice sheet, reaching a depth of 3035.22m in 2007 and ice that is approximately 720,000 years old.

Molodezhnaya Station

Once the summer home to as many as 400 residents, the collection of 70-some buildings called Molodezhnaya is now deserted. It was established in 1962 in the Thala Hills oasis, a region of lakes and ponds in the low, rounded **Thala Hills** 500m from **Cosmonauts Sea**. Many of its buildings were

CANINE COMPANIONS

In February 1958, the season after Syowa was built, its first wintering crew left by small plane to the relief ship *Soya*, which could not approach closer than 100km because of heavy pack ice. The station's 15 Sakhalin Island husky dogs had been chained up and given a bit of food since new station members were supposed to arrive immediately, but severe weather prevented planes from returning with the new wintering crew. Although the ship waited for weeks, it ultimately proved impossible to fly the men ashore, and winter was approaching.

The dogs were left to fend for themselves.

When the next team returned in January 1959, two dogs, Taro and Jiro, were found alive. Since neither penguins nor seals remain ashore in the region over winter, it is unknown how the dogs survived. Even the possibility that they ate their dead fellows does not explain the feat, since seven dogs were found still chained up, untouched.

For their amazing survival, Taro and Jiro became famous in Japan. Although Jiro died at Syowa the following year, Taro was returned to Japan in 1961, where he lived another nine years and received thousands of visitors weekly.

The dogs were later immortalized on Japanese postage stamps and in Koreyoshi Kurahara's film *Nankyoku Monogatari* (known outside Japan as *Antarctica*) – Japan's largest-grossing movie in 1983. In 2006 Disney made a version called *Eight Below*.

constructed using Arbolit, a special fire-resistant reinforced concrete, a precaution taken after the tragic 1960 fire at Mirnyy. The station gets its name from the *molodezh* (young people) who helped build it.

Molodezhnaya was the Soviet Union's (and then Russia's) main base of Antarctic research as well as its Antarctic Meteorological Centre from 1968. Numerous rockets were launched from here into the upper atmosphere for meteorology research between 1970 and 1984. The station closed in 1999 due to Russia's economic situation.

Near the station are two small Adélie **penguin rookeries** as well as a lonesome **cemetery**, about 6km east, in which the caskets are covered by steel vaults, which are themselves covered with rocks to secure them against high winds.

Mawson Station

The sign says: 'It's home, it's Mawson,' and for as many as 70 people living at the oldest continuously occupied station south of the Antarctic Circle, it is.

Australia's Mawson was established in 1954 on the southeastern shore of Horseshoe Harbour. Named after Douglas Mawson (see p151), it is most often approached through **Iceberg Alley**, a channel lined with huge tabular bergs that have run aground on underwater banks. **Horseshoe Harbour** is the best natural harbor for thousands of kilometers, a 90m-deep anchorage protected by two projecting arms of land. The station's high-latitude location makes it a good place for studying cosmic rays, done in an underground vault in solid rock, 20m below the surface.

Despite its capacity for 70, there are usually fewer than 25 people living at Mawson during the summer, and about 17 in winter. It was formerly the principal home of Australia's much-loved Antarctic huskies, before the Antarctic Treaty's Protocol on Environmental Protection forced their removal.

Visitors immediately notice two prominent features of Mawson's skyline: the 970m peaks of the nunatak **Mt Henderson** sticking out of the ice sheet 10km southeast and the 34m-tall **wind turbines**, installed in 2003. Mawson is the perfect place for this ambitious energy project, since the average monthly wind speed is 72km/h at the elevation of the turbine hubs, with gusts well above 180km/h. The turbines are designed to withstand 260km/h winds. If it's windy, the sound of the wind is louder than the turbines, which can provide 600 kilowatts

COLORED & STRIPED ICEBERGS

Every once in a great while, visitors to Antarctica – particularly East Antarctica – are treated to an exceptional wonder: a green iceberg. Scientists have learned that these beautiful jade or bottle-green icebergs are colored for the same reason that seawater is: they contain organic material from the degradation of marine plants and animals. The more organic material, the greener the ice or the seawater.

Under very special conditions (found primarily in East Antarctica) the organic matter in seawater at great depths freezes onto the underside of ice shelves floating on the ocean. For example, at the Amery Ice Shelf (a source of green icebergs) the base of the ice shelf is about 450m deep. At that depth and pressure, seawater slowly freezes to the underside of the ice shelf, forming 'marine ice.' At its greatest, the accumulation of marine ice can be tens of meters thick.

Icebergs that calve from the edge of the ice shelf are composed of two kinds of ice literally stuck together: glacial ice made of compressed snow that originated from the continent and flowed down to become the ice shelf, and marine ice from the seawater below. Under rare conditions an iceberg becomes unstable due to uneven melting and turns over, exposing its vibrant green marine underside. Marine ice is also unbelievably clear because of the absence of air bubbles from forming under such pressure.

While green icebergs are spectacular, also look for variations ranging from deep indigo to jade to yellow-brown, depending upon the amount of organic material trapped in the ice.

Though it is estimated that as many as 10% of all icebergs from East Antarctica are green, they are only rarely spotted. An even rarer phenomenon is the striped iceberg. These form when seawater fills up and freezes in crevasses occurring on the bottom side of ice shelves. The result is a bubbly, milky-blue iceberg with dark blue or green stripes.

of power and supply up to 80% of the station's needs.

A massive construction program modernized Mawson in the 1990s. Each structure is color-coded and stands out vividly from the Antarctic snow. The large building containing the living quarters, like its counterpart at Casey, is the **Red Shed**.

One of the few surviving buildings from 'old' Mawson is the small wooden **Weddell Hut**, the second building built at the station. Also known as 'the Carpenters' Hut,' it was originally erected at Heard Island.

The small **cemetery** contains the graves of men who died in 1963, 1972 and 1974.

Local traditions include an **Australia Day regatta** (January 26) of homemade wind-powered boats, held every summer when the sea ice breaks out. Station members in inflatable boats retrieve those that sink, capsize or take off in the wrong direction (most of them).

Scullin & Murray Monoliths

The coastline in this region is mainly unbroken ice cliffs 30m to 40m high, but it is interrupted by two spectacular massive rock features that hold the greatest concentration of breeding **seabird colonies** in East Antarctica. Because of this extraordinary birdlife, Scullin and Murray monoliths are an Antarctic Specially Protected Area. No landings are permitted; boats must remain at least 50m from shore.

Scullin Monolith, 160km east of Mawson, harbors Antarctica's highest concentration of breeding Antarctic petrels (160,000 pairs). Some 50,000 pairs of Adélie penguins nest on the monolith's lower slopes. Mawson, who discovered it in February 1931, named the crescent-shaped monolith for Australian Prime Minister James H Scullin. At about the same time, a group of Norwegian whalers named the feature for whaling captain Klarius Mikkelsen. As the result of a later compromise, the highest point on Scullin Monolith is 420m Mikkelsen Peak.

Murray Monolith, sometimes described as resembling an enormous loaf of bread, rises from the sea at an angle of more than 70 degrees to a height of 243m. On the same day in February 1931 that the Mawson expedition visited Scullin Monolith, its small boat was unable to land at this site due to rough seas, so a flag and a proclamation were simply thrown ashore, claiming the area for Britain. Mawson named it for George Murray, chief justice of South Australia and chancellor of the University of Adelaide. More than 20,000 pairs of Adélies occupy the lower slopes.

Lambert Glacier & Amery Ice Shelf

The Lambert Glacier, one of the world's largest glaciers, reaches up to 65km wide and 400km long. The Lambert drains about 8% of the Antarctic ice sheet into **Prydz Bay**. Named in 1957 for Bruce Lambert, Australia's director of National Mapping, it was originally called Baker Three Glacier for the photo reconnaissance aircrew that discovered it during Operation Highjump in 1946–47 (see p155). Eventually the Lambert may need to be renamed as a glacier tongue, as in recent years it was found to be afloat for much of its length; glaciers do not float.

The Amery Ice Shelf is the seaward extension of the Lambert Glacier, and is a source of beautiful jade-green icebergs (see boxed text).

Larsemann Hills

The Larsemann Hills, 11 rocky peninsulas discovered by Norwegian captain Klarius Mikkelsen in 1935, are an ice-free oasis extending 15km from the **Dålk Glacier**. Mikkelsen named the hills after young Lars Jr, son of expedition organizer Lars Christensen. The Larsemanns, which reach a maximum elevation of 160m, contain about 200 fresh and saline lakes, as well as unique species of flora.

BASES

China's **Zhongshan Station**, founded in 1989, accommodates about 60 people in summer and 22 winterovers. A quiet room in Zhongshan features a bust of Sun Yat-sen, first president of the Chinese republic, for whom the station is named. The station's most colorful feature: six large fuel tanks whose ends are painted with brightly colored masks from the Chinese national opera.

Nearby, Romania's first Antarctic base, summer-only **Law-Racoviţă base**, was originally an Australian base named for Phillip Law and established in 1986–87. It was handed over to Romania in February 2006, and the moniker Racoviţă was added

TERRITORIAL CLAIMS

East Antarctica includes regions claimed by Norway, Australia and France (but not recognized by the Antarctic Treaty).

Much of the Norwegian claim, called **Queen Maud Land** (also called by its Norwegian name, Dronning Maud Land) and extending from W 20° to E 45°, was explored by Norwegian whalers. Although exploration was only their second line of work, these whalers discovered much of the Queen Maud Land coast, naming sections for members of the Norwegian royal family.

Australia's claim, the **Australian Antarctic Territory** (AAT), extends from E 45° to E 160°, apart from the thin slice of France's Terre Adélie. Australians, including Mawson, Wilkins and Phillip G Law, explored much of this area, and names reflect many of its discoverers or their patrons.

Terre Adélie, France's Antarctic claim, extends from E 136° to E 142° and is wholly within Australia's claim. This section of the coast is distinguished by its French names.

to commemorate the first Romanian to visit Antarctica, explorer Emil Racoviţă, who was part of the 1897–98 *Belgica* expedition.

Russia's nearby **Progress II base** opened in 1989 and accommodates 77 people in summer, 20 in winter. An earlier Progress I nearby is now abandoned.

In April 2012, India opened **Bharati** station, housing up to 25 people on a promontory near the Broknes Peninsula.

Vestfold Hills

The Vestfold Hills is a 400 sq km oasis of ice-free rock. These hills, 25km across with a maximum elevation of 159m, are especially beautiful when viewed from the air, revealing long, black volcanic dikes striping the bare rock. The first woman to set foot in Antarctica, Caroline Mikkelsen, came ashore here on February 20, 1935 with her husband, Klarius Mikkelsen, captain of the Norwegian whaling support ship *Thorshavn*. The Mikkelsens named the Vestfolds for their home county in Norway, the center of the country's whaling industry.

The Vestfolds are biologically unique, dotted with a series of remarkable lakes, both freshwater and saline. Some of the hypersaline lakes are more than 13 times as salty as seawater, with freezing points as low as -17.5°C. In summer, when the ice on these lakes acts as a lid trapping solar energy absorbed by the saline water, the temperature of the bottom water can reach 35°C. Life in these lakes is highly specialized and rare. In **Deep Lake**, situated in a deep valley with its surface 51m below sea level, only two species have been found, an alga and a bacterium. Because no burrowing organisms disturb the lake-bottom sediment, cores taken here provide an unparalleled record going as far back as 5000 years.

At **Marine Plain**, fossils of whales and dolphins have been found. The area is protected by the Antarctic Treaty.

DAVIS STATION

Named after Captain John King Davis, master of ships used on expeditions led by Shackleton and Mawson, Australia's Davis is a colorful collection of buildings overlooking the sea and numerous islands. Opened in 1957 on the edge of the Vestfold Hills, Davis can accommodate 100 people, but usually there are about 80 in summer and 20 over winter.

During its first years, Davis accommodated very small wintering parties: in some cases, just four or five men stayed through the long polar night. In 1965 Davis was closed temporarily to allow Australia to concentrate its efforts on building Casey Station. It reopened in 1969 and has operated continuously ever since.

Compared to its two Australian sister stations, Mawson and Casey, Davis' climate is relatively mild, thanks to the moderating influence of the Vestfold Hills, which separate the station from the Antarctic ice sheet. Thus Davis' nickname: 'the Riviera of the South.'

Among the rocks near the blue meteorology building is a small **sculpture garden** unique to Antarctica. It was built by a Davis artist-in-residence, Stephen Eastaugh, who in 2002 was inspired by an enigmatic figure, 'Man Sculptured by Antarctica,' carved from wood by Hans, a plumber who overwintered in 1977. Nicknamed 'Fred the Head,' the sculpture is a 30-year-old work-in-progress being changed by Antarctic weather, an artistic counterpoint to the industrial/scientific aesthetic prevalent at most stations. Four small wood and metal sculptures by Eastaugh join Hans' enigmatic head in the sculpture garden.

Mirnyy Observatory

Russia's first station on the continent, located right on the Antarctic Circle, Mirnyy was opened in 1956. The first overwintering party had 92 members, and the station included a pigsty that supplied fresh pork.

Mirnyy (meaning 'peaceful') was named after the ship commanded by Mikhail Petrovich Lazarev on Bellingshausen's expedition. Tourists have visited only a few times.

Mirnyy's 200m main street was once officially called Ulitsa Lenina (Lenin St). On the morning of August 3, 1960, a fire fanned by 200km/h gusts killed eight and destroyed the station's meteorology building. The original station was replaced in 1970–71 and now lies under 2m of ice. In front of Mirnyy lies **Komsomolskaya Hill** (35m), named for the Young Communist League; beneath that, fronting the often-frozen sea, is a 25m ice cliff known as **Pravda Shore**.

Enormous Kharkovchanka tracked over-snow vehicles, used to make the traverse to Vostok 1400km inland, are parked here between trips. Their tracks measure a full meter wide, they sleep eight people in their berths, and their 500-horsepower engines can pull up to 45 tonnes.

NEARBY ISLANDS

A large **emperor penguin rookery** lies among the **Haswell Islands** just offshore. From this rookery in 1997, Swiss wildlife photographer Bruno Zehnder became lost in a whiteout and died of exposure.

Along with the men killed in the 1960 fire and dozens of others who have died at Mirnyy over the years, Zehnder now rests in an imposing **cemetery** on tiny **Buromskiy Island**. Buromskiy, formerly called Godley Island, is named after hydrographer Nicolay Buromskiy, also buried here. He died along with naval engineering student EK Zykov when the ice shelf collapsed during the unloading of *Lena* on February 3, 1957. A tall wooden Russian Orthodox cross on the island's crest has a bronze plaque reading: 'Bow your heads, all who come here. They gave up their lives in the struggle against the austere nature of Antarctica.' The coffins and memorials marking the graves of Russian, Czech, German, Austrian, Ukraine and Swiss members of Soviet and Russian Antarctic expeditions are bolted to the exposed rock because there's no soil. Visiting the cemetery is complicated by the many Adélie penguins nesting on the island.

Bunger Hills

When their discovery was announced to the world in 1946–47, the 952-sq-km Bunger Hills caused a sensation. Because they are an area of ice-free rock, newspaper headlines blared 'Antarctic Shangri-La.' The largest ice-free oasis on the East Antarctic coast, the hills are named for US Navy pilot David Bunger, who landed a seaplane on an unfrozen lake here in 1947 while on a photographic mission for Operation Highjump (p155). Dotted with numerous meltwater ponds, the Bunger Hills are bisected by the 145m-deep, 14-sq-km **Algae Lake**, covered by ice for 10 months annually. The hills reach a maximum elevation of 180m and are surrounded on all sides by 120m walls of ice.

Casey Station

Australia's Casey Station is located in a beautiful area known as the **Windmill Islands**, a group of more than 50 islands teeming with seabirds. It was a replacement station for the US's Wilkes Station, 3km to the north across the bay, which Australia took over in 1959. Wilkes had been built in 1957 for the International Geophysical Year and named for Lieutenant Charles Wilkes.

The original Casey Station, built in 1969, was a radical innovation in Antarctic design. To avoid Wilkes' problem of inundation with snow, it was built on stilts to allow snow to blow through underneath. It also had a long corrugated-iron tunnel on the windward side connecting all the buildings, which were constructed separately as a safety measure against fire. The wind blowing against the tunnel created so much noise that Casey residents who had grown used to it (nicknamed 'tunnel rats') sometimes found it hard to sleep during the rare calm periods. Casey was first known as 'Repstat', – replacement station – but was renamed to honor Australia's then Governor-General, Richard Casey, a staunch supporter

THEY COME FROM OUTTA SPACE *DR RALPH P HARVEY*

One special night in 1969, the world watched with amazement as humanity planted its first steps on the moon, changing forever the point from which we view our planet. As an eight-year-old viewer, I was filled with visions of a future exploring the planets, piloting spacecraft and fighting ferocious aliens.

On a cold summer's day six months later, something nearly as momentous occurred, this time witnessed by only a few Japanese glaciologists. They discovered the first concentration of Antarctic meteorites, nine specimens in all, near East Antarctica's Queen Fabiola Mountains. They had no idea their discovery would prove as important as the Apollo program in opening doors to the exploration of our solar system. Their discovery evolved into a collection of more than 45,000 specimens (as of early 2008) – our only current and continuous source of macroscopic extraterrestrial materials. While the Apollo program ended just three years later, the Antarctic search for meteorites continued to grow. In the end, I did end up exploring other planets – by going to one of the most otherworldly places on Earth and searching for rocks from outer space.

Why Antarctica?

Antarctica is the world's best place to look for meteorites, for two principal reasons. First, if you want to find objects that fall from the sky, spread out a giant white sheet and see what lands on it. Almost any rock you find on the East Antarctic ice sheet had to fall there. Second, a more subtle and dynamic mechanism concentrates meteorites in Antarctica. Meteorites falling randomly across the ice sheet get buried and travel with it as it flows toward the Antarctic coast. The vast majority of these embedded meteorites are lost to the Southern Ocean as the ice sheet calves icebergs. But in a few places, particularly where the ice sheet tries to squeeze through the Transantarctic Mountains, the flow of the ice can be dramatically slowed or stopped. If that happens where the ice is also exposed to the fierce winds of the plateau, massive amounts of ice sublimate, or change directly from solid to vapor. Where sublimation is strong, the loss of ice can be as much as several centimeters per day, producing beautiful deep-blue expanses of old glacial ice. Littered across this ice are meteorites, left behind because they can't evaporate. If we're really lucky, we find a place where this process has gone on for hundreds of thousands of years or more, allowing the meteorites to pile up until there are hundreds in an area the size of a football field.

The most consistent Antarctic meteorite recovery program has been **Antarctic Search for Meteorites** (ANSMET; http://geology.cwru.edu/~ansmet), whose annual expeditions have recovered over 20,000 specimens since 1976. Other nations, particularly Japan, Italy and China, currently support the active recovery of Antarctic meteorites, while several others (Belgium, Germany) joined International Polar Year activities.

Why Meteorites?

Why recover meteorites from anywhere, let alone Antarctica? Meteorites are rare scientific specimens – and outside of Antarctica, only a few are recovered each year. With the exception of a few lunar specimens, meteorites are the only samples we have of the extraterrestrial materials making up our solar system. Some represent the primitive building

of Australia's fledgling Antarctic program through the 1950s and '60s.

The original Casey Station was replaced in the late 1980s when corrosion threatened its metal supports. The current station was built 1km away and completed in 1988. It accommodates 88 people in summer and 19 in winter. The old Casey Station was dismantled from 1991 to 1993 and returned to Australia; today all that remains are drill holes in the rock where its supports once stood.

Landings are made at the **Casey wharf**, linked to the station by a 1.5km road. Visitors are likely to see the **Red Shed**, which provides kitchen, dining, recreation and living quarters, as well as a hospital and medical suite. Artifacts from the early days of the station and its predecessor, Wilkes, are on display here.

blocks from which our solar system formed, and are essentially unchanged since its birth 4.56 billion years ago. Others represent fragments of small planetary bodies broken up by impacts, providing samples from their deep interior. Still others are samples of intermediate planetoids with active and alien geological processes. A very small set of meteorites are pieces of the moon and Mars, knocked loose by giant impacts and sent on a collision course with Earth. Among these is the now-famous ALH84001 meteorite, a Martian sample within which some NASA researchers have suggested may be traces of ancient biological activity on Mars.

Like all Antarctic specimens, meteorites are collected only for scientific purposes and are protected by the Antarctic Treaty.

Life of a Meteor Hunter

The life of a meteorite hunter is scenic, cold and a little lonely. We camp near blue-ice areas on the margins of the high-altitude polar plateau, sometimes with little to see but ice and snow. Many of these areas are literally off the map, and we give them colorful, unofficial names such as Footrot Flats and Mare Meteoriticus. We live in double-walled Scott tents, depending on the round-the-clock sunshine to keep warm in temperatures as low as -40°C and winds that can blow at 60km/h for weeks. Most volunteers tolerate these conditions as a modest price for the privilege of being the first to see a visitor from space.

Far out on the ice sheet, we cruise slowly across the ice on snowmobiles and spot even the smallest speck. At sites closer to the Transantarctic Mountains, glacial moraines or fierce winds may carry in some earth rocks, so we walk or even crawl, sorting out the meteorites from what we call the 'meteorongs' and 'leaveorite' (leave 'er right there) specimens.

The Treasure

The quarry we hunt is rarely as glamorous or beautiful as the meteorites in museums. The average find is about 10g and smaller than a golf ball. They range from unweathered specimens still dressed in the glossy-black fusion crust they acquired during their fiery plunge through the atmosphere, to crumbling, rusty-grey fragments nearly indistinguishable from road gravel. To the meteorite hunter, of course, all meteorites are beautiful.

But there are too many specimens for sentimentality, so they get mundane names such as EET96538. In a typical season we recover between a few hundred and a thousand specimens, each one bagged quickly, cleanly and efficiently with sterile tongs to avoid contamination (and frozen fingers).

The specimens are shipped, still frozen, to the Johnson Space Center (JSC) in Houston, Texas for initial characterization and curation. Scientists knock off a few chips, look for minerals or textures that help define the kind of meteorite it is, and write up an initial description. Twice a year, the JSC lab issues the *Antarctic Meteorite* newsletter, detailing recently recovered specimens and offering samples to interested researchers worldwide. Sharing the 'treasure' this way has made ANSMET expeditions a unique example of cooperation in science, worthy of the international spirit shown by so many Antarctic endeavors.

Dr Ralph P Harvey has spent 25 seasons in Antarctica as the principal investigator of the Antarctic Search for Meteorites program.

A long-standing Casey tradition is the Saturday night candlelight dinner, when expeditioners dress up and enjoy a fine meal. The station **bar**, Splinters, has a pool table and dart board and serves home-brewed beer.

A large emperor penguin colony was sighted in late 1994 among the maze of icebergs grounded on offshore **Petersen Bank**. Despite more than 40 years of operations, including helicopter overflights during station resupply, Petersen Bank is so large that the penguins had never been seen before.

Australia achieved a long-desired goal when a long-range Airbus A319 left Hobart on December 9, 2007 and landed at the 4km **Wilkins Ice Runway** 70km southeast of Casey. The A$46.3 million air link supplements the Australian ship *Aurora Australis* by moving personnel and cargo to Antarctica quickly. The runway moves about 12m southwest annually as the glacier moves.

Dumont d'Urville Station

Colloquially known as 'Du-d'U' (doo-doo), France's Dumont d'Urville Station is located at a beautiful site on **Petrel Island**, overlooking the **Géologie Archipelago**. It is named for Dumont d'Urville, who is honored with a bust on station grounds.

A long curving boardwalk connects the landing jetty to the station. Dumont d'Urville was built in 1956 to replace Port Martín Station, 60km to the east, which burned down (without injuring anyone) in 1952, just two years after it opened.

The station's original accommodation building is preserved as a small **museum**. It has been restored with authentic radio equipment and portraits of the eight men who first overwintered here in 1953 in what had previously been a small field station called Base Marret.

Dumont d'Urville accommodates 36 winterers, 120 summer personnel and a host of Adélies which nest throughout the station, beneath and around the buildings. Emperor penguins from a nearby **rookery** were the subject for Luc Jacquet's 2005 hit *La marche de l'empereur* (March of the Penguins). A two-man film crew lived at the station for a year.

Antarctica's highest wind velocity, 327km/h, was recorded here in July 1972 – but even that isn't the world record. New Hampshire's Mt Washington recorded a gust of 372km/h in 1934.

In front of the station is Dumont d'Urville's **airstrip**, with abandoned equipment and vehicles, a control tower and a hangar. It was the focus of international attention in 1983 when construction began on what was planned to be a 1100m crushed-rock runway. Lion Island and two adjacent islets were dynamited to flatten them and provide material to fill in the sea between them. Greenpeace obtained photos of penguins killed by rock shrapnel. In early 1993 the airstrip was completed, at a cost of 110 million francs, but in January 1994 the nearby **Astrolabe Glacier** calved, causing an enormous wave that destroyed a building. In 1996 the government decided not to use the airstrip.

Commonwealth Bay & Cape Denison

Douglas Mawson's Australasian Antarctic Expedition (p151) was based at Commonwealth Bay (named by Mawson for the Commonwealth of Australia) from 1912 to 1914. Nearby Cape Denison commemorates one of the expedition's main supporters, Hugh Denison.

Already a veteran of Shackleton's *Nimrod* expedition, Mawson wanted to explore new territory west of Cape Adare. Mawson set up his base at Cape Denison, unaware that the roaring katabatics make the spot one of the windiest places on Earth. Eight men led by Frank Wild, another veteran of the *Nimrod* expedition, were landed at the Shackleton Ice Shelf, 2400km west of Cape Denison.

Battling wind speeds that occasionally reached more than 320km/h at Commonwealth Bay, the *Aurora* expedition systematically explored King George V Land, as well as neighboring Terre Adélie, during the summer of 1912–13. On one sledging trip the first Antarctic meteorite was found. The expedition also made the first radio contact between Antarctica and another continent, on September 25, 1912, using a wireless relay at a five-man station the expedition had established on Macquarie Island.

Despite those accomplishments and the comprehensive research done by the expedition, it is remembered primarily for the ordeal Mawson endured on a deadly dog-sledging journey. With British soldier Belgrave Ninnis and Swiss mountaineer and ski champion Xavier Mertz, Mawson left Cape Denison on November 10, 1912, to explore eastward. By December 14, after crossing two heavily crevassed glaciers (later named for Mertz and Ninnis), they had traveled 500km from their base. That afternoon, Ninnis disappeared down an apparently bottomless crevasse with his dog team, most of the party's food, all of the dog food and the tent. 'It seemed so incredible,' Mawson wrote later, 'that we half expected, on turning round, to find him standing there.'

They immediately began a harrowing trek home. Battling hunger, cold, fatigue and, possibly, vitamin A poisoning from the dog livers they were forced to eat, Mawson and Mertz struggled on. Mertz died on January 7, when they were still more than 160km out. Mawson sawed the remaining sledge in half with a pocketknife to lighten his load.

By now his body was literally coming apart: hair falling out, toenails loosened, even the thick soles of his feet sloughing off. Somehow he reached Cape Denison – a few hours after *Aurora* had sailed.

Six men remained hoping that the missing party might return. Although they radioed the ship, heavy seas prevented *Aurora* from reaching Cape Denison. They were forced to spend another winter, arriving home in Australia in late February, 1914.

From January 1995 to January 1996, Australians Don and Margie McIntyre wintered at Cape Denison, the first people to do so since Mawson. They lived in a 2.4m by 3.6m cabin they built; it has been removed.

The same furious katabatics that caused Mawson to call this the 'Home of the Blizzard' often make landing here impossible. They also make conservation of Mawson's huts much more difficult than it is for the historic buildings on Ross Island. In 2007 a small laboratory was built to help conserve the site's artifacts. Areas between the Main Hut and Boat Harbor where artifacts (building materials, domestic and scientific equipment, food, packaging, clothing and other historic detritus) are scattered on the ground and are off-limits to tourists. No more than 20 people at once may come ashore here.

Sights

Main Hut HISTORIC HUT

Mawson intended to have two separate huts, one housing 12 men, the other six. But it was decided instead to join the two, creating an accommodation area and a workshop. The larger building, about 53 sq m, was surrounded on three sides by a veranda, which held stores, food and biology equipment. Mawson's room, a darkroom and the cook's table and stove encircled a central dining table. Bunks were placed along the perimeter. A door on the northern side of the larger building connected to the 30-sq-m **workshop**.

Lighting consisted of acetylene lamps and skylights. Winter snowdrifts kept the quarters at a frosty 4°C to 10°C.

The entrance to the whole complex was through a 'cold porch' on the western veranda, with the door facing north to avoid the furious southern winds. The western veranda also contained a meat cellar, a roof door for entrance in winter and a latrine. Dogs were kenneled on the eastern veranda.

EXPLOSIVES WARNING

Explosives left over from Mawson's expedition lie approximately 50m southwest (or inland) of the Main Hut. Keep away.

Magnetograph House & Magnetic Absolute Hut HISTORIC HUT

Cape Denison's location close to the **South Magnetic Pole** makes it an ideal place to observe Earth's magnetic field. Magnetograph House and Magnetic Absolute Hut, northeast of the Main Hut, were where this work was conducted. A stone wall built on its windward side protected the magnetograph house, the best-preserved building at Cape Denison.

Transit Hut HISTORIC HUT

East of the Main Hut, this building was used as shelter while star-sighting to determine Cape Denison's exact position.

Memorial Cross LANDMARK

Erected in November 1913, this memorial atop **Azimuth Hill**, northwest of the Main Hut, pays tribute to Xavier Mertz and Belgrave Ninnis.

Leningradskaya Station

Perched atop the 304m Leningradsky nunatak behind a 220m seacliff, Leningradskaya opened in 1971. Resupplying the station was always difficult, however, because of heavy pack ice. Even icebreakers were sometimes trapped for months, so the station closed in 1991. The first tourists came by helicopter only in February 2002. Rusting machinery, old engines, empty fuel barrels and other litter in the rocky area around the base give it a junkyard feel.

Concordia Station & Dome Charlie (Dome C)

Well-named Concordia Station is a joint effort by France and Italy, which in 1993 agreed to build a new permanent Antarctic research station at a cost of €31 million. Construction began in 1998–99, and the station opened in 2005, when 12 men and one woman wintered over.

SUBGLACIAL LAKES *MARTIN J SIEGERT*

Subglacial lakes sit at the base of large ice sheets and remain liquid (as opposed to Antarctica's frozen lakes). The lakes occur due to geothermal heating from the earth, the insulating effect of the overriding ice, and the enormous pressure of the ice overburden (thought to be between 300 and 400 atmospheres, which allows the ice to melt at around -3°C). Meltwater collects in hollows, forming the lakes.

Subglacial lakes were discovered in the late 1960s and 1970s by British glaciologists using ice-penetrating radar. Over 150 subglacial lakes have been identified, most of which are about 3km to 5km in length. At Dome C, so many subglacial lakes have been discovered that it has been named the Antarctic 'Lake District.'

How water moves beneath the ice is of vital interest to scientists studying the flow of ice above, and how it varies when climate changes. Consequently, scientists were intrigued when, in 2006, satellite observations of the ice surface revealed a sudden drop in elevation over one of the Lake District's lakes, and a simultaneous rise above at least two other lakes located some 250km away. Calculations reveal that this was due to an 'outburst' of lake water, which flowed at a rate equivalent to the Thames in London for around 14 months. Hence, we now believe many subglacial lakes are connected, and that periodic discharges occur between them.

Exploring the Lakes

To identify life in the lakes, sterile equipment is necessary to protect the lake from contamination – and to ensure the experiment is not compromised. This is easier said than done, because the technology currently used to drill down through the ice sheet uses contaminants such as kerosene to keep the drill hole from freezing shut.

NASA is also interested in solving this problem, since its planned exploration of Europa, one of the moons of Jupiter, will present similar technical hurdles. Europa's several-kilometers-thick ice crust covers a liquid ocean which some scientists suspect may harbor life.

Lake Vostok was the first subglacial lake to be tapped in 2011–12.

A team from the US and Britain (www.ellsworth.org.uk) will deploy new drilling/probing technologies in 2012–13 at Lake Ellsworth, in West Antarctica. Tapping the lake will involve hot-water drilling and the insertion of a robotic probe with sampling instruments. The probe will connect to the surface with a power cable; and everything is designed to keep the lake and samples uncontaminated. See http://salegos-scar.montana.edu/for more information.

Martin J Siegert is Professor of Geosciences at the University of Edinburgh

Concordia is located at **Dome C**, formally known as Dome Charlie, a massive ice dome in Wilkes Land's vast snow plateau. As at many inland stations, low temperatures recorded here are impressive, frequently dropping below -80°C. Concordia is resupplied by regular flights and a thrice-yearly truck traverse from Dumont d'Urville, a 20-day, 2400km round trip.

Concordia consists of twin white cylindrical buildings, each with 36 faces and three stories. The galvanized steel-frame buildings, connected by an enclosed walkway about 10m long, contain 1500 sq m of living space. A third building houses a wastewater treatment plant, power plant and another workshop. Concordia's cylindrical buildings can each be raised periodically with six hydraulic jacks to avoid snow accumulation. Station activities are separated by building: the 'noisy' one includes the kitchen, dining room and workshop; the 'quiet' one has labs, bedrooms, a library, a hospital and a gym. Concordia has an extensive 'summer camp' of tents that provide additional accommodation.

Concordia accommodates an international team of as many as 16 people: nine scientists, five technicians, a cook and a doctor, with double that many Concordians during the month-long annual changeover. The station is considered by many to enjoy Antarctica's best cuisine, with fine wines and seven-course lunches on Sundays.

One of the deepest ice cores drilled so far – 3190m – came from Dome C and spans at least 740,000 years and maybe up to 940,000 years (see p199 for more on ice cores).

Lake Concordia, 50km long and 30km wide, lies beneath 4150m of ice about 100km north of Dome C. It is Antarctica's second-largest subglacial lake, after Lake Vostok.

Vostok Station

An outpost if ever there was one, Russia's awe-inspiring Vostok Station is located near the **South Geomagnetic Pole** (one of four poles defined by geomagneticians; see p134). Built in 1957 on ice that is 3.7km thick, the station is named for one of Bellingshausen's two ships, *Vostok* (East). It's the site of the **lowest temperature recorded on Earth**: -89.2°C on July 21, 1983. Vostok's record *high* temperature, set in 2002, is -12.3°C. Its first wintering crew gave Vostok its enduring nickname: 'the Pole of Cold.'

Vostok accommodates 30 people in summer, 18 in winter. No tourists (except members of an international expedition in 1989–90) have ever visited Vostok.

Vostok's most visible landmark is the 10m-tall **drilling tower** covered in reddish sheet metal. Ice-core researchers from several nations operate here throughout the summer, and in 1998 they extracted the deepest ice core ever recovered, reaching a depth of 3623m. These cores contain data about Earth's climate over the past 420,000 years and are invaluable for understanding climate trends.

As a result of its drilling program, Vostok also safeguards one of the world's most important repositories: the **Vostok Ice Core Vaults**. Two of the vaults sit at the snow's surface and three more lie beneath the snow; they all remain at a constant -55°C. Together they contain hundreds of 3m-long, 10cm-diameter ice cores that have been painstakingly extracted from the ice sheet since the 1990s. Stored in heavy cardboard tubes lining the walls of the vaults, the ice cores vary in appearance according to age. In 'younger' cores (less than 50,000 years old), air bubbles make the ice appear white. The oldest (and therefore deepest) cores have a rare, transparent beauty like pure crystal.

Most of Vostok's original buildings are nearly completely drifted-over; some lie buried under as much as 10m of snow. Nevertheless, many remain accessible, including a storeroom holding 1000 16mm movies.

Vostok was closed in 1962–63 for financial reasons, but it has been open almost continuously since then. From 1957 to 1995 Vostok was resupplied by tractor-train expeditions that took a month to travel the 1400km from Mirnyy on the coast. Now the US resupplies the station with Hercules flights in exchange for a share of the ice cores.

LAKE VOSTOK

By chance, the station sits atop the southern end of the enormous subglacial Lake Vostok, to which it gave its name. It was not until the late 1960s and early 1970s that echo sounding through the ice revealed the lake beneath the station. About the size of Lake Ontario, Lake Vostok is much larger than any other subglacial lake – in fact, it's one of the 10 largest lakes on Earth. It is 50km wide, and extends in a crescent shape more than 240km north from Vostok Station.

Lake Vostok is also deep, the discovery of which attracted huge scientific and media interest in the early '90s. The lake's depth has yet to be evaluated accurately, but data suggests that it is around 510m deep at the lake's southern end. The volume of water in Lake Vostok is in the order of several thousand cubic kilometers.

In January 2012 a Russian team that had been drilling for over 20 years tapped the surface of the lake, at an ice core depth of 3769.3 m. They let the lake water freeze in the plug hole and will return in the 2012–13 season to take more samples. This was the first time a subglacial lake had been breached.

Lake Vostok is possibly 20 million years old, and some scientists think its trough formed well before the ice sheets covered Antarctica. This may limit the possibility of hydrothermal activity, which would be beneficial to any organisms that might live in the lake. The lake's water, melted from the underside of the ice sheet, is probably around one million years old, which effectively marks the last time the lake was in contact with the atmosphere.

No one expects fish or other large creatures to live in Lake Vostok, but biologists do think they will find unique microbes. For life to exist in Lake Vostok it must endure permanent darkness, pressures around 350 atmospheres and temperatures below 0°C. This means that the life form must use chemicals to power biological processes. These organisms would have developed in complete isolation from the outside world

VOSTOK'S WINTEROVERS: VOSTOCHNIKI

Those who winter at Vostok, who are called 'Vostochniki,' are respected throughout Antarctica for their ability to endure not only Vostok's extreme cold, but also the lack of creature comforts at the spartan station. In the Antarctic lexicon, Vostok is a synonym for privation. It's a place where, as the BBC once said, 'science takes second place to survival.'

Newcomers gasp for breath at Vostok because, although the station sits at an elevation of 3488m, the low pressure of the atmosphere makes it feel like 5000m. Vostok's air contains just 60% of the oxygen in the air at sea level. Thanks to its elevation, Vostok is colder than the South Pole.

Even cooking is difficult at Vostok. Because of the altitude, water boils at 86°C instead of 100°C, so it takes three hours to boil potatoes, and up to 14 to cook beans and peas. Crackers, however, never go stale in the extremely dry air.

Amazing Heroics

Vostochniki manage with a remarkable stoicism that borders on the heroic. During the 1992 resupply traverse, one man underwent an emergency appendectomy with only a local anesthetic.

In April 1982 catastrophe struck when a fire destroyed the station's power plant, killing one man and nearly dooming the rest. The 20 survivors were left in the dark of winter, without electricity. For two weeks, they worked desperately to restore any power or light, which they eventually managed to do by digging an old diesel generator up from the snow and making it operational. From April until November the men crowded together in a single hut. During those eight months of winter their only heat came from candlelike warmers they made by twisting asbestos fibers into wicks that they dipped in diesel fuel.

The Vostochniki declined to call for help, knowing that a rescue attempt would endanger others. Most extraordinarily, they kept on working. Not content merely to survive, they carried on their normal station routine, taking measurements of the night sky, recording weather data, and operating the ice-coring drill.

for as long as one million years, and there is thus strong opinion that Lake Vostok must not be polluted. The means by which Lake Vostok is sampled will involve technological challenges (see boxed text p122).

Another hypothesis is that a complete record of ice-sheet history is available from the layer of sediments (probably tens of meters deep, possibly hundreds of meters deep) that lie across the lake floor.

Dome Argus (Dome A)

At 4093m above sea level, Dome A is the highest point of the Antarctic Plateau. Officially, it is named 'Dome Argus' after the mythological Greek shipbuilder.

Dome A is more than 1000km from the coast in all directions. It sits atop East Antarctica's relatively broad, flat plateau, which creates some of the world's strongest temperature inversion conditions. The heat lost at the ice surface due to radiative cooling must be replaced by heat from the overlying near-surface atmosphere; therefore, the air at Dome A's surface becomes extremely cold. Dome A's very calm air conditions also play a role in making this area so cold, since the strongest inversions form in environments with the weakest winds. Because it is so much higher than Vostok (3448m), meteorologists expect that Dome A may soon break Vostok's record for the lowest temperature ever recorded on Earth.

PLATO & KUNLUN STATION

Dome A was first visited in January 2005, by a Chinese team that installed an automatic weather station. In early 2008 a six-tractor caravan left China's Zhongshan Station, covering the 1300km traverse to Dome A in three weeks to set up the **Plateau Observatory** (PLATO). This automated facility is designed to take advantage of what many scientists consider to be the best site on Earth for astronomy. Dome A's high elevation, very low humidity and near absence of wind mean that PLATO's telescopes (from Australia, China, the US and the UK) operate in conditions usually found only in airborne or orbiting telescopes. PLATO is powered by solar panels in summer and six small diesel engines in winter. It transmits data via Iridium satellites. In 2012 China installed Antarctica's largest unmanned optical telescope, the AST3-1 (see p200 for more details).

In 2009 China opened its third Antarctic outpost, **Kunlun Station**, at Dome A. Astronomy is a major focus, but the ice beneath Dome A is 3130m thick and possibly as old as 1.2 million years at the bottom, so China plans to extract ice cores. Because of Dome A's extreme cold, and the difficulty in reaching and supporting it, the station currently operates for summer only, and can host 25 people. In the next decade facilities may be added that will allow it to remain open in winter.

SOUTH POLE

'Polies,' the residents of the US scientific research station here, like to boast that S 90° is a 'latitude with attitude.' Indeed, it is a near-mythical location, a place of extremes (high altitude, intense cold and very low humidity) where the blinding sun remains above the horizon for months at a time, then plunges beneath it for an equivalent period of darkness.

Known to Polies simply as 'Pole,' the South Pole was, just a few decades ago, off-limits to all but the US government program's scientists and support personnel. The only exceptions were a small number of other countries' government-sponsored expeditions that traversed over the plateau from the coast, and well-financed adventurers who passed through on private expeditions to cross the continent by ski or dog team. Today, 'ordinary' tourists can make the trip, though the cost is significant and not many stay more than a few hours.

History

SCOTT'S DISCOVERY EXPEDITION

Captain Robert Falcon Scott's *Discovery* expedition of 1901–04 (see p147) was the first to set off with the explicit goal of reaching the Pole, and to have a reasonable chance of doing so. After establishing a base at Ross Island with a large supporting party, Scott and two fellow Britons, Edward Wilson and Ernest Shackleton, set off on what they hoped would be the final push to the Pole.

Despite initial optimism and a large food depot laid by an advance party, the trio soon struck harsh reality, Antarctica-style. The men had never tried skiing or sled-dog driving, and their inexperience produced poor results. Through sheer willpower, they reached S 82°16´30˝ on December 30 before turning back (more than 725km from the Pole). Actually, Scott and Wilson reached that point, with Shackleton having been ordered to remain at camp to look after the dogs. This may not have been an intentional slight on Scott's part, but Shackleton smarted at the gesture.

The trip home was miserable. The remaining dogs were nearly worthless, and soon were hitched *behind* the sledge, which the men pulled themselves. On at least one occasion, a dog was carried *on* the sledge. As dogs weakened, they were shot and fed to the others. The men were also breaking down. Shackleton suffered badly from scurvy (but accounts that say he had to be carried on the sledge are incorrect).

SHACKLETON'S NIMROD EXPEDITION

Shackleton tried again in 1908. His *Nimrod* expedition was a close scrape with death, part of an emerging pattern for South Polar exploration. Shackleton and Eric Marshall, Jameson Adams and Frank Wild pioneered the route up to the polar plateau (which he claimed, and named, for King Edward VII) via the Beardmore Glacier, named for the expedition's patron.

By January 9, 1909, the foursome had trudged to within 180km of the Pole before being forced to turn back by dangerously dwindling food supplies. It was the hardest decision of Shackleton's life. He told his wife Emily later: 'I thought you'd rather have a live donkey than a dead lion.' The men returned to their base at Ross Island in extremely poor condition and with all their supplies exhausted.

Still, they had achieved a remarkable run, beating Scott's furthest south by 589km, discovering almost 800km of new mountain range, and showing the way to anyone attempting the Pole after them. They also found coal and fossils at Mt Buckley at the top of the Beardmore Glacier.

It was generally believed that the next expedition to tackle the Pole, strengthened by the knowledge gained from previous attempts, would most likely reach it.

FURTHEST SOUTH

The following notes describe successive penetrations leading up to Roald Amundsen's attainment of the Pole in December 1911, as well as subsequent landmark accomplishments.

1603 Gabriel de Castilla (Spain), aboard *Nuestra Señora de la Merced*, probably penetrated to S 64° in the Southern Ocean south of Drake Passage. Subsequently, several vessels reported being blown south of S 60° rounding Cape Horn in severe weather.

1773 James Cook (UK), with HMS *Resolution* and HMS *Adventure*, crossed the Antarctic Circle (S 66°33') off Enderby Land on January 17, and later reached a furthest south of S 71°10' off Marie Byrd Land on December 30, 1774.

1842 James Clark Ross (UK) with HMS *Erebus* and HMS *Terror*, reached S 78°10' in the Ross Sea on February 23.

1900 Hugh Evans (UK) and three others from *Southern Cross* sledged to S 78°50' on the Ross Ice Shelf on February 23. This was the first southern penetration by land.

1902 Robert Scott (UK) and two others sledged to S 82°17', near the foot of the Beardmore Glacier, on December 30.

1909 Ernest Shackleton (UK) and three others sledged up the Beardmore Glacier to S 88°23' on January 9.

1911 Roald Amundsen (Norway) and four others dog-sledged to S 90° on December 14.

1912 Robert Scott and four others sledged to S 90° on January 17.

1929 Richard Byrd (USA) and crew claimed to have flown over the Pole on November 29, but the navigation has been questioned. On February 15, 1947, Byrd definitely flew over it.

1956 John Torbert (USA) and six others flew across Antarctica via the South Pole (Ross Island to Weddell Sea and back, without landing) on January 13. On October 31, Conrad Shinn (USA), with an aircraft crew, landed at the South Pole to set up a base.

1958 Three modified Ferguson farm tractors, outfitted with rubber tracks, were the first motor vehicles to reach the Pole overland, on January 4, 1958, led by New Zealander Edmund Hillary of Mt Everest fame. Hillary's team was laying depots for the first successful crossing of the continent, by British explorer Vivian Fuchs' Commonwealth Trans-Antarctic Expedition. Fuchs and party reached the Pole by motor vehicles and dog sledges on January 20, and continued across Antarctica (from the Weddell Sea to the Ross Sea).

Private Expeditions

Many private expeditions have accomplished 'firsts' – some of them quite spectacular – and often pass through the South Pole. Traverses to the interior are now commonplace because private air transportation to the Antarctic has become routine.

Adventure tourism is an area of controversy. The official US government position on private expeditions is to refuse them any support, although they no longer get the chilly brush-off that once decreed that station members were not even to speak to such arriving 'guests.' The centenary of Amundsen's attainment of the Pole saw many private expeditions traipsing through.

ROALD AMUNDSEN

Roald Amundsen (p149) was a polar technician. His approach was slow, methodical and proven. He carried spare food, extra fuel and backups for all essential equipment. The team used skis and brought dogs to do the heavy pulling, saving the men's strength. He also pragmatically calculated the worn-out dogs as food for the others.

Leaving their base at the Bay of Whales on October 19, 1911, Amundsen and Olav Bjaaland, Helmer Hanssen, Sverre Hassel and Oscar Wisting set out on skis with four sledges, each pulled by 13 Greenland dogs.

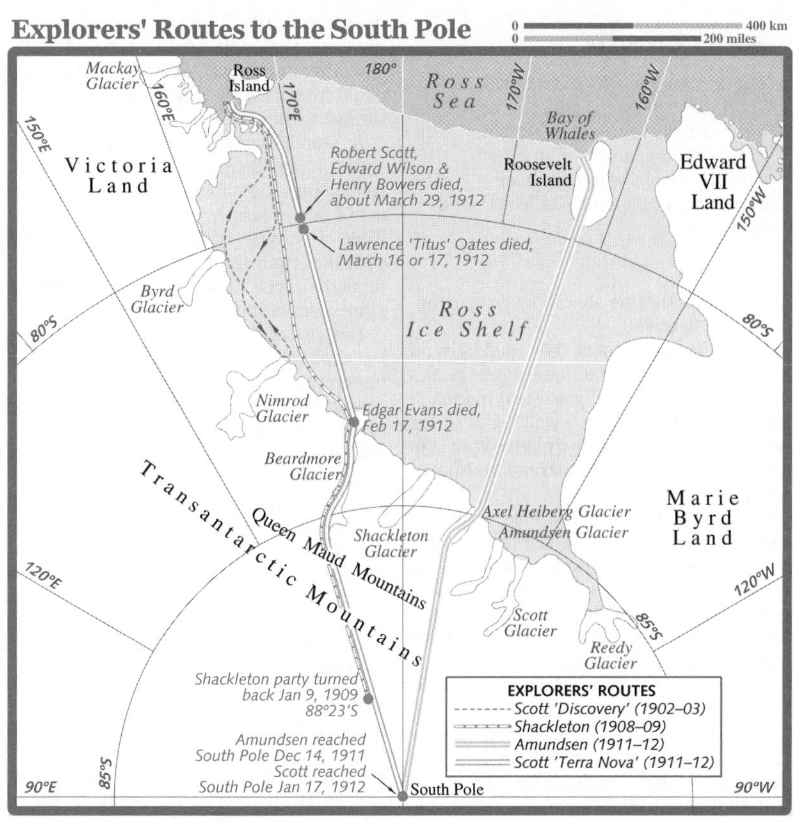

As Norwegians, they were well trained in the use of skis, and during his Arctic years Amundsen had developed excellent dog-driving skills. This served them well.

The five men climbed (and named) Axel Heiberg Glacier to the polar plateau and reached the South Pole on December 14, 1911. They camped in a dark green tent for three days at what they called *Polheim* and made weather observations and precisely calculated their position. Amundsen claimed the polar plateau for Norway, naming it King Haakon VII Land, and wrote a note for Scott that he left in the tent. Then, they turned for home, triumphant.

In contrast to Scott's desperate race against starvation just a month later, the Norwegians' return trip from 90°S to their coastal base seems little more than a bracing ski trek. 'On January 25, at 4am,' Amundsen laconically recorded in his diary, 'we reached our good little house again, with two sledges and 11 dogs; men and animals all hale and hearty.'

Amundsen's polar camp remains buried under the annual accumulations of snow, and by now should be about 12m below the snow surface. In 1993 a Norwegian group came to the Pole with hopes of recovering the tent, Norwegian flag and sledge for display at the 1994 Winter Olympics in Lillehammer. They gave up when one of the members fell 40m down a crevasse and was killed. The huts Amundsen left at his camp on the Ross Ice Shelf at the Bay of Whales disappeared long ago as pieces of the ice shelf calved and floated out to sea.

SCOTT'S TERRA NOVA EXPEDITION

With his renewed, detailed preparations and excellent financial support, Scott felt justifiably confident when he set sail for the south in 1910, on his *Terra Nova* expedition (p151). Unfortunately, as had Shackleton, Scott concluded from his earlier ill-fated attempts at

SCOTT ON FILM

The documentary *90° South: With Scott to the Antarctic* (1933) is 'camera-artist' Herbert Ponting's tribute to his lost companions, with superb cinematography of wildlife and the expedition's daily activities, all narrated by Ponting.

dog sledging that he should investigate another way to travel.

While laying depots he tried several methods including motor-sledges, ponies and dogs, but eventually selected manhauling. This brutal exercise – walking or skiing while pulling sledges heavily laden with supplies – is among the most strenuous human activities.

For the final push to the Pole, Scott had chosen a companion from his previous journey furthest south, Edward Wilson, along with Lawrence Oates and Edgar Evans. Henry Bowers was added only the night before – a tactical error, since the food, tent and skis had been planned for a four-man team.

What ensued is, perhaps, the most famous Antarctic story of all. The five exhausted men arrived at the Pole on January 17, 1912, to find that Amundsen had beat them by 35 days. Amundsen's dark-green tent, topped with the Norwegian flag, made that painfully clear. The grim photo Scott's party snapped of themselves tells it all: hollow-eyed despair darkens their faces.

Their return home was a haunting, desperate run of barely sighted depots, slow starvation, willing annihilation and incredible cold. A delirious Evans died on February 17. A month later, just before his 32nd birthday, his feet badly frostbitten and slowing the group's progress, Captain Lawrence 'Titus' Oates was in such bad shape that he prayed not to wake. The next morning, deeply disappointed to find himself among the living, Oates walked out of the tent in a raging blizzard, telling his companions, 'I am just going outside and may be some time.' They never saw him again.

Just two days later, from March 21 onwards, another blizzard pinned the survivors down – just 18km from a major cache of provisions they called One Ton Depot. They remained in their tent for 10 days, their supplies gradually dwindling to a single sputtering lamp. By its light, Scott scrawled his immortal words: 'It seems a pity, but I do not think I can write more... For God's sake, look after our people.' Scott's last entry was dated March 29. It is not known who was the last to die.

A search party sent out the following spring found them on November 12, 1912. Among the effects found in the tent with the men's bodies was Amundsen's letter to the King of Norway which Scott had brought with him from the Pole, as Amundsen had requested. Scott thus confirmed Amundsen's attainment of the Pole.

Despite being beaten to 90° South, Scott's last expedition accomplished a great deal of important science. In fact, the push to accomplish research had itself contributed to the polar party's destruction: the men dragged a sledge carrying among other items, 16kg of geological samples (ie rocks).

The search party buried the tent beneath a snow cairn. Because of the accumulating snowfall on the ice cap as it advances toward the sea, the bodies of Scott, Wilson, Bowers and their tent will eventually reach the sea through the *bottom* of the Ross Ice Shelf, making it extremely unlikely that they will be spotted by anyone.

FLIGHT OVER POLE

In 1929, American Richard E Byrd (p154) reported flying over the Pole with Bernt Balchen (chief pilot), Harold June (second pilot and radio operator) and Ashley McKinley (photo surveyor). They flew up the Liv Glacier to the polar plateau but due to the cold, thin air the plane was unable to climb, forcing the men to ditch 110kg of emergency rations. Balchen, an experienced Arctic pilot, gained a little more altitude by throwing the aircraft into a hard turn toward the towering rock face on his right and catching an updraft. It was a further suspense-filled four hours to the Pole; they arrived at 1:14am on November 29, 1929. Byrd dropped a rock wrapped in the American flag out the window of his Ford Trimotor plane *Floyd Bennett* and flew back to his camp at Little America. Although the navigation of Byrd's flight has been questioned, it is certain that Byrd was among the six men in two aircraft who flew over 90°S on February 15, 1947.

On neither of his flights did Byrd land, however, meaning that after Amundsen and Scott, the Pole lay untouched for another 44 years.

BIRTH OF A STATION

On October 31, 1956 an American ski-equipped plane set down on the ice, making it the first aircraft to land at the Pole. Pilot Conrad 'Gus' Shinn landed his Navy R4D (the military version of a DC-3) named *Que Sera Sera,* along with Admiral George Dufek and five other US Navy men who surveyed the area for a permanent scientific base.

Construction by the US Navy began the next month, and the first South Pole station was completed in February 1957. A group of 18 men under the co-leadership of scientist Paul Siple and naval officer Lieutenant John Tuck (joined by a malamute-husky named Bravo) spent the first winter at the South Pole, proving it was possible to survive a winter and measuring a low temperature of -74.5°C, at that time the coldest temperature ever recorded on Earth. They also studied the weather, atmosphere and seismology at the Pole. The station has operated continuously ever since.

Although no one owns the South Pole, and the Antarctic Treaty sets aside territorial claims made by seven countries, the US Amundsen-Scott South Pole Station sits astride all the lines of longitude, neatly occupying all time zones – and six of the seven Antarctic claims – at once.

FIRST WOMEN

The first women joined the US Antarctic Program in 1969, and the first women to reach the Pole arrived by US Navy aircraft on November 11 that year. The six of them – not wishing for one to later claim she had been first out of the aircraft – linked arms and walked out the back of the plane together. They spent a few hours visiting the station before flying back to McMurdo. Another two years passed before the first woman actually spent a 'night' at the Pole, in December 1971. Louise Hutchinson, a reporter for the *Chicago Tribune,* got to stay because weather delayed her flight out. Two years later, two American women, Nan Scott and Donna Muchmore, became the first women to work at the Pole. By 1979 the station had a female physician, Dr Michele Eileen Raney, the first woman to winter at S 90°. On January 6, 1995, Norwegian Liv Arnesen arrived at the Pole after skiing unaccompanied from the edge of the continent in 50 days, the first woman to accomplish the feat. In 2012, Felicity Aston was the first woman to ski across the whole continent alone.

FIRST TOURISTS

Tourists first arrived in 1968, when a chartered Convair flew over both poles from November 22 to December 3. The South Polar leg left Christchurch, landed at McMurdo Sound, then flew over the Pole at a low altitude and on to Argentina. The first tourist flight to land at the Pole was on January 11, 1988, when a pair of DHC-6 Twin Otters operated by Adventure Network International brought the first 15 paying passengers to 90°S – for a cool US$25,000 or US$35,000 each. The seven tourists who wished to be in the first plane, which landed 15 minutes before the other, paid the higher price.

Geography

Unlike its northern conjugate, which sits in the middle of the Arctic Ocean, the South Pole lies amid a mind-bending expanse of flat snow-covered ice called the **polar plateau**. All that lives here are a kind of algae and a bacterium that were both probably blown in from elsewhere. Just a handful of other animals have ever visited: huskies, hamsters used as experiment subjects, and skuas (that may actually deliberately cross the continent). Other critters (all invertebrates) have arrived accidentally in crates of vegetables, but even people survive here only with vast expenditures of time, money and energy.

The Pole itself is among the most isolated spots on Earth, surrounded by thousands of square kilometers unrelieved by a single feature. In every direction you look there is only unbroken horizon. The nearest protrusion through the ice is **Mt Howe**, a nunatak 290km away, home to a colony of bacteria and yeasts. The nearest settlement is China's Kunlun Station (at Dome A), 1070km away.

Climate

Temperatures on the polar plateau range from -82°C to -14°C. The mean temperature is -49.4°C. Winter wind chills can plummet to -110°C.

The elevation is 2835m, but the cold and polar location makes the average air pressure the equivalent of about 3230m, and thus a likely place to have altitude sickness.

The average **wind speed** is just 20km/h, a gentle breeze compared to the 320km/h katabatic winds on the coast. The extreme cold and very low humidity (3%) combine to make this the world's driest desert.

Very little snow falls; drifting snow is a result of already fallen snow being blown

ADJUSTING TO THE POLE

The South Pole sits at 2835m, but low barometric pressure can make it feel as high as 3350m. Just walking around – let alone doing heavy work – can be exhausting. Everybody 'sucks wind' their first few days in the oxygen-starved atmosphere.

Many visitors who fly in experience **altitude sickness** upon arrival. Shortness of breath, lethargy, painful headaches and poor sleep are among the symptoms. The first 24 hours are usually the worst, but for tourists visiting the Pole for a few hours, that doesn't help much.

Some recommend taking three or four aspirin on the flight to the Pole to ease the headache. Others find that gingko or Diamox (acetazolamide) is helpful.

With humidity just 3%, **dehydration** is a constant threat. Polie advice is to drink water constantly, lay off alcohol and cut back on caffeine. Hangovers, thanks to the dryness, are especially wicked.

To prevent **nosebleeds**, pack your nostrils with Vaseline. And when your fingertips crack in the dryness and won't heal, repair them with superglue.

around. The most common form of **precipitation** is ice crystals, also called 'diamond dust.' These often fall out of a clear sky, sometimes creating sundogs, sun pillars and other refractions around the sun and the moon.

The Sun's Cycle

Because the Pole is at the rotational axis of the earth, the sun and moon do not pass overhead each day. Instead, the sun appears to circle the horizon daily. Polies see the moon for about half of each lunar cycle as it similarly moves around the horizon. On the summer solstice (December 21) the sun is at its highest, approximately 23° above the horizon. On the winter solstice (June 21) the sun is at its furthest below the horizon.

The spectacular sunset lasts weeks before the sun dips below the horizon on about March 22 – although the extreme atmospheric refraction sometimes allows it to be seen for a day or two more, and occasionally causes it to appear to rise again briefly. Twilight lingers for another six or seven weeks. Then the darkness sets in, lightened only by the aurora australis (see the boxed text, p93), the moon and the stars. During the six-month polar night, the moon is visible for two weeks, then sets for two weeks before rising again and repeating the cycle. Because the moon provides so much silvery-grey light, some winterovers come to think of the moonlit periods as 'daytime.' The winterover crew is also treated to the green flash – a ray of green lights at the horizon – in March and early April.

Seven weeks of dawn precede sunrise on about September 22, when winterers rejoice. All year round, Polies can fall victim to a peculiar form of polar pathology called 'Big Eye,' a period of disorientation and sleeplessness caused by the lack of a regular light-dark cycle.

Station Life

Living at the South Pole is difficult. But Polies, clad in their grubby Carhartts (an American brand of clothing popular here for its extreme durability), take a special pride in meeting adversity head-on and actually seem to relish the challenges of working at S 90°.

Extreme cold limits the time one can spend outdoors, and the darkness and even colder temperatures of the polar winter can be hazardous. (Station members, however, routinely go outside even on the coldest and darkest days. Flag lines – bamboo poles with small flags attached to the top and spaced every 2m – guide the way to outlying buildings.)

During the summer (officially a month after sunrise, to a month before sunset, approximately late October to mid-February), showers are limited to two minutes' running water and can be taken only twice a week. One Polie doesn't mind: 'after you've taken a shower, it's like you've washed off a layer of oil, and I swear to God, I get colder when I'm clean than I do when I'm dirty.'

Fire is an omnipresent danger in the dry atmosphere, which can turn wood buildings into tinderboxes.

Amundsen-Scott Station uses New Zealand time (GMT+13) since resupply flights to the Pole and McMurdo Station originate in Christchurch, and this simplifies logistics.

ISOLATION & SENSORY DEPRIVATION

The isolation can be overwhelming. From mid-February to late October there are no scheduled flights, so the winter crew (normally approximately 50 winterover) is physically cut off from the rest of the world. Wintering at the Pole is in some ways similar to being an astronaut, albeit one who has a bit more room to walk around. The accommodation probably doesn't help much, since the rooms – which at least are private for winterovers – are smaller than the average prison cell.

A psychologist who has studied Antarctic winterovers and helped in their selection sums up their isolation like this: 'The normal ways we deal with things when we're fed up – either withdrawing and shutting the door or going out to seek other people – are not available.'

On cloudy and moonless winter nights sensory deprivation is severe, as one winterover describes: 'It was so dark I couldn't see my own hand in front of my face. I might as well have been walking with my eyes closed. It took my eyes at least three minutes to adjust enough so that I could see even very faint outlines of nearby buildings.'

Some station members combat this deprivation by finding the perfume-sample strips included in some magazine ads. It's a pleasing contrast to the pervasive smell of JP-8 (jet fuel), which is used to run furnaces and machinery because it operates better at cold temperatures than other fuels.

COMMUNICATIONS

Email and web access helps break the isolation (for about 12 hours a day, when a satellite is in range). Internet phone technology produces high-quality calls, and the station also has Iridium satellite telephones. Station members can also use high-frequency radio to patch telephone calls home via McMurdo.

FOOD & WATER

Polies eat well even though frozen, dried and canned food form the majority of meals. Cooking is challenging: because of the risk of fire, all stoves are electric, which take much longer than professional gas ranges. Most food is stored outdoors, where it freezes solid, so it can take up to two weeks for meat to defrost in the walk-in refrigerator!

One chef with a sense of humor tried (unsuccessfully) to start a new custom called 'Dog Day' by serving hot dogs for lunch on the day that Amundsen had to shoot his dogs on his journey to the Pole.

Through the long dark winter, chocolate is a favorite. One popular dessert, 'buzz bars,' is not what some people might guess; they're rather brownies with chocolate-covered espresso beans baked into them. 'Slushies' are very fresh snow with Coke or liquor added. Ice cream is also a local favorite, but since it's stored outdoors, it has to be warmed in a microwave before it can be eaten.

Despite all this, the Pole is a *very* good place to lose weight. Even with three meals a day plus copious snacks many people lose weight during their stay (losing 20kg is not uncommon in a 15-week summer!) because of the huge caloric expenditures. Many Polies, particularly those who work outdoors, can eat up to 5000 to 6000 calories per day without gaining weight. It's not unusual to see someone eat four or five steaks in a single meal.

To minimize complaints about the food, the chefs have installed a 'Whiner Alarm,' a copper-colored bell hung above the serving

SOUTH POLE WEATHER DATA

From Antarctic Meteorological Research Center records dating from 1957 through 2011.

AVERAGE SNOW ACCUMULATION (FALLEN AND DRIFTED)	27.4CM PER YEAR
Highest temperature	-12.3°C (December 25, 2011)
Lowest temperature	-82.8°C (June 23, 1982)
Average annual temperature	-49.4°C
Highest pressure	719.0 millibars (August 25, 1996)
Lowest pressure	641.7 millibars (July 25, 1985)
Average pressure	681.2 millibars
Average wind speed	14.8km/h
Peak wind speed	93.2km/h (September 27, 2011)

line and rung by kitchen staff when someone lets fly with an ill-considered remark about the chow.

Interestingly, the station gets its water from a well, an improvement over the former inefficient system of melting clean snow, which required large amounts of fuel and time. The well, more than 120m deep, is created by using waste heat from the power plant to make a hot-water 'drill.' Below the firn layer, the snow is no longer porous, so adding heat melts the ice, but the water can't seep out into the surrounding ice. As a result, a large pool of water is created that can be pumped out and used. Of course, the water is also very old, since the well is so deep. There's an unusual side benefit: the filtered water has yielded hundreds of thousands of micrometeorites for scientific study.

And yes, despite the thousands of cubic kilometers of ice outside, the galley has an ice machine for drinks!

RECREATION

Recreation is somewhat limited, although the gymnasium in the new station includes a basketball court that's one-third the size of those used by pros. Inventive Polies have also devised improvisations such as volleybag, a version of volleyball using a beanbag. Radio darts, played against other winter stations around the continent (scores are sent by radio), has been popular despite its heavy dependency on trust – one station (and frequent winner) was later found not to even have a dartboard! 'Dome sledding' used to be done on the back side of the Dome. The library houses more than 6000 videos and books. On Christmas Eve, the 4.4km Race Around the World circles the Pole in -23°C temperatures, challenging runners, walkers, skiers and even snowmobilers.

One popular hangout is the **hydroponic greenhouse**. As one veteran says, 'The lights, warmth, plants and humidity make it a nice place to get away from the normal reality of daily life at the South Pole.' While the garden's yield is modest – enough fresh vegetables for 60 winterers to enjoy a couple of salads a week – tending the plants can be a welcome diversion.

Then there's the unique membership known as the **300 Club**. To join, wait until the temperature drops below -100°F (-73°C). After steaming in a 200°F (93°C) sauna, run naked (shoes, however, are highly recommended) out of the station onto the snow. Some people push on even further, going around the Ceremonial Pole. While some claim that the rime of flash-frozen sweat acts as insulation, if you fall, the ice against your reddened skin feels as rough as rock. Induction into the club requires photographic documentation – but with so much steam rising from the hot bodies, most pictures turn out rather foggy.

Sights

At S 90° you'll probably visit the Ceremonial Pole and the Geographic Pole to take your 'hero pictures' first. You can also expect to be invited inside the station for a visit to the dining room and possibly a quick look around. The station **shop** sells souvenirs, and you can have letters or postcards stamped with the station's postmark.

Ceremonial South Pole LANDMARK

The resplendent flags of the original 12 Antarctic Treaty signatories surround this red-and-white-striped 'barber' pole, capped by a chromium globe, so it offers the perfect photo-op. But it's just for show.

Geographic South Pole LANDMARK

The Geographic South Pole (Geodetic Pole) marks the spot at one end of the Earth's axis of rotation (the other being the North Pole). The ice at the Pole moves about 10m per year in the direction of W 43° (toward Brazil), which means that the marker itself has to be recalculated and moved each summer. It is marked by a 4m steel pole topped by a medallion designed by the previous year's winterover crew; each design is unique. Since it sits at the intersection of all the time zones, a quick nip around the pole takes you right around the world. The American flag is planted about a meter from the Pole sign, which is also moved each year to adjust for the moving ice sheet. The sign reads:

> Geographic South Pole
>
> Roald Amundsen, December 14, 1911 'So we arrived and were able to plant our flag at the geographical South Pole'
>
> Robert F Scott, January 17, 1912 'The Pole, Yes, but under very different circumstances from those expected'
>
> Elevation: 9301ft (2835m)

Amundsen-Scott South Pole Station BASE

From 1975 to 2008, home at the Pole was known familiarly as 'the Dome,' or, affectionately, 'Dome, Sweet Dome.' Built from 1971 to 1975, the silver-grey aluminum geodesic

LOCAL KNOWLEDGE

WINTERING AT THE SOUTH POLE *KATHERINE L HESS*

Do you love winter? I mean, *really* love winter? How about spending it at the South Pole? The winter I was there, there were 60 of us – scientists, tradespeople and support staff. We all had to pass myriad physical, psychological and dental examinations that scrutinized our fitness to withstand the remoteness of the polar winter.

At Station Close on February 14, most of us watched as the last plane tipped its wings over the station in farewell. Then we convened for our first 'All-Hands Meeting,' where we reviewed rules and emergency procedures, then held the traditional screening of *The Thing* (both versions).

Here at 'Pole,' as we call it, the sun rises and sets once each year. Though the sun sets in late March, its image remains for a few days as the last of its rays are refracted over the horizon, with weather hopefully fair enough for us to watch the green flash for most of a day. Twilight lingers for weeks and stars come out a day at a time until it becomes truly 'nighttime' here. The darkness lasts four months, and auroras grace the skies quite frequently.

Time has less meaning here when daylight does not change on a diurnal cycle. Most support staff and construction workers keep a 7am to 5pm work schedule. In winter the cooks take Sundays off; volunteers pitch in to show off their favorite recipes. We all clean together on Mondays.

Winterovers each have a private room with internet and phone connections. Many rooms have a window. Some winter science projects require darkness, though, and light from station windows will significantly degrade data, so, for the winter season, all windows are covered. Station members decorate the cardboard shades in the Galley with artwork, poems and pictures of travel destinations or family members.

At sunset, temperatures start to dip to about -50°C; during winter the average is -60°C. Below -62°C, vehicles must be used with extreme caution to avoid damage. At that temperature, a winterover can actually hear her breath crystallizing as the exhalation visibly floats away.

No matter how cold it is, several winterovers work outside each day. Researchers commute between buildings and work under the stars to monitor weather, atmospheric dynamics and astrophysics. Others move frozen food and supplies between storage facilities, and the heavy equipment operator clears snowdrifts from behind any objects profiling the wind.

Photographing the auroras and starry skies is popular. So are our homemade film festivals. The winter version of the **South Pole International Film Festival** is the **Winter International Film Festival**. Entries can be instructional, dramatic, simple or graphic. Some have station members down on the floor laughing at themselves.

Our biggest party by far is **Midwinter's**, held on the solstice in June. It's a turning point for the season, though it will still be dark for another two months. We dress up in formal (or goofy) attire, have a huge meal and a big dance party. We also call around to the other Antarctic stations on the HF radio and exchange email greeting cards with group photographs. Each year the kitchen staff tries to outdo the previous year, creating a fancy banquet with food we never knew they could create during the winter, with special items saved just for the event.

By August even the really creative and strong-minded have trouble focusing on the adventure of the winter. The day-to-day routine can become repetitive and mundane.

It's always exciting to hear the first reports of light on the horizon – no matter how faint. However, until the sun rises well above the horizon, the temperature continues to drop, and September often brings the coldest temperatures of the year. Station Opening activities begin in late September and early October when we prepare for the arrival of the next year's crew.

Katherine L Hess, the 2007–08 South Pole Winter Site Manager, spent three summers (2004–07) at Pole as Communications Coordinator and wintered over in 2002–03 as Senior Meteorologist.

POLE POSITIONS

In addition to the Geographic (Geodetic) and the Ceremonial Poles, you may also hear about three other Poles.

South Magnetic Pole (which drifts toward the northwest by 5km to 10km a year and is estimated to be at S -64.354°, E 136.971° by 2013, off the coast near Commonwealth Bay) is where a magnetic compass needle will try to point straight down. Tourist ships frequently sail over it. In 1909 the South Magnetic Pole, then on land, was first reached by Douglas Mawson, Edgeworth David and Alistair Mackay.

South Geomagnetic Pole (estimated to be at S -80.252°, E 107.541° in 2013) is where the earth's electromagnetic field would manifest if it were the extension of a dipole magnet placed at the earth's center. Russia's Vostok station is nearby.

Pole of Maximum Inaccessibility (located at approximately E 83°, S 54°, though there is debate on this) is the point furthest from any Antarctic coast. This pole was reached in 1958 by a Soviet team, and a plaque and bust (of Lenin) still poke out above the snow, marking the spot.

Magnetic and Geomagnetic Pole locations are based on Geoscience Australia (www.ga.gov.au) data.

Dome was 50m in diameter at its base and 15m high. It covered three structures, each two stories high, which provided accommodations, dining, laboratory and recreational facilities. Although the Dome protected these buildings and their occupants from the wind, it did nothing about the cold; it was unheated. It had a packed snow floor and an opening at the top to let out water vapor. Over time, as the base became submerged in snow and ice, parts of the complex became unsafe. Occasional power brownouts and fuel leaks threatened station security, and the drifting snow began to crush the Dome. Because of all these problems, the US government built a new above-snow facility.

The old Dome complex was dismantled over several years, with the final pieces removed in 2010 and shipped to Port Hueneme, California, where the top portion sits in the new Seabee Museum.

Work on the new US$174 million station began in 1997 and required 80 construction workers (25% of them women) to work nine-hour days, six days a week. In the 24-hour summer daylight, three crews worked shifts round the clock. Workers described how, among the unusual hazards of construction here, touching metal barehanded burns like a hot stove. The station's normal winter population, meanwhile, nearly doubled with the extra staff devoted to construction. Hundreds of flights from McMurdo brought in the necessary building materials, which in turn had been planned, procured and shipped over many years to McMurdo. The station was built in phases, so the first group of occupants was able to take up residence in January 2003, and it was officially inaugurated in January 2008. Full summer operations began in October 2011 – during summer, the Pole can host up to 250 people.

The 6039-sq-m elevated station stretches 128m, facing the prevailing winds with an aeronautical design that helps scour snow from beneath it. The main **entrance**, sometimes called 'Destination Alpha,' faces the **skiway**. Another staircase entrance on the back of the station is 'Destination Zulu.' Two separate blue-grey, horseshoe-shaped modules are connected by flexible walkways and can be raised on stilts to prevent destructive snow buildup. They accommodate 150 people in summer and 50 in winter.

One module houses living quarters, a dining room, a bar, a hospital, a laundry, a store, a post office and a greenhouse (adding to the futuristic, space-station feeling of the new facility, the greenhouse is officially known as the 'food growth chamber'). In the other are offices, labs, computers, telecommunications, an emergency-power plant, conference rooms, music practice rooms and a gym. Cozy reading rooms and libraries are scattered throughout both units.

The new station has triple-pane windows, 200kg stainless-steel outside 'freezer' doors and a pressurized interior to keep out drafts. At one end, a four-story aluminum tower, familiarly known as 'the Beer Can,' contains a stairwell, cargo lift and utilities. Photovoltaic panels take advantage of the summer's

24 hours of sunlight. One wind turbine was added in the 2009–10 season, but the light winds of the polar plateau mean that the station would require a much larger windmill farm to support its needs.

Science Facilities LABORATORIES

Most of the scientific facilities at the Pole are off-limits to visitors, to avoid disrupting research. Other laboratories are off-limits because their instrumentation could be contaminated or decalibrated by unauthorized visitors. Still, it's interesting to know about the cutting-edge science being done at the Pole.

Clean Air Sector

Among the most important research is work on the notorious 'ozone hole,' the thinning of the atmosphere's ozone layer (see p162). Scientists at the **Atmospheric Research Observatory** (ARO), upwind of the station in the Clean Air Sector, study some of the purest air on Earth in the hope of learning about pollution and how it spreads around the globe. Another group in this observatory is using Lidar (light radar) to study the formation of polar stratospheric clouds, which act as the seeds for the depletion of ozone each spring.

Dark Sector

The South Pole is a world center for astronomy, thanks to its high altitude and thin, dry atmosphere. The centrifugal force of the Earth's rotation flattens out the atmosphere at both poles, and the extreme cold freezes water vapor out of the air. The astronomical instruments are located about 1km from the station in the 'Dark Sector,' where extraneous light, heat and electromagnetic radiation are prohibited, so as not to disturb the experiments. A new 8m **South Pole Telescope** (SPT), built at a cost of US$19 million, part of the **Dark Sector Laboratory**, achieved the milestone called 'first light' (when light passes through all parts of a telescope and it becomes operational) in 2007. The SPT seeks cosmic microwave background radiation to investigate the 'dark energy' that appears to be accelerating the expansion of the universe. The telescope also searches for the signature of primordial gravitational waves and tests models for the origin of the universe.

Another part of the Dark Sector Lab is **Background Imaging of Cosmic Extragalactic Polarization** (BICEP), an experiment designed to measure the polarization of the cosmic microwave background with unprecedented precision, helping to answer questions about the origin of the universe.

Also in the Dark Sector is the **Martin A Pomerantz Observatory** (MAPO), a two-story elevated structure named for a pioneering US Antarctic astrophysicist. MAPO has supported various telescopes and detectors, including the South Pole Upgrade DASI (SPUD), which studies the polarization of the cosmic gravitational-wave background.

IceCube

The amazing IceCube (www.icecube.wisc.edu) is a US$271 million, kilometer-sized neutrino observatory submerged beneath the ice. From 2005 to 2010, 86 holes were drilled 2450m deep into the ice with a hot-water drill. Then strings of 60 volleyball-sized instruments called digital optical modules (DOMs) were lowered down. This enormous underground array of about 5484 DOMs looks for ultrahigh-energy subatomic particles called neutrinos. The team searches for neutrinos that have passed through the core of the Earth (which they can do), thus the Earth becomes a telescope and the ice cap the detector. The neutrinos interact with atoms in the ice – perfectly transparent and superdark at that depth – creating blue flashes of light detected by the DOMs. Studying neutrinos in this way may increase our understandings of 'dark matter,' the power sources of galaxies, cosmic ray acceleration and the workings of supernovae (the massive explosions of stars), as well as the ability of neutrinos to change type. More than 36 institutions and 250 scientists worldwide use this data, see p201 for more.

Quiet Sector

Noise and other earth-shaking activities are banned in the Quiet Sector, where seismology is studied at the **South Pole Remote Earth Sciences Seismological Observatory** (SPRESSO), located 8km from the station, and operational since 2003. Instruments placed 300m beneath the surface detect earthquakes (and underground nuclear explosions) worldwide. Antarctica is so seismically 'quiet' and the seismometers are so sensitive that they can pick up vibrations up to four times quieter than previously observed. SPRESSO staff could easily detect when certain tractors used by Pole construction crews were left idling or shut down.

Understand Antarctica

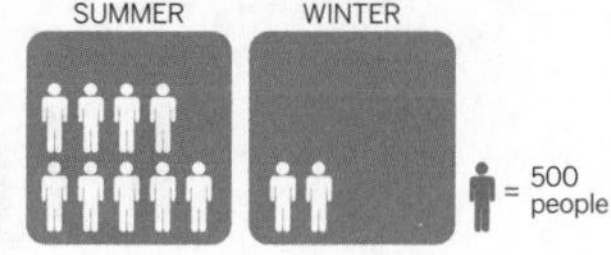

Antarctica Today

Antarctica & Climate Change

With global climate change melting its vast ice sheets, Antarctica, despite its remoteness, sits at the forefront of climate-change research.

In October 2011, NASA scientists discovered a rift in the Pine Island Glacier in West Antarctica that will ultimately yield a 900-sq-km iceberg. Such events interlock with other complex systems (eg ocean salinity and acidity), and there is a major push to better monitor and analyze these changes.

Local developments to combat climate change include the first zero-emission polar station: Belgium's Princess Elisabeth Antarctica Station, opened in 2009. Some other stations use wind turbines for power.

» Area: 14.2 million sq km
» Highest elevation: 4900m
» Lowest elevation: 2540m below sea level (but ice-covered)
» Highest temperature: 14.6°C
» Lowest temperature: -89.6°C
» Oldest ice core: c 800,000 years at bottom

Scientific Research

Antarctic science generates some of the world's most cutting-edge research. New technologies are allowing previously inaccessible areas of Antarctica to be studied. Sensors attached to animals gather data from deep below the sea and beam it to satellites; the Polar Earth Observing Network seismic array, completed in 2012, has sensors over one third of Antarctica.

Antarctica is uniquely placed for research in astronomy and physics. The IceCube neutrino detector, buried one cubic km below the Pole, made observations in 2012 that refute long-held understandings of Gamma Ray Bursts.

Antarctic Treaty & Political Governance

In 2012 Pakistan became the 50th country to join the Antarctic Treaty, which governs Antarctica. Treaty countries agree that Antarctica is a

Top Books

Endurance: Shackleton's Incredible Voyage (Alfred Lansing) Page-turner survival story.
The South Pole (Roald Amundsen) Triumph at 90° South.
Scott's Last Expedition (Robert F Scott) Firsthand (posthumous) account.
The Worst Journey in the World (Apsley Cherry-Garrard) Midwinter manhaul to Cape Crozier.
South (Ernest Shackleton) *Endurance* expedition from the leader's perspective.
At the Mountains of Madness (HP Lovecraft) Sci-fi on the Ice.

Top Albums

Antarctic Symphony Sir Peter Maxwell Davies' Symphony No 8
Sinfonia Antartica Ralph Vaughan Williams' Symphony No 7
Scott's Music Box: Music from Terra Nova Songs played on the expedition

continental makeup
(% of land)

if Antartica were 100 people

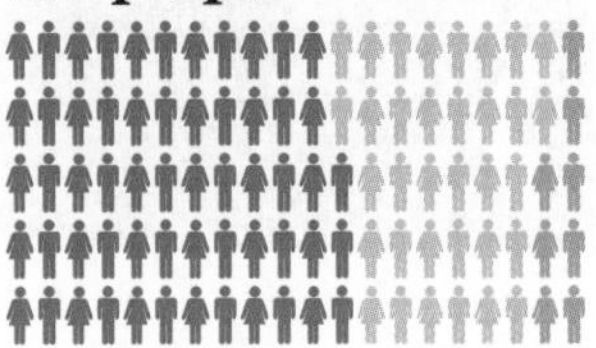

58 would be tourists
34 would be staff and crew
8 would be scientists

peaceful, free and demilitarized place of international cooperation and scientific research, open to all, with a minimum of human impact.

Though no country holds indisputable title over any part of Antarctica, seven nations have territorial claims. The claims are not internationally recognized, but nations attempt to strengthen them: for example, from 2007 to 2009 the UK, Chile and Argentina all filed for rights to Antarctica's ocean floor.

Occasionally disputes arise over resources and wildlife management. Whaling remains a contentious issue, with Japan continuing to hunt whales through a research loophole in the moratorium.

Environmental Issues Related to Tourism

Antarctica's largest industry by far is tourism. Tourist visitors and crew greatly outnumber scientists and support personnel, and mainly visit areas where wildlife is concentrated, increasing the risk to plants and animals. Accidental introduction of alien species via seeds and spores attached to clothing and gear is another major concern (see the boxed text, p161).

The Antarctic Treaty addresses tourism issues with guidelines for visitors and frequently visited places.

The 2011 to 2012 season saw a marked reduction in large cruise ships, following a 2011 ban on the use and carriage of heavy fuel oil (HFO). Designed to avoid the risk of leaks, the ban was the culmination of six years of negotiations, though the sinking of cruise ship *Explorer* in 2007 galvanized action.

As of 2012, all cruise-ship operators (but not all yachts) are members of the International Association of Antarctica Tour Operators (IAATO), which promotes clean Antarctic travel.

Tourists

» 2011-2: 26,519
» 2010-11: 33,824
» 2009-10: 36,875
» 2008-09: 37,858
» 2007-08: 46,091
» 2006-07: 37,552

Top Films

South (restored 1998; directed by Frank Hurley)
Frozen Planet (BBC Series, 2012)
La Marche de l'Empereur (*March of the Penguins;* 2005)
The Thing (1982; with a lesser remake in 2011)
Encounters at the End of the World (2007; Werner Herzog)
Shackleton's Antarctic Adventure (2001 IMAX film)
Scott of the Antarctic (1948) Starring John Mills.
Warren Miller's Storm (2003) Recreation of Shackleton's South Georgia crossing.

Cool Science

» Tapping 20 million–year-old subglacial Lake Vostok.

» Neutrino observatory IceCube tests models of the universe.

» Remote sensors explore the Gamburtsev Mountains, buried beneath the ice and the size of the Alps.

History

Antarctica, unlike any other continent, was postulated to exist long before it was actually discovered. The ancient Greeks, beginning with Pythagoras, believed the earth to be round. Aristotle refined the idea, suggesting that the symmetry of a sphere demanded that the earth's northern region should be balanced by a southern region – without it, the top-heavy globe might tumble over. This idea of earthly balance gave rise to the name we give the southern continent today: Antarktos, or 'opposite Arktos,' the constellation in the northern sky. In Egypt, Ptolemy agreed that geographical equilibrium required an unknown southern continent; a map he drew c AD 150 showed a large continent linking Africa and Asia.

The term 'antarctica' was used as a Latin adjective, but the proper name 'Antarctica' can be traced to one man. Edinburgh mapmaker John G Bartholomew (1860–1920) first used the term to label a map of 'the unexplored south polar continent' that he published in an 1890 atlas.

Explorers from the 15th and 16th centuries, like Vasco da Gama and Ferdinand Magellan, and James Cook in the 18th century, skirted the lands that rim the Southern Ocean, and slowly the peri-Antarctic archipelagos were discovered. But it wasn't until the 19th century with Fabian von Bellingshausen's circumnavigation and the far-flung activities of sealers and whalers that the continent itself was sighted in 1820 with humans landing on its shores in 1821. The race to find seals and whales heated up – and ultimately to explore and map the new terrain. Antarctica's heroic age of explorers from the 1890s to the 1920s intensified the push for geographic and scientific exploration, and encompassed Roald Amundsen's and Robert Scott's dramatic first and second attainments of the South Pole.

In 1954, Australia established the first permanent science station on the continent and by 1957–58, during the International Geophysical Year, 12 countries were operating 46 bases. This expanding activity made the Antarctica Treaty, signed in 1959, all the more relevant – the continent became reserved for clean peaceful science and exploration. In the ensuing years, despite some territorial claims, that has largely been the case. In the past decades, with the realization of Antarctica's central role in climate change and the continued unique opportunities for scientific observations, the discoveries way down under continue apace.

TIMELINE

1519

Portuguese explorer Fernão de Magalhães (Ferdinand Magellan), leading the first circumnavigation of the globe from 1519 to 1522, discovers and names Tierra del Fuego – and his namesake straits.

1531

French cartographer Oronce Finé is the first to use the term 'Terra Australis,' using that label on one of the earliest maps to show a vast southern circumpolar land mass.

1578

Francis Drake, sailing in *Pelican* (the name was later changed to *Golden Hind*) on the second voyage around the world, discovers the Drake Passage separating Tierra del Fuego and Antarctica.

The Explorers – Sea & Land

For a quick list of the 'furthest south' accomplishments of the various explorers, see p126.

The Sealers

During the sealing era from about 1780 to 1892, more than 1100 sealing ships visited Antarctic regions (both the peri-Antarctic islands, and the Antarctic Peninsula), compared to barely 25 exploration ships. The sealers came from Britain, the Cape Colony (now part of South Africa), France, Tasmania and New South Wales (in present-day Australia), New Zealand and the United States. Most were motivated by profit, not discovery, though a few firms, notably Enderby Brothers of London, spent vast sums on exploration.

Nearly a third of the peri-Antarctic islands were discovered by sealers. These hunters, however, considered their finds proprietary and kept the information to themselves (although drunken sailors were known to boast about newfound sealing grounds).

Sealing was an extremely hard life. Gangs were typically dropped off on a promising beach and left for months at a time while the ship continued in search of other sealing grounds. The sealers lived in tents, rude huts, or small caves among the rocks. All offered little shelter from the wind and weather, and the brutality of the seal-killing work itself impressed even the sealers.

Good reads: *Antarctica: The Extraordinary History of Man's Conquest of the Frozen Continent* (1990), editors of *Reader's Digest; Antarctica: The Complete Story* (2001), David McGonigal & Lynn Woodworth; and biography *The Last Explorer: Hubert Wilkins, Hero of the Great Age of Polar Exploration*, Simon Nasht.

Bellingshausen

In 1819, Czar Alexander I dispatched Fabian von Bellingshausen (1778–1852), a Baltic German and captain in the Russian Imperial Navy who had participated in the first Russian circumnavigation in 1803–06, on a voyage to the Southern Ocean. With his flagship *Vostok* (East), a newly launched corvette with a copper-sheathed hull, and the older, sluggish transport ship *Mirnyy* (Peaceful), he crossed the Antarctic Circle on January 26, 1820, and the next day became the first to sight the Antarctic continent. Through a heavy curtain of falling snow, at S 69°21´, W 2°14´, Bellingshausen saw 'an icefield covered with small hillocks.' Not realizing the importance of his discovery, however, he merely noted the weather and position in the ship's log before continuing.

The two ships sailed eastward, pushing further south than anyone before, reaching S 69°25´. They crossed the Antarctic Circle six more times, and circumnavigated the continent, eventually probing as far as S 69°53´, where they discovered Peter I Øy, the southernmost land known at that time. They also found a second piece of ice-free land, which Bellingshausen called Alexander Coast after the czar. It is now known to be an island joined to the Antarctic Peninsula by an ice shelf.

1603

Spaniard Gabriel de Castilla, commanding a fleet of three ships, penetrates to approximately 64°S, south of the Drake Passage. Spain's base at Deception Island is later named for him.

1773

On his second major voyage of exploration, Captain James Cook, a Yorkshireman, crosses the Antarctic Circle three times, penetrating as far south as 71°10'S – but never sees Antarctica.

1775

Cook discovers the eight southernmost islands of the South Sandwich Islands, naming them after the fourth Earl of Sandwich, First Lord of the Admiralty.

1786

Thomas Delano is the first of a stampede of British seal hunters to arrive at South Georgia after reading Cook's description of fur seals there.

Palmer

American sealer Nathaniel Brown Palmer (1799–1877), son of a shipyard owner, left his home of Stonington, Connecticut at age 14 to go to sea. On his second sealing voyage to the South Shetlands in 1820, commanding the sloop *Hero,* Palmer sailed south with a small fleet of other sealers. Upon his arrival in the South Shetlands, Palmer pushed south ahead of the others in search of a more secure anchorage. He anchored inside the caldera of Deception Island, almost certainly the first person to do so. On November 16 he saw Trinity Island to the southeast and probably the Antarctic Peninsula. The next day Palmer sailed to investigate, but due to heavy ice thought it imprudent to attempt a landing.

In January 1821, while searching for seal rookeries, Palmer took *Hero* south along the western side of the Antarctic Peninsula as far as Marguerite Bay.

A year later, commanding the sloop *James Monroe,* Palmer was searching for seals in the South Shetlands with British Captain George Powell of *Dove*. Finding no seals, they steered east, and on December 6, 1821, sighted a large island of a new archipelago now known as the South Orkney Islands.

Bellingshausen had a shipboard sauna constructed as a unique hygienic measure for his crew: heated cannonballs inside a tent on deck supplied the healthful steam for bathing and washing.

Weddell

Scotsman James Weddell (1787–1834), an upholsterer's son who became a master in the Royal Navy, rejoined the merchant service in 1819 and took command of the brig *Jane* on a sealing expedition to the recently discovered South Shetlands. Although the voyage was a financial failure, he independently discovered the South Orkney Islands, which had just been sighted by Nathaniel Palmer and George Powell.

THE EARLIEST ANTARCTIC LANDINGS *ROBERT HEADLAND*

Evidence suggests that in the summer of 1820–21 three sealing masters working from the South Shetlands independently landed on the Antarctic Peninsula – thus becoming the first humans on the continent. They were John Davis aboard *Cecilia,* a ship from Nantucket, on February 7, 1821, and John McFarlane and Joseph Usher aboard *Dragon* and *Caraquette* respectively, both from London but working out of Valparaiso, at unknown dates. Few details are known because no fur seals were found, thus the trips were of little interest to those involved.

Just two more continental landings by sealers during the rest of the century are known, one on the Antarctic Peninsula and the other in the vicinity of Cape Adare. Though other landings were probably made, the absence of seals meant they weren't recorded.

Robert Headland is a senior associate at the Scott Polar Research Institute

1819
English merchant Captain William Smith discovers the South Shetlands. Later in the year, he lands on King George Island, claiming the group for the British monarch.

1819
Antarctica's worst loss of life occurs off Livingston Island in the South Shetlands when the 74-gun *San Telmo,* a Spanish man-of-war, is lost with 650 officers, soldiers and seamen.

1820
On January 27, Fabian von Bellingshausen becomes the first person to sight the Antarctic continent. Through thickly falling snow at 69°21'S, 2°14'W, he sees 'an icefield covered with small hillocks.'

1821
Eleven crewmen from the sealing vessel *Lord Melville* spend the first recorded (and involuntary) winter in the Antarctic when they are left on King George Island in the South Shetlands.

On his next voyage, Weddell with *Jane* and the cutter *Beaufoy* reached the eastern end of the South Orkneys by late January 1823. At Saddle Island, Weddell went ashore collecting six skins of a new species of seal – now known as the Weddell. But by early February, Weddell had given up on finding a harvestable population of seals, so he changed course southward into a sea normally covered in impenetrable ice as far north as S 60°.

Constant gales soaked the crew, but on February 16, when they crossed the 70th parallel, the weather turned and they began a fine run south. Well aware of the remarkable conditions, Weddell noted: 'not a particle of ice of any description was to be seen.'

By February 20, they had reached an amazing S 74°15′ – a new southing record, 344km further than Cook. But the season was getting on and, despite open water to the south, Weddell ordered a retreat. A gun was fired in celebration and the sea named for King George IV (the name was changed in the next century to honor Weddell).

Wilkes

When American Lieutenant Charles Wilkes (1798–1877) accepted command of the US Exploring Expedition in 1838, little did he know the expedition was in for great hardship.

For a start, the six ships selected were ill-suited to polar exploration: warships *Vincennes, Peacock* and *Porpoise* had gun ports that admitted heavy seas; *Sea Gull* and *Flying Fish* were former New York pilot boats; while sluggish storeship *Relief* rounded out the sorry fleet.

After separating and undergoing numerous trials (gales blew out sails, boats were crushed by ice, men were injured and frozen, *Sea Gull* was lost off Chile with all hands) three vessels ultimately rendezvoused and, on January 16, 1840 – three days before Dumont d'Urville made his discovery – they sighted land near E 154°30′, putting a boat ashore three days later to confirm it. Separating again, *Vincennes* continued west, charting until the present-day Shackleton Ice Shelf, which Wilkes named Termination Land. Having followed the Antarctic coast for nearly 2000km, Wilkes announced the discovery of an Antarctic continent upon his return to Sydney.

Weddell's sailors' unenviable jobs were made more tolerable, perhaps, by their daily rum ration: three full wineglasses per man. The day that the expedition turned back, unhappy because they had found no seals and the voyage was unprofitable, they were cheered slightly by the day's extra rum ration.

Dumont d'Urville

Frenchman Jules-Sébastien-César Dumont d'Urville (1790–1842) was a veteran of two circumnavigations, when he sailed in 1837 with *Astrolabe* and *Zélée*. Although Dumont d'Urville hoped to reach the South Magnetic Pole, his orders from King Louis Philippe were simply to proceed as far south as possible in the Weddell Sea.

But the ice in the Weddell Sea that season extended far north and much to his frustration Dumont d'Urville was unable to penetrate nearly

1821

John Davis, an American sealer aboard the *Cecilia*, lands on the Antarctic Peninsula, becoming the first recorded human to step on the continent.

1821

American Nathaniel Brown Palmer, in the sloop *James Monroe*, with Briton George Powell in *Dove*, discovers the South Orkneys. Powell goes ashore and claims the group for the British crown.

1821

Fabian von Bellingshausen discovers Peter I Øy, the first land discovered south of the Antarctic Circle and thus the most southerly land known at the time

1823

Scotsman James Weddell penetrates the sea now named for him (originally named for King George IV), reaching a record 74°15'S – 344km further south than Cook.

as far south as Weddell had. At the end of February he discovered (or rediscovered, since sealers had probably already landed there) Louis Philippe Land and Joinville Island at the northern tip of the Antarctic Peninsula. By then, scurvy plagued his ships.

Following a year-long ethnological voyage in the Pacific, during which 23 men died of dysentery and fever, Dumont d'Urville and his crews headed south again and on January 19, 1840 saw what they felt certain was land (confirmed the next day). Unable to go ashore because of massive ice cliffs, they sailed west and landed on a group of islets just offshore. Chips of granite were hacked off as proof that they had found terra firma, and the discovery claimed for France and named for Dumont d'Urville's beloved wife, Adélie.

Returning to France in November 1840 to great acclaim, Dumont d'Urville and his men were rewarded with 15,000 francs (to share). Less than two years later, Dumont d'Urville, his wife and their son were killed in a train derailment.

One unsuccessful applicant for the position of Wilkes' expedition historian was Nathaniel Hawthorne, who later wrote *The Scarlet Letter*. Maybe he was lucky, for in the words of polar historian Laurence Kirwan (*The White Road*, 1959), it was 'the most ill-prepared, the most controversial, and probably the unhappiest expedition which ever sailed the Antarctic seas.'

Ross

Scotsman James Clark Ross (1800–62), considered one of the most dashing figures of his time, had joined the Royal Navy at the tender age of 11. Between 1818 and 1836, he spent eight winters and 15 summers in the Arctic, and in 1831, as second-in-command of a voyage led by his uncle, John Ross, he located the North Magnetic Pole. In 1839, he led a national expedition to explore the south and locate the South Magnetic Pole.

Sailing south from Hobart in *Erebus* and *Terror* (three-masted barques strengthened for ice navigation), Ross pushed through pack ice until he broke through to open water on January 9, 1841, becoming the first to reach 'the Victoria Barrier' (known today as the Ross Ice Shelf). The next day, Ross sighted land, an unexpected development. A boat was put ashore two days later on Possession Island, and the new territory claimed for Queen Victoria.

While continuing to search for the South Magnetic Pole, Ross discovered High (now Ross) Island, and named its two mountains for his ships: Erebus and Terror. Lying in Ross' path, however, was the formidable ice shelf towering 60m above the sea. The ships cruised along the Barrier for 450km, the sailors in awe. After calculating on January 22, 1841 that he had surpassed Weddell's furthest south, Ross turned for Hobart.

Sailing south again in November, Ross aimed for the eastern extremity of the Barrier, reaching a new record south of S 78°10′ on February 23, but winter's onset forced retreat.

After a disappointing third season in the Weddell Sea, the expedition reached England on September 2, 1843, after nearly 4½ years away. When Ross married later that year, his bride Anne's father set one con-

1831

Sailing in the brig *Tula* and accompanied by George Avery in the cutter *Lively*, Briton John Biscoe makes the first sighting of Antarctica in the Indian Ocean sector.

1839

English whaling captains John Balleny, in *Eliza Scott*, and Thomas Freeman, in *Sabrina*, discover a group of ice-smothered islands. Freeman disappears en route home.

1840

Frenchman Jules-Sébastien-César Dumont d'Urville discovers a stretch of Antarctic coast and a penguin species, and names both for his wife, Adélie.

1841

James Clark Ross reaches the sea that will bear his name, then discovers the enormous barrier of ice (today called the Ross Ice Shelf) that blocks progress further south.

dition: he must end his exploring days, a pledge Ross made and kept, with one exception. In 1847–48 he returned to the Arctic to search for John Franklin, who had disappeared in 1845 while trying to navigate the Northwest Passage.

In 1820, while still a young ensign on a survey ship in the eastern Mediterranean, Dumont d'Urville saw and sketched a remarkable statue recently unearthed on the island of Milos – the *Venus de Milo*. He helped France acquire it, and was awarded the Légion d'Honneur and promoted to lieutenant.

Bull

In 1893, Norwegian-born Henrik Johan Bull (1844–1930) persuaded Svend Foyn, wealthy inventor of the exploding harpoon gun, to back an expedition to assess the Ross Sea's whaling potential. Sailing in a refitted whaling steamer, *Antarctic* (later to be used by Nordenskjöld), Bull's expedition encountered many misfortunes and saw few whales. A £3000 profit made from sealing at Îles Kerguelen evaporated when the ship ran aground at Campbell Island.

On January 24, 1895, a party went ashore at Cape Adare in what was claimed to be the continent's first landing (although it was actually one of several disputed 'first landings,' see p142). Penguins, rock specimens, seaweed and lichens were collected. Bull continued sealing and whaling, and at the age of 62 was shipwrecked on Îles Crozet for two months.

De Gerlache

Belgian Adrien Victor Joseph de Gerlache de Gomery (1866–1934), a lieutenant in the Royal Belgian Navy, persuaded the Brussels Geographical Society to finance a scientific expedition to Antarctica. Sailing in a three-masted sealing ship rechristened *Belgica,* de Gerlache left Antwerp in 1897 with an international crew including a Norwegian who offered to join the expedition as first mate without pay: Roald Amundsen.

By early February, the expedition had discovered and mapped the strait that now bears de Gerlache's name on the western side of the Antarctic Peninsula, as well as the islands on the west side of that strait – Brabant, Liège, Anvers and Wiencke. Along the eastern side of the strait, they charted the Peninsula's Danco Coast, named for the ship's magnetician, who died during the expedition.

CRASH AT SEA

On March 13, 1842, when traveling together in darkness, Ross' *Erebus* and *Terror* were blown into a group of icebergs. To avoid collision with a berg, each ship put the helm over hard, but rising on an enormous wave, *Terror* landed on *Erebus,* breaking away *Erebus*' bowsprit, foretopmast, booms, yards and stays. One of *Erebus*' anchors was driven right though the hull's copper sheathing into the side of the ship. When they separated, *Erebus* was just 8m from the giant berg, but somehow managed to slip past, as did *Terror*.

1892

Norwegian Carl Anton Larsen explores both coasts of the northern Antarctic Peninsula, discovers Oscar II Land and makes the first use of skis in Antarctica.

1895

Sailing from Norway in 1893 in a refitted whaling steamer named *Antarctic,* Henrik Johan Bull goes ashore at Cape Adare, the first landing outside the Antarctic Peninsula region.

1897

Norwegian Roald Amundsen signs on to Adrien Victor Joseph de Gerlache de Gomery's Belgian Antarctic Expedition as a first mate – without pay.

1898

Joseph de Gerlache's ship *Belgica* is frozen into the pack ice. Trapped for 377 days, the expedition is the first to overwinter south of the Antarctic Circle.

Belgica crossed the Circle on February 15, 1898. By March 1, already deep into the heavy pack ice, she reached S 71°31´. The next day began a 377-day imprisonment in the ice. During this, the first time anyone had wintered south of the Antarctic Circle, the expedition underwent great hardships: midwinter darkness toyed with the men's sanity, and the lack of vitamin C made them ripe for scurvy.

In January 1899, they attempted to liberate themselves by hand-sawing a canal 600m from a stretch of open water back to the ship. They worked like dogs for a month. When they were within 30m of the ship, a wind shift tightened the pack ice, closing the hard-won canal within an hour. Two weeks later, the ice opened and they steamed into the polynya, only to be forced to wait another month until they could gain the open sea.

When Ross' expedition stopped in Hobart, their host, the governor of Van Diemen's Land (Tasmania) was John Franklin, himself a veteran Arctic explorer who would later sail Arctic waters again – in the same *Erebus* and *Terror* – before disappearing and triggering the greatest polar search in history.

Borchgrevink

Carsten Egeberg Borchgrevink (1864–1934), son of a Norwegian father and an English mother, sailed with Bull in the *Antarctic* in 1894. Landing at Cape Adare convinced Borchgrevink it was possible to survive an Antarctic winter ashore, so he decided to organize his own expedition to be the first to accomplish this feat – the British Antarctic Expedition of 1898–90.

Borchgrevink's *Southern Cross,* a converted Norwegian sealer, arrived at Cape Adare on February 17, 1899. Despite the loss of one life, the daring expedition was ultimately successful (see p91).

Photography was first used in Antarctica on de Gerlache's expedition. Ship's surgeon Frederick Cook recorded that 'as the ship steamed rapidly along, spreading out one panorama after another of a new world, the noise of the camera was as regular and successive as the tap of a stock ticker.'

Nordenskjöld

Swedish geologist Nils Otto Gustav Nordenskjöld (1869–1928) had previously led expeditions to the Yukon and Tierra del Fuego. In 1900, he was assigned to lead the Swedish South Polar Expedition, the first to winter in the Antarctic Peninsula region.

Under Nordenskjöld's leadership, experienced Antarctic explorer Norwegian Carl Larsen captained the *Antarctic,* the stout former sealer used by Henrik Bull. By late January 1902, they were exploring the western side of the Peninsula, making several important geographical discoveries before sailing back to the tip of the Peninsula. There, they crossed between the Peninsula and off-lying Joinville Island, naming the strait for their ship.

Next the expedition attempted to penetrate south into the Weddell Sea, but its infamous ice stopped them. Instead Nordenskjöld and five men set up a winter base in a small hut on Snow Hill Island in February 1902, while the *Antarctic* sailed to winter in the Falklands. It wasn't until November 1903 that Nordenskjöld and his men were finally reunited with Larsen and the crew of the *Antarctic*. For more on their harrowing adventure, see p87.

1899–1900

Borchgrevink's *Southern Cross* expedition is the first to winter ashore on the mainland. The 10 men have the entire continent to themselves (along with 90 sledge dogs, the first in Antarctica).

1902

Robert F Scott's *Discovery* expedition makes the first dedicated attempt to reach the South Pole, but the three-man party of Scott, Ernest Shackleton and Edward Wilson gets only to 82°16'30"S.

ARCHIVE PICS / ALAMY©

» *Terra Nova* in pack ice

1904

Norwegian Carl Anton Larsen establishes Grytviken whaling station on the shore of South Georgia's best harbor, on the island's protected north coast. The Antarctic whaling era begins.

Although Nordenskjöld's expedition is remembered primarily for its survival against nearly overwhelming odds, it also performed the most important research in Antarctica – including studies in botany, geology, glaciology and hydrography – undertaken up to that time.

Scott – the *Discovery* Expedition

Even as Nordenskjöld's men were struggling for survival, British explorer Captain Robert Falcon Scott (1868–1912) was working from a base on Ross Island. The son of an upper-middle-class brewer, Scott joined the Royal Navy's training ship *Britannia* as a cadet at age 13. He advanced through the ranks, and was promoted to commander in June 1900. A month later he was named leader of the British National Antarctic Expedition, and the well-financed enterprise sailed from England on August 6, 1901, in *Discovery,* a specially built wooden steam barque.

On January 3, 1902, *Discovery* crossed the Antarctic Circle, and six days later stopped briefly at Cape Adare. Penetrating the Ross Sea, Scott cruised along the Ross Ice Shelf, discovering King Edward VII Land on its eastern margin.

By mid-February 1902, Scott's men had established winter quarters at Hut Point on Ross Island. Although a hut was built ashore (p100), *Discovery,* frozen into the sea ice, served as the accommodations.

In a violent snowstorm during a sledge trip, young sailor George Vince slipped over a precipice to his death. The winter passed fairly quietly otherwise, the group's accommodations made cheerier by another Antarctic first: electric lights (powered by a windmill). With expedition member Ernest Shackleton as editor, they published Antarctica's first magazine, the monthly *South Polar Times,* and one issue of a more ribald alternative, the *Blizzard,* whose title page featured a figure holding a bottle, captioned 'Never mind the blizzard, I'm all right.'

To the cheers of *Discovery*'s men, Scott set out for the South Pole on November 2, 1902, with Shackleton, scientific officer Dr Edward A Wilson, 19 dogs and five supply sledges. Inexperience with skiing and dog-sledging, however, resulted in this initial foray being unsuccessful (for more details, see p125).

The following summer, after Scott led a sledging party in southern Victoria Land, the relief ships *Morning* and *Terra Nova* arrived. If *Discovery* could not be freed within six weeks, it was to be abandoned. After weeks of cutting and blasting, nature relented. A final charge, on February 16, 1904, released *Discovery* for the long journey home.

Bruce

Scotsman William Spiers Bruce (1867–1921), a physician, headed the Scottish National Antarctic Expedition, sailing in *Scotia,* a renamed

When the *Southern Cross* returned on January 28, 1900, Borchgrevink's group had proven a critical fact: humans could survive Antarctica's winter ashore, using a wooden hut as a base for exploration. They also produced excellent maps of the Ross Sea area, which would prove invaluable to later explorers.

Scott made the first flight in Antarctica, on February 4, 1902, to 240m in a tethered balloon called *Eva* at the Bay of Whales. Camera-toting expedition member Ernest Shackleton went up next, becoming Antarctica's first aerial photographer.

1908

Ross Island's Mt Erebus, 3794m high and the world's most southerly active volcano, is first climbed by a party from Ernest Shackleton's *Nimrod* expedition.

1909

Ernest Shackleton and companions – Jameson Adams, Eric Marshall and Frank Wild – reach their record south, 88°23'S, just 180km from the Pole. Dwindling provisions force them to turn back.

1909

Three men from Shackleton's *Nimrod* expedition – TW Edgeworth David, Douglas Mawson and Alistair Mackay – hike nearly 1600km to the South Magnetic Pole, the first time it is reached.

1911

Norwegians Roald Amundsen, Olav Bjaaland, Helmer Hanssen, Sverre Hassel and Oscar Wisting reach the South Pole on December 14 and claim the polar plateau for Norway.

Norwegian steam sealer. The expedition pushed south into the Weddell Sea in 1902–03, but by S 70°, *Scotia* was beset. After freeing themselves, the group headed north to winter at Laurie Island, where they set up a meteorological station on April 1, 1903, the oldest continuously operated base in the Antarctic (now called Orcadas, see p60).

In January 1904, Bruce penetrated the Weddell Sea to S 74° where he discovered Coats Land, which he named for the expedition's patrons, Andrew and James Coats. *Scotia* followed the coast for 240km, but the fast ice continually kept the ship two or three frustrating kilometers offshore.

Upon his death in 1921, Bruce's ashes were carried south and poured into the Southern Ocean.

Charcot

French physician Jean-Baptiste Etienne August Charcot (1867–1936) headed the French Antarctic Expedition along the west coast of the Peninsula. By February 19, 1904, he had discovered Port Lockroy on Wiencke Island. Sailing on, the expedition wintered at a sheltered bay

DRYGALSKI: INGENUITY ON THE ICE

Erich Dagobert von Drygalski (1865–1949), a geography professor and leader of a four-year expedition to Greenland, was given command of the German South Polar Expedition in 1898. Drygalski, aboard *Gauss,* a three-masted schooner, sighted land on February 21, 1902, in the region of 90°E and named it Kaiser Wilhelm II Land. On the same day, the ship was beset, soon becoming, in Drygalski's words, 'a toy of the elements.'

With *Gauss* trapped in a west-drifting pack, the men settled into a routine of scientific work by day, and card games, lectures, beer and music by night. Snow drifted up over the ship and its warm, humid interior became infused with a very German *Gemütlichkeit* (coziness). The expedition even published a shipboard newspaper, *Das Antarktische Intelligenzblatt* (The Antarctic Intelligencer).

A sledging party journeyed 80km to the Antarctic coast, discovering along the way a low volcano they named Gaussberg after their ship. On March 29, 1902, Drygalski ascended 480m in a large, tethered hydrogen balloon and used a telephone to report his observations to the ship.

When spring and then summer arrived, sawing, drilling and even dynamiting the 6m-thick ice had done nothing to free the ship. Drygalski noticed that cinders from the ship's smokestack caused the ice on which they landed to melt, since the dark ashes absorbed the sun's heat. He had his men lay a trail of coal ash, supplemented by rotting garbage, across the 600m of ice separating *Gauss* from open water.

The ingenious trick worked. Soon there was a 2m-deep channel filled with water. Two months passed, however, before – on February 8, 1903 – the bottom of the canal cracked open and the ship was freed.

1912

Robert F Scott, Henry Bowers, Edgar Evans, Lawrence 'Titus' Oates and Edward Wilson sledge to 90°S on January 17. On the return to their hut on Ross Island, all five men perish.

1912–13

A total of 10,760 whales are killed and processed this season in the Antarctic by six land stations, 21 factory ships and 62 catcher boats.

1913

Douglas Mawson staggers into his base at Cape Denison after his two companions perish on a sledging trip. Mawson arrives only a few hours after his relief ship, *Aurora,* departed.

1915–16

Ernest Shackleton's *Endurance* is crushed by Weddell Sea pack ice. Expedition members live on the ice for five months before sailing three small boats to Elephant Island in the South Shetlands.

on the north coast of Booth Island, a place he named Port Charcot for his father. After the spring breakup, the expedition sailed north, running into trouble on January 15, 1903, when their schooner, *Français,* struck a rock. Despite attempts at plugging the hole, the expedition was forced to disband in Argentina. Charcot headed home, where his wife Jeanne divorced him for desertion.

In 1908, Charcot again sailed south on a French government expedition in the newly built *Pourquoi Pas?* (Why Not?), which carried the name Charcot had christened his toy boats with as a child. The group continued the survey work on the western side of the Peninsula that Charcot had begun with *Français*. He discovered and named the Fallières Coast, circled Adelaide Island and proved its insularity, and discovered Marguerite Bay (named for his second wife, Meg).

The ship boasted electric lighting and a 1500-volume library, which proved invaluable during winter 1909, when the expedition was icebound in a bay at Petermann Island. The group set up a shore station, with huts for meteorological, seismic, magnetic and tidal research.

Twenty-six years later, Charcot and *Pourquoi Pas?* were again sailing treacherous waters, this time off Iceland, when a gale arose and claimed captain, ship and all but one of the 43-man crew.

Shackleton – The *Nimrod* Expedition

Anglo-Irishman Ernest Henry Shackleton (1874–1922), second of 10 children born to a doctor and his Quaker wife, lived by his family motto: *Fortitudine vincimus* (By fortitude we conquer). An indefatigable worker with a charming, forceful personality, Shackleton was badly stung by his own ill health during Scott's furthest south expedition in 1902 (p125).

Back in Scotland, Shackleton worked as a PR man for a big Glasgow steelworks. The works' owner, William Beardmore, took a liking to Shackleton and sponsored his next Antarctic expedition. The British Antarctic Expedition sailed from New Zealand in *Nimrod,* a three-masted sealing ship with 40 years' Arctic use. When Shackleton arrived at the Ross Ice Shelf in January 1908, he built his hut at Cape Royds on Ross Island (p103), before pushing for the Pole. Thwarted by diminished supplies, Shackleton and his men were forced to abandon their attempt only 180km from their goal.

> The Scottish National Antarctic Expedition achieved an important milestone: moving pictures were made in the Antarctic for the first time. Also, photographs document the first known use of bagpipes in the Far South; an emperor penguin has its head thrown back and beak agape, being serenaded by a kilted piper.

Amundsen

Norwegian Roald Engelbregt Gravning Amundsen (1872–1928) was already a veteran explorer by the time he sailed in 1910 from Christiana (modern-day Oslo) on his way to what only he and a few others knew was Antarctica. Amundsen had been with the first group to winter south of the Antarctic Circle, de Gerlache's *Belgica* expedition (p145). From

1928

Australian George Hubert Wilkins makes the first powered flight in Antarctica, flying his Lockheed Vega monoplane from a Deception Island airstrip for just 20 minutes before the weather closes in.

1929

Taking off from the expedition's base 'Little America' at the Bay of Whales on the Ross Ice Shelf, Richard Evelyn Byrd and three companions become the first people to fly over the South Pole.

1935

American Lincoln Ellsworth and Canadian Herbert Hollick-Kenyon complete the first trans-Antarctic flight. Intended to last just 14 hours, the 3700km flight is stretched to two weeks by poor weather.

1935

Norwegian Caroline Mikkelsen becomes the first woman to set foot on the continent when she lands at the Vestfold Hills with her husband Klarius, captain of a whaling ship, on February 20.

1903 to 1906 he accomplished the first navigation of the Northwest Passage, a goal sought by mariners for centuries. He spent three winters in the Arctic, learning from the native Inuit much about polar clothing, travel and dog-handling, which would later prove invaluable.

The Arctic was Amundsen's first interest. He had long dreamed of reaching the North Pole, but as he was planning an expedition the news reached him that American Robert E Peary claimed to have reached N 90° on April 6, 1909. Amundsen quickly, and secretly, turned his ambitions 180 degrees.

Amundsen's *Fram* (Forward), used by Norwegian explorer Fridtjof Nansen on his unsuccessful attempt to reach the North Pole, sailed from Norway on August 9, 1910. *Fram* had a diesel engine, allowing quick start-up (as opposed to a coal-fired steam engine), as well as a rounded hull so it would rise out of pressing ice floes (rather than being nipped like a standard hull). To prevent Robert Scott from learning of his plans, Amundsen revealed his intentions to just three members of the expedition, until he reached Madeira, where he stunned the others with the news. Soon after, he sent his infamous telegram to Scott in Melbourne: 'Beg leave to inform you *Fram* proceeding Antarctic Amundsen.'

Charcot used his inheritance of 400,000 gold francs and a Fragonard painting, *Le Pacha*, to finance construction of the three-masted schooner, *Français*, and to outfit it with laboratory equipment.

Amundsen established his base, Framheim (home of *Fram*), on the ice shelf at the Bay of Whales. In a small prefab wooden hut, nine men spent the winter. Outside, 15 identical tents served as store sheds and doghouses for the expedition's 97 North Greenland dogs. From Framheim, Amundsen had the advantage of starting 100km closer to the Pole than Scott would, but he would have to pioneer a new route up to the polar plateau from the Ross Ice Shelf.

On December 14, 1911, Amundsen and his men became the first explorers to reach the South Pole. For more on their finely executed journey, see p126.

OTHER SHACKLETON 'FIRSTS'

In addition to the polar party reaching a furthest south, Shackleton's *Nimrod* group:

» **Climbed Mt Erebus**: six men led by TW Edgeworth David reached the volcano's rim on March 10, 1908, after a five-day climb.

» **Reached the South Magnetic Pole**: Douglas Mawson and Alistair Mackay, with David again leading, hiked nearly 1600km, arriving on January 16, 1909.

» **Tested Antarctica's first motorcar**: an Arrol-Johnston, it proved no good in snow, but was useful for transporting loads across ice.

» **Published the first (and only) book in Antarctica**: 80 copies of *Aurora Australis*.

1946

The US Operation Highjump, the largest Antarctic expedition ever, sends 4700 men, 33 aircraft and 13 ships to the continent. Aerial photographs are taken along nearly three-quarters of the coast.

1947

Americans Edith ('Jackie') Ronne and Jennie Darlington become the first women to overwinter on Antarctica on the Ronne Antarctic Research Expedition to Stonington Island.

1954

Phillip Law and the Australian National Antarctic Research Expeditions establish Mawson Station in East Antarctica. Named after Douglas Mawson, it is the continent's first permanent scientific station.

1956

US Navy pilot Conrad 'Gus' Shinn flies Rear Admiral George Dufek and five others to the South Pole aboard R4D aircraft *Que Sera Sera*; they are the first people to arrive since Robert F Scott.

Scott – The *Terra Nova* Expedition

Scott's British Antarctic Expedition sailed from New Zealand on November 29, 1910, with the renewed goal of reaching the South Pole. Arriving at Ross Island in January 1911 aboard *Terra Nova,* the old Scottish whaler that had been one of the two relief ships sent at the end of the *Discovery* expedition, Scott found ice blocking the way to his old *Discovery* hut, so he established winter quarters at Cape Evans (p101),named after his second-in-command, Edward Ratcliffe Garth Russell 'Teddy' Evans. As soon as the hut was built, Scott commenced an ambitious program of depot-laying. He also introduced a useful Antarctic innovation: a telephone line was established between Cape Evans and Hut Point.

The next spring, on October 24, Scott dispatched a party with two motor-sledges, and eight days later followed with a larger group of men and 10 ponies. Various teams relayed supplies and laid depots. Despite finally reaching the pole on January 17, Scott's expedition was tragically unsuccessful – not only did they fail to reach the pole first (that triumph went to Roald Amundsen), but Scott and the four men travelling with him perished on their return journey. For more details, see p127.

Among those left at the edge of the continent were the infamous three-man midwinter trekkers to Cape Crozier (see p106) and a separate Northern Party, led by Victor Campbell. This party discovered Oates Land (memorializing Lawrence Oates) and spent a winter of terrible privation in a snow cave at Terra Nova Bay on the Ross Sea's western shore.

A six-man group led by geologist Griffith Taylor explored the mysterious, otherworldly Dry Valleys, which Scott had found on the *Discovery* expedition.

Amundsen's planning was meticulous: he took three or four backups of every critical item, and the team laid 10 extremely well-marked depots as far as 82°S, which together contained 3400kg of stores and food.

Mawson

Australian geologist Douglas Mawson (1882–1958) had been asked by Robert Scott to accompany *Terra Nova,* but he declined the invitation in favor of leading his own expedition. Already a veteran of Shackleton's *Nimrod* expedition, Mawson wanted to explore new territory west of Cape Adare.

The Australasian Antarctic Expedition sailed from Hobart on December 2, 1911, in *Aurora,* an old sealer. Its master was Captain John King Davis (who was also on the *Nimrod* expedition with Mawson and Shackleton). They reached the ice edge in January 1912, then headed west and followed the coast to new territories, which Mawson called King George V Land and claimed for the British crown. Mawson set up his base at Cape Denison on Commonwealth Bay and groundbreaking science and hair-raising adventures ensued (for more, see p120).

1957–58

Forty-six Antarctic stations (including one at the South Pole) operated by 12 countries contribute to the International Geophysical Year, modeled on the International Polar Years of 1882–83 and 1932–33.

1958

Englishman Vivian Fuchs' Commonwealth Trans-Antarctic Expedition (TAE) is the first to successfully cross the continent: from the Weddell Sea coast to the Ross Sea.

BETTMANN / CORBIS©

» Dr Vivian Fuchs

1959

The Antarctic Treaty, reserving Antarctica for peace, prohibiting nuclear explosions and guaranteeing the freedom of science, is signed by 12 nations on December 1. It comes into force in 1961.

In 1929–31, Mawson returned to Antarctica, leading the two summer voyages of the British, Australian & New Zealand Antarctic Research Expedition (BANZARE) to the west of Commonwealth Bay, where they discovered Mac.Robertson Land, named for Sir MacPherson Robertson, an expedition benefactor.

Filchner

With the Pole won by Amundsen, Bavarian army lieutenant Wilhelm Filchner (1877–1957) tackled another question: whether the Weddell and Ross seas were joined by a channel, as some geographers posited. Filchner hoped to cross the Antarctic continent, starting from the Weddell Sea, to solve this puzzle.

Sailing on May 4, 1911 in *Deutschland,* the Second German South Polar Expedition reached the Weddell Sea pack ice by mid-December. After 10 days of pushing through narrow leads, the ship penetrated to the sea's southern coast, William Bruce's Coats Land. Sailing west, Filchner reached new territory, calling it 'Prinz Regent Luitpold Land' (now Luitpold Coast). He also discovered a vast ice shelf, naming it 'Kaiser Wilhelm Barrier' for his emperor (who later insisted that it be renamed after Filchner). Filchner then tried to establish a winter base ('Stationseisberg') on the ice shelf, but these plans had to be hastily abandoned when a huge section of the shelf carrying the expedition's nearly completed hut calved into the sea.

The Antarctic winter closed in and the ship was beset and drifted for nine months. During this period of monotonous tedium, one crew member read an entire dictionary from A to Z. The ship's captain, Richard Vahsel, died of syphilis in August 1912 during the drift and was, as Filchner later wrote, 'committed to the sea in a sack, along with a heavy weight.'

On November 26, 1912, the disintegrating ice released the ship, which sailed to South Georgia and home.

POLAR ARTIFACTS ON THE BLOCK

Captain Scott's descendants auctioned artifacts from his last expedition in 1999. Parts of the Primus stove on which the three last members of the polar party may have cooked their final hot meal brought £27,600. A Union flag found with the bodies, possibly flown by the party at the Pole, sold for £25,300.

A centenary auction in March 2012 saw Scott's farewell letter to Sir Edgar Speyer fetch £163,250.

1961

Using only local anesthetic, Leonid I Rogozov, physician at Russia's Novolazarevskaya Station, successfully removes his own appendix in an emergency operation that lasts one hour and 45 minutes.

1965

Grytviken, South Georgia's last shore-based whaling station, closes as whales are commercially extinct. South Georgia's catch from 1904 to 1966 totaled 175,250 whales.

1966

Antarctica's highest peak, 4900m Vinson Massif in the Sentinel Range of the Ellsworth Mountains, is first climbed by four members of a private US expedition led by Nicholas Clinch.

1969

The first women to reach the South Pole arrive by US Navy aircraft and spend a few hours visiting the station before flying back to McMurdo.

Shackleton – The *Endurance* Expedition

After failing to reach the Pole on his *Nimrod* expedition, Shackleton set his sights on crossing Antarctica. The Imperial Trans-Antarctic Expedition would sail *Endurance* to the Weddell Sea coast, establish a base, and then trek across the continent via the Pole. At the top of the Beardmore Glacier, the crossing party would be met by another group, which would have landed at Ross Island (sailing *Aurora* from Hobart).

Endurance sailed from Plymouth on August 8, 1914, calling at Madeira, Buenos Aires and South Georgia, then pushing into the Weddell Sea pack ice. Soon *Endurance* was squeezing through ever-narrower leads.

By January 19, 1915, *Endurance* was caught. The incredible events that followed have grown to legend, and much of it was caught on film by expedition photographer Frank Hurley. The ship, inexorably crushed by the grinding ice floes, finally sank on November 21. Shackleton and his men lived on the pack ice for five months before they sailed three small open lifeboats to Elephant Island through freezing waters. Since the island was little more than a windswept rock, Shackleton and five others were forced to navigate another 1300km across open sea in the 6.9m *James Caird* (which the ship's carpenter had decked over with scavenged timbers) to seek help from whalers at South Georgia. After 16 exhausting days at sea, they landed at South Georgia, completing one of history's greatest navigational feats. Frank Worsley used a sextant in deep cloud cover and amid 15m waves.

Unfortunately, their South Georgian landfall was at King Haakon Bay, on the bleak, uninhabited southwest coast; the whaling stations were on the island's northeastern side (for more on how they survived, see p58).

When they reached Stromness, a ship was dispatched to pick up the three men left behind at King Haakon Bay. After three failed attempts over the next four months to pick up the 22 men stranded at Elephant Island, Shackleton enlisted the help of *Yelcho,* a steamer lent by the Chilean government, and recovered them all on August 30, 1916. Everyone on *Endurance* had survived.

Meanwhile, the Ross Sea party had encountered its own difficulties. *Aurora* had intended to winter at Ross Island, but a blizzard blew the ship from its moorings, stranding 10 men at Cape Evans. They spent a miserable winter with minimal supplies. *Aurora* was herself beset for 10 months, finally getting free on March 14, 1916. Shackleton met the ship in New Zealand and relieved the Cape Evans party on January 10, 1917.

Shackleton mounted a final journey to the Antarctic, the *Quest* expedition. Upon reaching Grytviken, South Georgia, he died of a heart attack on January 5, 1922 aboard his ship; he is buried at Grytviken.

1978

Emilio Marcos de Palma is born at Argentina's Esperanza Station on January 7, the first person born in Antarctica. Over the next five years, seven more children are born there.

1979

All 257 people aboard Air New Zealand Flight 901 are killed when their DC-10 flies into Mt Erebus in Antarctica's worst air tragedy.

1982

Fire destroys Vostok Station's power plant, killing one man. For eight months, the survivors' only heat comes from warmers made by twisting asbestos fibers into wicks dipped in diesel fuel.

1983

Russia's Vostok Station, located near the South Geomagnetic Pole, records the lowest-ever temperature on Earth: -89.6°C. Vostok's record high temperature, set in 2002, is a balmy -12.3°C.

Antarctic Aviators

Wilkins

Australian George Hubert Wilkins (1888–1958), a veteran of two Antarctic expeditions including one on Shackleton's *Quest,* mounted a well-funded expedition in 1928 (including a lucrative US$25,000 news-rights contract with American press lord William Randolph Hearst), and accomplished the first powered flights in Antarctica (p67).

Wilkins returned to the Antarctic the next summer, making more flights and discoveries. All told, he mapped 200,000 sq km of new territory. He later supported Lincoln Ellsworth with his flights.

Even as *Endurance* prepared to sail in 1914, the firestorm of WWI began engulfing Europe. Britain declared war on Germany on August 4, and Shackleton immediately offered *Endurance* and her crew for war service. Winston Churchill, then First Lord of the Admiralty, wired his thanks, but the expedition was told to proceed.

Byrd

American flier Richard Evelyn Byrd (1888–1957), a graduate of the US Naval Academy, claimed in 1926 to be the first to fly over the North Pole (the claim though has been questioned). In 1927, he was narrowly beaten by Charles Lindbergh in the era's greatest race: solo flight across the Atlantic. Soon after, he made it his goal to become the first to fly over the South Pole.

Byrd's United States Antarctic Expedition's base, Little America, was established at the Bay of Whales on the Ross Ice Shelf in January 1929.

They had three aircraft: a large aluminum Ford trimotor, *Floyd Bennett;* a smaller, single-engine Fairchild, *Stars and Stripes;* and a single-engine Fokker Universal named *The Virginian.* Near the Rockefeller Mountains (named for one of Byrd's sponsors) *The Virginian* blew/flew 800m – unmanned – in a blizzard, to its destruction. With winter's onset, the two remaining planes were cached in snow shelters.

The next season, on November 28, a field party working in the Queen Maud Mountains radioed Little America that the weather was clear, so *Floyd Bennett* took off. In the wee hours of November 29, Byrd and his crew of three piloted over the Pole. For more on the flight, see p128).

Byrd returned to the US as a national hero, feted with ticker-tape parades, a promotion to rear admiral, and a gold medal struck in his honor. He went on to lead four more Antarctic expeditions including the second USAE of 1933–35 (during which he nearly died of carbon monoxide poisoning while living alone at a tiny weather station) and the US's massive Operation Highjump (p155).

Byrd's was the best-funded private expedition to Antarctica in history. He raised nearly a million dollars from sponsors like Charles Lindbergh (US$1000) and the *New York Times,* which paid US$60,000 for exclusive rights.

Ellsworth

American Lincoln Ellsworth (1880–1951), scion of a wealthy Pennsylvania coal-mining family, had whetted his appetite for polar exploration in 1925, when he made the first flight toward the North Pole with Roald

1985

British scientists at Halley Station first measure ozone depletion of the Antarctic stratosphere, making headlines globally and spurring the international agreement on banning chlorofluorocarbons.

1989

Argentine navy supply ship *Bahía Paraíso* strikes a submerged rock pinnacle 3km from the US Palmer Station and spills 645,000L of fuel – Antarctica's worst environmental disaster to date.

1991

The Protocol on Environmental Protection to the Antarctic Treaty is adopted, designating Antarctica as a natural reserve and prohibiting any activity relating to mineral resources, other than scientific research.

1994

In accordance with the Protocol on Environmental Protection, the last sledge dogs leave Antarctica. For 95 years canines had proven themselves tireless workers, remarkable navigators and loyal companions on the Ice.

Amundsen. The flight failed, but he reached the North Pole in 1926, three days after Byrd's (disputed) flight.

In 1931, Ellsworth began a long, productive association with George Hubert Wilkins – with the goal of crossing Antarctica by air. Ellsworth bought a Northrop Gamma monoplane, which he named *Polar Star,* and for his pilot on the Ellsworth Antarctic Expedition he chose Bernt Balchen, chief pilot on Byrd's expedition. Ellsworth's third attempt, in November 1935, was successful (for more details, see p83).

During WWII, a German *Hilfskreuzer,* an armed merchant ship disguised to look like an innocent vessel from another nation, succeeded in a daring Antarctic raid that captured nearly the entire Norwegian whaling fleet – all without bloodshed or a single shot fired.

WWII & the Modern Era

WWII

WWII interrupted the plans of many explorers, although a secret Nazi expedition in 1938–39, led by Alfred Ritscher, was dispatched to Antarctica by Field Marshal Hermann Göring. Göring was interested both in claiming territory and in protecting Germany's growing whaling fleet. The expedition used seaplanes to overfly vast stretches of the ice sheet, dropping 1.5m darts inscribed with swastikas to establish sovereignty – claims that were never recognized.

Operations Highjump & Windmill

In 1946, the US launched Operation Highjump, history's largest Antarctic expedition. Officially called the US Navy Antarctic Developments Project, Highjump sent 4700 men, 33 aircraft, 13 ships and 10 Caterpillar tractors to the continent. It used helicopters and icebreakers for the first time in the Antarctic. Tens of thousands of aerial photographs were taken along nearly three-quarters of the continent's coast, although their usefulness for mapmaking was limited by a lack of ground surveys. The smaller, follow-up expedition the next year (later nicknamed Operation Windmill for its extensive use of helicopters) surveyed major features sighted by Highjump.

ANARE

In February 1954, Phillip Law and the Australian National Antarctic Research Expeditions (ANARE) set up Mawson Station in East Antarctica. Named after Douglas Mawson, this was the first permanent scientific station established on the continent, and the only one outside the Peninsula. Mawson remains one of Australia's three continental stations.

International Geophysical Year

The International Geophysical Year (IGY; July 1, 1957 to December 31, 1958) was declared to pursue global interest in the earth and atmospheric sciences. Sixty-six countries participated from locations around the

1997

Børge Ousland completes the first solo crossing of Antarctica, skiing 2845km from Berkner Island to Ross Island in 64 days. Using parasails, he skied as far as 226km in one day.

1999

Brazilian Amyr Klink completes the first solo circumnavigation of Antarctica in 77 days by sailing his 15m *Paratii* south of the Antarctic Convergence all the way around the continent.

2000

B-15, the largest iceberg ever recorded, measuring 298km by 37km, calves from the Ross Ice Shelf. It is about the size of Jamaica, more than twice the size of US state, Delaware.

2005

Dome A, the highest point on the East Antarctic plateau, is visited for the first time. A Chinese team installs an automated weather station.

world, but the IGY left its greatest legacy in Antarctica. Twelve countries established more than 40 stations on the continent and another 20 on the sub-Antarctic islands. Among these were the US base at the South Pole, created through a massive 84-flight airdrop of 725 tonnes of building materials, and the Soviet Vostok Station at the Geomagnetic South Pole. The international cooperation promoted by the IGY led to the creation of the Antarctic Treaty.

The Antarctic Treaty

In the wake of the IGY, scientists and diplomats codified the spirit of international cooperation in the unprecedented Antarctic Treaty. Signed in 1959 by the 12 nations active in the Antarctic during the IGY, it has governed the continent since 1961.

The Antarctic Treaty (www.ats.aq), which applies to the area south of S 60°, ensures that countries active in Antarctica consult on the uses of the continent. It is surprisingly short but remarkably effective, creating a natural reserve devoted to peace and science where there are no wars, where the environment is fully protected and where research is the priority.

During the IGY, many countries operated tractor traverses across the continental interior. The British Commonwealth Trans-Antarctic Expedition, led by Vivian Fuchs, was the first to cross the continent overland.

Subsequent legislation has further codified environmental protections. Chief among these, the Protocol on Environmental Protection to the Antarctic Treaty (Madrid Protocol; 1991) and its annexes established environmental principles for the conduct of all activities on the Ice, prohibited mining, and requires environmental impact assessments before new activities can be undertaken.

Similarly, the Convention for the Conservation of Antarctic Marine Living Resources (CCAMLR; 1980) protects the species inhabiting the ocean surrounding Antarctica and manages fishing.

The 50 (as of January 2012) Antarctic Treaty members represent about 80% of the world's population. Any state performing significant scientific research in Antarctica can become a 'consultative party,' or full voting member. They meet annually to discuss issues as diverse as scientific cooperation, environmental protection measures, management of tourism and the preservation of historic sites – and make decisions by consensus.

Seven nations (Argentina, Chile, the UK, Australia, France, New Zealand and Norway) have territorial claims, which are not internationally recognized. The Antarctic Treaty 'freezes' territorial claims, but countries have employed various methods to try to reinforce their sovereignty over large sections of Antarctica. These include flagpoles, plaques and stamps, while Argentina has sent pregnant women to the Ice to give birth. Most recently, from 2007 to 2009 the UK, Chile and Argentina all filed for rights to Antarctica's ocean floor in the vicinity of their claims.

2007

Antarctica's first expedition cruise ship – the 'Little Red Ship,' *Explorer* – sinks in the Bransfield Strait after hitting an iceberg. All aboard are rescued unhurt.

2007

The International Polar Year begins 50 years after the International Geophysical Year. Scientists from more than 100 countries begin an intensive, coordinated campaign to study the Arctic and Antarctic.

2008

The US's new elevated station at the South Pole is dedicated by a party of 40 'distinguished visitors' whose outdoor speeches are kept short by subzero temperatures.

2008

Satellite images capture the breaking up of large parts of the Wilkins Ice Shelf, at the base of the Antarctic Peninsula – just as predicted by climate-change models.

International Polar Year 2007–08 & Beyond

International Polar Year 2007–08 (IPY; www.ipy.org) was a coordinated international science program, like IGY, that ran from March 2007 to March 2009. It saw a multitude of international projects advancing polar science and cooperation. For example, the EU's Cryosat satellite and NASA's GRACE satellites measure the mass/gravity of ice sheets and the data is shared freely.

Developing on the IPY mentality of cooperation, in 2011 a US National Academy of Sciences committee proposed an international, multidisciplinary observation system in Antarctica. The committee foresees increased data-gathering and more accurate predictions – necessary in light of the rapid changes the continent (and the planet) is facing.

With the discovery of global climate change and Antarctica's central role in it (see the Environment chapter, p162), Antarctica has become a focus for research, and news of the changes in the ice and ecosystems hits international media regularly. On the Ice, new ecofriendly science bases are being inaugurated, like Belgium's Princess Elisabeth Antarctica Station and Germany's Neumayer III (both in 2009), and facilities like wind turbines are being added to existing stations (like McMurdo and Scott Base) to offset power needs and carbon footprints.

As tourism to the Antarctic has increased, so too have cruise-ship mishaps. In February 2007 *Nordkapp* ran aground in Deception Island's Neptunes Bellows, ripping a 25m gash along her hull. Nearby sister ship *Nordnorge* picked up the 280 passengers for transport home. Then, in November, *Explorer* hit an iceberg and sank, requiring the rescue of more than 150 people. *Explorer*'s sinking (with its fuel on board) highlighted the environmental risks of accidents in Antarctica and helped coalesce the final support needed to push through a ban on the use and carriage of heavy fuel oil in Antarctic waters (which took effect in 2011). Nonetheless, accidents continued to occur: in 2009 *Clelia II* ran aground and then in 2010 lost most of her power after being smacked by a huge wave. In 2012 *Plancius* suffered engine failure, stranding passengers and crew near South Georgia.

The 2011–12 season saw the centenaries of Amundsen's and Scott's attainments of the Pole and focused the spotlight on Antarctica. Media reports followed myriad international exhibitions and private expeditions to the Pole.

Between tourism and science (which is well-publicized over the internet), Antarctica and its mysteries are more accessible to more of the world than ever before. By maintaining environmental protections while developing technologies and international initiatives, much of what is revealed may come to serve humankind enormously in the century ahead.

Flowing into the Amundsen Sea at more than 3050m annually (8m per day), the Pine Island Glacier is believed to be Antarctica's fastest-moving glacier. In 2011–12 NASA scientists observed a rift that began the creation of a 900-sq-km iceberg.

2009

On February 15, Belgium's Princess Elisabeth Antarctica Station is inaugurated. Powered by the sun and wind, the station is the first zero-emission base on the ice.

2010

Neutrino detector IceCube is completed, with 5,484 digital optical modules buried in one cubic kilometer of ice below the South Pole. It searches for dark matter in outer space.

2012

Pakistan accedes to the Antarctic Treaty, bringing to 50 the number of signatories to the short but remarkably effective treaty, which applies to the area south of 60°S.

2012

Antarctica's largest subglacial lake, Vostok, is tapped by Russian scientists. The body of water, untouched for 200 million years, is the first subglacial lake to be explored.

Environment

Antarctica is a continent of extraordinary natural beauty, physical purity and serenity. Many of its features are, simply put, unique. Tourism and science are the primary activities in Antarctica today, each with attendant environmental issues. And the continent serves as a rare test case for many global issues, such as global warming.

The Land

Around 200 million years ago Antarctica was joined with Australia, Africa, South America, India and New Zealand in the supercontinent Gondwana. About 20 million years later, Gondwana began the enormously slow process of breaking into the pieces we recognize today, and the continents, subcontinent and islands began moving into their present positions. Antarctica arrived at the southern pole around 100 million years ago and had forests with mammals and dinosaurs. Fossil evidence includes conifer, fern and reptile species that have also been found in India, South America, Australia and Africa.

MELTING

Antarctica's ice sheets contain 90% of the world's ice, holding about 70% of the world's fresh water. If they melted, it is estimated the world's oceans would rise by more than 60m.

Between 34 and 24 million years ago, what is now known as the Drake Passage opened, and the isolation of the continent began. With falling CO2 levels, Antarctica began to cool dramatically.

Today the continent has a diameter of about 4500km and an area of about 14.2 million sq km (1.4 times the size of the US). This most isolated, arid and highest continent has an average elevation of 2250m, and is classified as a desert.

Antarctica is divided by the 2900km-long Transantarctic Mountains into East Antarctica (sometimes referred to as 'Greater Antarctica') and West Antarctica (or 'Lesser Antarctica'), with the directions deriving from 0° longitude. Antarctica's highest point is Vinson Massif (4900.3m).

The rocks of East Antarctica are at least three billion years old, among the oldest on Earth. Some of the oldest terrestrial rock, estimated to be 3.84 billion years old, was found in Enderby Land. West Antarctica is relatively new: only 700 million years old.

The Antarctic Peninsula separates the two great embayments into the continent, the Weddell and Ross Seas, each of which flows in a broad clockwise motion. Each also has its own ice shelf (Ronne Ice Shelf and Ross Ice Shelf, respectively), which are extensions of the great Antarctic ice sheet.

In September, Antarctica's late winter, the size of the continent effectively doubles with the freezing of the sea ice, which can extend more than 1000km from the coast. The Antarctic coastline is still far from being perfectly charted.

The Antarctic Ice Sheet

Satellite images show that ice covers 99.6% of Antarctica. The Antarctic ice sheet has an area of about 13.3 million sq km (1.7 times the size of Australia). This ice is up to 4775m thick in some locations and on average is about 2700m thick – giving it a total ice volume of about 28 million cu km. In some places its enormous weight has depressed the underlying landmass by nearly 1600m. Antarctica's continental shelf is about three times deeper than that of any other continent.

This enormous amount of ice has formed through the accumulation of snow over millions of years, and exists in a state of dynamic equilibrium. The amount of snow deposited in any one year is relatively very low – Antarctica is a desert and the driest continent on Earth. Because the snow has been deposited over so many years without melting, the ice sheet provides a natural archive that glaciologists and climatologists study for evidence of past environments and of climatic changes.

When snow is deposited it consolidates to form ice. Due to pressure created by its own weight, the ice flows from the high interior toward the Antarctic coast, where large slabs break off to form icebergs.

The Southern Ocean

The Southern Ocean encircles Antarctica in a continuous ring of mainly eastward-flowing water. This water comprises 10% of the world's oceans, and is the most biologically abundant ocean in the world.

As well as connecting the Atlantic, Pacific and Indian oceans, the Southern Ocean also isolates the Antarctic continent from warmer waters. The strong westerly winds around Antarctica help form the Antarctic Circumpolar Current. This, the world's longest current, extends from the sea surface to the ocean floor, and has an average eastward flow rate of 153 million cu m/sec – more than 100 times the combined flow of all the world's rivers and four times greater than the Gulf Stream. Deep waters from all of the world's oceans are upwelled here. And it separates polar waters and their ecosystems from subtropical ones.

For information on the Antarctic Convergence, see p49.

The Southern Ocean is also vital in the air–sea exchange of carbon dioxide. Its cold waters naturally absorb massive amounts of CO2, leading some scientists to study the possibility of deliberately increasing this uptake in order to minimize the impact of global warming.

The largest glacier in the world is the Lambert Glacier, which flows onto the Amery Ice Shelf in East Antarctica.

FAST FACTS

» **Average elevation, including the floating ice shelves**: 1958m; excluding ice shelves: 2194m.

» **Highest point**: Vinson Massif (4900.3m); highest point of Antarctic Plateau: Dome A (4093m); highest mountain on Antarctic Peninsula: Mt Jackson (3184m).

» **Average thickness of Antarctica's continental ice**: 1829m; average thickness of East Antarctic Ice Sheet: 2226m; West Antarctic Ice Sheet: 1306m.

» **Maximum depth of the ice sheet**: 4776m (measured near Dome C at S 69° 56', E 135°12').

» **Total volume of ice sheets and ice shelves**: 28 million cu km.

» **Total length of Antarctic coastline**: approximately 45,317km; ice shelves make up 18,877km (42% of total); ice 20,972km (46%); and rock 5468km (12%). The coast is dynamic and these totals vary over time.

» **Largest ice shelf**: Ross Ice Shelf (487,000 sq km, or roughly the size of France). It is several hundred meters thick, and like all ice shelves, it floats!

» **Area of Antarctica that is free of ice**: 44,890 sq km (about 0.4% of the continent; area slightly larger than Denmark).

» **Lowest bedrock elevation**: -2555m, in the Bentley Subglacial Trench (S 80°19', W 110°5').

OCEAN RIGHTS

The UN Convention on the Law of the Sea's 'Exclusive Economic Zone' gives a country exclusive use of the resources in its water (such as fish) and on the sea floor. In Antarctica, three of the seven countries claiming Antarctic territories have applied for these rights. If the rights are granted, the nations would still be bound by all of the Antarctic environmental rules, including the mining ban. A country could choose to impose even higher levels of environmental protection.

Scientists have proposed a monitoring network of Southern Ocean systems (atmosphere, land, ice, ocean and ecosystems), the Southern Ocean Observing System.

Environmental Issues

Despite its isolation, Antarctica is increasingly subject to the same threats and challenges as the rest of the planet. Some major impacts on the Antarctic environment are caused by people who have never even visited. Climate change and ozone depletion, pesticide residue, rubbish and fishing practices all affect Antarctica. As does the impact of visitors.

Antarctic Bottom Water forms when seawater is cooled by air and made saltier by ice formation. It sinks to the ocean floor because it's denser than surrounding water. Then it travels northward, mixing with warmer waters and affecting the world's heat balance. In 2012, research showed it's been disappearing – cause unknown.

Exploitation of Marine Life

Sealers were among the first to explore the Antarctic waters and millions of seals were slaughtered up until the end of the 19th century. Whaling became a major industry near the beginning of the 20th century, with most whale species being hunted to near extinction. Although commercial whaling is now prohibited in Antarctica and its surrounding waters, a loophole allowing whaling for research purposes permits the Japanese whaling fleet to catch 1000 whales a year. Commercial sealing is regulated by the 1978 Convention on the Conservation of Antarctic Seals, although it's unlikely sealing will return.

Commercial fishing was regulated in 1980 with the Convention for the Conservation of Antarctic Marine Living Resources (CCAMLR; www.ccamlr.org), which ensures that the Southern Ocean's living resources are treated as a single ecosystem. Measures under CCAMLR identify protected species, set catch limits, identify fishing regions, define closed seasons, regulate fishing methods and establish fisheries inspection. It applies south of the Antarctic Convergence, a zone much larger than the Antarctic Treaty area. But illegal fishing continues to be a problem (see p183).

Sampling of seal blubber and milk has shown a slow but steady accumulation of pesticides and other organic poisons, transported south from the industries and agriculture of the northern hemisphere.

Exploitation of Minerals

The Protocol on Environmental Protection prohibits all mining in Antarctica. Iron ore, coal and other minerals have all been found, but their quantities and qualities are still unknown. It is theorized that oil and natural gas exist beneath Antarctica's continental shelf, but no commercial-size deposits have ever been found. At present, exploiting any of these deposits would be highly uneconomical; the equivalent, in one scientist's words, of 'mining on the moon.'

Nevertheless, there was a knotty history to get to the current prohibition on mining, and in 2041 the criteria required to lift the ban become less stringent. If no action is taken, the ban will continue.

For more on the Protocol on Environmental Protection, see under Environmental Impact of Science.

Environmental Impact of Science

Most people in Antarctica and on its surrounding islands are either scientists or support staff at the scientific bases. While today's science bases are environmentally responsible, this wasn't always the case. Early on, scientific bases operated without much environmental awareness, burning waste, dumping barrels of oil, and building bases and airstrips in sensitive areas such as penguin rookeries. In 1961, the US's McMurdo Station installed a nuclear reactor. It was shut down in 1972 and shipped back to the US along with 101 drums of radioactive earth.

The situation changed in the 1980s when tourists on ships, the first independent visitors, noticed the damage and complained. In the late 1980s and 1990s NGOs, such as Greenpeace, wrote reports and brought independent journalists on expeditions. International pressure on the governments with scientific bases led to greener practices and an understanding that scientific research should be carried out while protecting the environment. A clean Antarctic has great scientific value; a contaminated one does not.

Throughout the '80s many stations were cleaned up, and this major international shift in attitude culminated in the 1991 signing of the Protocol on Environmental Protection. Also known as the Madrid Protocol, it came into force in 1998, and designates Antarctica as a 'natural reserve, devoted to peace and science.' It establishes environmental principles for the conduct of all activities; prohibits mining; and subjects all activi-

Many governments now have environmental officers and waste-management programs with environmental-awareness training for all staff in Antarctica. In some cases, they audit the environmental impact of their activities.

ALIENS IN ANTARCTICA

Worldwide, many non-native species (also called 'alien species' or 'aliens') have invaded and affected virtually every ecosystem. The cost includes the loss of native species and ecosystems. Native biodiversity on sub-Antarctic islands has been heavily impacted by invasive plants and vertebrates, including rats, giant mice, feral cats and weeds (for more examples, see www.issg.org/database).

While the Antarctic continent itself has, so far, escaped the ravages of biological invasion, non-native organisms, including terrestrial invertebrates and plants, and a marine crustacean, have been found surviving in the Antarctic Treaty region. The possibility of successful establishment and development of invasiveness is increasing as growing numbers of visitors from government programs, tourism and fisheries add to the chances of 'hitchhiking' organisms arriving in the Antarctic on equipment, containers, clothing or ships' hulls. The increasing number of connections between the Arctic and Antarctic regions mean that more organisms originate in a similar climate. Moreover, faster transport increases an organism's probability of arriving in good shape for survival.

In the longer term, climate change will make the receiving environment more 'hospitable' and hence increase the threat of biological invasion.

The issue has been spearheaded by the International Union for Conservation of Nature (IUCN) in Antarctic Treaty meetings since 1998, as well as by international projects during International Polar Year (IPY) 2007–08. One study estimates that during the 2007–08 season, 70,000 seeds arrived with visitors. About one-fifth of tourists and two-fifths of scientists accidentally carried seeds, and half those seeds hailed from very cold regions, making them ideal candidates for naturalization.

Prevention

Lessons learned in the rest of the world show that preventing the arrival of such non-native organisms is the best approach because of the difficulty and cost of eradicating invaders once they are established. The proactive, preventative approach of Antarctic Treaty parties (and responsible tour operators) includes cleaning boots, gear and clothing and checking Velcro areas – before going to Antarctica – and removing all seeds, soil, or other material of biological origin.

ties to prior assessment of their environmental impacts. Annexes to the protocol detail rules regarding conservation of Antarctic fauna and flora, waste disposal, marine pollution, management of protected areas, and liability arising from environmental emergencies.

The Ferocious Summer: Palmer's Penguins and the Warming of Antarctica by Meredith Hooper gives a clear explanation in layman's terms of some of the effects of climate change in Antarctica.

Environmental Impact of Tourism

Tourist visitors to the Antarctic far outnumber scientists and support personnel. Consequently, many regulations have been developed to mitigate the environmental impact of tourism.

The classic example of human impact in the Antarctic is a footprint in a moss bed, still visible a decade after it was made. Less obvious is the impact on 'invisible' wildlife, such as algae living inside rocks or flora underneath snow.

Animals can be affected even when they don't show it noticeably in their behavior. German researchers, for instance, found that heart rates of incubating Adélies increased markedly when they were approached by a human still 30m away, even though the birds showed no visible response.

The Protocol on Environmental Protection to the Antarctic Treaty studies the environmental impact of tourism through its Antarctic Site Inventory project, which began field work in 1994. The project is managed by Oceanites, Inc. (www.oceanites.org), the only nongovernmental, publicly supported organization conducting scientific research in Antarctica.

In August 2011 a ban on the use and carriage of heavy fuel oil (HFO) imposed by the International Maritime Organization was projected to reduce the number of voyages by 500-plus passenger cruise ships from 12 (in 2010–11) to five (in 2011–12). And 500-plus passenger ships may not land.

Land-based infrastructure for tourism such as hotels or hard-rock airstrips is opposed by all environmental NGOs because the environmental impact cannot be justified.

Protected Areas

An EU-funded project (www.ice2sea.eu) tracks ice changes and projects their contribution to sea levels. The European Space Agency (www.esa.int) uses ice-measuring satellite CryoSat to measure Antarctica's ice sheet.

The Antarctic Treaty System provides for Antarctic Specially Protected Areas (ASPAs), which are designed to preserve unique ecological systems, natural features or areas where research is either underway or planned.

No one is allowed to enter an ASPA without a specific permit. Many ASPAs are not marked, but tour leaders should tell you where they are.

Climate Change & Antarctica

The world's climate is influenced by many factors, including the amount of energy coming from the sun, the amount of greenhouse gases and aerosols in the atmosphere, and the properties of the Earth's surface, which determine how much solar energy is retained or reflected. Antarctica has proven central to many climate change discoveries, as well as vulnerable to many of its impacts.

Ozone Depletion

The spring ozone 'hole' over the Antarctic continent was discovered in 1985. During February and March in seven of the last 11 years, significant ozone decline was observed in northern latitudes. Stratospheric ozone depletion is caused by chlorine gas formed from various artificial chemicals such as chlorofluorocarbons (CFCs) and halons.

Sunlight (hence the spring-time hole) and cold temperatures are necessary to complete the release of chlorine gas to destroy the ozone.

Ozone depletion is significant because the hole allows substantially higher levels of ultraviolet-B (UV-B) radiation to reach Antarctica and the Southern Ocean in spring and early summer, the peak period of biological activity. Increased UV levels threaten plankton, the base of the Antarctic marine ecosystem, upon which all life (from fish to seabirds, penguins, seals and whales) depends. Researchers have found a 6% to 12% reduction in marine primary productivity during the period of the hole.

In addition, Antarctic animals and vegetation may become directly damaged by increased UV-B, or by the appearance of shorter wavelength UV-C, the most damaging form of this radiation. Nobody knows yet to what degree Antarctic life can adapt to withstand this increasing stress.

GUIDELINES FOR VISITORS TO THE ANTARCTIC

In 2005–07, Antarctic Treaty countries adopted guidelines designed to limit the cumulative impact of visitors. These site-specific rules for the 32 most visited sites in the Antarctic Peninsula, Ross Sea area and sub-Antarctic islands establish a visitor code of conduct, limit landings to certain size ships (some sites prohibit visits by ships carrying more than 200 passengers) and set daily limits on the number of hours a site can be visited.

In 2011, treaty parties established new guidelines, applicable everywhere on the Ice, as noted below. For the full regulations see www.ats.aq or ask your tour operator. For the rules related to wildlife, see the Wildlife chapter, p169.

Protected Areas

» Know the locations of areas that have been afforded special protection, and observe any restrictions on entry or on activities that can be carried out in and near them.

» Do not move, remove or damage historic sites or artifacts.

» Clean boots and clothes of snow and grit before entering sites.

Environment

» Do not discard garbage on land or at sea. Open burning is prohibited.

» Do not disturb or pollute lakes or streams.

» Do not take souvenirs or collect biological or geological specimens, including rocks, bones, eggs, fossils, or parts or contents of buildings.

Scientific Research

» Do not interfere with scientific research, facilities or equipment.

» Obtain permission before visiting Antarctic science and logistic-support facilities; confirm arrangements 24 to 72 hours before arriving, and comply strictly with the rules regarding such visits.

Safety

» Be prepared for severe and changeable weather. Be sure that your equipment and clothing meet Antarctic standards.

» Know your capabilities and the dangers posed by the Antarctic environment. Plan activities with safety in mind at all times.

» Take note of, and act on, advice and instructions from your leaders; do not stray from your group.

» Do not walk onto glaciers or large snowfields without proper equipment and experience; there is a real danger of falling into hidden crevasses.

» Do not enter emergency refuges (except in emergencies). If you use equipment or food from a refuge, inform the nearest research station or national authority once the emergency is over.

» Respect any smoking restrictions, and safeguard against fire, a hazard in Antarctica's dry environment.

The discovery of the ozone hole and its effects led to the negotiation of the Montreal Protocol on Substances that Deplete the Ozone Layer (entered into force in 1989), an international treaty designed to phase out the production of some substances responsible for ozone depletion. As a result, ozone depleting gases in the Antarctic stratosphere reached a maximum around the year 2000, and are now declining.

Warming Temperatures

Carbon dioxide and other greenhouse gases warm the surface of the Earth by trapping heat in the atmosphere, which under 'normal' circumstances keeps our planet habitable. However, the atmospheric concentrations of greenhouse gases such as carbon dioxide (CO2), methane (CH4) and nitrous oxide (N2O) have significantly increased since the beginning of the industrial revolution. This is mainly due to human activities such as the burning of fossil fuels, land-use changes and agriculture. The atmospheric concentration of CO2 is now far higher than at any time in the last 650,000 years. It has also been increasing faster in the last decade than it has since the beginning of continuous measurements around 1960. As a result, global temperatures (and sea levels) are rising.

The severity of the ozone hole varies from year to year, depending on the meteorological conditions of the stratosphere during the Antarctic winter. According to 2011 data, it is expected to recover over the next 50 years.

Global Impacts

The Intergovernmental Panel on Climate Change (IPCC; www.ipcc.ch) was established in 1988 by the World Meteorological Organization and the UN Environment Programme. IPCC assesses scientific information relevant to human-induced climate change, the impacts of human-induced climate change and options for adaptation and mitigation. Its latest report was released in 2007.

There are many observations of increasing air and ocean temperatures. Eleven of the 12 years between 2001 and 2011 rank among the 12 warmest years recorded since 1850; 2005 and 2010 were the warmest years on record. From 1906 to 2005, global temperature has increased by 0.74°C. Regional temperature changes have also been observed, including larger

ICEBERGS *DR JO JACKA*

The Antarctic ice sheet is the 'iceberg factory' of the Southern Ocean. The total volume of ice calved from the ice sheet each year is about 2300 cu km, and it has been estimated that there are about 300,000 icebergs in the Southern Ocean at any one time. Individual icebergs range in dimension from a few meters (often called 'growlers') to about 5m ('bergy bits') to kilometers.

From time to time particularly large icebergs break off the ice sheet. These can be tens of kilometers to even 100km long. At any one time there might be four or five gigantic icebergs in excess of 50km in length in the Southern Ocean, usually close to the Antarctic coast. In 2000, one of the world's biggest icebergs – about the size of Connecticut – broke free from the Ross Ice Shelf. It held enough freshwater to supply the world for over a year.

These larger icebergs are tabular in shape and form by calving from the large Antarctic ice shelves (eg the Ross, Filchner or Amery ice shelves). Typically, these icebergs are about 30m to 40m high (above sea level) and as much as 300m deep. After erosion from wind and waves, and melting from the warmer sea temperatures away from the Antarctic coast, the tabular icebergs become unstable and roll over to form jagged irregular icebergs, sometimes with spikes towering up to 60m into the air and with even greater protrusions deep under the ocean surface. Ultimately, icebergs melt completely as they drift to more northerly, warmer water.

Dr Jo Jacka, Chief Scientific Editor of the Journal of Glaciology

changes in Arctic and Antarctic temperatures (eg 2.8°C in the Antarctic Peninsula – the highest rise in the world).

Globally, sea level is rising at about 3.5mm each year. Sea level will rise at different rates in different places. Due to factors like the Earth's rotation, the shape of ocean basins, and ocean circulation, the loss of West Antarctica ice, for example, would cause a 15% higher-than-average sea rise along the coastal US.

Effects of climate change have been observed in many natural systems, on all continents and in most oceans. Glaciers are melting; frozen ground is thawing; and damage associated with coastal flooding is increasing. Regional changes include those in sea ice and pack ice, ocean salinity, wind patterns, droughts, precipitation, frequency of heat waves and intensity of tropical cyclones.

Antarctic ice cores reveal that levels of greenhouse gases in the atmosphere and the temperature are intimately linked.

Recent changes in climate have already had significant impacts on biodiversity and ecosystems, including changes in species distributions, population sizes, the timing of reproduction or migration, and higher frequency of pest and disease outbreaks.

Projections for the Future

The IPCC estimates that global temperature from the 1980s to the year 2100 will rise by between 1.8°C and 4°C if no additional mitigation measures are put in place. It is estimated that up to 30% of plant and animal species could become extinct if the global increase exceeds 1.5°C to 2.5°C. The average warming of inhabited continents is likely to be twice as much as it was during the 20th century.

Global average sea level is expected to rise by 0.4m to 2m during that time (but these calculations do not take into account the possibility that ice could be lost more rapidly).

Other projected changes include acidification of the oceans, reduced snow cover and sea ice, more frequent heatwaves and heavy precipitation, more intense tropical cyclones, and slower oceanic currents.

According to the International Union for Conservation of Nature (IUCN), there is compelling evidence that continued climate change will be catastrophic for much of our biodiversity. Modeling shows that the ranges occupied by many species will become unsuitable for them. Because species will shift habitats at different rates, the community structure of ecosystems will become very disrupted. The same could be true for humans.

Global sea level has risen by 17cm during the 20th century. A rise of 30cm to 50cm caused by melting ice sheets in Antarctica would flood Polynesian islands. If the West Antarctic ice sheet were to become destabilized and 'slide' into the sea, it could create a rise of up to 6m.

Impacts on Antarctica

Antarctica can be likened to an early warning system for global warming. The IPCC suggests that global warming will be greatest in the polar regions. Recent data shows a sustained atmospheric temperature increase of 2.8°C in the western Antarctic Peninsula region since the 1940s. Mean winter air temperatures since the 1950s have increased by 6°C; this is one of the fastest increases in the world.

Consistent with climate change is the rapid disintegration and collapsing of ice shelves in the Antarctic Peninsula and the breaking off of large icebergs. A 2012 study examined satellite data from 1972 to 2011, finding that ice shelves in West Antarctica are steadily losing their grip on land. For example, ESA's Envisat satellite observed the Larsen B ice shelf losing 4990 sq km of ice from 2002 to 2011.

Currently, melting in West Antarctica contributes 1mm to 2mm per year to global sea rise, but this could increase with the acceleration of ice loss in the region. Another 2012 study showed that simply thinning ice sheets (as opposed to calving) also accelerates glaciers' descents to the coast.

A further consequence of increased melting is a decrease in the salinity of the Ross Sea, since freshwater will be added to the sea water.

Scientists have also measured a 20% decline in Antarctic sea-ice extent since the 1950s. This directly influences the breeding success of penguins. In the Peninsula region (where the duration of sea-ice cover has decreased by over 80 days since 1978) the Adélie population has declined by 80%. This is due directly to warming and also because it affects krill reproduction, and hence the amount of food available to krill-feeding penguins.

With changes in climate, and therefore ecosystems, some penguin populations, like the Adélies, will dwindle. Chinstraps, which had been thought to be relatively safe since they inhabit more ice-free areas than the Adélies, were shown in a 2012 study also to be declining (a 36% decline in one colony was noted). As with the Adélies, chinstraps are krill-eaters, and so impacted upon by the ice reduction. Gentoo penguins have a more variable diet, and so their populations are not decreasing due to ice-melt (as of the time of writing).

Ironically, according to a 2012 study, climate change could harm Antarctic fur seal populations because as the weather warms it is also projected to get wetter and windier, making it harder for them to stay warm in their vulnerable early months of life.

International Response

In Rio de Janiero in 1992, 198 countries including the US signed the UN Framework Convention on Climate Change (http://unfccc.int), a voluntary agreement that contained no legally binding commitments to cut greenhouse gas emissions. A two-year negotiation then resulted in the Kyoto Protocol, which entered into force on February 16, 2005. This legally binding agreement aims to reduce greenhouse gases that cause climate change.

Despite continued debate about the protocol's costs and benefits, it is considered by many to be the most far-reaching agreement on the environment and sustainable development adopted so far. Most of the world's countries agreed to ratify and implement it, but not the USA.

The 2009 Copenhagen Summit and 2010 Cancun Agreements continued negotiations to develop next-step accords for keeping global warming below 2°C. In Cancun, nations set new climate goals which are not legally binding. This included the US (with a target of reducing emissions 17% below 2005 levels) and China. (US cap-and-trade legislation passed in the House in 2010, but failed to pass in the Senate.)

MEASURING THE ICE SHEET & CLIMATE CHANGE

Glaciologists measure the amount of snow falling on the ice sheet and compare this with the amount of ice flowing toward the coast (some moving as fast as 9m a day), and ultimately with the amount of ice breaking off as icebergs or melting in the warmer coastal margins of the continent. These quantities would be the same if there had been no change in the climate during the thousands of years since the ice in the icebergs was falling as snow. If they are different, then the climate has changed and more or less snow has fallen than in the past.

By flying over the ice sheet, or by traversing it with over-snow tractor trains, glaciologists use satellite surveying techniques to measure the ice's surface height. Ice thickness is measured using downward-looking radars. Global positioning satellites measure the positions of markers in the ice sheet (p196), which over time reveal the speed of the ice flow, and other satellites measure ice extents.

In December 2011 the 17th UN Framework Convention on Climate Change in Durban, South Africa, extended the Kyoto Protocol for five years, to 2017. The summit also agreed to set a new accord by 2015 to be implemented in 2020, and established a Green Climate Fund (up to $100 billion per year) to aid developing nations in combating climate change. The treaty's Clean Development Mechanism was expanded to include subsidies for carbon capture and sequestration technologies. Just after, however, Canada pulled out of the Kyoto Protocol, not having met its 2012 targets (thereby looking at multibillion-dollar fines).

Innovation in the private sector is another area of potential response to climate-change challenges, with technologies being developed and commercialized in China and the US, among other nations.

Despite earnest efforts both publicly and privately, emissions continue to increase, and results on reaching Kyoto targets have been mixed. It remains unclear whether – even with the adherence of the major emission-producing countries – the Kyoto targets would definitively reverse the situation.

In 2012 US researchers reported that data from NASA's GRACE satellites show shrinking ice caps and glaciers led to a 12mm increase in global sea levels from 2003 to 2010. That's 4.3 trillion tons of ice: enough to cover the United States 0.5m deep.

DISCOVERY

Wildlife

The isolated, seemingly barren continent of Antarctica is home to an astounding variety of wildlife – including many species found nowhere else on Earth. Many animals have evolved special characteristics that are uniquely suited to life on and around the Ice, and fossil records show bizarre extinct life forms and even dinosaurs (p95).

Today, the wild Southern Ocean contains blooms of zooplankton and phytoplankton which support a wealth of fish, crustaceans and squid. This food chain, with its rich swarms of krill, leads to top predators: whales, seals and seabirds, and of course, those ever-fascinating penguins. Since the Southern Ocean encircles Antarctica, much of this exceptional wildlife lives around the entire continent.

See also the full-color Wildlife Guide (p185) for more on Antarctic animals.

Whales

Whales (cetaceans) generally have long lifespans and are essentially divided into baleen whales (of which the blue whale is the largest) and toothed whales (dolphins, sperm whales and orcas). Baleen whales strain out small crustaceans like krill through the fibrous baleen plates that line their jaws.

Antarctica's whale species typically migrate north to warm waters for austral winter where they calve. The calves then migrate south with their mothers (repeating the migration together for several years until they are independent) to the food-rich edge of the sea ice in Antarctic spring.

Hunted to near-extinction, some species, like the mighty blue whale, are now so rare that a sighting will be reason to rejoice. Others, especially the minke, are still abundant.

The largest animal that permanently dwells on Antarctica is a wingless midge *(Belgica antarctica)* that grows to just over 1cm long. New Antarctic species are being discovered continuously: in 2012, 23 new animal species were identified around Antarctica's underwater hydrothermal vents.

Blue Whales

The blue whale *(Balaenoptera musculus)* is one of a group of baleen whales called rorquals (derived from the Norwegian *røyrkval*, meaning furrow whale), which have longitudinal folds running from below the mouth backwards, allowing their mouths to open very wide. Thus, they can gulp up to 50 tonnes of water, filtering out tiny crustaceans with 250 to 400 pairs of baleen plates. A single blue whale can eat as much as 4.5 tonnes of krill in one day.

The blue whale is the largest animal on Earth, reaching up to 200 tonnes and 33.5m. Blues are found in all oceans; the largest are found further south. The pygmy blue whale *(brevicauda)*, which grows to 25m, live further north. Blues are usually solitary or travel in pairs.

Commercial whaling severely reduced the species' numbers: 360,000 blue whales were killed in the 20th century alone. Current estimates put the blue whale population at 2300; they are classified as Endangered.

Fin Whales

The fin whale *(Balaenoptera physalus),* a baleen whale, is the second-largest whale species, after the blue. Female fin whales attain 27m in length in the southern hemisphere, with males reaching 25m. Unusually, the anterior part of the animal is asymmetrically colored: the left lower jaw is bluish-grey, the right is white.

Fin whales are found in all oceans. The highest population density is away from the sea ice, in temperate and cool waters. In Antarctic waters fin whales feed on krill.

Nearly 750,000 fin whales were killed in the 20th century in the southern hemisphere. They are classified as Endangered.

Humpback Whales

Humpback whales *(Megaptera novaeangliae)* are baleen whales that can be readily recognized by their enormous flippers, which can reach one-third of their total body length. (Its generic name *Megaptera* means 'Great wing.') Humpbacks are normally black, with varying amounts of white on the undersides of their flippers and flukes. Males reach a

TIPS FOR VIEWING WILDLIFE

When viewing Antarctic wildlife, it is important to keep your distance. The 2011 Guidelines for Visitors to the Antarctic require it – and it's important for your safety and that of the wildlife.

Although Antarctic animals may appear unconcerned by humans nearby, they may in fact be under considerable stress. People as far as 30m from a penguin rookery have been shown to increase the birds' heart rates significantly. And penguins may deviate from their usual path when approaching or leaving a colony for as long as three days after people visit. The further you stay from an animal, the more natural its behavior will be. For this reason, many biologists prefer to view wildlife through binoculars or telephoto lenses even when ashore.

Guidelines for Visitors to the Antarctic: Wildlife Rules (2011)

The taking of, or harmful interference with, Antarctic wildlife is prohibited, except in accordance with a permit.

» When in the vicinity of wildlife, walk slowly and carefully and keep noise to a minimum.

» Maintain an appropriate distance from wildlife. While in many cases a greater distance may be appropriate, in general don't approach closer than 5m (15m for fur seals). Abide site-specific distance guidelines.

» Observe wildlife behavior. If wildlife changes its behavior, stop moving or slowly increase your distance.

» Animals are particularly sensitive to disturbance when they are breeding (including nesting) or molting. Stay outside the margins of a colony and observe from a distance.

» Every situation is different. Consider the topography and the individual circumstances of the site, as these may have an impact on the vulnerability of wildlife to disturbance.

» Always give animals the right of way and do not block their access to the sea.

» Do not feed wildlife, or leave food or scraps lying around.

» Vegetation (including mosses and lichens) is fragile and very slow growing. Do not walk, drive or land on any moss beds or lichen-covered rocks; stay on established paths.

» Do not introduce any plants or animals into the Antarctic.

maximum length of 17.5m; females 19m. Adult humpbacks can reach 40 tonnes.

Humpbacks, found in all oceans, have the longest annual migration of any mammal, and often feed in groups (on krill and small fish). They can migrate from the Antarctic Peninsula to Mexico, up to 25,000 km.

Humpbacks were hunted to near extinction as late as the 1960s, but the population has bounced back. There are estimated to be 42,000 humpbacks today; they are classified as Least Concern.

Minke Whales

Following genetic studies, minke whales are now thought to be two separate species: the larger Antarctic minke whale *(Balaenoptera bonaerensis)* and the smaller dwarf *(B. acutorostrata),* or common, minke whale. Minke whales are the second-smallest of the baleen whales, although with a maximum length of 10.7m and a mass of up to 10 tonnes, they're still large animals.

In summer minkes are circumpolar in distribution, with the highest densities seen at the pack-ice edge. In winter most minkes move to lower latitudes. Minkes are the most abundant baleen whales in the Southern Ocean, with a population of possibly half a million. These krill-feeding rorquals are well-adapted to the ice: in heavy pack ice, they breathe through the cracks. Each year several hundred minkes are killed, ostensibly for scientific purposes, by Japanese whalers, although some of the meat is sold for human consumption (see the boxed text, p183).

Wildlife Reads

» *Complete Guide to Antarctic Wildlife* (2008), Hadoram Shirihai

» *The National Audubon Guide to Marine Mammals of the World* (2002), RR Reeves

» *Albatrosses and Petrels Across the World* (2003), Mike Brooke

» *Antarctic Underwater Field Guide* (www.oikonos.org/apfieldguide), David Cothran

Orca Whales

Orcas *(Orcinus orca),* also known as killer whales, are the largest members of the dolphin family. Their black-and-white markings and tall dorsal fins (especially in the adult male) are distinctive. Males reach 9m, females nearly 8m. Orcas can weigh 6 tonnes or more.

Orcas occur in all seas, but are more abundant in colder waters. They travel in schools or pods of up to 50 individuals. Orcas feed on squid, fish, birds and marine mammals, including penguins, dolphins and whales. They will tip up small ice floes to get to resting seals, and they have been observed working in teams to 'swamp' a floe, sending a wave surging across the ice to wash a seal into the water. Orcas have been spotted at sub-Antarctic Marion Island swallowing king penguins whole.

There are still many killer whales in the Southern Ocean. One estimate puts the summer population at 70,000. Recent observations suggest there may be three species of killer whales in the Southern Ocean, a smaller one *(O. glacialis)* being restricted to the Antarctic pack ice. They have not been caught commercially since 1979–80 (when Soviet whalers killed 916), but they are taken in small numbers for display in captivity.

Sei Whales

Sei whales *(Balaenoptera borealis),* part of the rorqual group of baleen whales, are the third-largest whales in the Southern Ocean. Females may reach 19.5m and 45 tonnes; males are slightly shorter and lighter.

Sei whales can be found in all oceans, but only larger individuals have been recorded south of the Antarctic Convergence. They occur in small schools of three to eight animals. Seis catch their prey (copepod crustaceans) by skimming not gulping water.

Seis were hunted to commercial extinction during the whaling era and have been completely protected since 1979. They number fewer than 10,000 today, and are considered Endangered.

Southern Right Whales

Whalers named the slow-moving, inshore-visiting southern right whale *(Eubalaena glacialis)* 'right' because it was relatively easy to row down and harpoon – and then it obligingly stayed afloat to yield its long baleen plates and lots of oil. Southern rights grow up to 17m in length and can weigh up to 90 tonnes. The whitish callosities on the jaw and forehead can be used to identify individuals.

Southern right whales occur in the southern oceans between S 20° and S 50°, and have been recorded around the more northerly of the southern islands. They feed on krill.

Southern rights were overexploited to commercial extinction as early as the mid-19th century, and full protection came only in 1935. There are estimated to be 7500 today, and they are classified as Endangered.

Sperm whales have powerful sonar and can dive to 3200m, remaining submerged for over an hour hunting prey including giant squid. Scientists calculate the size of squid eaten by whales, seals and seabirds by measuring the squid's indigestible beaks (mouth parts) when they are regurgitated, and then extrapolating.

Sperm Whales

The sperm whale *(Physeter macrocephalus)*, of *Moby Dick* fame, is an unmistakable species with its enormous flat-fronted head and narrow, tooth-filled lower jaw. The largest of the toothed whales, they have as many as 50 teeth (up to 25cm long) in the lower jaw, and the upper jaw (nearly always toothless) contains sockets the lower teeth fit into. Males can reach over 18m in length, females 11m, with males weighing as much as 57 tonnes.

Sperm whales occur in all of the world's oceans, but rarely in shallow seas. Most sperm whales south of S 40° are adult males. Schools of 20 to 25 individuals are made up of females and their young, joined by males during the October to December breeding season. Sperm whales eat mid- to deep-water squid, some of which reach 200kg; these veritable krakens of the deep are caught in absolute darkness at depths of 3km.

Sperm whales were much exploited in the past for their oil, ambergris and teeth. Now they are fully protected in the Southern Ocean. They are classified as Endangered.

Seals

Seven species of seals range from the sub-Antarctic and southern cool-temperate islands to the continent itself. Some are true (earless) seals and others have small flaps over their ears (fur seals) and are related to sea lions (which are present in the Falkland Islands). Some seals breed in colonies, others are restricted to the pack ice, and the elusive Ross Seal is hard to spot anywhere.

Seal populations are currently robust, despite 19th-century hunting, and none are endangered, though all are protected by the Convention for the Conservation of Antarctic Seals.

Blue whales are the loudest animals on Earth. They can emit low-frequency sounds louder than 180 decibels that can travel thousands of kilometers. Humpback whales are highly vocal in their breeding grounds: songs of up to 20 minutes are thought to be mainly produced by adult males.

Antarctic & Sub-Antarctic Fur Seals

Fur seals can be found on most of the circumpolar southern islands – in very large numbers at some of them. Vagrants have reached the southern continents. The Antarctic fur seal *(Arctocephalus gazella)* occurs further south than its slightly smaller relative, the sub-Antarctic fur seal *(A. tropicalis)*, with which it sometimes hybridizes. Males, at more than 200kg and 2m, far outweigh females, which weigh up to 55kg (at 1.3m).

Fur seals breed in harems, and males can be formidable opponents to rivals and human visitors alike. Male fur seals defend their beachfront territory and give off a strong musk scent when they are breeding. Pupping takes place in December. Fur seals eat squid, fish and crustaceans such as krill. Some Antarctic males kill penguins as well.

Fur seals are now showing a remarkable recovery in numbers since being overexploited for their coats early in the 19th century – so much so that at some localities, they are displacing breeding albatrosses and killing vegetation, leading to conservation dilemmas. Nearly two million Antarctic fur seals crowd the coastline of Bird Island off South Georgia.

Fur seals, related to sea lions, can walk on all-fours; and about one in 800 is of the 'blonde' variety, with markedly yellow- or cream-colored fur.

Crabeater Seals

The name 'crabeater' *(Lobodon carcinophaga)* comes from the German word *krebs*, which refers to crustaceans (like krill), not just crabs. They have specially adapted teeth with extra projections that form a sieve so they can strain out Antarctic krill, their almost-exclusive diet, from the water. These slim seals reach about 2.5m in length and 400kg.

Crabeaters breed in spring on the pack ice. The distribution of crabeaters is circumpolar, although they prefer pack ice to open sea. Crabeaters are considered the world's most abundant seal – some estimates put the population as high as 15 million.

Leopard Seals

Adult male leopard seals *(Hydrurga leptonyx)* reach a length of 2.8m and weigh 320kg. Females are even larger, at 3.6m and 500kg. Leopard seals have large heads with huge gapes, making them fearsome predators. They're found among the pack ice in summer and hauled-out on the more southerly sub-Antarctic islands in winter.

Leopards are often solitary, except during the breeding season. Because they live in the pack ice, little is known about their breeding behavior. Pups are born on the ice during summer. The leopards' diet includes penguins and other seals (especially pups), as well as fish, squid and krill.

Ross Seals

The Ross seal *(Ommatophoca rossii)* dwells in the densest pack ice and is consequently the least-often seen of all Antarctic seals. Named for its discoverer James Clark Ross (leader of the British Antarctic Expedition of 1839–43), this solitary animal is usually found hauled-out onto large floes, alone or in pairs. Females reach 2.4m and 200kg; males are slightly smaller.

When a Ross seal is disturbed, it rears back almost vertically, with its mouth open and throat inflated. They are also known for distinctive vocalizations: trilling, warbling or 'chugging.' The Ross seal feeds on squid and fish.

Elephant seals have huge reservoirs of blood (22% of their body mass) and can slow their hearts to just a single beat per minute. The deepest dive recorded is an amazing 1930m; they can stay down for two hours, and rest for surprisingly short intervals at the surface.

Southern Elephant Seals

The southern elephant seal *(Mirounga leonina)* is the world's largest seal. Males grow to 3 tonnes and 5m in length, females 900kg and 3m. They have a circumpolar distribution, and are found on most of the southern islands and on the Antarctic Peninsula.

Males spend winter at sea and first haul out in August, followed by females. Males fight to determine which will be 'beachmaster,' with mating rights to a harem of females. Their large proboscis helps create their fearsome roars. Adults use their thick blubber layer (for which they were once hunted) to survive while breeding, during which they do not feed.

Southern elephant seals are known for adaptations that allow them to feed at great depths for prolonged durations (their diet is predominantly squid and fish). They are elongated in shape and have enormous volumes of red blood cell-rich blood (useful for storing oxygen when diving), special cavities for storing extra blood, and muscles which also store oxygen.

Weddell Seals

The quintessential Antarctic seals, Weddell seals *(Leptonychotes weddellii)* reach 3.3m in length and a weight of 500kg and may live for 20 years. Females are slightly larger than males.

Weddell seals have a circumpolar distribution, living further south than any other mammal (except people). They live on fast ice (sea ice attached to shore or between grounded icebergs) year-round, though they are occasionally sighted in pack ice. In October, pups are born in colonies near cracks and holes in the ice that give their mothers access to the sea. Males defend their holes.

Studies have shown Weddells can dive to 720m and stay underwater for more than an hour. Because Weddells use their incisors and canines to keep their breathing holes open, they often wear down their teeth. They have been observed blowing air bubbles into cracks under the sea ice to flush out prey (fish, squid and crustaceans). Weddells are the best studied of the Antarctic seals, because they can be more easily approached over fast ice than can the pack-ice species.

Animals, especially seals and penguins, are becoming gatherers of data using remote sensors. Elephant seals dive under ice in winter, wand to over 900m, situations difficult for humans to duplicate. Small sensors attached to animals' bodies transmit data to a satellite when the animal resurfaces.

Birds

Approximately 45 species of birds breed south of the Antarctic Convergence, including nine of the 17 species of penguins, and many frequent the skies and waters of the Southern Ocean. Just a very few, however, come to land on the continent to breed.

Penguins

Penguin sexes are similarly marked but sometimes females are smaller. Chicks often huddle in groups called crèches, especially while parents are away hunting.

Penguins species are impacted by changes from global warming, and currently many scientists are studying how this is affecting population numbers and species distribution. See also p165 for Impacts on Antarctica in the Environment chapter.

Adélie Penguins

Adélies *(Pygoscelis adeliae),* the archetypical Antarctic penguin, were named by French explorer Dumont d'Urville after his wife. Purely black and white, thus similar to gentoos and chinstraps, Adélies have a distinctive white eye ring. They weigh 3.9kg to 5.8kg and are 46cm to 75cm in length. Adélies prefer krill, and dive up to 150m, but they usually remain closer to the surface.

Over 2.5 million pairs breed during summer in large colonies all around the Antarctic continent and at some of the more southerly sub-Antarctic islands. They create stone-lined nests and take turns protecting two eggs. They winter in the sea ice and, if possible, return to the same nest and mate the next year.

Emperor penguins eat fish, krill and squid, and capture their prey by pursuit-diving, often to amazing depths and durations: as much as 535m and 22 minutes, by far the deepest and longest dives known for any bird.

Chinstrap Penguins

Chinstraps *(Pygoscelis antarctica)* are black and white like Adélies, but have a distinctive black line below the chin – hence the name. They weigh 3kg to 6kg, with a length of 68cm. The second-most numerous penguin, after the macaroni, 7.5 million pairs of chinstraps have been identified.

Chinstraps feed on krill and fish near their colonies (around the Antarctic Peninsula and on islands south of the Antarctic Convergence). They lay two eggs in November and chicks fledge by early March. Chinstraps feed both chicks equally (unlike others who feed preferentially). They range north of the pack ice in winter.

Emperor Penguins

The emperor penguin *(Aptenodytes forsteri)* is the world's largest penguin, at over 1m (although ancient fossils have been found of penguins measuring 2m) and 40kg.

The known population is 595,000 breeding pairs in 44 locations, and they do not travel north of the Antarctic Convergence.

The emperor is the only Antarctic bird that breeds in winter. A single egg is incubated on the feet of the males, which group-huddle in the extreme winter cold to reduce heat loss. Meanwhile, females travel across the ice to find polynyas in which to feed. Incubation averages 66 days, and chicks become independent during November to January.

Gentoo Penguins

The black-and-white gentoo *(Pygoscelis papua)* which grows between 75cm and 90cm, can be distinguished from the slightly smaller Adélie and chinstrap by its orange bill and a white patch above and behind its eye. The estimated 300,000 breeding pairs are circumpolar, inhabiting the sub-Antarctic islands and the Antarctic Peninsula. Large populations occur at South Georgia (100,000 pairs), the Falkland Islands (70,000 pairs) and Îles Kerguelen (30,000 pairs).

At the more northerly sub-Antarctic islands, gentoos breed in winter, laying two eggs as early as July. On the more southerly islands and the Peninsula, laying occurs from October to December.

Gentoos can dive deeper than 100m for prey: krill, fish and squid. The species has been categorized as Near-threatened by the International Union for Conservation of Nature (IUCN).

ALBINO

Leucistic (or albinistic) penguins have whitish-beige, not black, plumage due to a genetic inability to produce melanin. Scientists estimate leucism rates on the Antarctic Peninsula at about 1:114,000 in Adélies, 1:146,000 in chinstraps and 1:20,000 in gentoos.

King Penguins

The king penguin *(Aptenodytes patagonicus)* is the world's second-largest penguin, weighing 9kg to 15kg, with a length of 80cm. It is estimated there are between one and 1.5 million pairs. They breed on seven sub-Antarctic island groups, eat primarily lanternfish and squid, and can dive to 300m for 15 minutes.

Kings often breed in very large colonies, close to the shore on rocky terrain. For about 55 days in summer, the parents take turns incubating a single egg on their feet. They can shuffle along slowly to avoid seals. The downy chick is uniformly dark brown, and was once described as the 'woolly penguin,' a species of its own. During the long breeding season (14 to 16 months) chicks are reared right through the winter (huddling in crèches to keep warm) and only fledge the following summer, making annual breeding impossible. They breed only twice every three years.

Macaroni Penguins

Orange tassels meeting between the eyes differentiate the macaroni *(Eudyptes chrysolophus)* from the slightly smaller (and lighter-billed) rockhopper. Macaronis weigh 5.3kg, with a length of 70cm. The krill-eating macaroni penguin is the most abundant of the sub-Antarctic and Antarctic penguins, with 11.8 million pairs in sometimes gigantic colonies on islands near the Antarctic Convergence and off the Peninsula. They have been known to travel up to 10,000km across the oceans during winter.

The summer-breeding macaroni lays two eggs, the first smaller than the second (extremely unusual for birds, but common to all the crested penguins). The first-laid ('A') egg is usually kicked out of the nest soon after the 'B' egg is laid and only one egg hatches. This system has prompted many studies.

IUCN has classified the macaroni as Vulnerable due to recent decreases at some sub-Antarctic breeding locales (attributed to temperature changes reducing available prey).

Rockhopper Penguins

'Rockies,' the smallest of the crested penguins (2.3kg to 2.7kg), have lemon yellow tassels that do not meet between the eyes. Two species are now recognized, the southern *(Eudyptes chrysocome)* and the northern (*E. moseleyi*), with longer, more luxuriant crests.

Rockhoppers (including both species, an estimated 3.7 million pairs) are both sub-Antarctic and southern cool temperate island breeders. The largest population (one million pairs) nests on the Falklands.

They can breed (in a two-egg system like the macaronis) among boulders on exposed shores, where their strong hopping and swimming abilities allow them to transfer from sea to nest sites.

Rockhoppers of both species have decreased dramatically, attributed to sea-temperature rises due to climate change (which affects the availability of prey), thus their IUCN Vulnerable status.

Royal Penguins

Royals *(Eudyptes schlegeli),* which resemble macaronis but have white faces, are found only at sub-Antarctic Macquarie Island. A census in 1984–85 found 848,700 breeding pairs, which is now regarded as an underestimate.

Two eggs (the first of which is discarded) are laid in often-huge coastal colonies in October with chicks fledging by February. In nonbreeding times they have been spotted as far away as Tasmania.

Royals have been classified Vulnerable due to their single breeding locality. Years ago, molting royal penguins, called 'fats,' were killed for their oil, but protest against this led to Macquarie Island being made the first sub-Antarctic island nature reserve.

The 'great' albatrosses' genus name *Diomedea* commemorates the Trojan hero Diomedes, whose companions were turned into large, white birds by the Greek gods.

Albatrosses

On the Southern Ocean, entrancing albatrosses will glide past your ship, but distinguishing the different species is not always easy (depending on the taxonomy, from eight to 17 albatrosses breed on the islands).

They all lay only one egg at breeding, and some only breed every two years. All albatrosses feed on squid, fish and crustaceans caught at the sea surface.

Today, many albatrosses are killed in Southern Ocean longline fisheries. Fishermen spool out baited longlines and the birds drown after they get hooked when diving for the bait. The Convention for the Conservation of Antarctic Marine Living Resources (CCAMLR; www.ccamlr.org) has addressed this problem in its jurisdiction by employing streamers to scare the birds away from bait, by ensuring that baited hooks sink faster, and by prohibiting longlining during daylight hours, shifting mortality away from albatrosses. Other dangers include trawl warps, land-based introduced predators and pollution. These issues are being addressed through initiatives like the Agreement on the Conservation of Albatrosses and Petrels (www.acap.aq) and by NGOs like BirdLife International (www.birdlife.org). At present, though, the future of all albatross is still a concern, with conservation statuses ranging from Vulnerable (grey-headed albatross) to Critically Endangered (Amsterdam albatross).

The **black-browed albatross** *(Thalassarche melanophrys)* is widespread in the southern seas and breeds at nine island groups including South Georgia and the Falklands. It is one of the smaller-sized group of albatrosses, sometimes known as mollymawks, but with a 2.5m wingspan and a weight to 5kg, it's still a big bird. They're white and have yellow bills with red-orange tips and dark lines through the eye, and their underwing pattern features a wide, dark leading edge

The **grey-headed albatross** *(Thalassarche chrysostoma)* can be identified by its greyish head; broad, dark leading edge to the underwing; and orange stripes on both upper and lower mandibles. The greyhead has a circumpolar breeding distribution and can be seen on such islands as South Georgia, and Campbell and Macquarie Islands.

The **royal albatross** (northern *Diomedea epomophora,* and southern *D. sanfordi*) belongs to the 'great' albatrosses of the Southern Ocean. They are primarily recognized at sea by their huge size and their all-white tail with mostly black upper wings and a dark edge to the upper mandible, which occur at adulthood. They breed on islands off New Zealand.

Shy albatrosses *(Thalassarche cauta)* are the largest of the Southern Ocean mollymawks, with a wingspan of up to 2.6m. Distinguishing features are a humpbacked appearance in flight, dark upperwings that are not as black as other mollymawks' and a narrow dark leading edge to the underwing in both adults and juveniles. The shy albatross is misnamed, since it will approach and follow ships. It breeds on islands south of New Zealand and around Tasmania. However, the bird (now considered to form four species) has a widespread at-sea distribution.

There are two species of **sooty albatrosses**: the dark-mantled *(Phoebetria fusca),* usually called the sooty, is uniformly chocolate brown, whereas the light-mantled *(P. palpebrata)* has a contrasting pale back. The dark-mantled sooty has a yellow sulcus along its lower mandible, whereas the light-mantled has a blue one. Both species have circumpolar at-sea distributions, but the light-mantled tends to occur further south, reaching the edge of the pack ice. This is mirrored by their breeding distribution. The paired courtship flights and haunting calls around misty cliffs make for one of the quintessential experiences of visits to Southern Ocean islands.

Grey-headed albatrosses breed every second year. On their year off, they can fly right around the Southern Ocean, with some making journeys as long as 12,000km.

The **wandering albatross** *(Diomedea exulans)* is distinguished from the mollymawk albatrosses by its huge size – with a wingspan of up to 3.5m. It has a white head, neck and body, a wedge-shaped tail, and large pink beak. Wanderers are found in 10 island groups in the Southern Ocean. They can cover vast tracts of the Southern Ocean, flying up to several thousand kilometers on a single foraging trip, so are aptly named. Indeed, young wanderers may not return to land for five years or more, staying at sea the whole time.

Other southern species include the **yellow-nosed albatross** (Atlantic *Thalassarche chlororhynchos* and Indian *T. carteri*), found on remote islands like the Tristan da Cunhas, and the **Amsterdam albatross** *(Diomedea amsterdamensis)*, one of the world's rarest birds, found only at Île Amsterdam.

Petrels

This group of seabirds got their name because of the habit of the small storm petrels pattering across the sea surface as if they were walking across it. 'Petrel' means 'little Peter,' the apostle who walked on the water with Christ on the Sea of Galilee. Except for the two biggest species, all petrels remain at sea, coming to land only to dig burrows in which to breed (so protecting themselves from predatory birds like skuas). Unfortunately, introduced cats and rats on many breeding islands have not been so easily thwarted, and many species are threatened as a consequence.

Many of these birds eat krill, fish and squid, caught mainly by surface-dipping while on the wing. Like albatrosses, some petrels are threatened by longline fishing (see p175.

Giant petrels are the largest of the petrel family. The northern giant petrel *(Macronectes halli)* and the southern giant petrel *(M. giganteus)* can be distinguished by the color of their bill tips: greenish in northerns, reddish-brown in southerns. Giant petrels can be seen in all parts of the Southern Ocean, with southerns occurring further south – some breed on the Peninsula and in Terre Adélie. Unlike albatrosses, giant petrels forage on both land and sea. On land they kill birds as large as king penguins and scavenge in seal colonies. At sea they eat fish, squid and crustaceans, and scavenge dead cetaceans and seabirds. Giant petrels are caught by tuna and toothfish longline-fishing from vessels in the Southern Ocean.

Antarctic fulmars *(Fulmarus glacialoides)* are a medium-sized petrel (800g, 1.2m wingspan), readily identified by their pale-grey plumage with white head and black flight feathers. The bill is pink with a dark tip and the dark eye is a distinguishing feature. Antarctic fulmars are a southerly species with a circumpolar distribution at sea and are commonly found on pack-ice fringes. They breed on the islands off the Peninsula, the South Orkney and South Sandwich Islands, along the Antarctic coastline and on Bouvetøya.

The **Antarctic petrel** *(Thalassoica antarctica)* is a boldly marked dark-brown-and-white petrel, a little smaller than the Antarctic fulmar. It breeds only on the Antarctic continent; the largest-known colony, Svarthamaren in Queen Maud Land, supports about 250,000 pairs.

Snow petrels *(Pagodroma nivea)* are unmistakable with their all-white plumage, black bill and small black eyes. They breed on the Antarctic continent and Peninsula, and on Bouvetøya, in no fewer than 298 breeding sites. The birds' at-sea distribution does not extend far north; they are very much denizens of the pack-ice zone, where they roost on icebergs.

Prions *(Pachyptila spp.),* also known as whalebirds, are small grey-blue-and-white birds. They can be distinguished from blue petrels by their black terminal band to the upper tail. All have a vague M shape visible on their upperparts when in flight. There may be as many as six species. Breeding takes place at many southern islands, with one or two species occurring together. They can be seen in all areas of the Southern Ocean north of the pack ice and in continental waters, often in very large flocks. Prions have suffered from predation by introduced cats and rats. Removal of these may eventually lead to population recoveries.

Storm petrels are the smallest and lightest seabirds in the world. The Wilson's storm petrel *(Oceanites oceanicus)* weighs only 35g to 45g. 'Willies' have a circumpolar distribution and breed on the more southerly sub-Antarctic islands, such as South Georgia, and on the Antarctic Peninsula and continent, as well as on islands near Cape Horn and in the Falklands. They have been regarded as the world's most abundant seabird; there are certainly several million of them. They are regular ship followers and associate with whales. Medium-sized black-bellied *(Fregetta tropica)* and white-bellied *(F. grallaria)* storm petrels are closely related; they are separated by the presence or absence of a black line down the center of an otherwise white under body. White-bellies breed on the more northerly islands of the Southern Ocean. Black-bellies breed on South Georgia, Îles Crozet and Kerguelen, and on islands along the Antarctic Peninsula. The small grey-backed storm petrel *(Garrodia nereis)* is distinctively marked with white underparts, a dark-brown head and back and a grey rump. Grey-backs have a discontinuous distribution in the Southern Ocean, with three centers near breeding localities in the South Atlantic Ocean, southern Indian Ocean and south of Australasia.

Other petrels that might be spied include: the **blue petrel** *(Halobaena caerulea),* superficially resembling prions, but for the white terminal band to the tail, which breeds at Islas Diego Ramirez, South Georgia, the Prince Edward Islands, Îles Crozet and Kerguelen, and Heard and Macquarie Is-

MUMIYO

Snow petrels can regurgitate their stomach oil as a defense mechanism. Deposits of this substance, called mumiyo, have built up around nest sites over thousands of years and can be radiocarbon dated. The oldest-known colony dates back an astounding 34,000 years.

lands, and has an at-sea circumpolar distribution; the **cape petrel** *(Daption capense)*, whose speckled dark brownish-black-and-white appearance gives it its other common name, 'pintado,' meaning 'painted' in Spanish, and which has a wide, circumpolar at-sea distribution and a wide breeding range: from the Antarctic continent to the more southerly sub-Antarctic islands; the **South Georgian diving petrel** *(Pelecanoides georgicus)*, which breeds at South Georgia, and on islands in the southern Indian Ocean and off New Zealand; the **common diving petrel** *(P. urinatrix)*, which breeds at a number of southern islands, from South Georgia to the Tristan da Cunha group and south of New Zealand; and the **white-chinned petrel** *(Procellaria aequinoctialis)*, which breeds at the Falkland Islands, South Georgia, Prince Edward Islands, Îles Crozet and Kerguelen and on New Zealand's sub-Antarctic islands, and has an at-sea distribution that is circumpolar, with a wide latitudinal range.

Other Birds

Cormorants

There is not yet firm agreement on how many species of cormorants *(Phalacrocorax spp.)* – or shags, which is their other commonly used name – inhabit the southern islands and the Antarctica Peninsula. There are probably as many as seven, or as few as two, depending on what taxonomic levels are used. All are reasonably similar; they are brown-black with long necks and wing plumage, and they have a distinctive fast-flapping flight.

Cormorants breed on the Antarctic Peninsula, on all the sub-Antarctic islands and on the islands south of New Zealand. They breed in summer, making nests of seaweed and terrestrial vegetation in colonies on cliff tops and ledges directly above the sea. Cormorants eat mainly benthic fish, caught by deep and long dives from the surface (rather than by plunging from a height above the water).

Kelp Gulls

The kelp, or Dominican, gull *(Larus dominicanus)* is the only gull of the Southern Ocean. It lives on the Antarctic Peninsula and at most sub-Antarctic islands, where it is resident year-round, generally in small numbers. Like most southern seabirds, kelp gulls breed in summer.

Diet includes scraps scavenged from penguin colonies and giant petrel kills, terrestrial invertebrates such as earthworms and moth larvae, and intertidal shellfish such as limpets.

Sheathbills

Sheathbills are not seabirds (their feet are not webbed) but are in their own family, allied to waders or shorebirds. They are Antarctica's only land-based bird, and they often strut and squabble around penguin colonies. The greater sheathbill *(Chionis alba)* – also known by the names American, snowy or pink-faced sheathbill – is found at South Georgia, the South Shetland and South Orkney Islands and along the Antarctic Peninsula; they migrate north to South America and the Falklands in winter. They have a thick, white plumage and sturdy bodies. Lesser or black-faced sheathbills *(C. minor)* are somewhat smaller, with noticeably shorter wings. They are strict residents of the four sub-Antarctic island groups of the southern Indian Ocean, each with its own subspecies.

Sheathbills nest in crevices in summer, usually near penguin colonies, where they scavenge eggs, spilled food being fed to chicks, and from carcasses killed by giant petrels. They also feed on intertidal life and on invertebrates in the peat.

Skuas

Skuas are large, heavily built gull-like birds, mainly brown but with conspicuous white flashes in their wings. South Polar skuas *(Catharacta maccormicki)* are marginally smaller than sub-Antarctic or brown skuas *(C. antarctica)* and have a paler plumage.

Sub-Antarctic skuas breed on most of the southern islands, whereas South Polars are found on the Antarctic continent. On the Antarctic Peninsula, both species occur, and hybrid pairs are regularly recorded.

Both species breed in summer, generally laying two mottled eggs in open nests on the ground. Skuas are aggressive hunters and prey upon the eggs and chicks of penguins and other colonial seabirds (including adults of smaller species), and feed on carrion. They also consume Antarctic krill, squid and fish.

In winter, both species leave their breeding areas and spend time at sea, occasionally reaching the northern hemisphere.

Terns

Several species of tern *(Sterna spp.)* may be seen in the Southern Ocean. The Antarctic *(S. vittata)* and the rarer Kerguelen *(S. virgata)* terns breed at a number of southern islands, the former are more widespread and occur on the Antarctic Peninsula as well. At sea you'll likely see Arctic terns *(S. paradisaea)*, long-distance migrants from the northern hemisphere. Kerguelens are resident on the few islands where they occur, whereas Antarctic terns migrate, several thousand reaching South African waters to spend the winter.

All three species are slender, long-winged grey-and-white birds, similar in size. Arctic terns have white foreheads and dark bills; the Antarctic and Kerguelen species are red-billed and have conspicuous black caps.

Antarctic and Kerguelen terns breed in summer, laying mottled eggs in open nests on the ground in loose colonies. They eat mainly small fish caught at the surface or by shallow dives within sight of land, often within the kelp-bed zone. The rare Kerguelen tern is considered Near Threatened and both breeding species are at risk from feral cats on islands where felines occur.

At sea, skuas chase smaller seabirds to force them to regurgitate or drop their prey (an act known as kleptoparasitism), often retrieving it spectacularly before it drops to the water.

Shearwaters

The great shearwater *(Puffinus gravis)*, with its dark cap and white band at the base of the upper tail, breeds only in the Tristan da Cunha group and Gough Island (except for a very few in the Falklands). The black-and-white little shearwater *(Puffinus assimilis)* is often seen in groups of two or three, usually close to breeding localities – the Tristan da Cunha group, Gough Island, Île St Paul and islands around Australia and New Zealand. It has a circumpolar at-sea distribution in the Southern Ocean. The sooty shearwater *(Puffinus griseus)* is all brown, apart from its silvery underwings. It has a circumpolar at-sea distribution, and breeds on islands off New Zealand and Cape Horn.

Fish & Benthic Species

The Southern Ocean supports more than 270 species of fish and the nutrient-rich area just north of the Antarctic Circumpolar Current gives rise to some of the world's most productive fisheries. Some of the species nearest the continent or on the ocean floor (benthic region) are very different from those of other oceans.

Scientists study several fascinating species like the Antarctic cod or toothfish *(Dissostichus mawsoni)* which survive in subzero waters without freezing because of 'antifreeze' proteins in their blood. Antarctic cod are not related to other 'cod' and can grow to 2m and 135kg. Their hearts beats once every six seconds.

Members of the ice fish family, Channichthyidae, such as the mackerel ice fish *(Champsocephalus gunnari)*, have no hemoglobin and are 'white-blooded.' Oxygen is carried in their blood plasma, but this has only 10% of the oxygen-carrying capacity of fish blood containing hemoglobin. To make up for this, ice fish have more blood, a larger heart, larger blood vessels and more gill surface area, and can even exchange oxygen through their tails.

All Antarctic fish grow slowly, with most coastal species requiring five to seven years before they can breed. This is of great importance when deciding sustainable catch limits. Due to initially uncontrolled fishing, several species (eg marbled notothon *(Notothenia rossii)* and mackerel ice fish) are now commercially extinct. Fisheries have targeted new species (eg Patagonian toothfish, *Dissostichus eleginoides*) and CCAMLR attempts to control practices with a system of annual quotas and inspections. Nevertheless, overfishing remains a threat.

The communities that inhabit the seafloor around Antarctica are called the benthos, and are as rich in plants and animals as a tropical coral reef. They comprise Antarctica's true indigenous flora and fauna, adapted to life in a cold ocean over tens of millions of years (such as Turquet's octopus, *Pareledone turqueti*). Nearly every time a deep-sea sample is brought up, it includes many species new to science.

Dogs were once widely used in Antarctica to pull sledges, but they were banned from the continent by the Antarctic Treaty's Protocol on Environmental Protection. The last were removed in 1994.

SLEDGING

Invertebrates

Antarctic Krill

Antarctic krill *(Euphausia superba)* is a 6cm-long planktonic crustacean that is found in sometimes-enormous swarms south of the Antarctic Convergence. There is also a smaller species, the ice krill *(E. crystallarophias)*. Krill is sifted out of the water by baleen whales, and eaten by many species of southern seabirds (especially penguins), squid, fish and crabeater seals. Without krill the ecosystem of the Southern Ocean would collapse.

Antarctic krill has been the target of fisheries and quotas are now set by CCAMLR, which also encourages research on krill and its predators.

Terrestrial Invertebrates

Antarctica's native land animals are all tiny invertebrates, many of them specially adapted. They include mites, lice, springtails, midges and fleas, many of which are parasites of seals and birds. Some mites, however, inhabit exposed soil and survive extreme cold and dryness. Studies on the continent have concentrated on the microbiota: ciliates, rotifers, tardigrades and nematodes (see p94 for more on nematodes).

Introduced invertebrates like slugs, snails, earthworms, spiders, isopods and aphids arrived on sub-Antarctic islands, some changing the ecosystem.

Plants

Antarctic plant species are more numerous than you would expect, but they are far smaller and less conspicuous than plants in other latitudes. Antarctica is home to nearly 400 species of lichen, 100 species of moss and liverworts and hundreds of species of algae – including 20 species of snow algae.

Terrestrial Plants

Antarctica's plants differ greatly from those found on sub-Antarctic islands. The continent supports only mosses, lichens and algae, along with two flowering plants, a hairgrass *(Deschampsia antarctica)* and a cushion plant or pearlwort *(Colobanthus quitensis)*, which have footholds on the comparatively milder Antarctic Peninsula. Interestingly, global warming is believed to be the cause for the observed spread of this grass.

Very large specimens of lichens (some more than 500 years old) and banks of moss more than 1m deep can be found, especially on the Peninsula. Radiocarbon dating shows the base of large moss banks to be as much as 7000 years old.

High rainfall and long hours of summer sunshine allow the islands to support diverse and at-times lush vegetation (epitomized by tussock grassland). South Georgia alone boasts at least 50 species of vascular plants – but no trees. The more northerly cool temperate islands, such as Tristan da Cunha and Gough, support a few native trees.

Marine Plants

The intertidal and subtidal areas of the southern islands support giant seaweeds such as bull kelp *(Durvillea antarctica)*, which form thick bands and protect shores from rough seas. These kelp 'forests' support fish, shellfish, octopus and crustaceans, which in turn provide food for inshore-foraging birds, such as cormorants and terns.

There are more than 100 species of plankton in the Southern Ocean. The productivity of all Antarctic ecosystems rests on the photosynthesis of the phytoplankton group, which are tiny single-celled plants or microscopic algae, floating in the upper layers of the Southern Ocean. Ice algae stains pack ice pink or brown, and snow algae grows atop certain areas of snow (see Pink Snow, p88). During algal blooms, the sheer density of phytoplankton is so great that they color the ocean.

Kerguelen cabbage *(Pringlea antiscorbutica)*, found on southern Indian Ocean islands, was used by shipwrecked 19th-century sealers to ward off scurvy (as its scientific name suggests).

Threats to Antarctic Wildlife

Antarctica's exploration was tied directly to the exploitation of its marine mammals, specifically seals and whales.

Nowadays, many of the threats to Antarctic wildlife come from ecosystem changes, like those caused by global warming (see p162 for more on ecosystem changes).

The Past

Whales

Antarctic whaling was established in 1904, with 183 whales killed the first season. By 1912–13, six land stations, 21 factory ships and 62 catcher boats killed and processed 10,760 whales. South Georgia was an important early catching ground; see p51). By the 1920s, advancing technology (particularly the stern slipway, which allowed the entire whale to be winched aboard a floating factory ship for processing) shifted predominance to pelagic, or open-ocean, whaling. Also, since they were at sea, pelagic factory ships avoided government limits on whale-hunting. By 1930–31 the annual kill had increased to 40,000. With the exception

ROCK ALGAE

In areas formed from large-grained sandstone (Victoria Land) the outer skin of the rocks themselves has been colonized by plants. These plants live within the rock, growing between the sand grains and forming separate layers of algae, fungus and lichen. Just enough light penetrates for photosynthesis to occur for a short period each year (sometimes only a few days) when meltwater is available. Acids excreted by the plants eventually dissolve the rock and the outer skin breaks off. The growth rate of these plants is so slow that some may be many thousands of years old.

of the years during WWII, whaling continued at this level for the next 20 years. As each targeted species was driven to near extinction whalers switched to a new species.

The International Whaling Commission (IWC; http://iwcoffice.org) was established in 1946 to regulate the 'orderly development of the whaling industry' worldwide. It agreed to a moratorium, which came into force in 1986, on all commercial catches.

For an idea of the numbers of whales caught, we can look to records from South Georgia, the main site of land-based operations. From 1904 to 1965, when whaling at South Georgia ceased, a total of 41,515 blue whales were caught, along with 87,555 fins, 26,754 humpbacks, 15,128 seis and 3716 sperm whales.

Seals

Nearly a third of the peri-Antarctic islands were discovered by sealers. Sealers often preceded explorers, thus becoming explorers themselves (for more history, see p141 and p50). The sealing trade was aggressive. The South Shetlands were discovered in 1819, and by 1823–24 fur sealing there was already over, due to the rapid influx of sealers and the near-extinction of the seals.

Fur seals were hunted for their thick pelts and elephant seals for their blubber, which could be rendered into oil.

Finfish & Krill

In the 1970s, fish (called finfish to distinguish them from shellfish) became commercially targeted. Species in the South Georgia area (Antarctic cod, ice fish) were caught in great numbers, mostly by the Soviet Union. Commercial extinction followed, from which these species have never recovered.

Simultaneously, world interest turned to krill (fished commercially since 1972). The catch reached a peak in the early 1980s at more than 400,000 tonnes per summer season. At first it was postulated that in their vast numbers, krill might solve the world's famine problems. However, although relatively easy to catch once a swarm has been identified, krill have proved costly to process and difficult to market. Krill possess some of the most powerful protein-digesting enzymes ever found, so they must be processed very rapidly or their tissues begin to break down, turning black and mushy. They become unfit for human consumption after three hours on deck and unfit for cattle feed after 10 hours. Krill also have high levels of fluorine in their outer shell, making them toxic unless the shell is completely removed.

Modern Era

Historically, whale oil was used for lighting, lubrication and tanning; in the early years, it was mainly a Norwegian and British industry.

Whales

In modern times, the IWC moratorium on commercial catches has come under pressure from whaling nations such as Japan and Norway.

In 1994 the IWC established the Southern Ocean Whaling Sanctuary to protect the primary feeding grounds of the majority of great whales and to provide an opportunity for depleted species to recover. The sanctuary does not allow commercial whaling, even if the worldwide moratorium were to be lifted. However, there is an exception for whaling for scientific purposes (see the boxed text Southern Ocean Whaling Controversy).

Seals

Seals are officially protected on land and ice shelves, where they can only be killed for scientific purposes (permit required). The Convention for the Conservation of Antarctic Seals extends this protection to the sea, the sea ice and the pack ice. It prohibits the commercial culling of fur, elephant and Ross seals and establishes closed areas and closed seasons for the other species.

Since the convention maintains catch limits for crabeater (175,000), leopard (12,000) and Weddell seals (5000), in theory commercial sealing could occur again; but the public outcry it would generate makes this unlikely.

Finfish & Krill

Fish and squid are caught in large numbers; around South Georgia, crabs are taken, too. The CCAMLR, which came into effect in 1982, placed limits on fishing, unless data showed that catches could be increased, taking into account the whole ecosystem. Inspection and scientific-observer schemes were put in place. With increased monitoring, however, there also came an increase in fisheries trying to work outside the law.

The only natural predator of leopard seals are orca whales.

The 1990s saw a rush on Patagonian toothfish or Chilean sea bass *(Dissostichus eleginoides)*. Due to its late sexual maturity, the toothfish is highly vulnerable to overfishing; additionally, longline fishing, which is used to catch them, causes the death of albatrosses and petrels (see p175). The Patagonian toothfish can grow to more than 240cm and 130kg, though most caught today weigh less than 10kg. CCAMLR reacted with a Catch Certification Scheme and Dissostichus Catch Documentation requirements. Individual countries tried to take action when illegal fishing took place within their exclusive economic zone. Nevertheless, since 1996 illegal fishing has exceeded legal fishing of toothfish.

SOUTHERN OCEAN WHALING CONTROVERSY

When the Southern Ocean Whaling Sanctuary was established by the International Whaling Commision (IWC) in 1994, Japan was the only nation of the 24 members to oppose it. An exception was then granted allowing whaling for research purposes. The Japanese whaling fleet is currently permitted to catch 1000 minke whales each year under this proviso. Conservation organizations and many scientists object to this practice as deceptive, as meat from the minkes is sold in markets, used in school-lunch programs and served in *kujira-ya* (whale restaurants). Sales figures from 2011–12, however, show a significant decline in the market for whale meat in Japan. Japan's Institute of Cetacean Research (ICR; www. Icrwhle.org) says that it sells the meat to help fund its research, which includes data collected on age, calves and gestation.

The practice has created a lot of contention. Every year, the activist group Sea Shepherd Conservation Society (www.seashepherd.org) tries to disrupt whale hunts by pursuing whaling ships and blocking slipways on vessels, preventing whalers from loading whales on board. Although Sea Shepherd's direct actions have been denounced by many governments, it does have wide support, with prominent celebrities, musicians and sports figures among its backers.

In 2007–08, two activists from the Sea Shepherd ship *Steve Irwin* boarded a whaling ship without permission and were detained. Later, Sea Shepherd claimed their captain had been shot at. The ICR whalers said they had been attacked with chemicals such as acids. Also in that season, Greenpeace's *Esperanza* chased the whaling factory ship *Nisshin Maru* more than 7400km.

While the Sea Shepherd Conservation Society maintains Japanese whaling in Antarctica is illegal, the organization has been accused of ecoterrorism by the ICR. In 2011, the ICR sued Sea Shepherd in a US Federal Court in Seattle, Washington (Sea Shepherd is based in Washington State, although many of its operations are based in Australia and its vessels currently fly Dutch flags). However, the judge denied the injunction and allowed continued activity by Sea Shepherd.

At the IWC's July 2012 meeting in Panama, a South American–led bid for an expanded South Atlantic Whale Sanctuary was up for a vote again, after a similar attempt in 2011 ended with Japan and other whaling nations walking out in protest. Despite support from Australia, New Zealand and the US, the vote fell short of the 75% majority required to pass. Japan, China, Russia and Norway were among the nations that voted against the measure.

A rarely-seen colossal squid caught in the Ross Sea by a New Zealand fishing boat in 2007 was 10m long and weighed nearly 500kg. Its two basketball-sized eyes, each measuring 27cm across, are the largest known eyes.

In spite of CCAMLR's efforts and a consumer boycott called for by environmentalists, toothfish is in danger of being fished (legally and illegally) to commercial extinction. In the UK, toothfish is known as Antarctic sea bass, Australian sea bass or Antarctic icefish.

Antarctic krill is canned or frozen and sold as 'Antarctic shrimp,' and also used as cattle and fish feed and in aquaculture. Advances in fishing technology coupled with growing interest in krill for nutriceutical uses may have contributed to recent rises in krill catches: 109,000 tonnes were caught in the 2006–07 season; 210,000 tonnes in 2010–11. Despite being well below CCAMLR limits, there is concern that the fisheries should be monitored and that krill (the base of the Southern Ocean food chain) are also facing pressure from climate change.

Antarctic Wildlife Guide

The remote, ice-covered Antarctic continent and its surrounding Southern Ocean are home to some of Earth's most unique creatures. These whales, penguins, seals and seabirds have evolved over eons to thrive in this exceptional environment. Antarctica remains one of the world's best places for observing animals in the wild at close range. As a visitor to their realm, there is nothing quite like seeing your first whale breach on the open water, or fearless penguin totter along the sea ice. Any Antarctica trip is equally a wildlife-viewing adventure, so come prepared for fleeting glimpses and marvelous encounters.

Adélie penguins and Weddell seal on the ice

FRANS LEMMENS / GETTY ©

Whales

The krill-rich waters of the Southern Ocean attract Earth's largest mammals: baleen whales, like the mighty blue whale and thriving minke, and toothed whales, like the orca and sperm whale. These magnificent cetaceans migrate to Antarctic waters each year before returning north to breed. Keep your eyes open as you cruise!

Humpback Whales

1 Humpback whales, with their stocky bodies, are slower than most other whales, but they are superactive at the ocean's surface. They breach and slap their enormous flippers, which can reach one-third of their total body length. (p169)

Orca (Killer Whales)

2 Spectacular to see in the wild, orcas can travel at up to 55km per hour. They are born into a pod of up to 50 closely related animals, which has its own 'dialect' of calls and hunts as a pack. (p170)

Minke Whales

3 These small whales are by far the most abundant baleen whales in the Southern Ocean. Fast swimmers and curious, minkes often approach slow-moving vessels, and can occasionally feed in large groups. (p170)

Blue Whales

4 The blue whale is the largest animal that has ever lived. This rare behemoth is distinctive in its habit of showing its flukes when diving. Only about 2300 are thought to exist, having been hunted to near extinction. (p168)

Fin Whales

5 The second-largest whale, adult fin whales can reach speeds of 37km per hour and may not feed at all in winter, relying on their accumulated blubber for energy. (p169)

Clockwise from top left

1. Humpback whale breaching 2. Orca and calf
3. Minke whale

FLIP DE NOOYER/FOTO NATURA/MINDEN PICTURES/CORBIS©

2

GORDON LO/GETTY©

Seals

Whether lolling in the sun or diving from the sea ice deep into Antarctica's icy waters, seals provide some of the best wildlife-viewing. Vast breeding colonies of elephant and fur seals pack the shores of the sub-Antarctic islands, and several of the seven Antarctic species dwell, hidden, in the pack ice.

Crabeater Seals

1 This krill-eating seal dwells year-round in the pack-ice zone, and with an estimated population of 15 million, is the most numerous of the world's larger animals (except humans). **Where to see**: pack ice (p172)

Weddell Seals

2 Placid, permanent dwellers of the Antarctic, Weddells are the world's southernmost dwelling mammal. They use their teeth to keep holes in the ice open for diving, and pups learn to swim at one week. **Where to see**: continental ice (p172)

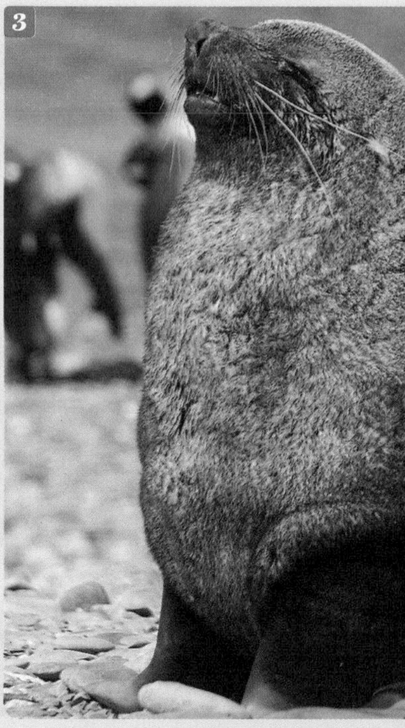

Fur Seals

3 The smallest seal, the fur seal is closely related to sea lions and dogs. They were hunted to near-extinction in the 19th century for their skins, but populations have since rebounded. **Where to see**: sub-Antarctic islands (p171)

Southern Elephant Seals

4 Named for the giant proboscis on the males, this largest of seals lumbers on land but is graceful at sea: they have been known to dive 2km deep, and remain submerged for two hours. **Where to see**: sub-Antarctic islands, Antarctic Peninsula (p71)

Leopard Seals

5 Built for speed, this long, sleek predator has a giant maw that opens to reveal supersharp canines and pointed molars. **Where to see**: southerly sub-Antarctic islands, pack ice (p172)

Clockwise from top left
1. Crabeater seal 2. Weddell seal and her pup
3. Antarctic fur seal

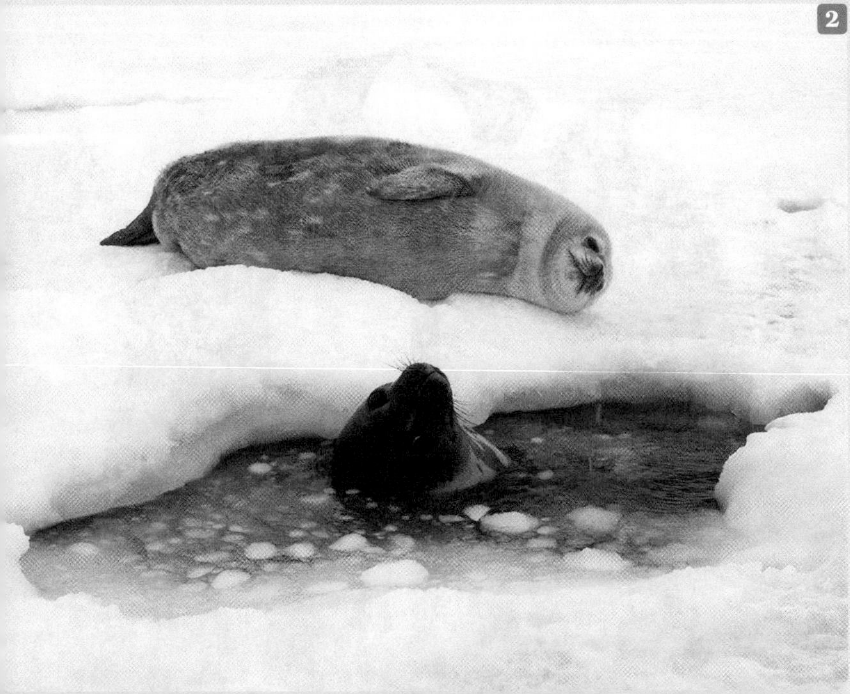

RICK PRICE/CORBIS©

STEVEN KAZLOWSKI/SCIENCE FACTION/CORBIS©

4

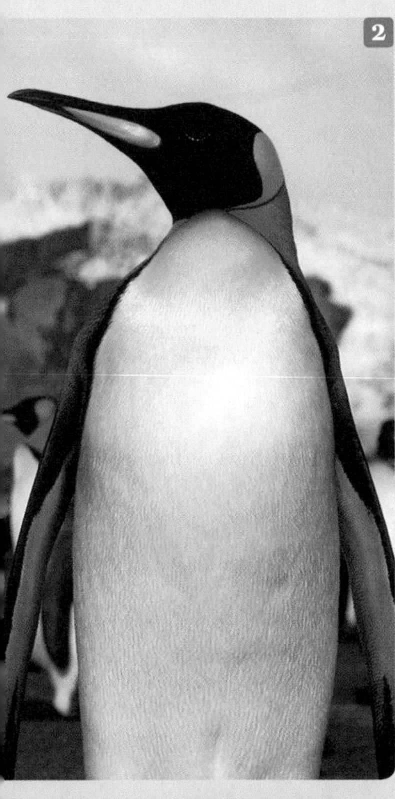

RALPH HOPKINS/LONELY PLANET IMAGES©

MICHAEL AW/LONELY PLANET IMAGES©

Penguins

For many, the word 'Antarctica' immediately conjures up the image of penguins. Nine distinct species roam the region – some live only on the southern islands and one, the lordly emperor penguin, sticks to the continent. Spot them diving for prey, or ashore (or on fast ice) breeding in colonies.

Emperor Penguins

1 Antarctica's colorful giant, with its golden blaze on the neck, is known for its winter breeding, deep diving and amazing survival skills. **Where to see**: Weddell Sea, Queen Maud Land, Enderby Land and Princess Elizabeth Land, Ross Sea. (p173)

King Penguins

2 Slightly smaller than the similarly marked emperors, the king penguin breeds in very large colonies close to the shore. **Where to see**: sub-Antarctic islands. (p174)

Chinstrap Penguins

3 Named for the thin black band under their heads, the acrobatic chinstrap can scoot quickly on its belly ('toboggan'), and leap great distances for a foothold. **Where to see**: Antarctic Peninsula, South Shetland, South Georgia, South Sandwich. (p173)

Macaroni Penguins

4 The world's most abundant penguin has a near-relative in the royal penguin. Distinguish macaronis from other crested species by their orange-plumed 'eyebrows' and black chins. **Where to see**: South Georgia, Crozet, Kerguelen, Antarctic Peninsula. (p174)

Adélie Penguins

5 This diminutive tuxedo-ed penguin masses in giant breeding colonies all around mainland Antarctica, but they range as far as 600km north in winter. **Where to see**: mainland shores, South Shetland, South Orkney, South Sandwich. (p173)

Clockwise from top left
1. Emperor penguins 2. King penguin
3. Chinstrap penguin 4. Macaroni penguins

Seabirds

You don't have to be an ornithologist to enjoy birdwatching around the Southern Ocean, with everything from incredible lone wanderers to cacophonous colony-dwellers. Only a very few species breed on the continent proper. On the open ocean, albatrosses wing gracefully alongside ships, and near land cormorants dive deep for their meals.

Albatrosses

1 Dramatically immortalized in Coleridge's 'The Rime of the Ancient Mariner,' this majestic bird with the greatest wingspan lives up to its reputation: foraging trips can take several days and extend hundreds of kilometers. **Where to see**: sub-Antarctic islands; at sea. (p175)

Skuas

2 The South Polar skua has the distinction of being the world's most southerly bird: several have actually turned up (lost?) at the Pole. The sturdy skua is both a scavenger and an aggressive hunter. **Where to see:** sub-Antarctic islands, Antarctic Peninsula. (p179)

Cormorants

3 Inshore-feeding birds, cormorants are not normally seen out of sight of land. Their presence alongside a ship in the mist is a sure sign of approaching terra firma. **Where to see:** sub-Antarctic islands, Antarctic Peninsula (p178)

Petrels

4 These seabirds come to land only to breed, and myriad species circle the skies of the Southern Ocean. The Antarctic petrel is unique in that it breeds only on the continent. **Where to see**: everywhere (p176)

Right
1. Cambell Island black-browed albatross
2. Great skua, Auckland Islands

Antarctic Science

Since its earliest exploration, Antarctica has been a land of discovery. Many of the initial expeditions were undertaken to discover whether the fabled Terra Australis Incognita existed, and then, once it had been identified, to determine its extent, properties, flora and fauna. In the modern era, with the creation of the Antarctic Treaty, Antarctica became the one protected continent in the world, reserved almost exclusively for scientific research.

Two key features of Antarctic science are that research findings are freely available to everyone and that many of the projects are internationally supported. This coordination has been arranged since 1957 through the Scientific Committee on Antarctic Research (SCAR; www.scar.org). More recently, information is being centrally gathered by Polar Information Commons (www.polarcommons.org).

As it turns out, Antarctica offers not only myriad opportunities to study a unique environment with specially adapted life forms, but it sits at the center of some of the great scientific questions of the modern age. It is particularly vulnerable to the effects of climate change, as well as being a source of weather and global patterns that affect the entire world, and also a superior place from which to monitor changes. Despite Antarctica's remoteness, much of the research done there is immediately relevant to Earth's populated areas.

The International Geophysical Year 1957–58 (p155) really kicked off modern Antarctic science, and International Polar Year 2007–08 (IPY; www.ipy.org; p157), the coordinated international science program, helped push polar science to the next level and integrate it more closely into our models of how the earth works.

Antarctic Journals & Websites

» *Antarctic Science*, Cambridge University Press

» *Polar Biology*, Springer

» *Arctic, Antarctic & Alpine Research*, University of Colorado

» **Australian Antarctic Data Centre** (http://data.aad.gov.au) Clearinghouse of Antarctic observations.

» **High-resolution image of Antarctica** (http://lima.usgs.gov)

Fields of Study

Many of the questions that stand to be answered by research in Antarctica are of a multidisciplinary nature and involve linked, complex systems. For example, how does climate change affect winds and atmospheric, land and ocean temperatures; how do they then interact with ice shelves and sheets; and how do they, in turn, affect sea level and, potentially, global climate? Therefore, many of the fields of study listed here are linked with other fields, both conceptually and in their information gathering. Cores taken of ice and land and ocean sediment, for example, are used across many disciplines, and by many nations.

Ecosystems

Antarctic ecosystems are, relatively speaking, simpler than those in other parts of the world. Thus it is easier to observe changes in the systems due to factors like global warming. Though Antarctic life evolved separately, starting with the opening of the Drake Passage millions of years ago, issues like pollution, increased UV radiation and climate change are impacting species and ecosystems, thus providing dynamic areas of study.

POLAR PROGRAMS

International Bodies

Council of Managers of National Antarctic Programs (COMNAP) www.comnap.aq
Offers full list of bases and programs.

Scientific Committee on Antarctic Research (SCAR) www.scar.org

International Polar Year 2007–08 www.ipy.org

European Polar Board www.esf.org/research-areas/polar-sciences.html

National Programs

Australia www.antarctica.gov.au

Britain www.antarctica.ac.uk

Chile www.inach.cl

China www.pric.gov.cn

France www.institut-polaire.fr

Germany www.awi.de

India www.ncaor.gov.in

Japan www.nipr.ac.jp

New Zealand www.antarcticanz.govt.nz

Norway www.npolar.no

Russia www.aari.aq

South Africa www.sanap.org.za

USA www.usap.gov, www.nsf.gov

Disciplines include biochemistry, biology, physiology, genomics and evolution.

Since the 1990s, for example, studies like the Palmer Station (http://oceaninformatics.ucsd.edu/datazoo/data/pallter) and McMurdo Dry Valleys (www.mcmlter.org) Long Term Ecological Research (LTER) projects have been recording data on these interactions, and are trying to answer the question: how will these ecosystems interact and alter in the face of increasing changes in the region?

Marine Life

The Census of Antarctic Marine Life (CAML; www.caml.aq), with its 17 ships and scientists from 20 nations, investigates the population numbers and distribution of Antarctic marine life. This study requires expensive infrastructure – icebreaker research vessels, scuba-diving facilities, laboratories at research stations and access to satellite data – promoting international research in which resources are shared.

Evolved characteristics for study include body shape and composition, cardiovascular control, body temperature, metabolism, oxygen levels when deep diving and resurfacing (without getting the bends), prey availability and adaptations to the rhythm of sea-ice formation and retreat.

The use of satellite transmitters and other electronic equipment has provided remarkable data: for example, while at sea, elephant seals spend almost 90% of the time submerged, making dives of up to two hours' duration and reaching depths of more than 975m. How they manage this is the subject of wide-ranging physiological research. Similarly, a tiny satellite transmitter on a bird's back can report on its position, while a small tube on its leg can collect data on the depth and timing of its dives for food. Even the oxygen consumption required for flying or swimming can be measured automatically.

Animal populations are being monitored both through direct counting, tagging individual animals, and, more recently, through satellite observations. For example, in 2012 satellite data revealed almost twice as many emperor penguins exist than were previously estimated (595,000 as opposed to 270,000); the first complete census of a species taken from space. In short, scientists study everything from breeding behavior and rates of growth to diet and the impact of climate change.

A great deal of research has been undertaken to establish the diversity, life histories and extent of fish stocks. Most research has concentrated on the two most abundant groups – the Antarctic cod *(Nototheniidae)* and the ice fish *(Channichthyidae)* – with interest focused on the evolution of the groups, their ability to survive in icy waters, their reproduction and growth rates, and their population age structure.

Every aspect of the life cycle and biology of krill, the single most important food of whales, seals and birds, has been studied.

Phytoplankton or algae contain chlorophyll, which can be detected by satellite. Plankton takes up carbon from carbon dioxide dissolved in the water, and when it dies takes the carbon down into the sediments. This has prompted considerable research on how much carbon can be taken out of the atmosphere by phytoplankton and what, if anything, can be done to increase the rate. Studies on the effects on phytoplankton of increases in springtime UV radiation continue.

The communities that inhabit the seafloor around Antarctica are called the benthos, and are as rich in plants and animals as a tropical coral reef. Research focuses on identification and the biochemistry and physiology of benthos.

Terrestrial Life

The relationships between Antarctic plants and those on the surrounding continents have interested botanists for almost 150 years. Research continues on how these lichens and mosses survive bizarre terrains and the extreme cold and desiccation of the Antarctic winter.

Invertebrates like mites and nematodes are also the subject of much research, in part because of how they survive extreme cold (many make antifreezes), a lack of water and oxygen (some put their metabolism into a special state), and high salt levels in the soil (see also Dry Valleys wildlife, p94).

There is increasing interest in how microbial communities survive in Antarctica. Where retreating glaciers reveal bare rock and soil, scientists use new technologies to both investigate the earliest stages of the colonization of these areas and to develop a better understanding of how complex communities develop. For example, in 2009 bacteria were discovered under an inland glacier with no light or heat and very little oxygen (they convert iron compounds for energy). In 2012 a new technology called SkyTEM (http://skytem.com) allowed the mapping of subsurface groundwater and rock, giving a view into under-ice microbial systems in the Dry Valleys that were previously inaccessible.

A joint IPY program is studying alien plant and invertebrate species carried to Antarctica and their effects on native ecosystems (see p161).

Lakes & Streams

Within the many ponds and lakes scattered around ice-free areas (some very saline, some that have almost no nutrients), the most developed animal is a small shrimp and the most complex plant is an aquatic moss. Many lakes are dominated by microbial communities. The simplicity of the systems attracts scientists: work has concentrated on the lakes in the

Science Reads

» *The Biology of Polar Regions*, DN Thomas et al (2008)

» *Biology of the Southern Ocean (2nd edition)*, G Knox (2006)

» *The Ferocious Summer*, M Hooper (2007)

» *Sea Ice: An Introduction to its Physics, Chemistry and Biology*, DN Thomas & GS Dieckmann, editors (2003)

» *Antarctic Meteorology and Climatology*, JC King & J Turner (1997)

» *Astronomy on Ice: Observing the Universe from the South Pole*, Martin A Pomerantz (2004)

» *Encyclopedia of the Antarctic*, B Riffenburgh, editor (2007)

HUMANS

It's not just the animals that scientists study. Research on humans stationed in Antarctica include studying the effects of the seasonal changes in the climate and UV light, the isolation experienced during winter, epidemiology, and the effects of diet and exercise on health.

For more on life on a science station, see p84.

Taylor and Wright Valleys (especially Lake Vanda), at the Vestfold and Bunger Hills regions, and at Signy Island. Additionally, the sediment at the bottom of lakes contains a record of how the lake has changed over a period as long as 10,000 years; this helps in determining the history of Antarctica's recent climate.

Subglacial Lakes

One of the areas of extreme interest and debate now is the drilling into subglacial lakes (p122) like enormous Lake Vostok (p123). This lake, which had been untouched for 200 million years, was tapped in 2012 by Russian scientists.

Antarctica contains one of the best climatic archives of the past. Terrestrial sediments cover the last 200,000 years and marine sediments cover millions of years. There are even older areas of ancient continental rocks. Current marine drilling projects include the **Integrated Ocean Drilling Program** (www.iodp.org) and **Antarctic Geologic Drilling** (www.andrill.org).

Geology, Geomorphology & Paleontology

Less than 0.5% of Antarctica's rock is accessible for direct examination. Some scientists say that the geology and topography under the ice (especially in East Antarctica) is less well known than the topography of Mars. In fact, the Dry Valleys are the best terrestrial analogue for Mars, and study there has possible applications for life under extraterrestrial frozen seas.

Understanding the connections between the southern continents, and how they broke apart and why, continues to fascinate geoscientists, as do the origins of the subglacial mountains like the Gamburtsev range, which lies under Dome A. In 2012, new data-gathering techniques revealed a previously unknown extension of the East Antarctic Rift System (a fracture that extends 2500km from India to Antarctica).

Antarctica's glacial and tectonic histories are interlinked, as without the high topography the ice sheet would have formed quite differently. Geomorphologists study Antarctic landforms and have mainly been concerned with the effects of the ice sheet on the underlying rock, as well as the study of glacial deposits, the remains of old beaches left when the sea level fell, and the formation of patterned ground.

Technology is developing to better observe these systems, and further study will be accomplished with airborne radar, long-range aircraft, laser observation, gravity and magnetic field data, and a new generation of clean, rapid drilling systems (for ice and sediment cores).

Seismology & Volcanology

The Polar Earth Observing Network (Polenet; www.polenet.org) seismic array was completed in 2012, placing sensors over about one-third of Antarctica. These sensors record seismic activity, giving insight into geological makeup, and offer GPS monitoring to the millimeter of bedrock uplift, for use in calculating changes in the ice sheets.

The South Pole Remote Earth Science and Seismological Observatory (p135) detects earthquakes worldwide, while the Mt Erebus Volcano Observatory (http://erebus.nmt.edu) studies the active volcano (p104).

Minerals & Soils

Are there vast deposits of precious metals and ores beneath the Antarctic ice sheet? Are there huge basins of gas and oil under the Weddell and Ross Seas? Antarctic geologists are working to determine how known mineral deposits (p160) were formed and what they can tell us about geological processes.

Antarctic soils are primitive, almost without organic matter, very dry, and with a high salt content. Scientists working on soils in the Dry Valleys have been able to show that some of them are at least five million years old, giving a possible date for the retreat of ice from these valleys.

The polygons, circles, stripes and sometimes even hummocks that can be seen throughout the Antarctic are called 'patterned ground.' They are formed by alternate freezing and thawing of water in the soil, which produces lateral sorting of coarse and fine particles.

Fossils

Fossils give us evidence of ancient life in Antarctica. Coal beds and plant fossils in the Transantarctic Mountains were reported by both Ernest Shackleton and Captain Robert Scott, clearly indicating that the Antarctic was not always covered with ice. Since then much more fossil evidence of preglacial periods has been uncovered. Antarctica even had dinosaurs (see p95).

Fossils provide evidence of the connections between the parts of the ancient supercontinent Gondwana, give indirect information about the changes in Antarctic climate over millions of years, and offer an insight into the evolution of present Antarctic species.

Many deposits contain fossil plants, petrified wood (sometimes in pieces as long as 20m) and fossil pollen, but fossils of animals are much less common. In some places ferns and other woodland species are also preserved in great detail.

Meteorites

Most of humankind's knowledge about meteorites comes from analysis of those found in Antarctica, which acts as a huge meteorite collector (see p118).

Ice & the Southern Ocean

The study of Antarctica's ice sheets, shelves and sea ice is critical to understanding climate change, sea-level rises and the interactions of myriad inter-related systems.

As Antarctica's ice shelves are lost along the continent's edges, continental ice moves more rapidly toward the sea. Both a 2002 and a 2012 study showed that a major contributor to this loss was warming ocean temperatures, which undermine ice shelves from subsurface cavities. Additionally, increasing winds are predicted to increase ocean upwelling rates, which would also increase subglacial melting.

For a description of the ice sheet, its dynamics and attempts to measure it, see p158.

Currently, there are many questions facing scientists regarding Antarctic ice, oceans and climate change. For instance, summer temperatures on the major ice sheets remain below freezing, so how will the ice sheet respond to rapid temperature changes? And what are the interactions between sea, land and atmospheric temperatures, winds, ice shelves and sheets, ocean salinity and acidity, ocean circulation, bottom waters, and carbon uptake?

Understanding the processes around the stormy waters of the Southern Ocean is also critical for understanding the world's systems. Southern Ocean circulation is central to global ocean circulation, and it is the site of upwelling to the surface of deep water from all oceans. Scientists study these processes and the effects of Antarctic bottom water.

Nuclear fallout from atomic bomb tests during the 1950s and '60s shows up clearly in ice cores drilled from the Antarctic ice sheets, and can be linked to specific events.

Cold waters can absorb more of the excess carbon dioxide generated by humankind. Plus, fresh water from ice melt is 10 times more acidic than sea water. Increases in carbon dioxide in Antarctica's waters will reduce the calcium carbonate that many marine organisms need for bone or shell, raising significant questions. Will organisms adapt? Migrate? Where will they be able to find cold temperatures? The international Census of Antarctic Marine Life studies the Southern Ocean, shedding light on these issues.

As part of the World Ocean Circulation Experiment (http://woce.nodc.noaa.gov), which is measuring worldwide current patterns in order to improve existing computer models for predicting climate change, several countries have placed current meters on the seafloor around Antarctica. A network of tidal gauges, which often report data via satellite, has also been installed at various Antarctic stations.

Currently, Antarctic sea-ice increases and decreases vary by region. Contrary to General Circulation Models, Antarctic sea ice is gaining an average of 1% per decade, and scientists are working to understand why. They expect it will decrease dramatically, especially as ozone depletion's net cooling is reversed (as the hole closes).

NEW OBSERVATIONS

Glaciers & Floating Ice Shelves

We now have enough historical data to study changes in glaciers over decades. Assessing 244 glaciers around the Antarctic Peninsula has shown that 87% have retreated over the past 50 years, and over 300 glaciers show an increased rate of flow into the sea. Satellite data also allows glaciologists to monitor giant icebergs calving.

Other research on the ice shelves concentrates on determining how quickly ice is moving off the continent, and how rapidly the shelf ice thins from the melting of its underside.

The long-term objective is to provide researchers with a computer model that will allow the loss of ice to the Southern Ocean to be accurately predicted and combined with other climate and ocean models. Investigating the underside of the ice shelves is now possible using remotely operated vehicles (ROVs).

Sea Ice

Antarctic sea-ice cover varies from a minimum of 4 million sq km in February to a maximum of 20 million sq km in September, and this huge seasonal change has enormous repercussions. The ice alters the exchange of heat, ocean and atmospheric circulation, and the marine ecosystem has to adapt to lower temperatures and a lack of light under the ice. Developing models of the way sea ice effects energy transfers between the sea and air is a major scientific concern.

Satellite observation of the sea ice began in 1979, and now the Sea Ice Mass Balance in the Antarctic project (Simba; http://utsa.edu/lrsg/Antarctica/SIMBA) uses radar and altimetry data to set a baseline for future measurements, which can help answer the question: how does all of this interact with the climate?

To verify satellite data, research must be undertaken inside the pack ice; new technologies include drifting buoys, which will give meteorological and oceanographic data and more information about ice movement.

Climatology & Weather Forecasting

Antarctica and the Southern Ocean are directly connected to the entire global climate system – atmosphere, global ocean circulation and overturning, and the rate of carbon dioxide uptake. To understand the world's system, we must understand Antarctica and the Southern Ocean. Furthermore, climate, glacial ice, sea ice and the ocean are all interconnected.

Using this understanding of interconnectedness, scientists reconstruct past climate conditions (paleoclimatology) to understand the present and to model predictions for the future. This is all accomplished through sediment drilling, studying ice cores and fossil records, and understanding changes in the earth's orbit and greenhouse gases.

Countries surrounding the Southern Ocean have a great interest in the current meteorology of Antarctica. The strong westerly winds and their associated weather systems drive storms across the Southern Ocean and beyond, while the seasonal formation and melting of sea ice has a major effect on southern-hemisphere weather. Antarctic bases and automated weather stations share daily meteorological observations; over 100 locations represent 12 nations.

Current modeling efforts include the **Community Earth System Model** (www.cesm.ucar.edu/working_groups/Polar) and the **Community Ice Sheet Model** (CISM; http://oceans11.lanl.gov/trac/CISM).

Atmospheric Science

Global warming and ozone depletion have made the study of atmospheric gases a major Antarctic discipline. Observations made from satellites, drones, constant-level balloons and self-sustaining blimps also have applications for other disciplines.

ICE CORES: DRILLING INTO THE PAST *DR JO JACKA*

As snow is deposited on the surface of the Antarctic ice sheet, different chemicals and gases that have dissolved and mixed in the snow and in the atmosphere become trapped in the ice. By drilling through the ice sheet and analyzing the ice and air trapped in the bubbles, glaciologists access an archive of past climate change, both locally and globally. Drilling is a difficult and highly skilled activity, often extending over years. The ice sheet is always moving, so the drill hole is continually being bent and squeezed shut unless it is kept open with drilling fluid.

The oxygen isotope ratio (or 'delta value') of melted ice samples is related to the temperature when the ice was deposited as snow. Thus, a climate history can be built up by measuring delta value from the surface of the ice sheet down. At Russia's Vostok Station, an ice core was drilled to a depth of 3623m. The ice at the bottom of this core is about 426,000 years old, and the delta values show several glacial cycles; that is, several ice ages and warmer interglacial periods. The oldest ice core (3km deep) came from Dome C: 800,000 years. They could get even older: the oldest ice estimate is about 1.5 million years, in the East Antarctic interior.

Air pockets between snow grains on the surface of the ice sheet become bubbles under high pressure deep down in the ice. These bubbles contain tiny samples of the atmosphere from earlier times. Analysis of the air trapped in the bubbles allows glaciologists to examine how the concentrations of different gases in the atmosphere have changed over time.

While some ice cores (such as Vostok's) give a climate history extending back hundreds of thousands of years, they cannot be dated accurately. Other cores, drilled at locations where the snow accumulation is relatively high, can provide very precise dating if the annual snow layer is thick enough, because several samples can be analyzed for each year of snow. This ice is (comparatively) not that deep, so data is for the past few thousand years.

Ice cores can be dated by counting annual layers (cycles of hydrogen peroxide); dating decay rates of natural isotopes; modeling changes in ice flow with age; and by their sulfate levels. Sulfate is blasted into the atmosphere by erupting volcanoes and is then distributed around the globe. By measuring sulfate concentration in the ice cores, glaciologists can 'see' past volcanic eruptions. By collaborating with volcanologists, they can then determine which sulfate signals in the ice correspond with which volcanic eruption and when that eruption occurred. They can also study world pollution.

For the world's ice core and climate data, visit www.ncdc.noaa.gov. These are three ice core programs: West Antarctic Ice Sheet Divide Ice Core (WAIS Divide; www.waisdivide.unh.edu), Dome Fuji Ice Core (www.ncdc.noaa.gov) and Epica (European Program for Ice Coring in Antarctica; www.esf.org).

Dr Jo Jacka, Chief Scientific Editor of the Journal of Glaciology

Atmospheric Chemistry & Ozone Depletion

Probably the most famous science project ever undertaken in Antarctica is the monitoring of stratospheric ozone at Britain's Halley Station. A paper published in *Nature* in 1985 provided such alarming evidence of the increasing rate of ozone destruction that it resulted in a worldwide agreement to ban chlorofluorocarbons (CFCs). It also stimulated a massive increase in research on polar chemistry. See the Environment chapter, p162, for more on ozone depletion.

Areas of open water in the ice, called polynyas, occur in the same places deep in the pack ice each year. We know little about these polynyas, as only the strongest icebreakers can reach them. Data suggests that they are very important in energy transfers between the sea and the atmosphere.

Greenhouse Gases & Global Warming

To measure global changes in greenhouse gases like carbon dioxide and methane, you need a site as far away from the industries that produce these gases as possible. Thus the US chose the South Pole for carbon-dioxide measurements in 1956. This series of measurements is still running and is one of the world's most important monitoring activities, and has been expanded to other sites around the globe.

Other gases identified as important contributors to warming (nitrous oxide, hydrofluorocarbons, perfluorocarbons and sodium hexafluoride) are also rising. For more on greenhouse gases, climate change and global warming, see p162.

Geomagnetism & Space Weather

The peculiar structure of the earth's magnetic field over Antarctica makes it the best place in the world to investigate how the sun's activities affect the ionosphere (the north pole has no landmass, so is not suited to year-round observations). The sun produces a continuous stream of electrically charged, high-energy particles called 'solar wind.' When it comes into contact with other particles or enters a magnetic field, its energy becomes channeled and discharged. The only visible signs of this discharge are the auroras seen at both poles.

To study this, physicists use auroral radar systems looking toward the South Pole. They utilize the overlap between the beams to create a 3D picture of the changes in the ionosphere above the Pole. This data has allowed the production of 'space weather' maps, plotting the timing and duration of magnetic 'storms' that can have devastating effects on the many satellites upon which we rely.

Recent studies have revealed that during the ice ages the sea level varied by more than 130m, and that carbon-dioxide rise preceded the end of the Ice Age.

The Space Weather Prediction Center (www.swpc.noaa.gov) and the NSF's Center for Integrated Space Weather Modeling (www.bu.edu/cism) work on these forecasts and try to monitor and understand solar cycles.

Astronomy

Incredibly stable atmospheric conditions above Antarctica's surface area (it's high, cold, dry and the thin atmosphere is transparent – there's no air or light pollution), plus its prime geographic location (objects stay in view, above the horizon), make Antarctica the best place on Earth for astronomical observations. Couple this with the very low sky noise (low wind and lack of solar heating during winter) at places like the South Pole and East Antarctica, and it's an astronomer's dream.

Recent technological advancements have catapulted Antarctica to the cutting edge of astronomy, taking some of the most sensitive measurements ever accomplished on Earth. The South Pole is now a major astronomical site with infrared telescopes (looking at star formation) and the massive new South Pole Telescope (p135).

In 2012, China installed the largest optical telescope (AST3-1) in Antarctica at their fully robotic Plato observatory at Dome A. The AST3-1 can be steered remotely, making large expanses of the night sky accessible throughout the Antarctic winter. It is the first of three telescopes that are expected to find planets around other stars and to make other observations formerly only possible from space.

A new branch of astronomy called helioseismography is making progress on the question of how the sun affects the earth.

Searching for the Origins of the Universe

Antarctic research (specifically using the telescopes at the Pole and data from high-altitude balloons) is also playing its part in unraveling the mysteries of where the universe came from. The South Pole Telescope was designed specifically to seek the dark energy believed to comprise 95% of the universe, and to help discover the mass of neutrinos. It is used to study cosmic microwave background radiation, believed to be the remaining echo of the Big Bang. Antarctica's sensitive instruments can make measurements that show whether there is a spatial structure to the background radiation.

Similarly, IceCube (p135) investigates the mystery of the acceleration of cosmic rays to extremely high energies by detecting neutrinos, nearly massless particles with no charge, which are traceable to their direction of origin. Almost immediately after going online, IceCube provided new information – in April 2012, data revealed that there were fewer neutrinos than expected for Gamma Ray Bursts (GRB) if they are the source of high energy cosmic rays. This will lead scientists to reevaluate both their GRB and cosmic ray models.

Antarctic Weather

» **Antarctic Mesoscale Prediction System (AMPS)** www.mmm.ucar.edu/rt/amps

» **Antarctic Meteorological Research Center** http://amrc.ssec.wisc.edu

» **NOAA's Climatic Data Center** www.ncdc.noaa.gov

Future of Antarctic Science

The increasing interest in developing global models to try to predict the world's future has shown Antarctica's importance very clearly. In Antarctica, the combination of direct observations and sophisticated modeling of data will lead to immense improvements in the accuracy of predictions about climate, evolution, astrophysics and more. A 2011 proposal called for a Southern Ocean Observing System (SOOS), which would become a part of the Global Ocean Observing System (www.ioc-goos.org),w

WARREN ZAPOL: US POLAR RESEARCH BOARD, US ARCTIC COMMISSION

Warren Zapol has been to Antarctica countless times and has led nine expeditions to study the diving mechanisms of the Weddell seal. This led to a treatment for hypoxic human newborns which is now used to save the lives of 10,000 babies each year in the US. In 2011 he chaired the National Academy of Sciences' Future Science Opportunities in Antarctica and the Southern Ocean Committee.

What are the hot spots for Antarctic science these days?

Tapping subglacial Lake Vostok: In 2012 a Russian team tapped the largest Antarctic subglacial lake. They reported that what came up with the drill 'smelled like marsh.' Why should that be? What might be surviving down there over millions of years?

Research on climate change: As ocean temperatures rise with global warming, this warmer water melts and destabilizes our ice shelves, glaciers and ice sheets. More so than the Arctic (where the ice is floating, so does not raise sea levels by melting), the Antarctic will impact sea levels (by 60m if all the ice goes!). The spot most tourists visit, the western side of the Antarctic Peninsula, is indeed one of the most rapidly warming places on Earth.

Gamburtsev Mountains imaging: This range is as large as the European Alps but is completely covered by the East Antarctic ice sheet. For the first time, using digital imaging such as ice-penetrating radar, scientists are mapping these mountains and gaining an understanding of how they were formed.

and create a comprehensive observational instrument network monitoring the atmosphere, ice sheet, sea ice and ocean.

Severe space weather (magnetic storms) on the sun can send high-energy particles toward Earth and disrupt GPS satellites and electrical power on the earth's surface. In one such event in 1859, auroras were visible around the world, and telegraph systems caught fire.

With scientists from over 30 countries now active in Antarctica, there is an increasing emphasis on investigating big issues that can only be tackled on a coordinated international scale. Additionally, new technologies are being developed such as DNA sequencing (currently being undertaken on the Weddell seal), sensor networks, and clean sampling of subglacial lakes.

These ambitious, cooperative efforts utilize Antarctica's special features to answer scientific questions. Using the latest tools, researchers can map the Antarctic more accurately than ever before to assess the changing continent and globe. With geographic information systems, scientists can synthesize widely differing types of data to gain better understanding of how glaciology interacts with meteorology and geology, and with modern databases, all of this data can be made available to the world's scientific and educational community.

At the same time, scientists and logistics support people must continue to provide light, transportation, heat, potable water and safety while making a minimal impact on the natural environment. Ever-evolving new, clean, energy-efficient technologies will help protect and preserve the continent and its scientific riches for the future.

Survival Guide

Accommodations

See the Planning Your Antarctic Adventure chapter, p21, for details of shipboard accommodations.

Children

Children are still relatively rare visitors to Antarctica. Antarctica's amazing landscapes and abundant wildlife are exciting for young people, but sea time ca be tedious. Help children learn about Antarctic topics before and during the voyage and encourage them to question ship staff. Meredith Hooper is a great author of children's Antarctic stories.

Climate

Antarctica is synonymous with cold, thanks to its polar location; high elevation; lack of a protective, water vapor–filled atmosphere; and permanent ice cover (which reflects about 80% of the sun's radiation back into space). The Antarctic Peninsula is warmest year-round.

» **Mean temperature in Antarctic interior**: -40°C to -70°C in coldest month; -15°C to -35°C in warmest month.

» **Coastal temperature**: -15°C to -32°C in winter; 5°C to -5°C in summer.

» **Precipitation**: Antarctica's interior, despite its ice cap, is the world's driest desert, since the extreme cold freezes water vapor out of the air. Annual snowfall on the polar plateau is equivalent to less than 5cm of rain. Antarctic blizzards are common, but are usually violently blown snow which has fallen over years and never melted, not falling snow.

» **Wind**: Antarctica experiences the strongest winds on Earth because of katabatics caused by denser, colder air rushing down off the polar plateau to the coast. These achieve velocities up to 320km/h. Winds on the plateau, by contrast, are usually very light.

Amundsen-Scott (US)

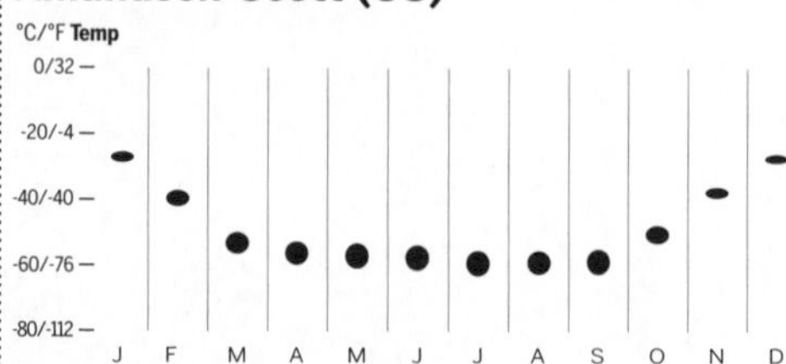

Mawson Station (AUS)

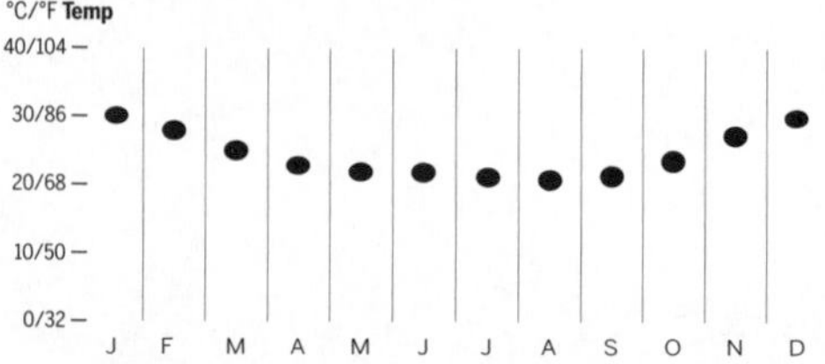

Electricity

Shipboard Each ship has its own type of electricity based on its country of origin; check with the tour operator before buying converters. Many ships are Russian, and use 220 volts, 50 hertz, with electrical sockets accommodating the standard European two round-pin plug.

Argentina: 220V/50Hz; V-shaped flat prongs and round-pin European-style prongs

Chile: 220V/50Hz; round-pin European-style prongs

Falkland Islands: 220V/50Hz; straight, flat, British-style prongs

Health

The following is an overview of common ailments that afflict travelers to Antarctica. See also p25 for information on planning for health and medical concerns.

Seasickness

The bane of many a traveler, seasickness is simply a natural response to the sea's motion.

» Eat lightly, but never have a completely empty stomach.

» Book a cabin that minimizes motion: midship, lower-deck cabins can be more comfortable.

» Fresh air and a view of the horizon usually help.

» Avoid reading, cigarette smoke, alcohol and diesel fumes.

» Ships' doctors dispense one or two commercial remedies, but plan ahead and bring your favored treatments, even if you've never been seasick before.

Commercial **motion-sickness remedies** must be taken before you start to feel seasick:

» Dimenhydrinate (Dramamine, Travel-Gum), meclizine (Antivert, Bonine): common choice, but often cause drowsiness.

» Promethazine (Phenergan): less drowsiness than motion sickness itself. Promotes adaptation to motion. Can still cause drowsiness, dizziness and dry mouth.

» Scopolamine (Transderm Scop/Travel Patch)

Non-medicinal remedies:

» Ginger

» Acupressure wrist bands

Other Ailments

Visitors to the South Pole and inland East Antarctica can experience **altitude sickness** amongst other maladies (see Adjusting to the Pole, p130).

» **Frostbite** is most likely to occur in the nose, cheeks, chin, fingers and toes. First signs are numbness and redness, followed by the development of waxy, white/yellow plaque. Dress in layers; wear a hat; keep dry (waterproof outer layer); change wet clothes, socks and gloves.

» **Hypothermia** occurs when the body loses heat faster than it can produce it, and core temperature falls; often due to a combination of wind, wet clothing, fatigue and hunger. Symptoms include exhaustion, numb skin (particularly in fingers, toes), shivering, slurred speech, irrational or violent behavior, lethargy, stumbling, dizzy spells, muscle cramps and violent bursts of energy. Get out of the wind and rain; change wet clothing for dry; drink hot liquids (not alcohol); eat high-calorie, easily digestible food; and if possible, take a warm (not hot) shower.

» **Dehydration** Antarctica's extremely dry environment can lead to dehydration. Signs include dark-yellow urine and/or fatigue. Drink at least 4L of water a day; avoid coffee and tea.

» **Sun exposure** Even on overcast days it's easy to get sunburned, and suffer eye pain, as the sun reflects off snow, ice and sea. Wear ultraviolet-filtering sunglasses and sunblock.

Insurance

Travel insurance is highly recommended as cancellation penalties are stiff and medical evacuations costly. Most tour companies offer supplemental insurance (check with your operator). Worldwide travel insurance is available at www.lonelyplanet.com/travel_services. Check the fine print: often known medical conditions are not covered.

» **US State Department** (www.travel.state.gov) Lists medical evacuation and travel insurance companies.

Internet Access

Ships offer different services: some have in-cabin wi-fi, others use a common computer for web access for a fee (eg €30 per 100 minutes). Speed is slower than on land, and coverage can break up based on location and weather/atmospheric conditions.

Maps

» **Downloadable satellite images**: http://lima.usgs.gov

» **Graham Land and South Shetlands Islands**, **British Antarctic Survey/UK Antarctic Heritage Trust** (www.ukaht.org; UK£12) Best visitors' map for the Antarctic Peninsula. Reverse-side *Scotia Sea* (1:4 million), shows southern Tierra del Fuego, Falkland Islands, South Sandwich Islands, South Georgia and northern Antarctic Peninsula. Also good: *Brabant Islands to Argentine Islands* (UK£10). Available through UKAHT and at Port Lockroy.

» **Antarctica Satellite Map**, **National Geographic Society** (http://shop.nationalgeographic.com; US$11) Detailed digital mosaic of 4500 satellite scans, up-to-date information.

» **Ocean Explorer series** includes Antarctica, South Georgia and Falkland Islands (each US$10 to US$13). Available, along with many other maps, at the **Antarctic Connection** (www.antarcticconnection.com).

Money

Each ship runs its onboard economy differently, but in general you sign for items and pay at the end of the trip. These bills can usually be settled with cash, traveler's checks or credit cards; check with your operator.

» **ATMs/banks**: no access in Antarctica; take cash and credit cards.

» **Currencies on land**: Chile and Argentina each have their own currency (with the same name: peso). Falkland Islands uses British pound (£) or local pound (FK£).

» **Bases**: national currency or US dollars, euros and British pounds.

» **Tipping**: some tips are included in some cruises (check with your operator). Although optional, when not included in your fare, it's considered appropriate to tip crew and staff for good service. Near the end of the voyage most tour operators distribute guidelines (eg US$7 to US$10 per day).

Post

Send postcards (to others or yourself!) from Antarctica for the novelty, understanding that service is slow (often two to three months). Some stations don't accept tourist mail.

Telephone & Fax

Ship communications use International Maritime Satellite (INMARSAT), often for a significant fee (€5 per minute). Coverage can be disrupted based on location and weather/atmospheric conditions. Iridium phones also work in Antarctica. Standard mobile phones don't work at sea or in Antarctica.

Time

There are no time zones in Antarctica The summer sun stays up as long as 20 hours a day; in winter it's the reverse. Most ships' clocks are based on ports of departure/disembarkation.

» **Chile**: GMT -4 hours

» **Argentina**: GMT -3 hours

Travelers with Disabilities

The physical challenges of shipboard life, Zodiac boats and icy landing sites can make Antarctica difficult for everyone, no matter their physical limitations. Nevertheless, disabled travelers may be able to make special arrangements with a tour operator, especially if an able-bodied traveler accompanies them. Check with tour operators to see whether they can meet your needs (eg some ships have elevators and helicopters).

Visas

No single government controls Antarctica, so visitors do not need visas. All tour operators, yachts, researchers and independent expeditioners of countries that are signatories of the Antarctic Treaty must have a permit from their country (permit rules vary).

» Cruise-ship passengers are covered under permits applied for by the operator.

» Japanese nationals must register with their Ministry of the Environment if they are on a tour authorized by any country other than Japan.

» Yacht passengers/crew, expeditioners, researchers and anyone visiting by air should check with their national government to ensure their paperwork is in order.

If uncertain about your status, check with your tour operator. Also, you may need visas for countries you visit before/after your cruise.

Work

Scientists usually go to Antarctica on specific research proposals. Support personnel are selected by national programs (usually hiring only citizens/work-eligible people). Contact your country's national Antarctic program (for a list, see p194). The US is Antarctica's largest employer; personnel are hired by private contractor **Lockheed Martin** (www.lockheedmartin.com). It recruits about 600 people for US bases, from chefs, clerks, hairstylists to construction.

Transportation

GETTING THERE & AWAY

Most visitors reach Antarctica via group tours on a ship, but there are some alternatives. Some tours can be booked online at www.lonelyplanet.com/travel_services.

Entering Antarctica

See Visas, p206 for information on permit requirements.

Air

Flights to the Interior

Antarctic Logistics & Expeditions (ALE; www.antarctic-logistics.com) owns pioneering tour operator **Adventure Network International** (ANI; www.adventure-network.com), which was the first company to offer flights to Antarctica's interior.

Using Ilyushin IL76 aircraft, ALE flies from Punta Arenas, Chile, to its new runway at Union Glacier (4½ hours). An older, secondary runway is 70km southeast at Patriot Hills. ALE's private camp (opened in 2010) sits at the base of Mt Rossman.

» Emperor penguin rookery US$38,250

» Vinson Massif with guided climb US$38,000

» South Pole Fly-In (four hours at 90°S) US$42,950

» Guided 65-day ski trip from continent edge to Pole US$63,950

The Antarctic Company (TAC; www.antarctic-company.info) operates Ilyushin IL76 aircraft from Cape Town to Novo Airbase (six hours), 15km southwest of Russia's Novolazarevskaya Station in East Antarctica. TAC also provides support for non-governmental organizations, private expeditions and adventure travelers.

» Queen Maud Land (three days) €15,600

» Meet the emperors (10 days) from €23,000

» Pole to coast (10 days) €37,000

White Desert (www.white-desert.com) flies 12-passenger Gulfstream G-IV and Ilyushin IL76 aircraft from Cape Town to Novo Airbase. It uses a temporary camp, powered by wind and solar energy, and offset flights with a carbon program.

» Three-day safari €25,200

» Emperors and mountains €37,400

» Emperors and the South Pole €56,000

Flights to King George Island

Aerovías DAP (www.dapantartica.cl) flies from Punta Arenas, Chile, to Frei Station on King George Island (South Shetland Islands) in summer (weather permitting), using 10-passenger Beechcraft King Air turboprops and 70-passenger BAE-146s.

» Day visit US$3960

» Overnight visit US$4960

CLIMATE CHANGE & TRAVEL

Every form of transport that relies on carbon-based fuel generates CO_2, the main cause of human-induced climate change. Modern travel is dependent on airplanes, which might use less fuel per kilometer per person than most cars but travel much greater distances. The altitude at which aircraft emit gases (including CO_2) and particles also contributes to their climate change impact. Many websites offer 'carbon calculators' that allow people to estimate the carbon emissions generated by their journey and, for those who wish to do so, to offset the impact of the greenhouse gases emitted with contributions to portfolios of climate-friendly initiatives throughout the world. Lonely Planet offsets the carbon footprint of all staff and author travel.

Fly-Cruise

AntarcticaXXI (www.antarcticaxxi.com) flies from Punta Arenas, Chile, to Frei Station on King George Island (1½ hours) using 70-passenger BAE-146 aircraft. Passengers transfer to 68-passenger *Ocean Nova* for several days of cruising the South Shetlands and Antarctic Peninsula before their return flight. Fares begin at US$9700.

Several cruise companies also offer fly-cruises.

Overflights

Australia's Qantas airlines and **Croydon Travel** (www.antarcticaflights.com.au) offer day-long flights over the continent (with guides) on a Boeing 747 once or twice per summer. All seats, except Economy Center, rotate. Prices range from Economy Centre A$999, Economy Premium A$2599 to First Class A$7299.

Passengers move about the plane for views from several vantage points. But you get what you pay for: some tickets don't provide direct window access at any time, so you may have to look over someone's shoulder.

Sea

Nearly all visitors arrive by sea, most of them by ship from Ushuaia. For information on booking your trip, including costs, see p21.

Cruise Ships

Below are some of the oldest, most established companies cruising to Antarctica. For more, visit **International Association of Antarctica Tour Operators** (IAATO; http://iaato.org).

Abercrombie & Kent (www.abercrombiekent.com) *Le Boreal* (199 passengers). All balcony cabins; luxury travel.

Antarctic Shipping S.A. (www.antarctic.cl) *Antarctic Dream* (80 passengers). Kayak, fly-cruise options.

Aurora Expeditions (www.auroraexpeditions.com.au) *Polar Pioneer* (56 passengers); *Marina Svetaeva* (100 passengers). Carries two helicopters; scuba diving, kayaking, mountain climbing and camping.

Compagnie du Ponant (www.ponant.com) Sails 264-passenger luxury boats; French operator.

Fathom Expeditions (www.fathomexpeditions.com) Various small-ship cruises.

Hapag-Lloyd Kreuzfahrten (www.hlkf.de) Luxury ice-strengthened ships: *Hanseatic* (188 passengers); *Bremen* (164 passengers). Some Ross Sea/Macquarie Island trips.

Heritage Expeditions (www.heritage-expeditions.com) *Spirit of Enderby* (50 passengers). Carries two hovercraft; NZ's sub-Antarctic islands, Macquarie Island, Ross Sea.

Holland America (www.hollandamerica.com) *Prinsendam* (835 passengers). Cruise only (no landing), 68-day trip from Fort Lauderdale, FL; four days in Antarctica.

Lindblad Expeditions (www.expeditions.com) *National Geographic Endeavour* (110 passengers); *National Geographic Explorer* (148 passengers). Kayaking.

Mountain Travel-Sobek (www.mtsobek.com) Kayaking, fly-cruise packages.

Oceanwide Expeditions (www.oceanwide-expeditions.com) Sails 46- to 52-passenger vessels; scuba diving.

One Ocean Expeditions (www.oneoceanexpeditions.com) *Akademik Ioffe* (96 passengers); *Akademik Sergey Vavilov* (107 passengers). Kayaking and camping.

Quark Expeditions (www.quarkexpeditions.com) Sails 107- to 189-passenger ships, including a carbon-neutral cruise on *Ocean Diamond*. Camping, kayaking, skiing, snowshoeing and climbing; fly-cruise packages.

Rederij Bark Europa BV (www.barkeuropa.com) Three-masted tall-ship *Europa* with professional crew of 14 plus 48 'voyage crewmembers;' trips include one from Ushuaia to Cape Town.

Students on Ice (www.studentsonice.com) Tours for high-school and college students.

WildWings/WildOceans Travel (www.wildwings.co.uk) Bird- and wildlife-focused tours; some to NZ sub-Antarctic Islands.

Zegrahm Expeditions (www.zeco.com) Antarctic Peninsula cruises on several vessels; occasional Ross Sea cruises.

SUSTAINABLE TRAVEL

All of the cruise companies listed, most of the yachts, and many of the air operations, are members of **International Association of Antarctica Tour Operators** (IAATO; http://iaato.org), which promotes environmentally responsible travel to the continent. Its website lists guidelines for vessel operators and visitors.

Starting in 2012, **Quark Expeditions** (www.quark-expeditions.com) will work with a carbon-credit trading company to offset emissions from its ship *Ocean Diamond* (the first carbon-neutral Antarctic cruise). Flight-adventure company **White Desert** (www.white-desert.com) does the same with its flights, and will even offset your flights to Cape Town, where they are based.

Yacht Cruises

In three decades of Antarctic cruising, there have been just over 200 yacht voyages to the continent. Several hundred fare-paying passengers visit Antarctica by yacht each year.

Although the national Antarctic programs cannot regulate yacht tourism – since Antarctica is open to everyone – permits are required and most research stations require advance notice of several weeks or even months for a visit.

Visitors on yachts must follow the same rules as those aboard cruise ships; see the **IAATO website** (www.iaato.org).

The following yachting agencies manage a number of Antarctic yachts: **Club Croisiere Pen Duick** (www.club-croisiere.com), **Ocean Voyages Inc** (www.oceanvoyages.com).

Evohe (www.evohe.com) 25m steel ketch; 12 passengers.

Fernande (www.fernandexp.com) 21m aluminum ketch; 10 passengers.

Golden Fleece (www.goldenfleecexp.co.fk) 19.5m steel schooner; skippered by Jérôme Poncet, highly experienced Antarctic yachtsman; IAATO member; eight passengers.

Kotick (www.kotick.net) 15.8m steel sloop; IAATO member; five passengers.

Le Sourire (www.lesourire.com.ar) 19.6m aluminum cutter; IAATO member; eight passengers.

Northanger (www.northanger.org) 15.6m steel ketch; four passengers.

Ocean Expeditions (www.ocean-expeditions.com) *Australis:* 23m steel motor sailor, nine passengers; *Philos:* 14m steel schooner, five passengers; IAATO member.

Pelagic Expeditions Ltd (www.pelagic.co.uk) *Pelagic:* 16.5m steel sloop, six passengers; *Pelagic Australis:* 23m aluminum sloop, 10 passengers; IAATO member.

Sarah W Vorwerk (www.sarahvorwerk.net) 16m steel sloop, eight passengers.

Seal (www.expeditionsail.com) 17m aluminum cutter; six passengers; IAATO member.

Spirit of Sydney Expeditions (www.spiritofsydney.net) 18m aluminum cutter; eight passengers; IAATO member.

Tiama (www.tiama.com) 15.2m steel cutter; six passengers; IAATO member.

Tooluka (www.tooluka.com) 14.2m steel sloop; six passengers.

Vaihéré (www.vaihere.com) 23.9m steel schooner; 10 passengers; IAATO member.

Xplore (www.xplore-expeditions.com) 20.4m steel cutter-rigged sloop; eight passengers; IAATO member.

> **SAILING RESOURCES**
>
> » *The Antarctic Pilot,* 6th edition (2004), Britain's Hydrographer of the Navy; the most comprehensive resource; available from New York Nautical (www.newyorknautical.com).
>
> » *Sailing Directions (Planning Guide & Enroute) for Antarctica,* 6th edition (2007), US National Imagery and Mapping Agency, also available from New York Nautical.
>
> » *Southern Ocean Cruising* (2007), Sally & Jérôme Poncet; available from Environmental Research & Assessment (www.era.gs).

Resupply Vessel

The 110-passenger French resupply ship *Marion Dufresne II* sails from Réunion to France's Terres Australes et Antarctiques Françaises (Crozet, Kerguelen, St Paul and Amsterdam Islands), to deliver personnel and provisions to research stations. Guides accompany tourists (about 30 each year) on landings; the voyage lasts a month. Fares start at €8030; book with Paris travel agency **Mer et Voyages** (www.mer-et-voyages.com).

Tours

All cruises/packages are guided tours. You can also book through third-party organizations, like universities, to have particular expert guides. **Harvard Museum of Natural History Travel Program** (www.hmnh.harvard.edu/travel) has top-notch guides and small groups.

GETTING AROUND

Zodiacs, generically known as RIBs (rigid inflatable boats; other name-brands are Naiad, Avon and Polarcirkel) are the backbone of tourist travel once in the Antarctic. These small (nine to 16 passengers), inflatable boats powered by outboard engines have a shallow draft which is ideal for cruising among icebergs and landing in otherwise inaccessible areas.

Zodiacs are very stable in the water, and are designed to stay afloat even if one or more of their six separate air-filled compartments are punctured.

Zodiac safety:

» No smoking.

» Wear a life jacket.

» Wet-weather gear is critical, as is a waterproof backpack (or waterproof bag inside the pack), because of the boat's flying spray.

» Use care entering and exiting Zodiacs.

» Check with your driver before standing, and follow all crew instructions.

Glossary

Several of these entries are taken (with permission) from Bernadette Hince's *Antarctic Dictionary* (2000).

ANARE – Australian National Antarctic Research Expeditions

Antarctic Convergence – region where the colder Antarctic seas meet the warmer waters of the north; also called the Polar Front

ASPA – Antarctic Specially Protected Area

aurora australis – the southern lights

BAS – British Antarctic Survey

beachmaster – territorial male seal who guards and breeds with a *harem*

berg – an iceberg

boondoggle – (American) fun trip away from station; see also *sleigh ride*

brash ice – the wreckage of larger pieces of ice

cairn – pyramid of stones or pieces of ice or cut snow raised as a marker

calve – the breaking off of an iceberg from a glacier or ice shelf

Camp – Falkland Islands term for the countryside; all areas outside of Stanley

CCAMLR – Convention for the Conservation of Antarctic Marine Living Resources

crèche – group of penguin chicks huddling in a small group, especially while parents are away hunting

factory ship – ocean vessel equipped for processing fish, whales, seals etc

fast ice – sea ice attached to the shore or between grounded *bergs*

fata morgana – mirage of vertically-stacked images

GPS – global positioning system; a satellite-based system that employs triangulation to determine geographic location to within about 10m

green flash – ray of green light at the horizon at sunset/sunrise

growler – small *berg* or piece of ice awash with waves

guano – bird excrement; also the remains of whale meat and bones that were dried and turned into a meal after the oil extraction process

halo and horizontal-parenthely – appearance of circles around the sun

harem – group of female seals jealously guarded on a breeding beach by a *beachmaster*

IAATO – International Association of Antarctica Tour Operators, the industry trade association

Ice, the – Antarctica

IGY – International Geophysical Year, which ran from July 1, 1957 to December 31, 1958

INMARSAT – International Maritime Satellite; used for ship communications

IPY – International Polar Year 2007–08

IWC – International Whaling Commission; set up in 1946 to regulate the harvesting of whales

katabatic – gravity-driven wind caused by colder, heavier air rushing down from the polar plateau

lead – a section of open water within pack ice between large floes

manhaul – archaic term meaning to pull a sledge carrying supplies and food on a South Polar journey, while either skiing or walking

moon dog – 'false moon,' or paraselena: an optical phenomenon caused by the refraction of moonlight by ice crystals suspended in the air; see *sun dog*

mumiyo – regurgitated stomach oil of petrels, used as a defense mechanism

NGO – nongovernmental organization

NSF – National Science Foundation; the part of the US government in charge of the US Antarctic program

nacreous clouds – (polar stratospheric cloud) iridescent clouds

nilas – thin crust of floating ice that bends with waves but does not break

nunatak – mountain or large piece of rock sticking up through an ice sheet

OAE – old Antarctic explorer; used to describe someone who has worked at an Antarctic station

oasis – area of bare rock without ice or snow caused by a retreating or thinning ice sheet and ablation of any snow that does fall

pancake ice – discs of young sea ice

PI – principal investigator; the lead scientist on a project

polynya – area of open water within the pack ice that remains free of ice throughout the winter

refugio – refuge hut

rookery – colony of breeding animals, usually birds

SANAP – South African National Antarctic Programme

sastrugi – furrows formed on snow surface by the wind

SCAR – Scientific Committee on Antarctic Research; originally the Special Committee on Antarctic Research

snow bridge – crustlike lid that often covers a crevasse

sun dog – 'false sun,' or more correctly, a parhelion: an optical phenomenon caused by the refraction of sunlight by tiny ice crystals, themselves known as 'diamond dust,' suspended in the air

sun pillar – vertical shaft of light from the rising or setting sun, also caused by ice crystals in the atmosphere

tabular berg – iceberg with vertical sides and a flat top, indicating that it has calved relatively recently

tide crack – crack separating sea ice from the shore

try-pot – cauldron for rendering the blubber of whales, seals or penguins into oil

UKAHT – UK Antarctic Heritage Trust

USAP – US Antarctic Program

whiteout – condition in which overcast sky descends to the horizon, causing a blurring between ground and sky and eliminating all points of perspective; described by pilots as 'like flying in a bowl of milk'

winterovers – station members who remain in Antarctica through the long dark winter

Zodiac – an inflatable rubber dinghy powered by an outboard engine and used for making shore landings

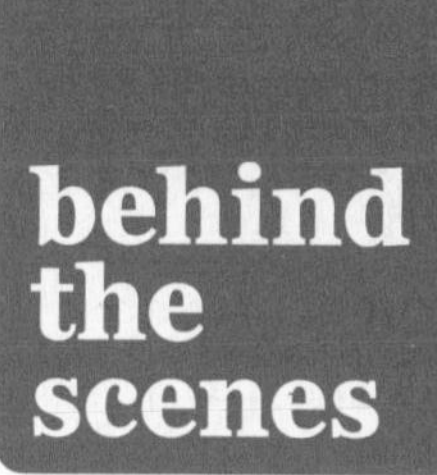

SEND US YOUR FEEDBACK

We love to hear from travelers – your comments keep us on our toes and help make our books better. Our well-traveled team reads every word on what you loved or loathed about this book. Although we cannot reply individually to postal submissions, we always guarantee that your feedback goes straight to the appropriate authors, in time for the next edition. Each person who sends us information is thanked in the next edition – the most useful submissions are rewarded with a selection of digital PDF chapters.

Visit **lonelyplanet.com/contact** to submit your updates and suggestions or to ask for help. Our award-winning website also features inspirational travel stories, news and discussions.

Note: We may edit, reproduce and incorporate your comments in Lonely Planet products such as guidebooks, websites and digital products, so let us know if you don't want your comments reproduced or your name acknowledged. For a copy of our privacy policy visit lonelyplanet.com/privacy.

OUR READERS

Many thanks to the travelers who used the last edition and wrote to us with helpful hints, useful advice and interesting anecdotes: Richard L Huber, Heike Luci Kohler

AUTHOR THANKS

Alexis Averbuck

I offer untold gratitude to Diana Laird who inspired me to live on the Ice and always shares her science and friendship unstintingly. Rachel Averbuck reminded me to go – and remains a faithful guide in life's bardos. David Zapol brings intelligence, enthusiasm and humor to all things Antarctic and otherwise. Warren Zapol shared his erudition, and hilarious OAE anecdotes. Thank you to Jenny, Jacob, Patti and David for their unfailing support. Patty Kline, birder extraordinaire, provided avian guidance. IAATO (Steve Wellmeier), COMNAP, SCAR, the Antarctic Meteorological Research Center, the NSF (Peter West), Geoscience Australia, the Government of South Georgia and the South Sandwich Islands, and the Falkland Islands Tourist Board were invaluable in verifying my data. Boundless thanks to Kathleen Munnelly for her unwavering vision and her comprehensive knowledge of both Antarctica and Lonely Planet. Gratitude, finally, to Ruthie, Amelia, Oren, Redmond, Eli, Eva, Elliot, Noah and Timothy for their constant illumination and inspiration. I dedicate this book to Evelyn Averbuck who inspires me to live my largest life.

ACKNOWLEDGMENTS

Climate map data adapted from Peel MC, Finlayson BL & McMahon TA (2007) 'Updated World Map of the Köppen-Geiger Climate Classification', *Hydrology and Earth System Sciences*, 11, 163344.

Cover photograph: Gentoo penguin on a floating iceberg, Momatiuk Eastcott, Corbis.

THIS BOOK

This 5th edition of Lonely Planet's *Antarctica* guidebook was researched and written by Alexis Averbuck. The Ushuaia, Argentina, section was researched and written by Carolyn McCarthy. The previous four editions were written by Jeff Rubin, with John Cooper contributing the Wildlife chapter. This guidebook was commissioned in Lonely Planet's Oakland office, and produced by the following:

Commissioning Editor Kathleen Munnelly
Coordinating Editors Fionnuala Twomey, Tasmin Waby
Coordinating Cartographers Hunor Csutoros, Brendan Streager
Coordinating Layout Designer Sandra Helou
Managing Editor Bruce Evans
Senior Editors Andi Jones, Susan Paterson
Managing Cartographers Alison Lyall, Mark Griffiths
Managing Layout Designer Chris Girdler
Assisting Editors Paul Harding, Saralinda Turner
Cover Research Naomi Parker
Internal Image Research Nicholas Colicchia

Thanks to Ryan Evans, Larissa Frost, Gerard Walker, Tara Baker, Trent Paton, Colette Harfouche, Judith McNaughtan

000 Map pages
000 Photo pages

000 Map pages
000 Photo pages

000 Map pages
000 Photo pages

how to use this book

These symbols will help you find the listings you want:

- Sights
- Beaches
- Activities
- Courses
- Tours
- Festivals & Events
- Sleeping
- Eating
- Drinking
- Entertainment
- Shopping
- Information/Transport

These symbols give you the vital information for each listing:

- Telephone Numbers
- Opening Hours
- Parking
- Nonsmoking
- Air-Conditioning
- Internet Access
- Wi-Fi Access
- Swimming Pool
- Vegetarian Selection
- English-Language Menu
- Family-Friendly
- Pet-Friendly
- Bus
- Ferry
- Metro
- Subway
- London Tube
- Tram
- Train

Reviews are organised by author preference.

Look out for these icons:

- TOP CHOICE — Our author's recommendation
- FREE — No payment required
- A green or sustainable option

Our authors have nominated these places as demonstrating a strong commitment to sustainability – for example by supporting local communities and producers, operating in an environmentally friendly way, or supporting conservation projects.

Map Legend

Sights
- Beach
- Buddhist
- Castle
- Christian
- Hindu
- Islamic
- Jewish
- Monument
- Museum/Gallery
- Ruin
- Winery/Vineyard
- Zoo
- Other Sight

Activities, Courses & Tours
- Diving/Snorkelling
- Canoeing/Kayaking
- Skiing
- Surfing
- Swimming/Pool
- Walking
- Windsurfing
- Other Activity/Course/Tour

Sleeping
- Sleeping
- Camping

Eating
- Eating

Drinking
- Drinking
- Cafe

Entertainment
- Entertainment

Shopping
- Shopping

Information
- Post Office
- Tourist Information

Transport
- Airport
- Border Crossing
- Bus
- Cable Car/Funicular
- Cycling
- Ferry
- Metro
- Monorail
- Parking
- S-Bahn
- Taxi
- Train/Railway
- Tram
- Tube Station
- U-Bahn
- Other Transport

Routes
- Tollway
- Freeway
- Primary
- Secondary
- Tertiary
- Lane
- Unsealed Road
- Plaza/Mall
- Steps
- Tunnel
- Pedestrian Overpass
- Walking Tour
- Walking Tour Detour
- Path

Boundaries
- International
- State/Province
- Disputed
- Regional/Suburb
- Marine Park
- Cliff
- Wall

Population
- Capital (National)
- Capital (State/Province)
- City/Large Town
- Town/Village

Geographic
- Hut/Shelter
- Lighthouse
- Lookout
- Mountain/Volcano
- Oasis
- Park
- Pass
- Picnic Area
- Waterfall

Hydrography
- River/Creek
- Intermittent River
- Swamp/Mangrove
- Reef
- Canal
- Water
- Dry/Salt/Intermittent Lake
- Glacier

Areas
- Beach/Desert
- Cemetery (Christian)
- Cemetery (Other)
- Park/Forest
- Sportsground
- Sight (Building)
- Top Sight (Building)

OUR STORY

A beat-up old car, a few dollars in the pocket and a sense of adventure. In 1972 that's all Tony and Maureen Wheeler needed for the trip of a lifetime – across Europe and Asia overland to Australia. It took several months, and at the end – broke but inspired – they sat at their kitchen table writing and stapling together their first travel guide, *Across Asia on the Cheap*. Within a week they'd sold 1500 copies. Lonely Planet was born.

Today, Lonely Planet has offices in Melbourne, London and Oakland, with more than 600 staff and writers. We share Tony's belief that 'a great guidebook should do three things: inform, educate and amuse'.

OUR WRITERS

Alexis Averbuck

Alexis Averbuck lived at McMurdo Station through a summer and winter, experiencing both townie life and incredible boondoggles. She observed diving emperor penguins and Weddell seals from beneath the ice. She reveled in multi-week sunsets and sunrises reflecting off mountains and sea ice. Midwinter she camped in an ice trench watching the *aurora australis*. Alexis explored ice caves, flew over Mt Erebus, and, ultimately, made it to the geographic South Pole. And she made friends.

Antarctica changed her life irrevocably. A travel writer for 20 years, Alexis has crossed the Pacific by sailboat, written books on her journeys through Asia and the Americas, and now lives on the island of Hydra. She also specializes in Greece and France for Lonely Planet.

Antarctica inspired her to paint, because some things are simply beyond words. See her work at www.alexisaverbuck.com.

Read more about Alexis at:
lonelyplanet.com/members/alexisaverbuck

Contributing Author

Carolyn McCarthy wrote the Ushuaia section of this book. As well as writing about her favorite destination of Patagonia, Carolyn has contributed to over a dozen Lonely Planet titles. She has also written for *National Geographic*, *Outside* and *Lonely Planet Magazine*. You can follow her Americas blog at www.carolynswildblueyonder.blogspot.com.

Published by Lonely Planet Publications Pty Ltd
ABN 36 005 607 983
5th edition – November 2012
ISBN 978 1 74179 459 5

10 9 8 7 6 5 4 3 2 1
Printed in China